BusinessEthicsNow

BusinessEthicsNow

Andrew W. Ghillyer, PhD

McGraw Hill Education

CHIEF PRODUCT OFFICER, SVP PRODUCTS & MARKETS: **G. Scott Virkler**
VICE PRESIDENT, GENERAL MANAGER, PRODUCTS & MARKETS: **Michael Ryan**
VICE PRESIDENT, CONTENT DESIGN & DELIVERY: **Betsy Whalen**
MANAGING DIRECTOR: **Susan Gouijnstook**
DIRECTOR: **Michael Ablassmeir**
DIRECTOR, PRODUCT DEVELOPMENT: **Meghan Campbell**
LEAD PRODUCT DEVELOPER: **Kelly Delso**
PRODUCT DEVELOPER: **Laura Hurst Spell**
DIRECTOR, CONTENT DESIGN & DELIVERY: **Terri Schiesl**
PROGRAM MANAGER: **Mary Conzachi**
CONTENT PROJECT MANAGERS: **Christine A. Vaughan; Evan Roberts**
BUYER: **Jennifer Pickel**
DESIGN: **Jessica Cuevas**
CONTENT LICENSING SPECIALISTS: **Ann Marie Jannette; Jacob Sullivan**
COVER IMAGE: **©kay/Getty Images**
TYPEFACE: **11/13 StixMathjax Main**
COMPOSITOR: **SPi Global**
PRINTER: **LSC Communications**

BUSINESS ETHICS NOW, FIFTH EDITION

2 3 4 5 6 7 8 9 LMN 21 20 19 18

ISBN   978-1-259-53543-7
MHID   1-259-53543-6

Library of Congress Cataloging in Publication Data

Names: Ghillyer, Andrew, author.
Title: Business ethics now / [Andrew W. Ghillyer].
Other titles: BusinessEthicsNow
Description: Fifth edition. | New York, NY : McGraw-Hill Education, [2018]
Identifiers: LCCN 2016047732 | ISBN 9781259535437 (alk. paper)
Subjects: LCSH: Business ethics.
Classification: LCC HF5387 .G493 2018 | DDC 174/.4—dc23 LC record available at https://lccn.loc.gov/2016047732

mheducation.com/highered

Dedication

To Princess Megan

© imagedepotpro/Getty Images RF

Acknowledgments

McGraw-Hill and Andrew Ghillyer would like to thank all the instructors whose insights help shape this text. Their contributions and suggestions ensure that this textbook includes what students and instructors need—both in the classroom and in today's ever-changing business environment.

Patrick Conroy, *Delgado Community College*

Linda Hartman, M.S., *Southeast Community College, Nebraska*

Jessica McManus Warnell, *Mendoza College of Business, University of Notre Dame*

Lori Whisenant, JD, LLM, *University of Kansas*

Raza Mir, *William Paterson University*

David Dyson, Ph.D., *Oral Roberts University*

Dr. John Hood, *Mount Olive College*

Dr. Deborah M. Houston, *Mount Olive College*

Lisa Machado, *Southeast Community College*

Lyna Matesi, *University of Wisconsin–Stevens Point*

Dr. Raven Davenport, *Houston Community College*

Dr. David J. Hill, *Mount Olive College*

Melanie Jacks Hilburn, *Lone Star College, North Harris*

Deborah Kane, *Butler County Community College*

Eivis Qenani, Ph.D., *California Polytechnic State University, San Luis Obispo*

About the
[AUTHOR]

Dr. Andrew W. Ghillyer is the former vice president of academic affairs for Argosy University in Tampa, Florida, and is an adjunct instructor in all aspects of business ethics, management, and leadership. His operational management experience spans more than 30 years across a wide range of industries, including chief operating officer of a civil engineering software company and director of international business relations for a global training organization. Dr. Ghillyer also served on the Board of Examiners for the Malcolm Baldrige National Quality Award for the 2007 award year. He received his doctorate in management studies from the University of Surrey in the United Kingdom.

© luoman/Getty Images RF

Ch. 1
UNDERSTANDING
ETHICS

© BJI/Lane Oatey/blue jean images/Getty Images RF

Ch. 2
DEFINING BUSINESS
ETHICS

© Dave and Les Jacobs/Blend Images LLC RF

Ch. 5
CORPORATE
GOVERNANCE

© Abel Mitja Varela/Getty Images RF

Ch. 7
BLOWING THE
WHISTLE

© John Lund/Drew Kelly/Blend Images LLC RF

BusinessEthicsNow

BRIEF TABLE OF CONTENTS

© sam74100/Getty Images

© Digital Vision RF

PART 2 The Practice of Business Ethics

3 > Organizational Ethics

© Bloomberg/Getty Images

4 > Corporate Social Responsibility

5 > Corporate Governance

© John Aikins/Corbis RF

7 > Blowing the Whistle

© Frank Rumpenhorst/EPA/Corbis

8 > Ethics and Technology

© Dave and Les Jacobs/Blend Images, LLC

© Stockbyte/Getty Images RF

Welcome to
BusinessEthicsNow

WHAT'S NEW

connect connect.mheducation.com

Continually evolving, McGraw-Hill Connect® has been redesigned to provide the only true adaptive learning experience delivered within a simple and easy-to-navigate environment, placing students at the very center.

- Performance Analytics—Now available for both instructors and students, easy-to-decipher data illuminates course performance. Students always know how they're doing in class, while instructors can view student and section performance at a glance.

- Mobile—Available on tablets, students can now access assignments, quizzes, and results on the go, while instructors can assess student and section performance anytime, anywhere.

- Personalized Learning—Squeezing the most out of study time, the adaptive engine within Connect creates a highly personalized learning path for each student by identifying areas of weakness and providing learning resources to assist in the moment of need.

This seamless integration of reading, practice, and assessment ensures that the focus is on the most important content for that individual.

LEARNSMART®

LearnSmart, the most widely used adaptive learning resource, is proven to improve grades. By focusing each student on the most important information they need to learn, LearnSmart personalizes the learning experience so they can study as efficiently as possible.

SMARTBOOK®

SmartBook—an extension of LearnSmart—is an adaptive eBook that helps students focus their study time more effectively. As students read, SmartBook assesses comprehension and dynamically highlights where they need to study more.

Instructor Library

The Connect Instructor Library is your repository for additional resources to improve student engagement in and out of class. You can select and use any asset that enhances your lecture.

Instructor's Resources

Specially prepared Instructor's Manual, Test Bank, and PowerPoint slide presentations provide an easy transition for instructors teaching with the book the first time.

Throughout the book:

© McGraw-Hill Education

1 Understanding Ethics

UPDATED *THINKING CRITICALLY* Three Cups of Tea

UPDATED *THINKING CRITICALLY* The Man Who Shocked the World

2 Defining Business Ethics

UPDATED *ETHICAL DILEMMA* Three-Card Monte

NEW *INTERNET EXERCISE* Compliance Initiative

UPDATED *INTERNET EXERCISE* Ethics Resource Center

NEW *THINKING CRITICALLY* Marriott

UPDATED *THINKING CRITICALLY* BELA

3 Organizational Ethics

UPDATED *THINKING CRITICALLY* Boosting Your Resume

UPDATED *THINKING CRITICALLY* A Loss of Privacy

4 Corporate Social Responsibility

NEW *FRONTLINE FOCUS* An Improved Reputation

UPDATED *THINKING CRITICALLY* Sustainable Capitalism

NEW *THINKING CRITICALLY* Monsanto

5 Corporate Governance

UPDATED *ETHICAL DILEMMA* 20/20 Hindsight

NEW *ETHICAL DILEMMA* A Spectacular Downfall

NEW *THINKING CRITICALLY* Tesco

UPDATED *THINKING CRITICALLY* SocGen

NEW *THINKING CRITICALLY* Valeant Pharmaceuticals

6 The Role of Government

UPDATED *ETHICAL DILEMMA* The Bribery Gap

UPDATED *INTERNET EXERCISE* Transparency International

UPDATED *THINKING CRITICALLY* Ponzi Schemes

UPDATED *THINKING CRITICALLY* India's Enron

UPDATED *THINKING CRITICALLY* "Off-Label" Marketing

© sam74100/Getty Images

PART 1

DEFINING BUSINESS ETHICS

1 Understanding Ethics

2 Defining Business Ethics

In Chapter 1, we begin by exploring how people live their lives according to a standard of "right" or "wrong" behavior. Where do people look for guidance in deciding what is right or wrong or good or bad? Once they have developed a personal set of moral standards or ethical principles, how do people then interact with other members of their community or society as a whole who may or may not share the same ethical principles?

In Chapter 2, with a basic understanding of ethics, we can then examine the concept of business ethics, where employees face the dilemma of balancing their own moral standards with those of the company they work for and the supervisor or manager to whom they report on a daily basis. We examine the question of whether the business world should be viewed as an artificial environment where the rules by which you choose to live your own life don't necessarily apply.

© BJI/Lane Oatey/blue jean images/Getty Images RF

UNDERSTANDING ETHICS

After studying this chapter, you should be able to:

1-1 Define *ethics*.

1-2 Explain the role of values in ethical decision making.

1-3 Understand opposing ethical theories and their limitations.

1-4 Discuss ethical relativism.

1-5 Explain an ethical dilemma, and apply a process to resolve it.

FRONTLINE FOCUS
Doing the Right Thing

Megan is a rental agent for the Oxford Lake apartment complex. The work is fairly boring, but she's going to school in the evening, so the quiet periods give her time to catch up on her studies, plus the discounted rent is a great help to her budget. Business has been slow since two other apartment complexes opened, and Oxford Lake's vacancies are starting to run a little high.

The company recently appointed a new regional director to "inject some energy and creativity" into its local campaigns and generate new rental leases. Her name is Kate Jones, and based on first impressions, Megan thinks Kate would rent her grandmother an apartment as long as she could raise the rent first.

Kate's first event is an open house, complete with free hot dogs and colas and a clown making balloon animals for the kids. Ads run in the paper and on the radio attract a good crowd.

The first applicants are Michael and Tania Wilson, an African-American couple with one young son, Tyler. Megan takes their application. They're a nice couple with a stable work history, more than enough income to cover the rent, and good references from their previous landlord. Megan advises them that they will do a background check as a standard procedure and that things "look very good" for their application.

After they leave, Kate stops by the rental office and asks, "How did that couple look? Any issues with their application?"

"None at all," answers Megan. "I think they'll be a perfect addition to our community."

"Don't rush their application through too quickly," replies Kate. "We have time to find some more applicants, and, in my experience, those people usually end up breaking their lease or skipping town with unpaid rent."

QUESTIONS

1. What would be "the right thing" to do here? How would the Golden Rule relate to Megan's decision?
2. How would you resolve this ethical dilemma? Review the three-step process in 'Resolving Ethical Dilemmas' for more details.
3. What should Megan do now?

> Ethics is about how we meet the challenge of doing the right thing when that will cost more than we want to pay.
>
> **The Josephson Institute of Ethics**

>> What Is Ethics?

The field of **ethics** is the study of how we try to live our lives according to a standard of "right" or "wrong" behavior—in both how we think and behave toward others and how we would like them to think and behave toward us. For some, it is a conscious choice to follow a set of moral standards or ethical principles that provide guidance on how they should conduct themselves in their daily lives. For others, where the choice is not so clear, they look to the behavior of others to determine what is an acceptable standard of right and wrong or good and bad behavior. How they arrive at the definition of what's right or wrong is a result of many factors, including how they were raised, their religion, and the traditions and beliefs of their **society**.

Ethics The manner by which we try to live our lives according to a standard of "right" or "wrong" behavior—in both how we think and behave toward others and how we would like them to think and behave toward us.

Society A structured community of people bound together by similar traditions and customs.

Culture A particular set of attitudes, beliefs, and practices that characterize a group of individuals.

Value System A set of personal principles formalized into a code of behavior.

Intrinsic Value The quality by which a value is a good thing in itself and is pursued for its own sake, whether anything comes from that pursuit or not.

>> Understanding Right and Wrong

Moral standards are principles based on religious, **cultural**, or philosophical beliefs by which judgments are made about good or bad behavior. These beliefs can come from many different sources:

- Friends.
- Family.
- Ethnic background.
- Religion.
- School.
- The media—television, radio, newspapers, magazines, the Internet.
- Personal role models and mentors.

Your personal set of morals—your *morality*—represents a collection of all these influences as they are built up over your lifetime. A

© BananaStock/PunchStock RF

strict family upbringing or religious education would obviously have a direct impact on your personal moral standards. These standards would then provide a moral compass (a sense of personal direction) to guide you in the choices you make in your life.

HOW SHOULD I LIVE?

You do not acquire your personal moral standards in the same way that you learn the alphabet. Standards of ethical behavior are absorbed by osmosis as you observe the examples (both positive and negative) set by everyone around you—parents, family members, friends, peers, and neighbors. Your adoption of those standards is ultimately unique to you as an individual. For example, you may be influenced by the teachings of your family's religious beliefs and grow to believe that behaving ethically toward others represents a demonstration of religious devotion. However, that devotion may just as easily be motivated by either fear of a divine punishment in the afterlife or anticipation of a reward for living a virtuous life.

Alternatively, you may choose to reject religious morality and instead base your ethical behavior on your experience of human existence rather than any abstract concepts of right and wrong as determined by a religious doctrine.

When individuals share similar standards in a community, we can use the terms *values* and *value system*. The terms *morals* and *values* are often used to mean the same thing—a set of personal principles by which you aim to live your life. When you try to formalize those principles into a code of behavior, then you are seen to be adopting a **value system**.

THE VALUE OF A VALUE

Just as the word *value* is used to denote the worth of an item, a person's values can be said to have a specific "worth" for them. That worth can be expressed in two ways:

1. An **intrinsic value**—by which a value is a good thing in itself and is pursued for its own sake, whether anything good comes from that pursuit or not. For example, happiness, health, and self-respect can all be said to have intrinsic value.

2. An **instrumental value**—by which the pursuit of one value is a good way to reach another value. For example, money is valued for what it can buy rather than for itself.

VALUE CONFLICTS

The impact of a person's or a group's value system can be seen in the extent to which their daily lives are influenced by those values. However, the greatest test of any personal value system comes when you are presented with a situation that places those values in direct conflict with an action. For example:

1. *Lying is wrong*—but what if you were lying to protect the life of a loved one?
2. *Stealing is wrong*—but what if you were stealing food for a starving child?
3. *Killing is wrong*—but what if you had to kill someone in self-defense to protect your own life?

How do you resolve such conflicts? Are there exceptions to these rules? Can you justify those actions based on special circumstances? Should you then start clarifying the exceptions to your value system? If so, can you really plan for every possible exception?

It is this gray area that makes the study of ethics so complex. We would like to believe that there are clearly defined rules of right and wrong and that you can live your life in direct observance of those rules. However, it is more likely that situations will arise that will require exceptions to those rules. It is how you choose to respond to those situations and the specific choices you make that really define your personal value system.

Superman has become a fictional representation of personal integrity. Can you find examples of individuals with personal integrity in your own life?

© Swim Ink 2 LLC/Corbis

DOING THE RIGHT THING

If you asked your friends and family what ethics means to them, you would probably arrive at a list of four basic categories:

1. Simple truth—right and wrong or good and bad.
2. A question of someone's personal character—his or her integrity.
3. Rules of appropriate individual behavior.

4. Rules of appropriate behavior for a community or society.

The first category—*a simple truth*—also may be expressed as simply *doing the right thing*. It is something that most people can understand and support. It is this basic simplicity that can lead you to take ethical behavior for granted—you assume that everyone is committed to doing the right thing, and it's not until you are exposed to unethical behavior that you are reminded that, unfortunately, not all people share your interpretation of what "the right thing" is, and even if they did, they may not share your commitment to doing it.

The second category—*personal integrity,* demonstrated by someone's behavior—looks at ethics from an external rather than an internal viewpoint. All our classic comic-book heroes—Superman, Spider-Man, Batman, and Wonder Woman, to name just a few—represent the ideal of personal integrity where a person lives a life that is true to his or her moral standards, often at the cost of considerable personal sacrifice.

Rules of appropriate individual behavior represent the idea that the moral standards we develop for ourselves impact our lives on a daily basis in our behavior and the other types of decisions we make.

Rules of appropriate behavior for a community or society remind us that we must eventually bring our personal value system into a world that is shared with people who will probably have both similar and very different value systems. Establishing an ethical ideal for a community or society allows that group of people to live with the confidence that comes from knowing they share a common standard.

Each category represents a different feature of ethics. On one level, the study of ethics seeks to understand how people make the choices they make—how they develop their own set of moral standards, how they live their lives on the basis of those standards, and how they judge the behavior of others in relation to those standards. On a second level, we then try to use that understanding to develop a set of ideals or principles by which a group of ethical individuals can combine as a community with a common understanding of how they "ought" to behave.

> **Instrumental Value** The quality by which the pursuit of one value is a good way to reach another value. For example, money is valued for what it can buy rather than for itself.

PROGRESS ✓ QUESTIONS

1. What is the definition of *ethics*?
2. What is a moral compass, and how would you apply it?
3. Explain the difference between intrinsic and instrumental values.
4. List the four basic categories of ethics.

THE GOLDEN RULE

For some, the goal of living an ethical life is expressed by the **Golden Rule**: *Do unto others as you would have them do unto you,* or *treat others as you would like to be treated.* This simple and very clear rule is shared by many different religions in the world:

- Buddhism: "Hurt not others in ways that you yourself would find hurtful."—Udana-Varga 5:18
- Christianity: "Therefore all things whatsoever ye would that men should do to you, do ye even so to them."—Matthew 7:12
- Hinduism: "This is the sum of duty: do naught unto others which would cause you pain if done to you."—Mahabharata 5:1517

The Golden Rule Do unto others as you would have them do unto you.

Virtue Ethics A concept of living your life according to a commitment to the achievement of a clear ideal— *what sort of person would I like to become, and how do I go about becoming that person?*

Utilitarianism Ethical choices that offer the greatest good for the greatest number of people.

Universal Ethics Actions that are taken out of *duty* and *obligation* to a purely moral ideal, rather than based on the needs of the situation, since the universal principles are seen to apply to everyone, everywhere, all the time.

Of course, the danger with the Golden Rule is that not everyone thinks like you, acts like you, or believes in the same principles that you do, so to live your life on the assumption that your pursuit of an ethical ideal will match others' ethical ideals could get you into trouble. For example, if you were the type of person who values honesty in your personal value system, and you found a wallet on the sidewalk, you would try to return it to its rightful owner. However, if you lost your wallet, could you automatically expect that the person who found it would make the same effort to return it to you?

>> Ethical Theories

The subject of ethics has been a matter of philosophical debate for over 2,500 years—as far back as the Greek philosopher Socrates. Over time and with considerable debate, different schools of thought have developed as to how we should go about living an ethical life.

Ethical theories can be divided into three categories: virtue ethics, ethics for the greater good, and universal ethics.

© Dimitris Tavlikos/Alamy RF

VIRTUE ETHICS

The Greek philosopher Aristotle's belief in individual character and integrity established a concept of living your life according to a commitment to the achievement of a clear ideal—*what sort of person would I like to become, and how do I go about becoming that person?*

The problem with **virtue ethics** is that societies can place different emphasis on different virtues. For example, Greek society at the time of Aristotle valued wisdom, courage, and justice. By contrast, Christian societies value faith, hope, and charity. So if the virtues you hope to achieve aren't a direct reflection of the values of the society in which you live, there is a real danger of value conflict.

ETHICS FOR THE GREATER GOOD

As the name implies, *ethics for the greater good* is more focused on the outcome of your actions rather than the apparent virtue of the actions themselves— that is, a focus on the greatest good for the greatest number of people. Originally proposed by a Scottish philosopher named David Hume, this approach to ethics is also referred to as **utilitarianism**.

The problem with this approach to ethics is the idea that the ends justify the means. If all you focus on is doing the greatest good for the greatest number of people, no one is accountable for the actions that are taken to achieve that outcome. The 20th century witnessed one of the most extreme examples of this when Adolf Hitler and his Nazi party launched a national genocide against Jews and "defective" people on the utilitarian grounds of restoring the Aryan race.

UNIVERSAL ETHICS

Originally attributed to a German philosopher named Immanuel Kant, **universal ethics** argues that there are certain and universal principles that should apply

>> What do you stand for, or what will you stand against?

Your personal value system will guide you throughout your life, both in personal and professional matters. How often you will decide to stand by those values or deviate from them will be a matter of personal choice, but each one of those choices will contribute to the ongoing development of your values. As Lawrence Kohlberg's work on Ethical Reasoning points out, your understanding of moral complexities and ethical dilemmas grows as your life experience and education grow. For that reason, you will measure every choice you make against the value system you developed as a child from your parents, friends, society, and often your religious upbringing. The cumulative effect of all those choices is a value system that is unique to you. Of course, you will share many of the same values as your family and friends, but some of your choices will differ from theirs because your values differ.

   The great benefit of having such a guide to turn to when faced with a difficult decision is that you can both step away from the emotion and pressure of a situation and, at the same time, turn to a system that truly represents who you are as a person—someone with integrity who can be counted on to make a reasoned and thoughtful choice.

Check List

---

to all ethical judgments. Actions are taken out of *duty* and *obligation* to a purely moral ideal rather than based on the needs of the situation, since the universal principles are seen to apply to everyone, everywhere, all the time.

   The problem with this approach is the reverse of the weakness in ethics for the greater good. If all you focus on is abiding by a universal principle, no one is accountable for the consequences of the actions taken to abide by those principles. Consider, for example, the current debate over the use of stem cells in researching a cure for Parkinson's disease. If you recognize the value of human life above all else as a universal ethical principle, how do you justify the use of a human embryo in the harvesting of stem cells? Does the potential for curing many major illnesses—Parkinson's, cancer, heart disease, and kidney disease—make stem cell research ethically justifiable? If not, how do you explain that to the families who lose loved ones waiting unsuccessfully for organ transplants?

> **Ethical Relativism** Gray area in which your ethical principles are defined by the traditions of your society, your personal opinions, and the circumstances of the present moment.

>> Ethical Relativism

When the limitations of each of these theories are reviewed, it becomes clear that there is no truly comprehensive theory of ethics, only a choice that is made based on your personal value system. In this context, it is easier to understand why, when faced with the requirement to select a model of how we ought to live our lives, many people choose the idea of **ethical relativism**, whereby the traditions of their society, their personal opinions, and the circumstances of the present moment define their ethical principles.

   The idea of relativism implies some degree of flexibility as opposed to strict black-and-white rules.

PROGRESS ✔ QUESTIONS

5. What is the Golden Rule?
6. List the three basic ethical theories.
7. Identify the limitations of each theory.
8. Provide an example of each theory in practice.

Key Point !

Why is the issue of accountability relevant in considering alternate ethical theories?

Applied Ethics The study of how ethical theories are put into practice.

Ethical Dilemma A situation in which there is no obvious right or wrong decision, but rather a right or right answer.

It also offers the comfort of being a part of the ethical majority in your community or society instead of standing by your individual beliefs as an outsider from the group. In our current society, when we talk about peer pressure among groups, we are acknowledging that the expectations of this majority can sometimes have negative consequences.

>> Ethical Dilemmas

Up to now we have been concerned with the notion of ethical theory—how we conduct ourselves as individuals and as a community in order to live a good moral life. However, this ethical theory represents only half of the school of philosophy we recognize as ethics. At some point, these theories have to be put into practice, and we then move into the area of **applied ethics**.

The basic assumption of ethical theory is that you as an individual or community are in control of all the factors that influence the choices that you make. In reality, your ethical principles are most likely to be tested when you face a situation in which there is no obvious right or wrong decision but rather a right or right answer. Such situations are referred to as **ethical dilemmas**.

As we saw earlier in our review of value systems and value conflicts, any idealized set of principles or standards inevitably faces some form of challenge. For ethical theories, that challenge takes the form

PEER PRESSURE

In the days before the dominance of technology in the lives of teenagers and young adults, concerns over *peer pressure* (stress exerted by friends and classmates) focused on bullying, criminal behavior, drug use, and sexual activity. The arrival of smartphones and the ability to send text messages to a wide audience and post short videos on the Internet have brought a new element to concerns over peer pressure at school. A 2008 survey by the National Campaign to Prevent Teen and Unplanned Pregnancy found that 20 percent of teens ages 13 to 19 said they have electronically sent or posted online nude or seminude pictures or videos of themselves. Nearly 50 percent of the teen girls surveyed said "pressure from guys" was the reason they shared sexually explicit photos or messages, and boys cited "pressure from friends."

Incidents of "sexting" have increased so quickly that local communities and law enforcement agencies have been caught unprepared. While many consider the incidents to be examples of negligent behavior on the part of the teens involved, the viewing and distribution of such materials could result in charges of felony child pornography and a listing on a sex offender registry for decades to come. In one case, 18-year-old Philip Alpert was convicted of child pornography after distributing a revealing photo of his 16-year-old girlfriend after they got into an argument. He will be labeled a "sex offender" until he is 43 years old.

Unfortunately, the dramatic increase in the number of incidents of sexting has brought about tragic consequences. Cincinnati teen Jessie Logan killed herself after nude pictures she had sent to her boyfriend were sent to hundreds of students. Even though only five teens were involved in sending the pictures, their unlimited access to technology allowed them to reach several hundred

© Punchstock/Brand X Pictures RF

students in four school districts before the incident was stopped. At the time of writing this case, 20 states now have legislation in place to deter teens from sexting without charging them as adult sex offenders.

QUESTIONS

1. In what ways does giving in to peer pressure constitute ethical relativism?
2. How could you use your personal value system to fight back against peer pressure?

3. How would you communicate the risks of sexting to students who are struggling to deal with peer pressure?

4. Is a change in the law the best option for addressing this problem? Why or why not?

Sources: Satta Sarmah, "'Sexting' on the Rise among Teens," http://rye.patch.com, May 21, 2010; "Sexting Bill Introduced at Statehouse," www.onntv.com, May 13, 2010; "Sex and Tech: Results from a Survey of Teens and Young Adults," www.thenationalcampaign.org, October 20, 2010; and http://cyberbullying.org/state-sexting-laws.pdf.

of a dilemma in which the decision you must make requires you to make a right choice knowing full well that you are:

- Leaving an equally right choice undone.
- Likely to suffer something bad as a result of that choice.
- Contradicting a personal ethical principle in making that choice.
- Abandoning an ethical value of your community or society in making that choice.

>> RESOLVING ETHICAL DILEMMAS

By its very definition, an ethical dilemma cannot really be resolved in the sense that a resolution of the problem implies a satisfactory answer to the problem. Since, in reality, the "answer" to an ethical dilemma is often the lesser of two evils, it is questionable to assume that there will always be an acceptable answer—it's more a question of whether or not you can arrive at an outcome you can live with.

Joseph L. Badaracco Jr.'s book *Defining Moments* captures this notion of living with an outcome in a discussion of "sleep-test ethics":[1]

> The sleep test . . . is supposed to tell people whether or not they have made a morally sound decision. In its literal version, a person who has made the right choice can sleep soundly afterward; someone who has made the wrong choice cannot. . . . Defined less literally and more broadly, sleep-test ethics rests on a single, fundamental belief: that we should rely on our personal insights, feelings, and instincts when we face a difficult problem. Defined this way, sleep-test ethics is the ethics of intuition. It advises us to follow our hearts, particularly when our minds are confused. It says that, if something continues to gnaw at us, it probably should.

When we review the ethical theories covered in this chapter, we can identify two distinct approaches to handling ethical dilemmas. One is to focus on the practical consequences of what we choose to do, and the other focuses on the actions themselves and the degree to which they were the right actions to take. The first school of thought argues that the ends justify the means and that if there is no harm, there is no foul. The second claims that some actions are simply wrong in and of themselves.

So what should you do? Consider this three-step process for solving an ethical problem:[2]

Step 1. *Analyze the consequences.* Who will be helped by what you do? Who will be harmed? What kind of benefits and harm are we talking about? (Some are more valuable or more harmful than others: Good health, someone's trust, and a clean environment are very valuable benefits, more so than a faster remote control device.) How does all of this look over the long run as well as the short run?

Step 2. *Analyze the actions.* Consider all the options from a different perspective, without thinking

© Stockbyte/PunchStock RF

about the consequences. How do the actions measure up against moral principles such as honesty, fairness, equality, respecting the dignity of others, and people's rights? (Consider the common good.) Are any of the actions at odds with those standards? If there's a conflict between principles or between the rights of different people involved, is there a way to see one principle as more important than the others? Which option offers actions that are least problematic?

Step 3. *Make a decision.* Take both parts of your analysis into account, and make a decision. This strategy at least gives you some basic steps you can follow.

PROGRESS ✓ QUESTIONS

9. Define *ethical relativism.*

10. Define *applied ethics.*

11. What is an ethical dilemma?

12. Explain the three-step process for resolving an ethical dilemma.

Ethical Reasoning Looking at the information available to us in resolving an ethical dilemma, and drawing conclusions based on that information in relation to our own ethical standards.

If a three-step model seems too simple, Arthur Dobrin identified eight questions you should consider when resolving an ethical dilemma:[3]

1. *What are the facts?* Know the facts as best you can. If your facts are wrong, you're liable to make a bad choice.
2. *What can you guess about the facts you don't know?* Since it is impossible to know all the facts, make reasonable assumptions about the missing pieces of information.
3. *What do the facts mean?* Facts by themselves have no meaning. You need to interpret the information in light of the values that are important to you.
4. *What does the problem look like through the eyes of the people involved?* The ability to walk in another's shoes is essential. Understanding the problem through a variety of perspectives increases the possibility that you will choose wisely.

! Key Point

Apply Dobrin's eight questions to an ethical dilemma you have faced in the past. Would applying this process have changed your decision? Why or why not?

5. *What will happen if you choose one thing rather than another?* All actions have consequences. Make a reasonable guess as to what will happen if you follow a particular course of action. Decide whether you think more good or harm will come of your action.
6. *What do your feelings tell you?* Feelings are facts too. Your feelings about ethical issues may give you a clue as to parts of your decision that your rational mind may overlook.
7. *What will you think of yourself if you decide one thing or another?* Some call this your conscience. It is a form of self-appraisal. It helps you decide whether you are the kind of person you would like to be. It helps you live with yourself.
8. *Can you explain and justify your decision to others?* Your behavior shouldn't be based on a whim. Neither should it be self-centered. Ethics involves you in the life of the world around you. For this reason you must be able to justify your moral decisions in ways that seem reasonable to reasonable people. Ethical reasons can't be private reasons.

The application of these steps is based on some key assumptions: First, that there is sufficient time for the degree of contemplation that such questions require; second, that there is enough information available for you to answer the questions; and third, that the dilemma presents alternative resolutions for you to select from. Without alternatives, your analysis becomes a question of finding a palatable resolution that you can live with—much like Badaracco's sleep test—rather than the most appropriate solution.

ETHICAL REASONING

When we are attempting to resolve an ethical dilemma, we follow a process of **ethical reasoning**. We look at the information available to us and draw conclusions based on that information in relation to our own ethical standards. Lawrence Kohlberg developed a framework (see Figure 1.1) that presents the argument that we develop a reasoning process over time, moving through six distinct stages (classified into three levels of moral development) as we are exposed to major influences in our lives.[4]

Level 1: Preconventional. At this lowest level of moral development, a person's response to a perception of right and wrong is initially directly linked to the expectation of punishment or reward.

- *Stage 1: Obedience and punishment orientation.* A person is focused on avoidance of punishment

Level	Stage	Social Orientation
Preconventional	1	Obedience and punishment
	2	Individualism, instrumentalism, and exchange
Conventional	3	"Good boy/nice girl"
	4	Law and order
Postconventional	5	Social contract
	6	Principled conscience

Figure 1.1 • Lawrence Kohlberg's Stages of Ethical Reasoning

and deference to power and authority—that is, something is right or wrong because a recognized authority figure says it is.

- *Stage 2: Individualism, instrumentalism, and exchange.* As a more organized and advanced

form of Stage 1, a person is focused on satisfying his or her own needs—that is, something is right or wrong because it helps the person get what he or she wants or needs.

Level 2: Conventional. At this level, a person continues to become aware of broader influences outside of the family.

- *Stage 3: "Good boy/nice girl" orientation.* At this stage, a person is focused on meeting the expectations of family members—that is, something is right or wrong because it pleases those family members. Stereotypical behavior is recognized, and conformity to that behavior develops.
- *Stage 4: Law-and-order orientation.* At this stage, a person is increasingly aware of his or her membership in a society and the existence of codes of behavior—that is, something is right or wrong because codes of legal, religious, or social behavior dictate it.

THE OVERCROWDED LIFEBOAT

In 1842, a ship struck an iceberg, and more than 30 survivors were crowded into a lifeboat intended to hold seven. As a storm threatened, it became obvious that the lifeboat would have to be lightened if anyone were to survive. The captain reasoned that the right thing to do in this situation was to force some individuals to go over the side and drown. Such an action, he reasoned, was not unjust to those thrown overboard, for they would have drowned anyway. If he did nothing, however, he would be responsible for the deaths of those whom he could have saved. Some people opposed the captain's decision. They claimed that if nothing were done and everyone died as a result, no one would be responsible for these deaths. On the other hand, if the captain attempted to save some, he could do so only by killing others and their deaths would be his responsibility; this would be worse than doing nothing and letting all die. The captain rejected this reasoning. Since the only possibility for rescue required great efforts of rowing, the captain decided that the weakest would have to be sacrificed. In this situation it would be absurd, he thought, to decide by drawing lots who should be thrown overboard. As it turned out, after days of hard rowing, the survivors were rescued and the captain was tried for his action.

QUESTIONS

1. Did the captain make the right decision? Why or why not?
2. What other choices could the captain have made?
3. If you had been on the jury, how would you have decided? Why?

© Hulton-Deutsch Collection/Corbis

4. Which ethical theory or theories could be applied here?

Source: Adapted from www.friesian.com/valley/dilemmas.htm.

Level 3: Postconventional. At this highest level of ethical reasoning, a person makes a clear effort to define principles and moral values that reflect an individual value system rather than simply reflecting the group position.

- *Stage 5: Social contract legalistic orientation.* At this stage, a person is focused on individual rights and the development of standards based on critical examination—that is, something is right or wrong because it has withstood scrutiny by the society in which the principle is accepted.

- *Stage 6: Universal ethical principle orientation.* At this stage, a person is focused on self-chosen ethical principles that are found to be comprehensive and consistent—that is, something is right or wrong because it reflects that person's individual value system and the conscious choices he or she makes in life. While Kohlberg always believed in the existence of Stage 6, he was never able to find enough research subjects to prove the long-term stability of this stage.

Kohlberg's framework offers us a clearer view into the process of ethical reasoning—that is, that someone can arrive at a decision, in this case the resolution of an ethical dilemma—on the basis of a moral rationale that is built on the cumulative experience of his or her life.

Kohlberg also believed that a person could not move or jump beyond the next stage of his or her six stages. It would be impossible, he argued, for a person to comprehend the moral issues and dilemmas at a level so far beyond his or her life experience and education.

Real World Applications

Michelle takes her managerial role very seriously. Sometimes managers are called on to make tough decisions—firing nonperformers and letting people go when cost cuts have to be made. She has always found a way to come to terms with the tough decisions: "As long as I can sleep at night, then I know I have made the best decision I can under the circumstances." Lately, however, the material in her business ethics class has made her reconsider some of her previous decisions. "Am I really making the best decision or just the decision I can live with?" How do you think most managers would answer that question?

PROGRESS ✓ QUESTIONS

13. What are the eight questions you should consider in resolving an ethical dilemma?
14. What assumptions are we making in the resolution of a dilemma? What should you do if you can't answer these eight questions for the dilemma you are looking to resolve?
15. What are Kohlberg's three levels of moral development?
16. What are the six stages of development in those three levels?

>> Conclusion

Now that we have reviewed the processes by which we arrive at our personal ethical principles, let's consider what happens when we take the study of ethics into the business world. What happens when the decision that is expected of you by your supervisor or manager goes against your personal value system? Consider these situations:

- As a salesperson, you work on a monthly quota. Your sales training outlines several techniques to "up sell" each customer—that is, to add additional features, benefits, or warranties to your product that the average customer doesn't really need. Your sales manager draws a very clear picture for you: If you don't make your quota, you don't have a job. So if your personal value system requires that you sell customers only what they really need, are you willing to make more smaller sales to hit your quota, or do you do what the top performers do and "up sell like crazy" and make every sale count?

- You are a tech-support specialist for a small computer software manufacturer. Your supervisor informs you that a bug has been found in the software that will take several weeks to fix. You are instructed to handle all calls without admitting the existence of the bug. Specific examples are provided to divert customers' concerns with suggestions of user error, hardware issues, and conflicts with other software packages. The bug, you are told, will be fixed in a scheduled version upgrade without any admission of its existence. Could you do that?

How organizations reach a point in their growth where such behavior can become the norm, and how employees of those organizations find a way to work in such environments, is what the field of business ethics is all about.

FRONTLINE FOCUS
Doing the Right Thing—Megan Makes a Decision

Kate was right; they did receive several more applications at the open house, but each one was less attractive as a potential tenant than the Wilsons. Some had credit problems, others couldn't provide references because they had been "living with a family member," and others had short work histories or were new to the area.

This left Megan with a tough choice. The Wilsons were the best applicants, but Kate had made her feelings about them very clear, so Megan's options were fairly obvious—she could follow Kate's instructions and bury the Wilsons' application in favor of another couple, or she could give the apartment to the best tenants and run the risk of making an enemy of her new boss.

The more Megan thought about the situation, the angrier she became. Not giving the apartment to the Wilsons was discriminatory and would expose all of them to legal action if the Wilsons ever found out—plus it was just plain wrong. There was nothing in their application that suggested that they would be anything other than model tenants, and just because Kate had experienced bad tenants like "those people" in the past, there was no reason to group the Wilsons with that class.

Megan picked up the phone and started dialing. "Mrs. Wilson? Hi, this is Megan with Oxford Lake Apartments. I have some wonderful news."

QUESTIONS

1. Did Megan make the right choice here?
2. What do you think Kate's reaction will be?
3. What would have been the risks for Oxford Lake if Megan had decided not to rent the apartment to the Wilsons?

[For Review]

1. **Define ethics.**

   Ethics is the study of how we try to live our lives according to a standard of "right" or "wrong" behavior—in both how we think and behave toward others and how we would like them to think and behave toward us. For some, it is a conscious choice to follow a set of moral standards or ethical principles that provide guidance on how they should conduct themselves in their daily lives. For others, where the choice is not so clear, they look to the behavior of others to determine what is an acceptable standard of right and wrong or good and bad behavior.

2. **Explain the role of values in ethical decision making.**

   Values represent a set of personal principles by which you aim to live your life. Those principles are most often based on religious, cultural, or philosophical beliefs that you have developed over time as a collection of influences from family, friends, school, religion, ethnic background, the media, and your personal mentors and role models. When you try to formalize these principles into a code of behavior, then you are seen to be adopting a value system that becomes your benchmark in deciding which choices and behaviors meet the standard of "doing the right thing."

3. **Understand opposing ethical theories and their limitations.**

   Ethical theories can be divided into three categories: virtue ethics (focusing on individual character and integrity); ethics for the greater good, also referred to as utilitarianism (focusing on the choices that offer the greatest good for the greatest number of people); and universal ethics (focusing on universal principles that should apply to all ethical judgments, irrespective of the outcome). Each category is limited by the absence of a clear sense of accountability for the choices being made. As we have seen in this chapter, individual character and integrity can depend on many influences and are therefore unlikely to be a consistent

   standard. Utilitarianism only focuses on the outcome of the choice without any real concern for the virtue of the actions themselves, and human history has produced many atrocities that have been committed in the name of the "end justifying the means." At the other end of the scale, staying true to morally pure ethical principles without considering the outcome of that choice is equally problematic.

4. **Discuss ethical relativism.**

   In the absence of a truly comprehensive theory of ethics and a corresponding model or checklist to guide them, many people choose to approach ethical decisions by pursuing the comfort of an ethical majority that reflects a combination of the traditions of their society, their personal opinions, and the circumstances of the present moment. This relativist approach offers more flexibility than the pursuit of definitive black-and-white rules. However, the pursuit of an ethical majority in a peer pressure situation can sometimes have negative consequences.

5. **Explain an ethical dilemma, and apply a process to resolve it.**

   An ethical dilemma is a situation in which there is no obvious right or wrong decision, but rather a right or right answer. In such cases you are required to make a choice even though you are probably leaving an equally valid choice unmade and contradicting a personal or societal ethical value in making that choice. There is no definitive checklist for ethical dilemmas because the issues are often situational in nature. Therefore, the best hope for a "right" choice can often fall to the "lesser of two evils" and an outcome you can live with. Arthur Dobrin offers eight questions that should be asked to ensure that you have as much relevant information available as possible (in addition to a clear sense of what you don't know) as to the available choices, the actions needed for each choice, and the anticipated consequences of each choice.

[Key Terms]

Applied Ethics 8

Culture 4

Ethical Dilemma 8

Ethical Reasoning 10

Ethical Relativism 7

Ethics 4

The Golden Rule 6

Instrumental Value 5

Intrinsic Value 4

Society 4

Universal Ethics 6

Utilitarianism 6

Value System 4

Virtue Ethics 6

Review Questions

1. Why do we study ethics?

2. Why should we be concerned about doing "the right thing"

3. If each of us has a unique set of influences and values that contribute to our personal value system, how can that be applied to a community as a whole?

4. Is it unrealistic to expect others to live by the Golden Rule?

5. Consider how you have resolved ethical dilemmas in the past. What would you do differently now?

6. What would you do if your resolution of an ethical dilemma turned out to be the wrong approach and it actually made things worse?

Review Exercises

How would you act in the following situations? Why? How is your personal value system reflected in your choice?

1. You buy a candy bar at the store and pay the cashier with a $5 bill. You are mistakenly given change for a $20 bill. What do you do?

2. You are riding in a taxicab and notice a $20 bill that has obviously fallen from someone's wallet or pocketbook. What do you do?

3. You live in a small Midwestern town and have just lost your job at the local bookstore. The best-paying job you can find is at the local meatpacking plant, but you are a vegetarian and feel strongly that killing animals for food is unjust. What do you do?

4. You are having a romantic dinner with your spouse to celebrate your wedding anniversary. Suddenly, at a nearby table, a man starts yelling at the young woman he is dining with and becomes so verbally abusive that she starts to cry. What do you do?

5. You are shopping in a department store and observe a young man taking a watch from a display stand on the jewelry counter and slipping it into his pocket. What do you do?

6. You are the manager of a nonprofit orphanage. At the end of the year, a local car dealer approaches you with a proposition. He will give you a two-year-old van worth $10,000 that he has just taken as a trade-in on a new vehicle if you will provide him with a tax-deductible donation receipt for a new van worth $30,000. Your current transportation is in very bad shape, and the children really enjoy the field trips they take. Do you accept his proposition?

Internet Exercises

1. Visit the Center for the Study of Ethics in the Professions (CSEP) at the Illinois Institute of Technology: http://ethics.iit.edu.

   a. What is the stated mission of CSEP?

   b. Identify and briefly summarize a current CSEP research project.

   c. Explain the purpose of the "NanoEthicsBank."

   d. Do you think that an "Ethics Bowl" competition at your institution would be useful in discussing the issues of professional ethics? Why or why not?

2. In these days of increasing evidence of questionable ethical practices, many organizations, communities, and business schools are committing to ethics pledges as a means of underscoring the importance of ethical standards of behavior in today's society. Using Internet research, find two examples of such pledges and answer the following questions:

   a. Why did you select these two examples specifically?

   b. Why did each entity choose to make an ethical pledge?

   c. In what ways are the pledges similar and different?

   d. If you proposed the idea of an ethics pledge at your school or job, what do you think the reaction would be?

[Team Exercises]

1. **Take me out to the cheap seats.**

   Divide into two groups, and prepare arguments *for* and *against* the following behavior: *My dad takes me to a lot of baseball games and always buys the cheapest tickets in the park. When the game starts, he moves to better, unoccupied seats, dragging me along. It embarrasses me. Is it OK for us to sit in seats we didn't pay for?*

2. **Umbrella exchange.**

   Divide into two groups, and prepare arguments *for* and *against* the following behavior: *One rainy evening I wandered into a shop, where I left my name-brand umbrella in a basket near the door. When I was ready to leave, my umbrella was gone. There were several others in the basket, and I decided to take another name-brand umbrella. Should I have taken it, or taken a lesser-quality model, or just gotten wet?*

3. **A gift out of the blue.**

   Divide into two groups, and prepare arguments *for* and *against* the following behavior: *I'm a regular customer of a men's clothing mail-order company, and it sends me new catalogs about six times a year. I usually order something because the clothes are good quality with a money-back guarantee, and if the item doesn't fit or doesn't look as good on me as it did in the catalog, the return process is very easy. Last month I ordered a couple of new shirts. When the package arrived, there were three shirts in the box, all in my size, in the three colors available for that shirt. There was no note or card, and the receipt showed that my credit card had been charged for two shirts. I just assumed that someone in the shipping department was recognizing me as a valuable customer—what a nice gesture, don't you think?*

4. **Renting a dress?**

   Divide into two groups, and prepare arguments *for* and *against* the following behavior: *My friend works for a company that manages fund-raising events for nonprofit organizations—mostly gala benefits and auctions. Since these events all take place in the same city, she often crosses paths with the same people from one event to the other. The job doesn't pay a lot, but the dress code is usually very formal. To stretch her budget and ensure that she's not wearing the same dress at every event, she buys dresses, wears them once, has them professionally dry-cleaned, reattaches the label using her own label gun, and returns them to the store, claiming that they were the wrong color or not a good fit. She argues that the dry-cleaning bill is just like a rental charge, and she always returns them for store credit, not cash. The dress shop may have made a sale, but is this fair?*

Source: Exercises 1 and 2 adapted from Randy Cohen, *The Good, the Bad, and the Difference: How to Tell Right from Wrong in Everyday Situations* (New York: Doubleday, 2002), pp. 194–201.

Thinking Critically

>> THREE CUPS OF TEA: MISMANAGEMENT OR FRAUD?

In April 2011, exposés by journalist Jon Krakauer and *60 Minutes* correspondent Steve Kroft cast a dark shadow over the work of Greg Mortenson, a medic, mountaineer, and education advocate whose charity work in Pakistan and Afghanistan had been documented in two best-selling books, *Three Cups of Tea* and *Stones into Schools.* The success of *Three Cups of Tea* (over 5 million copies of the book have been sold) had led to large donations to Mortenson's charity, the ambitiously named Central Asia Institute (CAI), which was originally founded with a $1 million donation by Swiss physicist and fellow mountaineer Dr. Jean Hoerni in 1996.

Source: DoD photo by Sgt. 1st Class William A. Jones, U.S. Army

Three Cups of Tea, written in the third person as an account of Mortenson's life by coauthor David Oliver Relin, begins with Mortenson failing to climb K2, the second-highest mountain on earth, in honor of his little sister Christa, who died in 1992. Exhausted and disoriented in unfamiliar surroundings, Mortenson stumbles into a village that he believes to be Askole. The village is actually Korphe, but the villagers welcome him and take care of him (with multiple cups of tea) while he recuperates from his extreme exhaustion. Mortenson is inspired by their generosity and promises to return and to build them a school.

Fast forward to 2011. Mortenson's charity, CAI, had received over $72 million in donations since 2003 (including $100,000 donated by President Barack Obama from his Nobel Peace Prize in 2009—an award for which, ironically, Mortenson was also nominated) and had $23 million in reserves. Mortenson had given over 500 speaking engagements in the preceding four years, and the CAI had, it claimed, built over 170 schools in Central Asia and was actively supporting dozens more. *Three Cups of Tea* had become required reading for all western military personnel assigned to Central Asia.

Subsequent investigative reporting by Krakauer and CBS correspondent Steve Kroft alleged that much of Mortenson's story was either significantly embellished or fabricated—he didn't lose his way descending from K2; he wasn't rescued by the villagers of Korphe; and he was never captured by the Taliban in 1996 as he claimed in *Three Cups of Tea.* It was further alleged that he was mismanaging the CAI and using it as his "personal ATM." Specific details were later made public in court records that appeared to support these allegations:

- In 2009–2010 Mortenson and his family charged personal items to CAI in the amount of $75,276 that included "LL Bean clothing, iTunes, luggage, luxurious accommodations, and even vacations."
- CAI spent more than $2 million on private charter flights for Mortenson's speaking engagements, even when he was reimbursed for travel fees by event organizers.
- Standard speaking fees started at $15,000 in 2008, with 25 percent of that going to the Penguin Speakers Bureau (Penguin was Mortenson's publisher). In subsequent years, that rate increased to $35,000, with Penguin Speakers Bureau getting the same 25 percent. Mortenson kept the balance of all fees.
- On average, only 41 percent of donations went to CAI's work in Central Asia—much of the rest went to bulk purchases ($3 million) of his books at full retail price to keep them on the best-seller lists (with Mortenson keeping the royalties), to travel expenses, and to advertising costs for the books ($5 million).

Mortenson's defenders argued that he was "more of a founding visionary than the disciplined CEO necessary to run a $20 million-a-year charity." However, investigations by the attorney general of the State of Montana in response to a civil lawsuit verified most of the allegations made against Mortenson. CAI responded by agreeing to a repayment amount by Mortenson of $1 million, by removing him from day-to-day operations (though he remained in a "visionary" capacity with the organization), and by appointing a new, larger board of directors. Other civil litigation was ongoing.

CONTINUED >>

Mortenson, by contrast, blamed his coauthor's "artistic license" and "time compression" in telling his story as being at the root of much of the confusion and misinformation surrounding CAI. Penguin Publishing, the publisher, admitted that minimal fact checking was performed in reviewing the first draft of the book.

Krakauer, who's 2011 report on *Byliner.com,* "Three Cups of Deceit," had brought the original allegations against Mortenson, wrote a follow-up piece for *The Daily Beast* in April 2013. The CAI, it appeared, had dismissed most of the issues raised as nothing more than growing pains for the organization. Mortenson was still very much the public face of the charity, at an annual salary of over $180,000. Krakauer's follow-up report went on to present a list of evidence of continued financial mismanagement in addition to Mortenson's persistent attempts to run CAI as his own fiefdom, even in the face of stricter board oversight.

In November 2015, under increasing pressure from declining donations and persistent media scrutiny, Mortenson announced his retirement from CAI as both an employee and nonvoting member of the board. While donations had fallen from $22.8 million in 2010 to only $2.2 million in 2014, Mortenson had continued to draw an annual salary, earning $194,000 in 2014. As part of the announcement, Mortenson stated that he had agreed to consult with CAI for its overseas programs occasionally, which prompted Krakauer to comment: "I am concerned CAI apparently does not intend to sever all ties with Mortenson, which suggests that the board still doesn't comprehend the harm Mortenson has done."

QUESTIONS

1. Based on the evidence presented in this case study, was Mortenson's work at the CAI an example of deliberate fraud or mismanagement? Defend your position.
2. How does the conduct of the CAI board relate to this case?
3. From a business ethics perspective, which was worse, the conduct of the CAI board or the conduct of Mortenson himself? Why?
4. Why would CAI want to keep Mortenson in a "visionary" capacity?
5. If Mortenson's claims have misled donors, should the CAI return the money? Why or why not?
6. What should be done to restore the reputation of the CAI?

Sources: Matt Volz, "Greg Mortenson, 'Three Cups of Tea' Author, Must Repay Charity $1 Million: Report," *Associated Press,* April 5, 2012; Alex Heard, "The Trials of Greg Mortenson," *Outside Online,* February 12, 2012; Katha Pollitt, "The Bitter Tea of Greg Mortenson," *The Nation,* April 27, 2011; Nicholas D. Kristoff, "Three Cups of Tea, Spilled," *The New York Times,* April 20, 2011; Peter Hessler, "What Mortenson Got Wrong," *The New Yorker,* April 21, 2011; Jon Krakauer, "Three Cups of Deceit," *Byliner,* April 2011; Jon Krakauer, "Is It Time to Forgive Greg Mortenson?" *The Daily Beast,* April 8, 2013; and Eleanor Goldberg, "Disgraced 'Three Cups of Tea' Author to Retire from Charity He Founded," *The Huffington Post,* November 20, 2015.

Thinking Critically 1.2

>> THE MAN WHO SHOCKED THE WORLD

In July 1961, a psychologist at Yale University, Dr. Stanley Milgram, a 28-year-old Harvard graduate with a PhD in social psychology, began a series of experiments that were destined to shock the psychological community and reveal some disturbing insights into the capacity of the human race to inflict harm on one another. Participants in the experiments were members of the general public who had responded to a newspaper advertisement for volunteers in an experiment on punishment and learning.

The "teacher" in the experiment (one of Milgram's team of researchers) instructed the participants to inflict increasingly powerful electric shocks on a test "learner" every time the learner gave an incorrect answer to a word-matching task. The shocks started, in theory, at the low level of 15 volts and increased in 15-volt increments up to a potentially fatal shock of 450 volts. In reality, the voltage machine was an elaborate stage prop, and the learner was an actor screaming and imitating physical suffering as the voltage level of each shock appeared to increase. The participants were told about the deception at the end of the experience, but during the experiment they were led to believe that the voltage and the pain being inflicted were real. The teacher used no force or intimidation in the experiment other than maintaining an air of academic seriousness.

The experiment was repeated more than 20 times using hundreds of research subjects. In every case the majority of the subjects failed to stop shocking the learners, even when they believed they were inflicting a potentially fatal voltage and the learner had apparently stopped screaming with pain. Some did plead to stop the test, and others argued with the teacher that the experiment was going wrong, but in the end, the majority of them obeyed the instructions of the teacher to the letter.

It's important to remind ourselves that these research participants were not criminals or psychopaths with a documented history of sadistic behavior. They were average Americans who responded to an ad and came in off the street to take part. What

© Hulton Archive/Getty Images

Milgram's research appears to tell us is that people are capable of suspending their own individual morality to someone in authority—even killing someone just because they were instructed to do it.

Milgram's research shocked the academic world and generated heated debate about the ethical conduct of the study and the value of the results in comparison to the harm inflicted on the research participants who were led to believe that it was all really happening. That debate continues to this day, even though subsequent repetitions of the study in various formats have validated Milgram's original findings. Almost 50 years later, we are faced with research data that suggest ordinary human beings are capable of performing destructive and inhumane acts without any physical threat of harm to themselves. As Thomas Bass commented, "While we would like to believe that when confronted with a moral dilemma we will act as our conscience dictates, Milgram's obedience experiments teach us that in a concrete situation with powerful social constraints, our moral senses can easily be trampled."

In 2015, Magnolia Pictures released the movie *Experimenter,* starring Peter Sarsgaard as Milgram. The movie documents Milgram's surprise and alarm at how many of the study participants were willing to proceed to the highest level of electric shocks, despite their personal reservations, because the formal design of the experiment required them to. It also examines the objections and concerns that Milgram's research prompted in the academic community, resulting in Milgram's denial for tenure at Harvard after his research approaches were deemed to be unethical.

QUESTIONS

1. Critics of Milgram's research have argued that the physical separation between the participant and the teacher in one room and the learner in the other made it easier for the participant to inflict the shocks. Do you think that made a difference? Why or why not?

2. The treatment of the participants in the study raised as much criticism as the results the study generated. Was it ethical to mislead them into believing that they were really inflicting pain on the learners? Why?

3. The participants were introduced to the learners as equal participants in the study—that is, volunteers just like them. Do you think that made a difference in the decision to keep increasing the voltage? Why?

4. What do you think Milgram's research tells us about our individual ethical standards?

5. Would you have agreed to participate in this study? Why or why not?

6. Do you think if the study were repeated today we would get the same kind of results? Why?

Sources: A. Cohen, "Four Decades after Milgram, We're Still Willing to Inflict Pain," *The New York Times,* December 29, 2008; A. Altman, "Why We're OK with Hurting Strangers," www.time.com, December 19, 2008; and www.magpictures.com/experimenter/.

Thinking Critically

>> **LIFE AND DEATH** • Elder Suicide or Dignified Exit? A Letter from Ohio

I'm 80. I've had a good life—mostly pretty happy, though certainly with its ups and downs. My wife died seven years ago. My children are healthy and happy, busy with their kids, careers, friends. But I know they worry about me; they

© Pixtal/AGE Fotostock RF

feel increasingly burdened with thoughts about how to care for me when I can no longer care for myself, which—let's not kid ourselves—is coming all too soon. I live four states away from them so either they will have to uproot me and move me close to them or I'll have to go live in a nursing home. I don't relish either option. This town has been my home for nearly my whole adult life, and I don't fancy leaving. On the other hand, I do not want to live among strangers and be cared for by those who are paid minimum wage to wash urine-soaked sheets and force-feed pudding to old people.

I'm in decent health—for the moment. But things are slipping. I have prostate cancer, like just about every other man my age. It probably won't kill me . . . but having to get up and pee four or five times a night, standing over the bowl for long minutes just hoping something will come out, this might do me in. My joints are stiff, so it doesn't really feel good to walk. I've got bits and pieces of skin cancer here and there that need to be removed. These things are all treatable, or so they say (there are pills to take and procedures to have done). But it seems to me a waste of money. Why not pass my small savings on to my grandkids, to give them a jump on college tuition?

What I don't understand is why people think that it is wrong for someone like me to just call it a day, throw in the towel. How can it be possible that I don't have a right to end my own life, when I'm ready? (But apparently I don't.)

I'm tired and I'm ready to be done with life. I'd so much rather just quietly die in my garage with the car running than eke out these last few compromised years. (Even better would be a quick shot or a small dose of powerful pills—but, alas, these are not at my disposal.)

But if I do myself in, I will be called a suicide. My death will be added to the statistics: another "elder suicide." How sad! (Doesn't the fact that so many elderly people commit suicide—and with much greater rates of success, I must say, than any other demographic group—tell you something?) Why can't this society just come up with a humane, acceptable plan for those of us ready to be finished? Why can't we old folks go to city hall and pick up our End-of-Life Packet, with the financial and legal forms to bring things into order for our children, with assistance on how to recycle all our unneeded furniture and clothes, and with a neat little pack of white pills: When ready, take all 10 pills at once, with plenty of water. Lie down quietly in a comfortable place, close your eyes, and wait.

How can choosing my own end at my own time be considered anything other than a most dignified final exit?

— Anonymous, June 2003

QUESTIONS

1. Should people have the moral right to end their lives if they so please?
2. Does being near the end of one's life make the decision to end it justified?
3. What might the phrase "right to die" mean?
4. Do people have the right to seek assistance in dying?
5. Do people have the right to give assistance in dying?
6. What kind of restrictions, if any, should there be on assisted suicide?

Source: Jessica Pierce, *Morality Play: Case Studies in Ethics* (New York: McGraw-Hill, 2005).

[References]

1. Joseph L. Badaracco Jr., *Defining Moments: When Managers Must Choose between Right and Right* (Cambridge, MA: Harvard Business School Press, 1997), pp. 41–42.

2. The Center for Business and Ethics, Loyola Marymount University, www.ethicsandbusiness.org/strategy.htm.

3. Arthur Dobrin, *Ethics for Everyone: How to Increase Your Moral Intelligence* (New York: Wiley, 2002), pp. 31–32.

4. Lawrence Kohlberg, *Essays in Moral Development,* Vol. I, *The Philosophy of Moral Development* (New York: Harper & Row, 1981); Lawrence Kohlberg, *Essays in Moral Development,* Vol. II, *The Psychology of Moral Development* (New York: Harper & Row, 1984).

© Dave and Les Jacobs/Blend Images LLC

DEFINING BUSINESS ETHICS

After studying this chapter, you should be able to:

2-1 Define the term *business ethics*.

2-2 Identify an organization's stakeholders.

2-3 Discuss the position that business ethics is an oxymoron.

2-4 Summarize the history of business ethics.

2-5 Identify and propose a resolution for an ethical dilemma in your work environment.

2-6 Explain how executives and employees seek to justify unethical behavior.

FRONTLINE FOCUS

The Customer Is Always Right

Carol was the shift leader at a local fast-food restaurant. She started working there as a summer job for gas money for the old Honda Civic she used to drive. That was more years ago than she cared to remember, and she had managed to upgrade her car to something far more reliable these days. She enjoyed working for this company. The job was hard on her feet, but when she hit the breakfast, lunch, or dinner rush, she was usually too busy to notice.

Today was an important day. Dave, the store manager, had called an "all staff meeting" to discuss the new healthy menu that the company had launched in response to public pressure for healthier lunch choices—lots of salads and new options for their side items. It was going to take a lot of work to get her staff up to speed, and Carol expected that a lot of the customers would need extra time to work through all the new options, but overall she liked the new menu. She thought that the new lower-priced items would bring in a lot of new customers who were looking for something more than burgers and fries.

The company had sent a detailed information kit for the new menu, and Dave covered the material very thoroughly. As he finished the last PowerPoint slide, he asked if anyone had any questions. Since they had been in the meeting for over an hour, her team was very conscious of all the work that wasn't getting done for the lunch rush, so no one asked any questions.

As a last comment Dave said: "This new menu should hopefully bring in some new customers, but let's not forget what we're doing here. We're here to make money for our shareholders, and to do that, we have to make a profit. So we're only going to make a limited number of these new items. If they run out, offer customers something from the regular menu and don't forget to push the "up-size" menu options and ice creams for dessert—those are still our most profitable items. And if someone wants one of these new healthy salads, make sure you offer them an ice cream or shake to go with it."

Carol was amazed. The company was making a big push for this new menu and spending a ton of money on advertising, and here was Dave planning to sabotage it just because he was afraid that these lower-priced items would hurt his sales (and his bonus!).

QUESTIONS

1. Look at Figures 2.1 and 2.2, and identify which stakeholders would be directly impacted by Dave's plan to sabotage the new healthy menu.
2. Describe the ethical dilemma that Carol is facing here.
3. What should Carol do now?

A large company was hiring a new CEO. The four leading candidates worked inside the company so the board decided to ask each candidate a very basic question. The comptroller was brought in. "How much is 2 plus 2?" "This must be a trick question, but the answer is 4. It will always be 4." They brought in the head of research and development, an engineer by training. "How much is 2 plus 2?" "That depends on whether it is a positive 2 or a negative 2. It could be 4, zero, or minus 4." They brought in the head of marketing. "The way I figure it, 2 plus 2 is 22." Finally, they brought in legal counsel. "How much is 2 plus 2?" they asked. He looked furtively at each board member. "How much do you want it to be?"

Tom Selleck, Commencement Speech, Pepperdine University, 2000

>> Defining Business Ethics

Business ethics involves the application of standards of moral behavior to business situations. Just as we saw in our review of the basic ethical concepts of right and wrong in Chapter 1, students of business ethics can approach the topic from two distinct perspectives:

1. A *descriptive* summation of the customs, attitudes, and rules that are observed within a business. As such, we are simply documenting what is happening.
2. A *normative* (or *prescriptive*) evaluation of the degree to which the observed customs, attitudes, and rules can be said to be ethical. Here we are more interested in recommending what should be happening.

Business Ethics The application of ethical standards to business behavior.

Stakeholder Someone with a share or interest in a business enterprise.

In either case, business ethics should not be applied as a separate set of moral standards or ethical concepts from general ethics. Ethical behavior, it is argued, should be the same both inside and outside a business situation. By recognizing the challenging environment of business, we are acknowledging the identity of the key players impacted by any potentially unethical behavior—the stakeholders. In addition, we can identify the troubling situation where your personal values may be placed in direct conflict with the standards of behavior you feel are expected of you by your employer.

>> Who Are the Stakeholders?

Figure 2.1 maps out the relevant **stakeholders** for any organization and their respective interests in the ethical operation of that organization. Not every stakeholder will be relevant in every business situation—not all companies use wholesalers to deliver their products or services to their customers, and customers would not be involved in payroll decisions between the organization and its employees.

Of greater concern is the involvement of these stakeholders with the actions of the organization and the extent to which they would be impacted by unethical behavior. As Figure 2.2 illustrates, the decision of an organization such as WorldCom in the late 1990s to hide the extensive debt and losses it was accumulating in its aggressive pursuit of growth and market share can be seen to have impacted all its stakeholders in different ways.

FIG. 2.1 Stakeholder Interests

Stakeholders	Interest in the Organization
Stockholders or shareholders	• Growth in the value of company stock • Dividend income
Employees	• Stable employment at a fair rate of pay • A safe and comfortable working environment
Customers	• "Fair exchange"—a product or service of acceptable value and quality for the money spent • Safe and reliable products
Suppliers/vendor partners	• Prompt payment for delivered goods • Regular orders with an acceptable profit margin
Retailers/wholesalers	• Accurate deliveries of quality products on time and at a reasonable cost • Safe and reliable products
Federal government	• Tax revenue • Operation in compliance with all relevant legislation
Creditors	• Principal and interest payments • Repayment of debt according to the agreed schedule
Community	• Employment of local residents • Economic growth • Protection of the local environment

FIG. 2.2 Stakeholder Impact from Unethical Behavior

Stakeholders	Interest in the Organization
Stockholders or shareholders	• False and misleading financial information on which to base investment decisions • Loss of stock value • Cancellation of dividends
Employees	• Loss of employment • Not enough money to pay severance packages or meet pension obligations
Customers	• Poor service quality (as WorldCom struggled to combine the different operating and billing systems of each company it acquired, for example)
Suppliers/vendor partners	• Delayed payment for delivered goods and services • Unpaid invoices when the company declared bankruptcy
Federal government	• Loss of tax revenue • Failure to comply with all relevant legislation
Creditors	• Loss of principal and interest payments • Failure to repay debt according to the agreed schedule
Community	• Unemployment of local residents • Economic decline

PROGRESS ✔ QUESTIONS

1. Explain the term *business ethics*.
2. Explain the difference between a descriptive and prescriptive approach to business ethics.
3. Identify six stakeholders of an organization.
4. Give four examples of how stakeholders could be negatively impacted by unethical corporate behavior.

>> An Ethical Crisis: Is *Business Ethics* an Oxymoron?

Our objective in identifying the types of unethical concerns that can arise in the business environment and the impact that such unethical behavior can have on the stakeholders of an organization is to develop the ability to anticipate such events and ultimately to put the appropriate policies and procedures in place to prevent such behavior from happening.

Unfortunately, over the past two decades, the ethical track record of many organizations would lead us to believe that no such policies or procedures have been in place. The standard of **corporate governance**, the extent to which the officers of a corporation are fulfilling the duties and responsibilities of their offices to the relevant stakeholders, appears to be at the lowest level in business history:

Corporate Governance The system by which business corporations are directed and controlled.

- Several prominent organizations (all former "Wall Street darlings")—Enron, WorldCom, Lehman Brothers, Bear Stearns—were found to have hidden the true state of their precarious finances from their stakeholders.
- Others—Adelphia Cable, Tyco, Merrill Lynch—were found to have senior officers who appeared to regard the organization's funds as their personal bank accounts.
- Financial reports are released that are then restated at a later date.
- Products are rushed to market that have to be recalled at a later date due to safety problems (Takata air bags).
- Organizations are being sued for monopolistic practices (Microsoft), race and gender discrimination (Walmart, Texaco, Denny's), and environmental contamination (GE).
- CEO salary increases far exceed those of the employees they lead.
- CEO salaries have increased while shareholder returns have fallen. According to the High Pay Centre, for example, Bob Dudley, the chief executive of oil giant BP, received a 20 percent pay increase to nearly $20 million in 2015, despite laying off 7,000 employees and overseeing a performance deficit of $6.5 billion.

It is understandable, therefore, that many observers would believe that the business world lacks any sense of ethical behavior whatsoever. Some would even argue that the two words are as incompatible as *government efficiency, Central Intelligence Agency,* or *authentic reproduction,* but is *business ethics* really an **oxymoron?**

It would be unfair to brand every organization as fundamentally unethical in its business dealings. There's no doubt that numerous prominent organizations that were previously held as models of aggressive business management (e.g., Enron, Global Crossing, HealthSouth, IMClone, Tyco, and WorldCom) have later been proved to be fundamentally flawed in their ethical practices. This has succeeded in bringing the issue to the forefront of public awareness. However, the positive outcome from this has been increased attention to the need for third-party guarantees of ethical conduct

Oxymoron The combination of two contradictory terms, such as "deafening silence" or "jumbo shrimp."

Code of Ethics A company's written standards of ethical behavior that are designed to guide managers and employees in making the decisions and choices they face every day.

and active commitments from the rest of the business world. Institutions such as the Ethics and Compliance Officer Association (now part of the Ethics and Compliance Initiative (ECI)), the Ethics Resource Center (also part of the ECI), and the Society of Corporate Compliance and Ethics, among others, now offer organizations clear guidance and training in making explicit commitments to ethical business practices.[1]

So while these may not be the best of times for business ethics, it could be argued that the recent negative publicity has served as a wake-up call for many organizations to take a more active role in establishing standards of ethical conduct in their daily operations. One of the key indicators in this process has been the increased prominence of a formal **code of ethics** in an organization's public statements. The Ethics Resource Center (ERC) defines a code of ethics as:[2]

A central guide to support day-to-day decision making at work. It clarifies the cornerstones of your organization—its mission, values and principles—helping your managers, employees and stakeholders

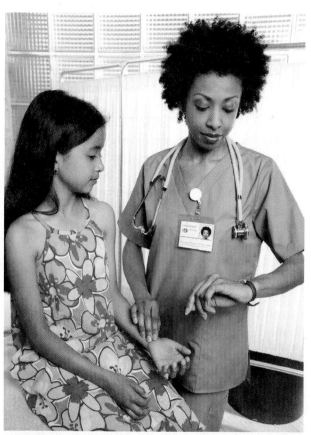

© Custom Medical Stock Photo/Alamy

© BananaStock/PunchStock RF

How do conversations regarding ethics change when your business is closely linked to human well-being? Should ethical standards be different for a hospital or day care center?

understand how these cornerstones translate into everyday decisions, behaviors and actions. While some may believe codes are designed to limit one's actions, the best codes are actually structured to liberate and empower people to make more effective decisions with greater confidence.

PROGRESS ✔ QUESTIONS

5. Define the term *oxymoron* and provide three examples.

6. Is the term *business ethics* an oxymoron? Explain your answer.

7. Define the term *corporate governance*.

8. Explain the term *code of ethics*.

The code of ethics can be seen to serve a dual function. As a message to the organization's stakeholders, the code should represent a clear corporate commitment to the highest standards of ethical behavior. As an internal document, the code should represent a clear guide to managers and employees in making the decisions and choices they face every day. Unfortunately, as you will see in many of the case studies and discussion exercises in this book, a code of ethics can be easily sidestepped or ignored by any organization.

> **Key Point**
>
> Does your company have a code of ethics? Where is it published? How frequently does the company promote it?

THE FORD PINTO

Forty years after its production, the Ford Pinto is still remembered as a dangerous firetrap.

In the late 1960s, the baby boom generation was starting to attend college. With increasing affluence in America, demand for affordable transportation increased, and foreign carmakers captured the market with models like the Volkswagen Beetle and Toyota Corolla. Ford needed a competitive vehicle, and Lee Iacocca authorized production of the Pinto. It was to be small and inexpensive—under 2,000 pounds and under $2,000. The production schedule had it in dealers' lots in the 1971 model year, which meant that it went from planning to production in under two years. At the time, it was typical to make a prototype vehicle first and then gear up production. In this case, Ford built the machines that created the shell of the vehicle at the same time as it was designing the first model. This concurrent development shortened production time but made modifications harder.

The compact design used a so-called saddlebag gas tank, which straddled the rear axle. In tests, rear impacts over 30 mph sometimes caused the tank to rupture in such a way that it sprayed gas particles into the passenger compartment, somewhat like an aerosol. Canadian regulations demanded a greater safety factor, and models for export were modified with an extra buffer layer. However, the Pinto met all U.S. federal standards at the time it was made.

Ford actively campaigned against stricter safety standards throughout the production of the Pinto. The government embraced cost–benefit analysis, and Ford's argument against further regulations hinged on the purported benefits. Under pressure, the National Highway

← **ETHICAL**   **DILEMMA** →

© AP Photo

Traffic Safety Administration came up with a figure that put a value of just over $200,000 on a human life. Using this figure, and projecting some 180 burn deaths a year, Ford argued that retrofitting the Pinto would be overly problematic.

At one point, more than 2 million Pintos were on the road, so it is not surprising that they were involved in a number of crashes. However, data began to indicate that some kinds of crashes, particularly rear-end and rollover crashes, were more likely to produce fires in the Pinto than in comparable vehicles. A dramatic article in *Mother Jones* drew on internal Ford memos to show that the company was aware of the safety issue and indicted the company for selling cars "in which it knew hundreds of people would needlessly burn to death." It also claimed that installing a barrier between the tank and the

CONTINUED >>

passenger compartment was an inexpensive fix (less than $20). In 1978, in an almost unprecedented case in Goshen, Indiana, the state charged the company itself with the criminal reckless homicide of three young women. The company was acquitted, largely because the judge confined the evidence to the particular facts—the car was stalled and rammed at high speed by a pickup truck—but Ford was faced with hundreds of lawsuits and a severely tarnished reputation.

Under government pressure, and just before new standards were enacted, Ford recalled 1.5 million Pintos in 1978. The model was discontinued in 1980.

Lee Iacocca said that his company did not deliberately make an unsafe vehicle, that the proportion of deadly accidents was not unusually high for the model, and that the controversy was essentially a legal and public relations issue.

QUESTIONS

1. Should a manufacturer go beyond government standards if it feels there may be a potential safety hazard with its product?

2. Once the safety issue became apparent, should Ford have recalled the vehicle and paid for the retrofit? Should it have invited owners to pay for the new barrier if they so chose? If only half the owners responded to the recall, what would the company's obligation be?

3. Is there a difference for a consumer between being able to make a conscious decision about upgrading safety features (such as side airbags) and relying on the manufacturer to determine features such as the tensile strength of the gas tank?

4. Once Pintos had a poor reputation, they were often sold at a discount. Do private sellers have the same obligations as Ford if they sell a car they know may have design defects? Does the discount price absolve sellers from any responsibility for the product?

Source: K. Gibson, *Business Ethics: People, Profits, and the Planet* (New York: McGraw-Hill, 2006), pp. 630–32.

>> The History of Business Ethics

Figure 2.3 documents a brief history of business ethics. It illustrates several dramatic changes that have taken place in the business environment over the past five decades:

- The increased presence of an employee voice has made individual employees feel more comfortable speaking out against actions of their employers that they feel to be irresponsible or unethical. They are also more willing to seek legal resolution for such issues as unsafe working conditions, harassment, discrimination, and invasion of privacy.
- The issue of corporate social responsibility has advanced from an abstract debate to a core performance-assessment issue with clearly established legal liabilities.
- Corporate ethics has moved from the domain of legal and human resource departments into the organizational mainstream with the appointment of corporate ethics officers with clear mandates.
- Codes of ethics have matured from cosmetic public relations documents into performance-measurement documents that an increasing number of organizations are now committing to share with all their stakeholders.

- The 2002 Sarbanes-Oxley Act has introduced greater accountability for chief executive officers and boards of directors in signing off on the financial performance records of the organizations they represent.

PROGRESS ✓ QUESTIONS

9. Identify a major ethical dilemma in each of the past five decades.
10. Identify a key development in business ethics in each of the past five decades.
11. Which decade saw the most development in business ethics? Why?
12. Which decade saw the most ethical dilemmas? Why?

>> Resolving Ethical Dilemmas

So what does all this mean for the individual employee on the front lines of the organization, dealing with stakeholders on a daily basis? In most cases, the code of ethics that is displayed so prominently for all stakeholders to see (and, presumably, be reassured

FIG. 2.3 A Brief History of Business Ethics

Decade	Ethical Climate	Major Ethical Dilemmas	Business Ethics Developments
1960s	Social unrest. Antiwar sentiment. Employees have an adversarial relationship with management. Values shift away from loyalty to an employer to loyalty to ideas. Old values are cast aside.	• Environmental issues. • Increased employee-employer tension. • Civil rights issues dominate. • Honesty. • The work ethic changes. • Drug use escalates.	• Companies begin establishing codes of conduct and values statements. • Birth of social responsibility movement. • Corporations address ethics issues through legal or personnel departments.
1970s	Defense contractors and other major industries riddled by scandal. The economy suffers through recession. Unemployment escalates. There are heightened environmental concerns. The public pushes to make businesses accountable for ethical shortcomings.	• Employee militancy (employee versus management mentality). • Human rights issues surface (forced labor, substandard wages, unsafe practices). • Some firms choose to cover rather than correct dilemmas.	• Ethics Resource Center (ERC) founded (1977). • Compliance with laws highlighted. • Federal Corrupt Practices Act passed in 1977. • Values movement begins to move ethics away from compliance orientation to being "values centered."
1980s	The social contract between employers and employees is redefined. Defense contractors are required to conform to stringent rules. Corporations downsize and employees' attitudes about loyalty to the employer are eroded. Health care ethics are emphasized.	• Bribes and illegal contracting practices. • Influence peddling. • Deceptive advertising. • Financial fraud (savings and loan scandal). • Transparency issues arise.	• ERC develops the U.S. Code of Ethics for Government Service (1980). • ERC forms first business ethics office at General Dynamics (1985). • Defense Industry Initiative established. • Some companies create ombudsman positions in addition to ethics officer roles. • False Claims Act (government contracting).
1990s	Global expansion brings new ethical challenges. There are major concerns about child labor, facilitation payments (bribes), and environmental issues. The emergence of the Internet challenges cultural borders. What was forbidden becomes common.	• Unsafe work practices in developing countries. • Increased corporate liability for personal damage (cigarette companies, Dow Chemical, etc.). • Financial mismanagement and fraud.	• Federal sentencing guidelines (1991). • Class-action lawsuits. • Global Sullivan Principles (1999). • In re Caremark (Delaware Chancery Court ruling regarding board responsibility for ethics). • International Guidelines requiring voluntary disclosure. • ERC establishes international business ethics centers. • Royal Dutch/Shell International begins issuing annual reports on its ethical performance.
2000s		• Cyber crime. • Increased corporate liability. • Privacy issues (data mining). • Financial mismanagement. • International corruption. • Loss of privacy—employees versus employers. • Intellectual property theft.	• Business regulations mandate stronger ethical safeguards (Federal Sentencing Guidelines for Organizations; Sarbanes-Oxley Act of 2002). • Anticorruption efforts grow. • Shift to emphasis on corporate social responsibility and integrity management. • Formation of international ethics centers to serve the needs of global business. • OECD Convention on Bribery (1997–2000).

Source: Adapted from Ethics Resource Center, "Business Ethics Timeline." Copyright © 2002, Ethics Resource Center.

by) offers very little guidance when employees face ethical conflicts in the daily performance of their work responsibilities. When employees observe unethical behavior (e.g., fraud, theft of company property, or incentives being paid under the table to suppliers or vendor partners) or are asked to do something that conflicts with their own personal values (selling customers products or services they don't need or that don't fill their needs), the extent of the guidance available to them is often nothing more than a series of clichés:

- Consult the company code of ethics.
- Do what's right for the organization's stakeholders.
- Do what's legal.
- Do what you think is best ("use your best judgment").
- Do the right thing.

© PNC/The Image Bank/Getty Images RF

What would you do if your supervisor had too much to drink?

However, in many cases, the scenario the employee faces is not a clear-cut case of right and wrong, but a case of right versus right. In this scenario, the **ethical dilemma** involves a situation that requires selecting between conflicting values that are important to the employee or the organization. For example:[3]

Ethical Dilemma A situation in which there is no obvious right or wrong decision, but rather a right or right answer.

- You have worked at the same company with your best friend for the past 10 years—in fact, he told you about the job and got you the interview. He works in the marketing department and is up for a promotion to marketing director—a position he has been wanting for a long time. You work in sales, and on your weekly conference call, the new marketing director—someone recruited from outside the company—joins you. Your boss explains that although the formal announcement hasn't been made yet, the company felt it was important to get the new director up to speed as quickly as possible. He will be joining the company in two weeks, after completing his two weeks' notice with his current employer. Should you tell your friend what happened?
- You work in a small custom metal fabrication company that is a wholly owned subsidiary of a larger conglomerate. Your parent company has announced cost-cutting initiatives that include a freeze on pay increases, citing "current market difficulties." At the same time, the CEO trades in the old company plane for a brand-new Gulfstream jet. Your colleagues are planning to strike over the unfair treatment—a strike that will cause considerable hardship for many of your customers who have come to rely on your company as a quality supplier. Do you go on strike with them?
- At a picnic given by your employer for all the company's employees, you observe that your supervisor—who is also a friend—has had a bit too much to drink. As you're walking home after the party, she stops her car and asks if you'd like a ride home. Do you refuse her offer, perhaps jeopardizing the friendship, or take a chance on not getting home safely?

RESOLUTION

Resolution of an ethical dilemma can be achieved by first recognizing the type of conflict you are dealing with:

- *Truth versus loyalty.* Do you tell the truth or remain loyal to the person or organization that is asking you not to reveal that truth?
- *Short term versus long term.* Does your decision have a short-term consequence or a longer-term consequence?
- *Justice versus mercy.* Do you perceive this issue as a question of dispensing justice or mercy? (Which one are you more comfortable with?)
- *Individual versus community.* Will your choice affect one individual or a wider group or community?

In the examples used above, both sides are right to some extent, but since you can't take both actions, you are required to select the better or higher right based on your own resolution process. In the first example, the two rights you are facing are:

- It is right, on the one hand, to tell your friend the truth about not getting the promotion. After all, you know the truth, and what kind of world would this be if people did not honor the truth? Perhaps your friend would prefer to hear the truth from you and would be grateful for time to adjust to the idea.

• It is right, on the other hand, not to say anything to your friend because the person who told you in the first place asked you to keep it secret and you must be loyal to your promises. Also, your friend may prefer to hear the news from his supervisor and may be unhappy with you if you tell.

In this example you are faced with a truth versus loyalty conflict: Do you tell your friend the truth or remain loyal to the person who swore you to secrecy?

Once you have reached a decision as to the type of conflict you are facing, three resolution principles are available to you:

• *Ends-based.* Which decision would provide the greatest good for the greatest number of people?
• *Rules-based.* What would happen if everyone made the same decision as you?
• *The Golden Rule.* Do unto others as you would have them do unto you.

None of these principles can be said to offer a perfect solution or resolution to the problem since you cannot possibly predict the reactions of the other people involved in the scenario. However, the process of resolution at least offers something more meaningful than "going with your gut feeling" or "doing what's right."

PROGRESS ✓ QUESTIONS

13. Give four examples of the clichés employees often hear when faced with an ethical dilemma.
14. List the four types of ethical conflict.
15. List the three principles available to you in resolving an ethical dilemma.
16. Give an example of an ethical business dilemma you have faced in your career, and explain how you resolved it, indicating the type of conflict you experienced and the resolution principle you adopted.

Life Skills

>> Making tough choices

What happens when your personal values appear to directly conflict with those of your employer? Three options are open to you: (1) Leave and find another job (not as easy as it sounds); (2) keep your head down, do what you have been asked to do, and hold onto the job; and (3) talk to someone in the company about how uncomfortable the situation is making you feel and see if you can change things. All three options represent a tough choice that you may face at some point in your career. The factors that you will have to consider in making that choice will also change as you move through your working life. Making a job change on the basis of an ethical principle may seem much less challenging to a single person with fewer responsibilities than to a midlevel manager with a family and greater financial obligations.

The important point to remember here is that while an ethical dilemma may put you in a tough situation in the present, the consequences of the choice you make may remain with you far into the future. For that reason, make the choice as objectively and unemotionally as you can. Use the checklists and other tools that are available to you in this book to work through the exact nature of the issue so that you can resolve it in a manner that you can live with.

>> Justifying Unethical Behavior

So how do supposedly intelligent, and presumably experienced, executives and employees manage to commit acts that end up inflicting such harm on their companies, colleagues, customers, and vendor partners? Saul Gellerman identified "four commonly held rationalizations that can lead to misconduct":[4]

1. *A belief that the activity is within reasonable ethical and legal limits—that is, that it is not "really" illegal or immoral.* Andrew Young is quoted as having said, "Nothing is illegal if a hundred businessmen decide to do it." The notion that anything that isn't specifically labeled as wrong must be OK is an open invitation for the ethically challenged employer and employee— especially if there are explicit rewards for such creativity within those newly expanded ethical limits. The Porsches and Jaguars that became the vehicles of choice for Enron's young and aggressive employees were all the incentives needed for newly hired employees to adjust their viewpoint on the company's creative practices.

2. *A belief that the activity is in the individual's or the corporation's best interests—that the individual would somehow be expected to undertake the activity.* In a highly competitive environment, working on short-term targets, it can be easy to find justification for any act as being "in the company's best interest." If landing that big sale or beating your competitor to market with the latest product upgrades can be seen to ensure large profits, strong public relations, a healthy stock price, job security for hundreds if not thousands of employees, not to mention a healthy bonus and promotion for you, the issue of doing whatever it takes becomes a much more complex, increasingly gray ethical area.

3. *A belief that the activity is safe because it will never be found out or publicized—the classic*

© Jon Lund/Blend Images LLC RF

companies to avoid up to $695 billion in taxes. Should any one of these companies ever need any of the money being held overseas, rather than "repatriating" the funds (and paying taxes), the company simply borrows the money from its subsidiary as a short-term loan (and pays no taxes). HP has used this strategy to borrow funds from subsidiaries in Belgium and the Cayman Islands.

QUESTIONS

1. Summarize the positions of both critics and supporters of these tax strategies.
2. Supporters and critics of these tax strategies agree that corporations are making use of legal financial options that are available to them under current tax law. However, does that equate to ethical business conduct? Why or why not?

3. The French chairman and CEO of Louis Vuitton, Bernard Arnault, announced that he would leave France for Belgium, allegedly to avoid the new highest-income tax rate of 75 percent. Is that any different from what corporations are doing? Why or why not?
4. Is there a potential solution that would represent a more ethical business approach to the payment of corporate taxes? Explain your answer.

Sources: "Corporate Tax Avoidance: The Price Isn't Right," *The Economist,* September 21, 2012; Geoff Lye, "Tax Avoidance: It May Be Legal but Is It Responsible?" *SustainAbility,* October 16, 2012; Jesse Drucker, "Google Revenues Sheltered in No-Tax Bermuda Soar to $10 Billion," *Bloomberg,* December 10, 2012; "Google Coughs up £130 Million Back Taxes," *The Register,* January 23, 2016; and Renae Merle, "How U.S. Companies Are Avoiding $695 Billion in Taxes," *The Washington Post,* March 4, 2016.

Real World Applications

Jane enjoyed her job as a human resource generalist— helping to recruit and hire new employees and seeing those employees succeed in the organization was very rewarding. Occasionally an employee performed below expectations and would be asked to leave the company. Today was one of those days. Steve had been caught falsifying sales reports to make sure he hit his monthly quota, and Jane had been asked to sit in on the meeting in which Steve's manager confronted him with the news. What amazed Jane was Steve's response: "Everybody does it in some form or another. As far as this company is concerned, you're only as good as your last quarter, and sometimes you have to bend the rules a little to meet that expectation." Is Steve's statement a valid defense? Why or why not?

crime-and-punishment issue of discovery. Every unethical act that goes undiscovered reinforces this belief. Companies that rely on the deterrents of audits and spot checks make some headway in discouraging unethical behavior (or at least prompting people to think twice about it). Gellerman argues, "A trespass detected should not be dealt with discreetly. Managers should announce the misconduct and how the individuals involved were punished. Since the main deterrent to illegal or unethical behavior is the perceived probability of detection, managers should make an example of people who are detected."

4. *A belief that because the activity helps the company, the company will condone it and even protect the person who engages in it.* This belief suggests some confusion over the loyalty being demonstrated here. Companies engaged in unethical behavior— willingly or otherwise—may protect the identity of the personnel involved but only for as long as it is in the company's best interests to do so. Once that transgression is made public and regulatory bodies get involved, most cases would seem to suggest that the situation rapidly becomes one of every man for himself. As illustrated by the Enron case, once the extent of the fraud became public, everyone involved suddenly became eager to distance him- or herself from both the activity and any key personnel in direct contact with that activity.

> ## Key Point !
>
> Which of the four rationalizations for unethical behavior do you think gets used the most? Why?

>> Conclusion

It is unfortunate that the media have been given so much material on unethical corporate behavior over the past two decades. Unethical CEOs have become household names to the extent that the term *business ethics* seems to be more of an oxymoron now than ever before. In such a negative environment, it is easy to forget that businesses can and do operate in an ethical manner and that the majority of employees really are committed to doing the right thing in their time at work. The organizations that build an ethical culture based on that fundamental belief can be seen to succeed in exactly the same manner as their more "creative" counterparts, with increased revenue, profits, and market share. In the following chapters we examine how they attempt to do just that.

However, as we will see in the following chapters, the challenge of building and operating an ethical business requires a great deal more than simply doing the right thing. The organization must devote time to the development of a detailed code of ethics that offers "guidance with traction" as opposed to traditional general platitudes that are designed to cover a multitude of scenarios with a healthy mix of inspiration and motivation.

Of greater concern is the support offered to employees when they are faced with an ethical dilemma. This involves not only the appointment of a designated corporate ethics officer with all the appropriate policies and procedures for bringing an issue to his or her attention but also the creation and ongoing maintenance of a corporate culture of *trust*.

FRONTLINE FOCUS
The Customer Is Always Right—Carol Makes a Decision

Rachel, one of Carol's brightest team members, identified the problem that Dave had created for them right away: "So we have a new menu that's supposed to bring in new customers, but we're only going to make a few healthy items to ensure that we sell lots of our unhealthy but more profitable items—is that it?"

"Looks like it," said Carol.

"Well, I hope I'm not working the drive-thru window when we start to run out of the new items," said Rachel. "Can you say 'bait and switch'?"

Fortunately, the new menu items wouldn't start until next week, so Carol had time to work on this potential disaster. She couldn't believe that Dave was being so shortsighted here. She understood his concern about sales, but healthier menu items would bring in new customers, not reduce his sales to existing ones. Sure, some might switch from their Jumbo Burger to a salad once in a while, but the new sales would more than make up for that. Plus, advertising items and then deliberately running out just wasn't right. She'd run out of things before—if there had been a run on a particular item or Dave had messed up the supply order—but she had never deliberately not made items just to push customers toward more profitable items before, and she didn't plan to start now.

For the first week of the new menu choices, Carol worked harder than she had done in a long time. She covered the drive-thru window through the breakfast, lunch, and dinner rushes, and when Dave made his trips to the bank for change or to their suppliers when he forgot something in the supply order, she ran in the back and made extra portions to make sure they never ran out. It was a close call once or twice when she was making things to order, but the customers were never kept waiting.

At the end of the week, she had all the information she needed. Sales were up—way up—the new items were a big hit. She had been able to sell everything she had made without affecting the sales of their traditional items. Now all she had to do was confess to Dave.

QUESTIONS

1. Did Carol make the right choice here?
2. What do you think Dave's reaction will be?
3. What would the risk have been for the restaurant if they had implemented Dave's plan and deliberately run out of the new items?

[For Review]

1. **Define the term *business ethics*.**

   Business ethics involves the application of standards of moral behavior to business situations. The subject can be approached from a descriptive *perspective (documenting what is happening) or a* prescriptive *perspective (recommending what should be happening). In either case, the expectation is that business ethics should not be a separate set of standards from general ethics. Ethical behavior, it is argued, should be the same both inside and outside a business situation.*

2. **Identify an organization's stakeholders.**

   An organization's stakeholders are any companies, institutions, or individuals that have a connection with or vested interest in the efficient and ethical operations of that organization. Depending on the market or industry in which the organization conducts business, those stakeholders can include shareholders, employees, customers, suppliers, wholesalers, creditors, community organizations, and the federal government.

3. **Discuss the position that business ethics is an oxymoron.**

   It would be unfair to brand every organization as fundamentally unethical in its business dealings. There's no doubt that numerous prominent organizations that were previously held as models of aggressive business management (Enron, Global Crossing, HealthSouth, IMClone, Tyco, and WorldCom) have later been proved to be fundamentally flawed in their ethical practices. This has succeeded in bringing the issue to the forefront of public awareness. However, the positive outcome from this has been increased attention to the need for third-party guarantees of ethical conduct and active commitments from the rest of the business world.

4. **Summarize the history of business ethics.**

   Several dramatic changes have taken place in the business environment over the past five decades:

   - *The increased presence of an employee voice has made individual employees feel more comfortable speaking out against actions of their employers that they feel to be irresponsible or unethical. They are also more willing to seek legal resolution for such issues as unsafe working conditions, harassment, discrimination, and invasion of privacy.*
   - *The issue of corporate social responsibility has advanced from an abstract debate to a core performance-assessment issue with clearly established legal liabilities.*
   - *Corporate ethics has moved from the domain of legal and human resource departments into the organizational mainstream with the appointment of corporate ethics officers with clear mandates.*
   - *Codes of ethics have matured from cosmetic public relations documents into performance-measurement documents that an increasing number of organizations are now committing to share with all their stakeholders.*
   - *The 2002 Sarbanes-Oxley Act has introduced greater accountability for chief executive officers and boards of directors in signing off on the financial performance records of the organizations they represent.*

5. **Identify and propose a resolution for an ethical dilemma in your work environment.**

   Resolution of an ethical dilemma can be approached in two stages: recognizing the type of conflict you are dealing with and then selecting a resolution principle based on that conflict type. Conflict types can be grouped into four categories:

   - *Truth versus loyalty.* Do you tell the truth or remain loyal to the person or organization that is asking you not to reveal that truth?
   - *Short term versus long term.* Does your decision have a short-term consequence or a longer-term consequence?
   - *Justice versus mercy.* Do you perceive this issue as a question of dispensing justice or mercy? (Which one are you more comfortable with?)
   - *Individual versus community.* Will your choice impact one individual or a wider group or community?

   Three resolution principles can then be considered:

   - *Ends-based.* Which decision would provide the greatest good for the greatest number of people?
   - *Rules-based.* What would happen if everyone made the same decision as you?
   - *The Golden Rule.* Do unto others as you would have them do unto you.

6. **Explain how executives and employees seek to justify unethical behavior.**

   When their conduct or decisions are questioned as being unethical, most executives and employees seek to rationalize their behavior with four common justifications:

   - *A belief that the activity is within reasonable ethical and legal limits—that is, that it is not "really" illegal or immoral.*

- A belief that the activity is in the individual's or the corporation's best interests—that the individual would somehow be expected to undertake the activity.
- A belief that the activity is safe because it will never be found out or publicized—the classic crime-and-punishment issue of discovery.
- A belief that because the activity helps the company, the company will condone it and even protect the person who engages in it.

[Key Terms]

Business Ethics 24

Corporate Governance 25

Oxymoron 26

Code of Ethics 26

Ethical Dilemma 30

Stakeholder 24

[Review Questions]

1. Based on the history of business ethics reviewed in this chapter, do you think the business world is becoming more or less ethical? Explain your answer.

2. How would you propose the resolution of an ethical dilemma using the Golden Rule?

3. Why should a short-term or long-term consequence make a difference in resolving an ethical dilemma?

4. Of the four commonly held rationalizations for unethical behavior proposed by Saul Gellerman, which one do you think gets used most often? Why?

5. Is it ever acceptable to justify unethical behavior? Why or why not?

6. Explain what "doing the right thing" in a business environment means to you.

[Review Exercises]

You are returning from a business trip. As you wait in the departure lounge for your flight to begin boarding, the gate attendant announces that the flight has been significantly overbooked and offers incentives for passengers to take later flights. After several minutes, the offer is raised to a free round-trip ticket anywhere in the continental United States plus meal vouchers for dinner while you wait for your later flight. You give the offer serious consideration and realize that even though you'll get home several hours later than planned, the inconvenience will be minimal, so you give up your seat and take the free ticket and meal vouchers.

1. Since you are traveling on company time, does the free ticket belong to you or your company? Defend your choice.

2. If the later flight was actually the next day (and the airline offered you an accommodation voucher along with the meal vouchers) and you would be late getting into work, would you make the same choice? Explain your answer.

3. If the offer only reached a $100 discount coupon on another ticket, would you still take it? If so, would you hold the same opinion about whether the coupon belonged to you or your company?

4. Should your company offer a clearly stated policy on this issue, or should it trust its employees to "do the right thing"? Explain your answer.

[Internet Exercises]

1. Locate the website for the Ethics Compliance Initiative (ECI) and review the 'Ethics & Compliance Toolkit'. The 'PLUS Ethical Decision Making Model' lists seven steps to ethical decision making. What are they?

2. The Ethics Resource Center (www.ethics.org) is also part of the ECI.

a. What is the stated goal of the ECI's research arm?
b. List the three categories of ECI research.
c. Identify the topic of the most recent Global Business Ethics Survey.

[Team Exercises]

1. **Thanks for the training!**
   Divide into two groups, and prepare arguments *for* and *against* the following behavior: *You work in the IT department of a large international company. At your annual performance review, you were asked about your goals and objectives for the coming year, and you stated that you would like to become a Microsoft Certified Systems Engineer (MCSE). You didn't get much of a pay raise (yet another cost-cutting initiative!), but your boss told you there was money in the training budget for the MCSE course—you're attending the training next week. However, after receiving the poor pay raise, you had polished your résumé and applied for other positions. You received an attractive job offer from another company for more money, and, in the last interview, your potential new boss commented that it was a shame you didn't have your MCSE certification because that would qualify you for a higher pay grade. The new company doesn't have the training budget to put you through the MCSE training for at least two years. You tell the interviewer that you will complete the MCSE training prior to starting the new position in order to qualify for the higher pay grade. You choose not to qualify that statement with any additional information on who will be paying for the training. You successfully gain the MCSE certification and then give your two weeks' notice. You start with your new company at the higher pay grade. Is that ethical?*

2. **What you do in your free time . . .**
   Divide into two groups, and prepare arguments *for* and *against* the following behavior: *You are attending an employee team-building retreat at a local resort. During one of the free periods in the busy agenda, you observe one of your colleagues in a passionate embrace with a young woman from another department. Since you work in HR and processed the hiring paperwork on both of them, you know that neither one of them is married, but your benefit plan provides coverage for "life partners," and both of them purchased health coverage for life partners. As you consider this revelation further, you are reminded that even if they have both ended their relationships with their respective partners, the company has a policy that expressly forbids employees from dating other employees in the company. Both you and the colleague you observed have applied for the same promotion—a promotion that carries a significant salary increase. What is your obligation here? Should you report him to your boss?*

3. **Treatment or prevention?**
   Divide into two groups, and prepare arguments for *treatment* (Group A) and *prevention* (Group B) in the following situation: *You work for a local nonprofit organization that is struggling to raise funds for its programs in a very competitive grant market. Many nonprofits in your city are chasing grant funds, donations, and volunteer hours for their respective missions—homelessness, cancer awareness and treatment, orphaned children, and many more. Your organization's mission is to work with HIV/AIDS patients in your community to provide increased awareness of the condition for those at risk and also to provide treatment options for those who have already been diagnosed. Unfortunately, with such a tough financial situation, the board of directors of the nonprofit organization has*

determined that a more focused mission is needed. Rather than serving both the prevention and treatment goals, the organization can only do one. The debate at the last board meeting, which was open to all employees and volunteers, was very heated. Many felt that the treatment programs offered immediate relief to those in need, and therefore represented the best use of funds. Others felt that the prevention programs needed much more time to be effective and that the funds were spread over a much bigger population who might be at risk. A decision has to be reached. What do you think?

4. **Time to raise prices . . .**

Divide into two groups, and prepare arguments *for* and *against* the following behavior: *You are a senior manager at a pharmaceutical company that is facing financial difficulties after failing to receive FDA approval for a new experimental drug for the treatment of Alzheimer's disease. After reviewing your test data, the FDA examiners decided that further testing was needed. Your company is now in dire financial straits. The drug has the potential to revolutionize the treatment of Alzheimer's, but the testing delay could put you out of business. The leadership team meets behind closed doors and decides the only way to keep the company afloat long enough to bring the new drug to market is to raise the prices of its existing range of drug products. However, given the financial difficulties your company is facing, some of those price increases will exceed 1,000 percent. When questions are raised about the size of the proposed increases, the chief executive officer defends the move with the following response: "Look, our drugs are still a cheaper option than surgery, even at these higher prices; the insurance companies can afford to pick up the tab; and, worst-case scenario, they'll raise a few premiums to cover the increase. What choice do we have? We have to bring this new drug to market if we are going to be a player in this industry."*

Thinking Critically

>> MARRIOTT: WI-FI AS A SERVICE OR REVENUE STREAM?

In October 2014, the Marriott hotel chain admitted to deliberately jamming guests' mobile Wi-Fi and personal hotspots and forcing business travelers to pay for the company's own Wi-Fi service. Prices charged ranged from the normal $14.95 per day to fees as high as $1,000 per device per day for exhibitors using hotel conference space.

Complaints to the Federal Communications Commission led to a $600,000 settlement, but a combative press release restated the company's argument that it was trying to protect customers from "rogue wireless hotspots," and called for a formal ruling on the issue from the FCC.

Marriott was by no means the sole transgressor. Despite clear instructions from the FCC on its website that Wi-Fi jamming is illegal, many other hotel companies and conference centers have fallen foul of the FCC's stance on the issue:

© E. Audras/PhotoAlto RF

- In August 2015, Smart City Holdings, LLC, a trade show and convention telecom services provider, was fined $750,000 for blocking customer Wi-Fi services at several sites and charging them $80 per day for access.
- In November 2015, the FCC proposed a $25,000 fine against Hilton Worldwide Holdings "for its apparent obstruction of an investigation into whether Hilton engaged in the blocking of consumers' Wi-Fi devices." The case referenced an incident at the Hilton Anaheim near Disneyland, where convention attendees were asked to pay a $500 fee to access the hotel's Wi-Fi system.
- In the same notice, the FCC proposed a $750,000 fine against M.C. Dean, the systems integration company, for allegedly blocking Wi-Fi hotspots at the Baltimore Convention Center.

While the position from the FCC's enforcement bureau is clear, the position from Wi-Fi experts is more complex. Using guest security as grounds to generate additional revenue may be nothing new in the hospitality industry, and for many smaller properties, that extra revenue can mean the difference between profit and loss on an annual basis. However, hotel IT specialists back that up with an argument that personal Wi-Fi hotspots not only present security risks but also drain the performance of the network as a whole as multiple access points overwhelm the capacity of the system.

Wi-Fi administrators raise another issue, criticizing the FCC for opening a "Pandora's box" with their Marriott ruling. The eagerness to show strong enforcement against a clear attempt to squeeze extra revenue from guests may be valid, they argue, but outside of the hospitality industry, the ability to jam Wi-Fi signals is needed for safe and effective operation of facilities. What happens in a hospital, for example, if visitors disrupt wireless medical equipment when using their personal Wi-Fi hotspots? What happens if journalists overwhelm a multimillion-dollar Wi-Fi system at a sports stadium media event? Must the stadium owners pay for the repairs? Since the FCC position clearly prohibits jamming of any kind, that would appear to be the case.

For the hospitality industry, however, Wi-Fi administrators argue that the guest security claim is especially weak. Making an investment in higher-grade systems hardware would allow guests to use their personal Wi-Fi hotspots without

CONTINUED >>

impacting the capacity of the system as a whole. Of course, for companies seeking to generate extra revenue, asking them to spend more money and forgo Wi-Fi revenue in return seems like a very tough sell.

QUESTIONS

1. What is the FCC's position on Wi-Fi jamming?
2. What is the position of hotels and convention centers?
3. Is there room for negotiation? Would less exorbitant fees draw less anger?
4. How should these companies balance their obligation to shareholders to make money against the obligation to provide good customer service?
5. Is the FCC being too extreme in its position? Why or why not?
6. Is there potential for an equitable resolution of this issue? Why or why not?

Sources: Mariella Moon, " Marriott Is No Longer Fighting for Permission to Block Wi-Fi Hotspots," *Engadget,* January 31, 2015; Lee Badman, "FCC-Marriott WiFi Blocking Fine Opens Pandora's Box," *Network Computing,* October 7, 2014; Christopher Elliott, "The FCC Is Cracking Down on Hotels' Wi-Fi Blocking," *Fortune,* November 4, 2015; "Hotel Wi-Fi: Knock Your Block Off," *Economist,* October 10, 2014; and Larry Loeb, "FCC Fines Hilton, Others in Wi-Fi Blocking Crackdown," *InformationWeek,* November 5, 2015.

Thinking Critically 2.2

>> UNEQUIVOCAL DEDICATION TO BUSINESS ETHICS?

At a time of increasing skepticism that businesses can be both successful and ethical, 17 companies, which between them accounted for almost $1 trillion in global sales, came together as the charter members of the Business Ethics Leadership Alliance (BELA). Formed in December 2008, the founding membership represented a wide range of industries, including retail, airlines, financial services, and computers. Some of the names may be familiar to you:

- Accenture
- Avaya
- CACI International
- Crawford
- Dell
- Dun & Bradstreet
- Ecolab
- Fluor
- General Electric

- Jones Lang Lasalle
- NYK Line
- PepsiCo
- Sempra Energy
- Southern Co.
- The Hartford
- United Airlines
- Walmart

Working with the Ethisphere Institute, an international think tank that dedicates itself to "the creation, advancement and sharing of best practices in business ethics, corporate social responsibility, anti-corruption and sustainability," BELA appears to take a very clear position and invites public and private companies to join it in making an explicit pledge to four core values: (1) legal compliance, (2) transparency, (3) identification of conflicts of interest, and (4) accountability.

Responding to a situation where "through the cacophony of media stories, political finger-pointing, infuriating reports of greed, and compelling stories of hardship, the business community as a whole has been characterized as a barrel full of bad apples that has the ability to spoil the global economy," the alliance members present themselves as "a growing quorum made up of some of the world's most recognizable companies joining together to affirm an unequivocal dedication to business ethics." In addition, they see it as their responsibility to "reestablish ethics as the foundation of everyday business practices."

Response to the new alliance was mixed. Optimists appeared to see this new organization as a step in the right direction, arguing that "a public so badly burned by ethical shortcomings in so many American companies will be cynical for years to come, but BELA is to be applauded for trying to turn the situation around." There were certainly some large companies getting involved —Walmart, GE, Dell, and PepsiCo—and they appeared to be committing to specific changes in their business practices that directly correlated to many of the ethical problems identified at companies such as Enron, WorldCom, Tyco, and many others.

However, many cynics saw this as just a public relations exercise for companies that had their own business practices brought into question in the past and were seeking redemption through a commitment to a new ethical philosophy. For example, Walmart paid $11 million to the Department of Justice in settlement of a case involving the

© Thinkstock Images/Comstock/Getty Images RF

hiring of illegal immigrants by its cleaning contractors in 2005. Other class-action suits are pending against the world's largest retailer. In 2006, Sempra Energy agreed to pay more than $377 million in response to allegations of manipulation of the price of natural gas during the 2001 California energy crisis.

Since its founding, the face of BELA has changed dramatically. Membership has grown, though a couple of prominent charter members have left, and the format now focuses on key products:

- The Ethics Quotient, a 125+ question survey "based on Ethisphere's proprietary methodology," that enables members to benchmark their programs and practices.
- The World's Most Ethical Companies award that recognizes performance in three areas—"promoting ethical business standards and practices internally, enabling managers and employees to make good choices, and shaping future industry standards by introducing tomorrow's best practices today."
- Compliance Certification Programs—offering "an independent validation of your current program and efforts."

QUESTIONS

1. Visit the website for BELA at www.ethisphere.com/bela. Define the three areas of performance for the World's Most Ethical Companies in detail, and explain which one you think will be the hardest for members to achieve and why.

2. Do you think it was a good idea to welcome founding members with such widely publicized ethical transgressions in their past? Why or why not?

3. BELA is a U.S.-driven initiative at the moment. Do you think it will achieve a wider global acceptance over time? Why or why not?

4. Are the three key products enough to establish a credible reputation as an ethical company? What other options would you consider adding and why?

5. Cynics could argue that this is simply a public relations exercise for companies that have performed unethical business practices in the past. Optimists could argue that this is, at the very least, a step in the right direction of restoring the ethical reputation of business as a whole. What do you think?

6. According to the rules of BELA, members will be audited every two years to make sure they are in compliance with BELA standards, and they face removal from the alliance should that audit provide evidence of failure to comply. Do you think the threat of removal from the alliance will keep members in line? Why or why not?

Sources: F. Guerrera and J. Birchall, "U.S. Groups in Ethical Standards Push," *Financial Times,* December 8, 2008; P. Faur, "17 U.S. Companies Form Business Ethics Leadership Alliance," www.communitelligence.com, December 10, 2008; "Business Ethics Leadership Alliance Forms to Affirm Core Business Ethics Principles, Supply and Demand Chain Executive," www.sdcexec.com, December 12, 2008; and C. MacDonald, "Business Ethics Leadership Alliance: What's in a Promise?" http://businessethicsblog.com/2008/12/12/business-ethics-leadership-alliance-whats-in-a-promise/; and www.ethisphere.com/bela/.

Thinking Critically

>> TEACHING OR SELLING? • Drugmakers Worried about Conflicts of Interest Modify Their Approach to Sponsorship of Continuing Education

In response to increasing criticism over its sponsorship of physician-education courses (and the suggestion of undue influence on doctors' prescriptions and procedures), the drugmaker Pfizer announced in July 2008 that it would no longer pay marketing communications companies to arrange continuing medical education (CME) courses, which doctors must take to maintain their licenses. Pfizer said it would support medical education only when it was put on by hospitals and professional medical associations. Zimmer Holdings, a medical device manufacturer that manufactures hip, knee, and elbow implants, suspended funding of all CME activity. The company said it will restrict the way it funds courses in the future by identifying an independent third party, such as a professional society, to organize educational programs.

© Siede Preis/Getty Images RF

"We understand that even the appearance of conflicts in CME is damaging, and we are determined to take actions that are in the best interests of patients and physicians," Dr. Joseph M. Feczko, Pfizer's chief medical officer, said in a press release.

Industry support for CME has quadrupled since 1998, to $1.2 billion a year, according to the Accreditation Council for Continuing Medical Education (ACCME), an organization in Chicago that approves CME providers. More than half of that is funneled to marketers, with the rest going to hospitals, medical associations, and other nonprofit entities.

As industry money for continuing education proliferates, so do worries that many of the courses have become at least partly aimed at promoting products. The industry and its outside marketers say they ensure that the courses remain free of commercial influence. But some medical experts argue that when employees of communications firms are beholden to pharmaceutical and device companies, they will produce CME courses that are slanted in favor of their sponsors, even if they don't realize what they are doing. "There's not only a perception of bias, there's a reality," says Dave Davis, a vice president of the Association of American Medical Colleges.

In January 2010, Pfizer appeared to modify its 2008 position by announcing a $3 million grant to Stanford University to create continuing medical education courses that the company claims will come with "no conditions, and the company will not be involved in developing the curriculum." However, critics have argued that the curriculum will most likely focus on at least two areas in which Pfizer has major product lines: smoking cessation and heart disease.

QUESTIONS

1. Where is the conflict of interest in this CME relationship?

2. Do you think doctors are likely to be influenced by such promotional tactics? Why or why not?

3. If the pharmaceutical company is paying for the event, shouldn't it have the right to promote its products at the event? Why or why not?

4. Pfizer stated in 2008 that it would only support medical education put on by hospitals and professional medical associations. How can it then justify the Stanford grant?

5. Has Pfizer simply replaced one conflict of interest with another? Why or why not?

6. Propose an alternative approach to ensure that CME is provided without a conflict of interest.

Sources: Arlene Weintraub, "Teaching Doctors or Selling to Them," *BusinessWeek,* July 31, 2008; Duff Wilson, "Using a Pfizer Grant, Courses Aim to Avoid Bias," *The New York Times,* January 11, 2010; and Jacob Goldstein, "Stanford's Continuing Medical Ed., Brought to You by Pfizer," *The Wall Street Journal,* January 11, 2010.

[References]

1. The Ethics and Compliance Officer Association, www.theecoa.org; Ethics Resource Center, www.ethics.org ; and Society of Corporate Compliance and Ethics, www.corporatecompliance.org.

2. ERC, "Creating a Workable Company Code of Ethics," www.ethics.org, 2003.

3. Institute of Global Ethics, www.globalethics.org/bds/reading.html.

4. Saul W. Gellerman, "Why 'Good' Managers Make Bad Ethical Choices," *Harvard Business Review,* July–August 1986.

THE PRACTICE OF BUSINESS ETHICS

With a clearer understanding of the issues relating to business ethics and the key players involved, we can now examine how the practice of business ethics affects an organization on a daily basis.

Chapter 3 examines how each functional department within an organization manages the challenge of building and maintaining an ethical culture.

Chapter 4 explores the topic of corporate social responsibility (CSR) where we change from the internal perspective of the organization to an external one and look at how an organization should interact with its stakeholders in an ethical manner.

Chapter 5 addresses the challenges in maintaining an ethical culture within an organization. What policies and procedures should be put into place to ensure that the company conducts itself in an ethical manner, and what should be the consequences when evidence of unethical conduct is found?

Chapter 6 steps outside the organizational framework and examines the legislation the government has put into place to enforce ethical conduct.

Chapter 7 examines how employees who find evidence of unethical conduct in their companies go about bringing that information to the attention of the companies' senior management or the appropriate regulatory authorities.

Chapter 8 explains the ethical debate over employee surveillance and the extent to which technology not only facilitates the prevention of unethical behavior but also jeopardizes the rights of individual employees.

© Image Source/Getty Images RF

ORGANIZATIONAL ETHICS

After studying this chapter, you should be able to:

3-1 Define *organizational ethics*.

3-2 Explain the respective ethical challenges facing the functional departments of an organization.

3-3 Discuss the position that a human resource (HR) department should be at the center of any corporate code of ethics.

3-4 Explain the potential ethical challenges presented by generally accepted accounting principles (GAAP).

3-5 Determine potential conflicts of interest within any organizational function.

FRONTLINE FOCUS
Just Sign the Forms

Matt, a new employee at TransWorld Industries (TWI), showed up bright and early for his first day of orientation. He was very excited. He had applied for several jobs in the area, but TWI was the one he really wanted. He had friends there, and they had told him that the company seemed to be growing very quickly with lots of new products coming online. To Matt, growth meant new opportunities, and he was looking forward to applying to the management-training program as soon as he finished his 90-day probationary period.

Scott, Matt's new boss, was waiting for him as soon as he reached the factory floor. "Hey, Matt, very punctual; I like that," said Steve, looking at this watch.

"Listen, kid, I know HR gave you a list of things to be checked off today—payroll paperwork, training videos, parking pass, ID, and all that stuff—but we could really use an extra pair of hands around here. Your position was vacant for quite a while, and we've built a nasty backlog of work that needs to get caught up ASAP.

"We could really use your help on the Morton6000—you've worked with one of those before, right?"

Matt nodded, not quite sure where this was going.

"Well, here's the deal," said Scott. "The way I see it, all those videos are going to do is tell you not to harass any of the young babes around here (which won't be difficult since none of them are young or babes), not to insult anyone's race, and not to do anything unethical, which you weren't going to do anyway, right?"

Matt nodded again, still not sure where this was going.

"So I think all that time spent watching TV would be put to better use on that backlog of work on the Morton6000. We can book the shipments, get paid by the customers that have been waiting very patiently, and you can make a good impression on your first day—sound good to you, kid?"

"But what about the videos?" asked Matt.

"Oh, don't worry about them," said Scott. "We keep them here in the office. You just sign the forms saying you watched the videos and take them up to HR after lunch when you do all your other paperwork, OK?"

QUESTIONS

1. HR requires that these training videos be viewed for a reason. What risks is Scott taking here? Review the four reasons (found in the "Ethics in Human Resources" section of this chapter) why HR should be directly involved in any code of ethics.
2. Do you think Scott's argument for skipping the training videos is justified?
3. What should Matt do now?

I very much doubt that the Enron executives came to work one morning and said, "Let's see what sort of illegal scheme we can cook up to rip off the shareholders today." More likely, they began by setting extremely high goals for their firm . . . and for a time exceeded them. In so doing they built a reputation for themselves and a demanding expectation among their investors. Eventually, the latter could no longer be sustained. Confronting the usual judgmental decisions which one presented to executives virtually every day, and not wanting to face reality, they gradually began to lean more and more towards extreme interpretations of established accounting principles. The next thing they knew they had fallen off the bottom of the ski jump.

Norman R. Augustine, retired chairman of Lockheed Martin Corp., in his 2004 acceptance of the Ethics Resource Center's Stanley C. Pace Leadership in Ethics Award

>> Defining Organizational Ethics

In Chapter 2, we proposed business ethics as an area of study separate from the general subject of ethics because of two distinct issues:

1. Other parties (the stakeholders) have a vested interest in the ethical performance of an organization.
2. In a work environment, you may be placed in a situation where your personal value system may clash with the ethical standards of the organization's operating culture.

Organizational Culture The values, beliefs, and norms that all the employees of that organization share.

Value Chain The key functional inputs that an organization provides in the transformation of raw materials into a delivered product or service.

Key Point

How would you describe the culture of your company? What "values, beliefs, and norms" do your employees share?

Organizational culture can be defined as the values, beliefs, and norms shared by all the employees of that organization. The culture represents the sum of all the policies and procedures—both written and informal—from each of the functional departments in the organization in addition to the policies and procedures that are established for the organization as a whole.

In this chapter, we can begin to examine individual departments within an organization and the ethical dilemmas that members of those departments face each day. To simplify this examination, we consider an organization in terms of its functional areas within a value chain (see Figure 3.1).

A **value chain** is composed of the key functional inputs that an organization provides in the transformation of raw materials into a delivered product or service. Traditionally, these key functions are identified as:

- Research and development (R&D), which develops and creates product designs.
- Manufacturing, which sources the components and builds the product.
- Marketing (and advertising).
- Sales.
- Customer service.

Supporting each of these functional areas are the line functions:

- Human resources management (HRM), which coordinates the recruitment, training, and development of personnel for all aspects of the organization.
- Finance, which can include internal accounting personnel, external accounting personnel, and external auditors who are called upon to certify the accuracy of a company's financial statements.
- Information systems (IS or IT), which maintain the technology backbone of the organization—data transfer and security, e-mail communications, internal and external websites, as well as the individual hardware and software needs that are specific to the organization and its line of business.

FIG.3.1 A Representative Company Value Chain

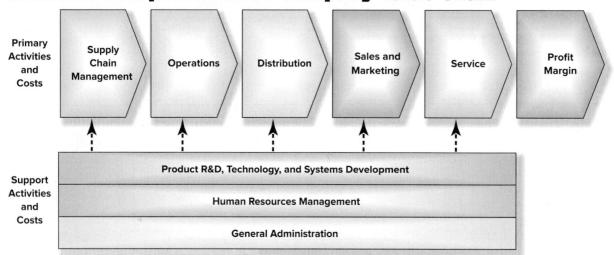

Sources: Adapted with permission of the Free Press, a division of Simon & Schuster Adult Publishing Group, from *Competitive Advantage: Creating and Sustaining Superior Performance,* by Michael Porter. Copyright © 1995, 1998 by Michael E. Porter. All rights reserved. And from A. A. Thompson Jr. and A. I. Strickland III, *Crafting & Executing Strategy: The Quest for Competitive Advantage: Concepts and Cases,* 14th ed. (New York: Irwin McGraw-Hill, 2005), p. 99.

- Management, the supervisory role that oversees all operational functions.

Each of these functional line areas can represent a significant commitment of resources—personnel, dollars, and technology. From an ethical perspective, employees in each area can face ethical challenges and dilemmas that can be both unique to their departmental responsibilities and common to the organization as a whole.

The functional areas of sales, customer service, information technology, and management typically have operational policies that reflect the overall ethical culture of the organization. They will be addressed in subsequent chapters in this text. In this chapter, we focus on five specific organizational areas: R&D, manufacturing, marketing (including advertising), human resources (HR), and finance (including accounting and auditing).

PROGRESS ✓ QUESTIONS

1. Explain the term *organizational culture*.
2. Define the term *value chain*.
3. List the five key functional areas within an organization.
4. List the four primary line functions.

>> Ethical Challenges by Organizational Function

ETHICS IN RESEARCH AND DEVELOPMENT

R&D professionals carry the responsibility for the future growth of the organization. Without new products to sell, organizations can lose their customers to competitors that are offering better, faster, and/or cheaper products. R&D teams incorporate customer feedback from market research, competitive feedback from closely monitoring the competition, and strategic input from the organization's senior management team to develop a product design that, hopefully, will allow the organization to capture and maintain a leading position in its market.

However, alongside this responsibility comes an equally critical commitment to the consumer in the provision of a product that is of the highest quality, safety, and reliability. Defective products not only put consumers at risk but also generate negative press coverage (damaging the organization's reputation) and very expensive lawsuits that can put the organization at risk of bankruptcy.

When we consider these opposing objectives, the potential for ethical dilemmas is considerable. As professionals in their respective fields of science, engineering, and design, R&D teams are tasked with

A FIRM PRODUCTION DATE

Scott Kelly, XYZ's marketing vice president, was shouting on the telephone to Tom Evers, director of new-product development in XYZ's R&D laboratories: "We're going to kick off a major ad campaign timed to make people want your new model appliance, just before we start delivering them to dealers, and I want to be sure your production date is firm and not one of those best estimates you've stuck us with in the past." Taking a quick breath, he continued: "You people in R&D don't have much credibility with marketing! You don't tell us what you're up to until it's too late for us to advise you or interact in any way. I still remember the money you spent on that water purifier we didn't want. And it didn't help your credibility when you tried to keep the project alive after we told you to kill it!"

Tom assured Scott that the schedule for starting production was absolutely firm. "We've run extensive tests, including life tests, and everything definitely indicates 'go'! We're going to do a small pilot production run and test those pilot units in employee homes. That's a purely routine confirmation, so I can assure you that the production

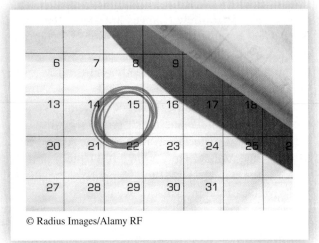

© Radius Images/Alamy RF

CONTINUED >>

date is locked in. Go ahead with your ad campaign—we're giving you a sure winner this time."

But Tom was wrong. A glitch appeared near the end of the pilot test and very close to the production date. In a hastily called engineering meeting, to which marketing was not invited, a quick-fix design change was approved. Another short pilot production run would be made, and the revised units would again be tested in employee homes. A delay of one to two months, perhaps longer, for start of production was indicated. With this schedule set, Tom arranged a meeting to apprise marketing of the problem and the new production schedule.

Scott exploded as soon as Tom began his account of the production delay. "You gave me a firm production date! We've got a major ad campaign under way, and its timing is critical. We'll have customers asking for these new models, and the dealers won't have them. We'll look silly to our customers, and our dealers will be upset."

"Now wait," Tom interrupted, "I didn't give you the production date as absolutely firm. I remember cautioning you that a problem could develop in the pilot run and suggested you allow for it in kicking off the ad campaign. I told we'd do our best to make the date but that

there's always an element of chance with a new machine. We're better off having customers asking dealers where the new models are than being out there with a big quality problem."

QUESTIONS

1. Tom was obviously overconfident in the final stages of the testing process, but was his behavior unethical? Why or why not?
2. Given Scott's concerns over R&D's credibility, should he have taken Tom's production date as being absolutely firm?
3. In fact, Scott was so skeptical of Tom's production date that he recorded their original conversation without Tom's knowledge and then produced the recording when Tom denied giving a firm production date. Tom responded: "You taped my conversation without telling me! That's unethical." Was it?
4. Has Scott's behavior damaged future relations between marketing and R&D? In what way? How could this situation have been avoided?

Source: Adapted from W. Gale Cutler, "When R&D Talks, Marketing Listens—on Tape," *Research Technology Management* 37, no. 4 (July–August 1994), p. 56.

making a complex set of risk assessments and technical judgments in order to deliver a product design. However, if the delivery of that design does not match the manufacturing cost figures that are needed to sell the product at a required profit margin, then some tough decisions have to be made.

If "better, cheaper, faster" is the ideal, then compromises have to be made in functionality or manufacturing to meet a targeted cost figure. If too many features are taken out, marketing and advertising won't have a story to tell, and the salespeople will face difficulties in selling the product against stiff competition. If too few changes are made, the company won't be able to generate a profit on each unit and meet its obligations to shareholders who expect the company to be run efficiently and to grow over the long term.

For the R&D team, the real ethical dilemmas come when decisions are made about product quality. Do we use the best materials available or the second best to save some money? Do we run a full battery of tests or convince ourselves that the computer simulations will give us all the information we need?

ETHICS IN MANUFACTURING

The relationship between R&D and manufacturing is often a challenging one. Managers complain about

designs being thrown "over the wall" to manufacturing with the implication that the product design may meet all the required specifications, but now it falls to the manufacturing team to actually get the thing built.

The pressures here are very similar to those in the R&D function as manufacturers face the ethical question, "Do you want it built fast, or do you want it built right?" Obviously, from an organizational perspective, you want both, especially if you know that your biggest competitor also is racing to put a new product on the market (and if it gets there before you do, all your sales projections for your product will be worthless).

Here again, you face the ethical challenges inherent in arriving at a compromise—which corners can be cut and by how much. You want to build the product to the precise design specifications, but what if there is a supply problem? Do you wait and hold up delivery, or do you go with an alternative (and less reliable) supplier? Can you be sure of the quality that alternative supplier will give you?

ETHICS IN MARKETING

Once the manufacturing department delivers a finished product, it must be sold. The marketing process (which includes advertising, public relations, and sales) is responsible for ensuring that the product reaches the hands of a satisfied customer. If the marketers did their research correctly and communicated the data to the R&D team accurately, and assuming the finished product meets the original design specifications and the competition hasn't beaten you to market with their new product, this should be a slam dunk, but with all these assumptions, a great deal can go wrong.

Opinions on the marketing process vary greatly in relation to how close you are to the process itself. Marketers see themselves as providing products (or services) to customers who have already expressed a need for and a desire to purchase those products. In this respect, marketers are simply communicating information to their customers about the functionality and availability of the product, and then communicating back to the organization the feedback they receive from those customers.

Critics of marketing tend to see it as a more manipulative process whereby unsuspecting customers are induced by slick and entertaining commercials and advertisements in several different media—magazines, radio, television, the Internet, and so forth—to buy products they don't really need and could quite easily live without.

From an ethical standpoint, these opposing arguments can be seen to line up with distinct ethical theories. Marketers emphasize customer service and argue that since their customers are satisfied, the good outcome justifies the methods used to achieve that outcome no matter how misleading the message or how unnecessary the product sold. As reviewed in Chapter 1, this represents a view of ethics called **utilitarianism**. Critics argue that the process itself is wrong irrespective of the outcome achieved—that is, how can you be proud of an outcome when the customer never needed that product to begin with and was manipulated, or at the very least influenced, by a slick ad campaign into feelings of envy, inadequacy, or inequality if he or she didn't rush out and buy it? On this side of the debate we are considering **universal ethics**.

Utilitarianism Ethical choices that offer the greatest good for the greatest number of people.

Universal Ethics Actions that are taken out of *duty* and *obligation* to a purely moral ideal, rather than based on the needs of the situation, since the universal principles are seen to apply to everyone, everywhere, all the time.

© McGraw-Hill Education/Jill Braaten, photographer

What role does marketing play in the perception that coffee brewed at Starbucks is superior to coffee brewed at home?

Real World Applications

From his first marketing course at college, Mike always believed that marketers had the responsibility of accurately describing the features and benefits of their product or service to their customers. If those features and benefits didn't meet the needs of those customers, Mike always assumed that survey data would be fed back to the designers to fix that. After only a year in the industry, Mike's viewpoint has changed. The job of the marketing department is to support the sales team with messages, brochures, and ads that help convince prospective customers that buying the company's product or service is the right choice. Whether it really is the right choice for them, or whether they need that product or service at all, never comes up for discussion. What happened?

These opposing positions become more complex when you consider the responsibility of a corporation to generate profits for its stockholders. Long-term profits come from sales growth, which means selling more of what you have or bringing new products or services to the market to increase your overall sales revenue. To do that, you must find ways to sell more to your existing customer base and, ideally, find more customers for your products and services. Unless you are selling a basic commodity in a developing country that has a desperate need for your product, at some point you reach a place where customers can survive without your product or service, and marketing must now move from informing customers and prospects about the product or service to persuading or influencing them that their lives will be better with this product or service and, more importantly, they will be better with your company's version.

Marketing professionals abide by a code of ethics adopted by the American Marketing Association (AMA). That code speaks eloquently about doing no harm, fostering trust, and improving "customer confidence in the integrity of the marketing exchange system," and establishes clear ethical values of honesty, responsibility, fairness, respect, openness, and citizenship. These are all honorable standards for any profession, but the question remains as to whether or not encouraging people to buy things they don't need is truly an ethical process.

Philip Kotler explored this debate further in his classic article, "Is Marketing Ethics an Oxymoron?"[1] His concern over the pressures of expanding consumption (the constant growth we discussed earlier in this section) was further complicated by the issue of reducing the side effects of that consumption, specifically in products that are perceived as harmful to the body—cigarettes, alcohol, junk food—as well as to the environment—nonrecyclable packaging or products that leach chemicals into landfills such as batteries or electrical equipment.

In response to these pressures, Kotler makes the following observation:

As professional marketers, we are hired by . . . companies to use our marketing toolkit to help them sell more of their products and services. Through our research, we can discover which consumer groups are the most susceptible to increasing their consumption. We can use the research to assemble the best 30-second TV commercials, print ads, and sales incentives to persuade them that these products will deliver great satisfaction. And we can create price discounts to tempt them to consume even more of the product than would normally be healthy or safe to consume. But, as professional marketers, we should have the same ambivalence as nuclear scientists who help build nuclear bombs or pilots who spray DDT over crops from the airplane. Some of us, in fact, are independent enough to tell these clients that we will not work for them to find ways to sell more of what hurts people. We can tell them that we're willing to use our marketing toolkit to help them build new businesses around substitute products that are much healthier and safer. But, even if these companies moved toward these healthier and safer products, they'll probably continue to push their current cash cows. At that point, marketers will have to decide whether to work for these companies, help them reshape their offerings, avoid these companies altogether, or even work to oppose these company offerings.

5. Identify the three functional components of the marketing process.
6. Explain why marketers feel that their involvement in the production and delivery of goods and services is an ethical one.
7. Explain the opposing argument that marketing is an unethical process.
8. Which argument do you support? Provide an example to explain your answer.

>> Ethics in Human Resources

The human resources function within an organization should ideally be directly involved in the relationship between the company and the employee throughout that employee's contract with the company:

- The creation of the job description for the position.
- The recruitment and selection of the right candidate for the position.
- The orientation of the newly hired employee.
- The efficient management of payroll and benefits for the (hopefully) happy and productive employee.

© Digital Vision RF

What ethical issues might arise for a human resources professional when privy to an employee's personal and professional history?

- The documentation of periodic performance reviews.
- The documentation of disciplinary behavior and remedial training, if needed.
- The creation of a career development program for the employee.

Finally, if the employee and the company eventually part ways, the HR department should coordinate the final paperwork, including any severance benefits, and should host an exit interview to ensure that anything that the organization can learn from the departure of this employee is fed back into the company's strategic plan for future growth and development.

Every step of the life cycle of that company–employee contract has the potential for ethical transgressions. Most HR professionals see their direct involvement in this contract as acting as the conscience of the organization in many ways. If the right people are hired in the first place, it is believed, many other problems are avoided down the road. It's when organizations fail to plan ahead for vacancies and promotions that the pressure to hire someone who was needed yesterday can lead to the gradual relaxation of what may be clearly established codes of ethics.

Consider the following ethical transgressions:[2]

- You are behind schedule on a building project, and your boss decides to hire illegal immigrants to help get the project back on track. They are paid in cash "under the table," and your boss justifies the decision as being "a 'one-off'—besides, the INS [Immigration and Naturalization Service] has bigger fish to fry than a few undocumented workers on a building site! If we get caught, we'll pay the fine—it will be less than the penalty we would owe our client for missing our deadline on the project."
- Your company has hired a new regional vice president. As the HR specialist for her region, you are asked to process her payroll and benefits paperwork. Your boss instructs you to waive the standard one-year waiting period for benefits entitlement and enroll the new VP in the retirement and employee bonus plan immediately. When you raise the concern that this request violates current company policy, your boss informs you that this new VP is a close friend of the company president and advises you that, in the interests of your job security, you should "just do it and don't ask questions!"
- On your first day as the new HR specialist, you mention to your boss that the company

Accounting Function The function that keeps track of all the company's financial transactions by documenting the money coming in (credits) and money going out (debits) and balancing the accounts at the end of the period (daily, weekly, monthly, quarterly, annually).

appears to be out of employee handbooks and both the minimum wage and Occupational Safety and Health Administration (OSHA) posters that are legally required to be posted in the employee break room. Your boss laughs and says, "We've been meaning to get around to that for years—trust me, there will always be some other crisis to take priority over all that administrative stuff."

In each of these scenarios, accountability for the transgression would ultimately end with the HR department as the corporate function that is legally responsible for ensuring that such things don't happen.

For this reason, many advocates of ethical business conduct argue that HR should be at the center of any corporate code of ethics—not as the sole creator of the code, since it is a document that should represent the entire organization, but certainly as the voice of reason in ensuring that all the critical areas are addressed.[3]

1. *HR professionals must help ensure that ethics is a top organizational priority.* The recent business scandals have shown that simply relying on the presence of an ethical monitor will not prevent unethical behavior. HR should be the ethical champion in the organization, including hiring a formal ethics officer if necessary.
2. *HR must ensure that the leadership selection and development processes include an ethics component.* The terrible metaphor of a fish rotting from the head is relevant here. HR must be involved in hiring leaders who not only endorse and support but also model the ethical standards needed to keep the company out of danger. The biggest challenge here is convincing the leadership team that it's not just the rank-and-file employees who should be put through ethics training.
3. *HR is responsible for ensuring that the right programs and policies are in place.* As we will learn in future chapters in this book, financial penalties for unethical behavior are now directly connected to evidence of efforts to actively prevent unethical conduct. The absence of appropriate policies and training programs can increase the fines that are levied for unethical behavior.
4. *HR must stay abreast of ethics issues (and in particular the changing legislation and sentencing guidelines for unethical conduct).* Response to

recent corporate scandals has been swift and frustratingly bureaucratic. Organizations now face reams of documentation that are designed to regulate ethical behavior in the face of overwhelming evidence that organizations cannot, it would seem, be trusted to do it on their own.

PROGRESS ✓ QUESTIONS

9. Explain why HR personnel might consider themselves to be the conscience of the organization.
10. Select one of the ethical transgressions listed in the HR sections, and document how you would respond to that situation as the employee.
11. Why is HR's involvement in the selection of the leaders of the company so important to ethical business conduct?
12. Why have ethics policies and ethics training suddenly become so important?

>> Ethics in Finance

The finance function of an organization can be divided into three distinct areas: financial transactions, accounting, and auditing:

1. The financial transactions—the process by which the flow of money through an organization is handled—involve receiving money from customers and using that money to pay employees, suppliers, and all other creditors (taxes and the like), with hopefully enough left over to create a profit that can be either reinvested back into the business or paid out to owners/shareholders. Part of this function may be outsourced to specialists such as Paychex or ADP, for example.
2. The **accounting function** keeps track of all those financial transactions by documenting the money coming in (credits) and money going out (debits) and balancing the accounts at the end of the period (daily, weekly, monthly, quarterly, annually). The accounting function can be handled by accounting professionals who are hired by the company, outside accounting firms that are contracted by the company, or usually a combination of the two.
3. When an organization's financial statements, or books, have been balanced, they must then be reported to numerous interested parties. For small businesses, the most important customers are government agencies—state income and sales taxes

and federal taxes the IRS collects on the profits generated by the business. In addition, lenders and creditors will want to see financial statements that have been certified as accurate by an impartial third-party professional. That certification is offered by the **auditing function**—typically handled by certified professional accountants and/or auditing specialists.

As an organization grows and eventually goes public by selling stock in the organization on a public stock exchange, the need for certified financial documents becomes even greater. Existing and potential investors will make the decision to invest in the shares of that organization based on the information presented in those certified financial statements—specifically, the profit and loss statement and the balance sheet. Investors look to those documents for evidence of financial stability, operational efficiency, and the potential for future growth. Many organizations are large enough to maintain their own internal auditors to monitor the accuracy of their financial functions.

ALL IN A DAY'S WORK: INTERNAL AUDITORS' ROLES

According to the Institute of Internal Auditors:[4]

> Internal auditors are grounded in professionalism, integrity, and efficiency. They make objective assessments of operations and share ideas for best practices; provide counsel for improving controls, processes and procedures, performance, and risk management; suggest ways for reducing costs, enhancing revenues, and improving profits; and deliver competent consulting, assurance, and facilitation services.

> **Auditing Function** The certification of an organization's financial statements, or "books," as being accurate by an impartial third-party professional. An organization can be large enough to have internal auditors on staff as well as using external professionals—typically certified professional accountants and/or auditing specialists.

Internal auditors are well disciplined in their craft and subscribe to a professional code of ethics. They are diverse and innovative. They are committed to growing and enhancing their skills. They are continually on the lookout for emerging risks and trends in the profession. They are good thinkers. And to effectively fulfill all their roles, internal auditors must be excellent communicators who listen attentively, speak effectively, and write clearly.

Sitting on the right side of management, modern-day internal auditors are consulted on all aspects of the organization and must be prepared for just about anything. They are coaches, internal and external stakeholder advocates, risk managers, controls experts, efficiency specialists, and problem-solving partners. They are the organization's safety net.

It's certainly not easy, but for these skilled and competent professionals, it's all in a day's work.

A DIFFERENT PERSPECTIVE

You work for a mortgage servicing company—making sure that mortgage payments get processed accurately and the funds forwarded to the mortgage holder. Lately your company has been dealing with as many foreclosure notices as payments, and the market is starting to turn in an interesting direction. Customers whose houses are worth 30 or 40 percent less than they paid for them just a couple of years ago are starting to question whether it makes sense to continue to pay for an asset (their home) that may remain "upside down" for many years to come. They can still afford the mortgage payment they are currently making, but since the house is worth so much less than what they paid for it, they are starting to feel that they are throwing good money after bad.

The company's growing concern over this new phenomenon was the topic of an all-staff meeting earlier this week. Senior leaders reminded everyone that mortgages are a legal contract and that homeowners have a legal obligation to make the payments to which they agreed. After the meeting, however, several of your

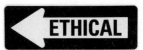 

© Jupiter Images Corporation RF

CONTINUED >>

colleagues shared some of the case histories they are currently working on.

Several common issues are starting to come up with these cases:

- Because of multibillion-dollar bailouts for banks, many people see themselves as victims of predatory lending practices with no apparent willingness on the part of the banks that received those bailout funds to help the individual homeowners.
- Media coverage of mortgage modification programs is reporting that banks are unwilling or unable to help, so what's the point in even trying?
- Because pools of mortgages have been sliced and diced into complicated financial derivatives, no one is even sure who the mortgage holder is anymore.
- The foreclosure process is so backed up in many cities that it can take as long as two years—that's a lot of time to live rent-free while you are saving up funds to move somewhere else—and with so many homes in foreclosure, rental property is attractively cheap these days.

You recall from your business ethics course in college that the elements of trust and consumer confidence in business are built on the belief that each party to a financial transaction has an ethical as well as a legal obligation to fulfill its part of the transaction, but it's clear that people are starting to feel that predatory lending practices now give them an excuse to ignore that ethical obligation.

QUESTIONS

1. Which ethics theories are being applied here?
2. If homeowners made poor financial decisions—taking too much equity out of their houses or buying at the wrong time—do the predatory lending practices of the banks and mortgage companies justify walking away from those mortgages?
3. Are homeowners really "throwing good money after bad" in making payments on mortgages for homes that are worth much less than the mortgage?
4. Would you walk away from your mortgage in this situation? How would you justify that decision?

Sources: Roger Lowenstein, "Walk Away from Your Mortgage," *The New York Times,* January 10, 2010; Glenn Setzer, "Stop Paying Your Mortgage and Walk Away?" www.mortgagenewsdaily.com, March 11, 2008; and David Streitfeld, "Owners Stop Paying Mortgages, and Stop Fretting," *The New York Times,* May 31, 2010.

>> Ethical Challenges

For internal employees in the finance, accounting, and auditing departments, the ethical obligations are no different from those of any other employee of the organization. As such, they are expected to maintain the reputation of the organization and abide by the code of ethics. Within their specific job tasks, this would include not falsifying documents, stealing money from the organization, or undertaking any other form of fraudulent activity related to the management of the organization's finances.

However, once we involve third-party professionals who are contracted to work for the company, the potential for ethical challenges and dilemmas increases dramatically.

GAAP

The accounting profession is governed not by a set of laws and established legal precedents but by a set of generally accepted accounting principles, typically referred to as **GAAP** (pronounced *gap*). These principles are accepted as standard operating procedures within the industry, but, like any operating standard, they are open to interpretation and abuse. The taxation rates that Uncle Sam expects you to

GAAP The generally accepted accounting principles that govern the accounting profession—not a set of laws and established legal precedents but a set of standard operating procedures within the profession.

pay on generated profits may be very clear, but the exact process by which you arrive at that profit figure is far from clear and places considerable pressure on accountants to manage the expectations of their clients.

CREATIVE BOOKKEEPING TECHNIQUES

Corporations try to manage their expansion at a steady rate of growth. If they grow too slowly or too erratically from year to year, investors may see them as unstable or in danger of falling behind their competition. If they grow too quickly, investors may develop unrealistic expectations of their future growth. This inflated outlook can have a devastating effect on your stock price when you miss your quarterly numbers for the first time. Investors have shown a pattern of overreacting to bad news and dumping their stock.

It is legal to defer receipts from one quarter to the next to manage your tax liability. However, accountants face ethical challenges when requests are made for far more illegal practices, such as falsifying accounts, underreporting income, overvaluing assets, and taking questionable deductions.

These pressures are further compounded by competitive tension as accounting firms compete for client business in a cutthroat market. Unrealistic delivery deadlines, reduced fees, and fees that are contingent on providing numbers that are satisfactory to the client are just some examples of the ethical challenges modern accounting firms face.

Accurate financial statements that present an organization as financially stable, operationally efficient, and positioned for strong future growth can do a great deal to enhance the reputation and goodwill of an organization. The fact that those statements have been certified by an objective third party to be "clean" only adds to that. However, that certification is meant to be for the public's benefit rather than the corporation's. This presents a very clear ethical predicament. The accounting/auditing firm is paid by the corporation, but it really serves the general public, who are in search of an impartial and objective review.

The situation can become even more complex when the accounting firm has a separate consulting relationship with the client—as was the case with Arthur Andersen and its infamous client Enron. Andersen's consulting business generated millions of dollars in fees from Enron alone. If the auditing side of its business chose to stand up to Enron's requests for creative bookkeeping policies, those millions of dollars of consulting fees, as well as additional millions of dollars in auditing fees, would have been placed in serious jeopardy. As we now know, the senior partners on the

Enron account chose not to stand up to Enron, and their decision eventually sank Arthur Andersen entirely.

With so many ethical pressures facing the accounting profession, and a guidebook of operating standards that is open to such abuse, the last resort for ethical guidance and leadership is the Code of Conduct issued by the American Institute of Certified Public Accountants (AICPA).

PROGRESS ✓ QUESTIONS

13. List the three primary areas of the finance function in an organization.
14. Explain how the accounting profession is governed by GAAP.
15. Why would audited accounts be regarded as being "clean"?
16. What key decision brought about the demise of Arthur Andersen?

Life Skills

>> Being Ethically Responsible

Review the company value chain in Figure 3.1. Consider the company you currently work for, or one that you hope to work for in the future. The department in which you work holds a specific place and function in that value chain, and the extent to which you interact with the other departments on that chain in a professional and ethical manner has a great deal to do with the long-term growth and success of the organization.

Of course, that's easy to say but a lot harder to do. Balancing departmental goals and objectives (to which you are held accountable) with larger company performance targets can be a challenge when resources are tight and you are balancing fierce competition in a tough economy. In that kind of environment, an organization's commitment to ethical conduct can be tested as the pressure to close deals and hit sales targets increases. Ethical dilemmas develop here when business decisions have to be made that will negatively affect one department or another. In addition, you may face your own dilemmas when you are tasked with obligations or responsibilities that conflict with your own value system.

In those situations, remain aware of the bigger picture and consider the results for all the stakeholders involved in the decision—whether it's your colleagues at work or your family members and friends. You may be the one making the decision, but others will share the consequences.

>> Conflicts of Interest

The obligation that an auditing firm has to a paying client while owing an objective, third-party assessment of that client's financial stability to stakeholders and potential investors represents a potentially significant **conflict of interest**. We examine the government's response to this conflict of interest in more detail in Chapter 6 when we review the Sarbanes-Oxley Act of 2002 and the impact that legislation has attempted to have on the legal enforcement of ethical business practices.

Conflict of Interest
A situation in which one relationship or obligation places you in direct conflict with an existing relationship or obligation.

Key Point

What kinds of conflicts of interest might arise in your company?

However, as the value chain model we reviewed at the beginning of this chapter shows us, the potential for conflicts of interest within an organization can go far beyond the finance department:

- At the most basic level, simply meeting the needs of your organization's stakeholders can present conflicts of interest when you consider the possibility that what is best for your shareholders (increased profits) may not be best for your employees and the community if the most efficient means to achieve those increased profits is to close your factory and move production overseas.
- Selling a product that has the potential to be harmful to your customers represents an equally significant conflict of interest. The convenience of fast food carries with it the negative consequences of far more calories than you need to consume in an average day. McDonald's, for example, has responded with increased menu choices to include salads and alternatives to french fries and soda, but the Big Mac continues to be one of its best-selling items.
- Selling a product that has the potential to be harmful to the environment also carries a conflict of interest. Computer manufacturers such as Dell and Hewlett-Packard offer plans to recycle your old computer equipment rather than throwing it into a landfill. Fast-food companies like McDonald's

have changed their packaging to move away from clamshell boxes for their burgers. Beverage companies such as Nestlé are producing bottles for their bottled water that use less plastic to minimize the impact on landfills.

These attempts to address conflicts of interest all have one thing in common. Whether they were prompted by internal strategic policy decisions or aggressive campaigns by customers and special interest groups, the decisions had to come from the top of the organization. Changing the way an organization does business can sometimes begin with a groundswell of support from the front line of the organization (where employees interact with customers), but eventually the key decisions on corporate policy and (where appropriate) capital expenditure have to come from the senior leadership of the organization. Without that endorsement, any attempts to make significant changes tend to remain as departmental projects rather than organizationwide initiatives.

© Tanya Constantine/Digital Vision/
Getty Images RF

Conflicts of interest do not just happen in large corporations. What are the potential conflicts that arise by this employee informing her friend that a sale next week will save her 30 percent, but not informing other customers?

>> Conclusion

The Ethics Resource Center (ERC), a nonprofit U.S. organization devoted to the advancement of organizational ethics, surveyed more than 3,000 American workers in its 2005 National Business Ethics Survey (NBES). The findings showed that more than half of U.S. employees had observed at least one example of workplace ethical misconduct in the past year and 36 percent had observed two or more. This represents a slight increase from the results of the 2003 survey. During the same period, willingness to report observed misconduct at work to management declined to 55 percent, a decrease of 10 percentage points since 2003. Types of misconduct employees observed most include:[5]

- Abusive or intimidating behavior toward employees (21 percent).
- Lying to employees, customers, vendors, or the public (19 percent).
- Situations that placed employee interests over organizational interests (18 percent).
- Violations of safety regulations (16 percent).
- Misreporting of actual time worked (16 percent).

Behavior such as the Ethics Resource Center documented in the NBES represents the real organizational culture more than any corporate statements or policy manuals. Employees learn very quickly about "the rules of the game" in any work environment and make the choice to "go with the flow" or, if the rules are unacceptable to their personal value systems, to look for employment elsewhere.

Of greater importance for the organization as a whole is the fact that any unethical behavior is allowed to persist for the long term. Explanations for the behavior (or for the failure to address the behavior) are plentiful:

- "That's common practice in this industry."
- "It's a tough market out there, and you have to be willing to bend the rules."
- "They're not in my department."
- "I don't have time to watch their every move—head office gives me too much to do to babysit my people."

- "If I fire them for a policy violation, the union rep would be on my back in a heartbeat."
- "If I fire them for a policy violation, I'd be one short—do you know how long it would take me to find a replacement and train him?"
- "The bosses know they do it—if they turn a blind eye, why shouldn't I?"
- "They don't pay me to be a company spy—I've got my own work to do."

So if bending the rules, stretching the truth, breaking the rules, and even blatantly lying have become a depressingly regular occurrence in your workplace, the question must be asked as to where the pressure or performance expectation comes from to make this behavior necessary. The answer can be captured in one word: *profit*.

This doesn't mean that nonprofit organizations don't also face problems with unethical behavior or that the pursuit of profit is unethical. What it means is that the obligation to deliver profits to owners or shareholders has created a convenient "get out of jail free" card, where all kinds of behavior can be justified in the name of meeting your obligations to your shareholders. You, as an individual, wouldn't normally do this, but you have a deadline or quota or sales target to meet, and your boss isn't the type to listen to explanations or excuses, so maybe just this once if you *(insert ethical transgression here),* you can get over this hurdle—just this once. Unfortunately, that's how it started for the folks at Enron, and that's how it could start for you. They fudged the numbers for one quarter and managed to get away with it, but all that did was raise investor expectations for the next quarter, and they found themselves on a train they couldn't get off.

As we shall see in the next chapters, if the organization doesn't set the ethical standard, employees will perform to the ethical standards of the person who controls their continued employment with the company—their boss.

How well companies set ethical standards can be measured by the extensive legislation that now exists to legally enforce (or at least attempt to enforce) ethical behavior in business.

FRONTLINE FOCUS

Just Sign the Forms—Matt Makes a Decision

Matt really wanted this job, and he really wanted to make a good first impression with Scott. Plus, Scott was right; he wasn't going to harass anyone or insult others based on their race, and he certainly wasn't going to risk his chances at the management-training program by doing anything unethical. What was the worst that could happen? If anyone from HR ever found out that he didn't watch the training videos, he could show how the company had benefited from his making up the backlog on the Morton6000, and he was sure that Scott would back him up.

Matt signed the forms and got to work.

Three months later, Matt finished his probationary period and met with the HR director to review his performance and, Matt hoped, discuss his application for the management-training program. The HR director was very friendly and complimentary about Matt's performance over the last 90 days. But he had one question for Matt: "The production log for the Morton6000 shows that you made a big dent in our backlog on your first morning here. I'm curious how you managed to do that when your paperwork shows that you spent three hours watching training videos as part of your new employee orientation."

QUESTIONS

1. What should Matt tell the HR director?
2. What do you think the HR director's reaction will be?
3. What are Matt's chances of joining the management-training program now?

[For Review]

1. **Define *organizational ethics*.**

    Organizational ethics can be considered as an area of study separate from the general subject of ethics because of two distinct issues:

    *   *Other parties (the stakeholders) have a vested interest in the ethical performance of an organization.*

    *   *In a work environment, you may be placed in a situation where your personal value system may clash with the ethical standards of the organization's operating culture (the values, beliefs, and norms shared by all the employees of that organization).*

2. **Explain the respective ethical challenges facing the functional departments of an organization.**

    The functional line areas of an organization—R&D, manufacturing, marketing, HR, and finance—face operational and budgetary pressures that present ethical challenges over what they should do as opposed to what the company may be asking them to do:

    *   *Research and development (R&D) carries the burden of developing products or services that are sufficiently better, faster, or cheaper than the competition to give the company a leading position in the market. However, market pressures often prompt instructions from senior management to lower costs and/or escalate deadlines that can prevent the designers and engineers from doing all the quality testing they would normally want to do.*

    *   *People in manufacturing share the same challenge: Do we build the best-quality product and price it accordingly, or do we build a product that meets a price point that is lower than our competition, even if it means using poorer-quality materials?*

    *   *The marketing challenge is more directly aligned to the debate between universal ethics and utilitarianism. Do you build a product that customers really need and focus your marketing message on showing customers how that product meets their needs (universal), or do you build a product that you think you can sell at a healthy profit and offer gainful employment to your workers and then focus your marketing message on convincing customers to buy a product they may not need (utilitarianism).*

    *   *For HR, there is a potential ethical dilemma at every step of the life cycle of an employee's contract with an organization. From recruitment and hiring to eventual departure from the company (either voluntarily or involuntarily), HR carries the responsibility of corporate compliance to all prevailing employment legislation. Any evidence of discrimination, harassment, poor working conditions, or failure to offer equal employment opportunities presents a significant risk for the company, and HR must combat managers willing to bend the rules to meet their department goals in keeping the company in compliance.*

    *   *Whether it is fraudulent financial transactions, poor accounting practices, or insufficient auditing procedures, poor financial management has featured in every major financial scandal over the past 50 years. Investors trust companies to use their invested capital wisely and to generate a reasonable return. Checks and balances are stipulated under GAAP (generally accepted accounting principles) to ensure that corporate funds are managed correctly, but as cases such as Enron have shown, those checks and balances are often modified, overruled, or ignored completely.*

3. **Discuss the position that a human resource (HR) department should be at the center of any corporate code of ethics.**

   Most HR professionals see their direct involvement in every aspect of an employee–employer relationship as acting as the corporate conscience of the organization in many ways. If the right people are hired in the first place, then many other problems are avoided down the road, it is believed. When organizations fail to plan ahead for vacancies and promotions, the pressure to hire someone who was needed yesterday can lead to the gradual relaxation of what may be clearly established codes of ethics.

4. **Explain the potential ethical challenges presented by generally accepted accounting principles (GAAP).**

   The accounting profession is governed not by a set of laws and established legal precedents but by a set of generally accepted accounting principles, typically referred to as GAAP (pronounced gap). These principles are accepted as standard operating procedures within the industry, but, like
   any operating standard, they are open to interpretation and abuse. The taxation rates that Uncle Sam expects you to pay on generated profits may be very clear, but the exact process by which you arrive at that profit figure is far from clear and places considerable pressure on accountants to manage the expectations of their clients.

5. **Determine potential conflicts of interest within any organizational function.**

   Any situation in which one relationship or obligation places you in direct opposition with an existing relationship or obligation presents a conflict of interest. Selling the product with the highest profit margin for the company rather than the product that best meets the customer's need is one example. McDonald's promotion of a new, healthier menu while continuing to sell its most unhealthy but best-selling Big Mac places it in a conflict of interest. Hiring someone who has the minimum qualifications but is available now as opposed to waiting for a better-qualified applicant who won't be available for another month is another example.

[Key Terms]

Accounting Function 54

Auditing Function 55

Conflict of Interest 58

GAAP 56

Organizational Culture 48

Universal Ethics 51

Utilitarianism 51

Value Chain 48

[Review Questions]

1. Consider the functional departments we have reviewed in this chapter. Which department do you think faces the greatest number of ethical challenges? Why?

2. Provide three examples of unethical behavior that you have observed at the company you work for (or a company you have worked for in the past). What were the outcomes of this behavior?

3. Philip Kotler argues that professional marketers "should have the same ambivalence as nuclear scientists who help build nuclear bombs." Is that a valid argument? Why or why not?

4. Should the HR department be the ethics champion in the organization? Why or why not?

5. What are "creative bookkeeping techniques"? Provide three examples.

6. Would you leave your position with a company if you saw evidence of unethical business practices? Why or why not? What factors would you consider in making that decision?

Review Exercises

Ambush Marketing. As billboards, radio commercials, print ads, and 30- or 60-second TV spots become increasingly lost in the blurred onslaught of advertising, larger companies are increasingly turning to more creative means to get the name of their product or service in front of the public's increasingly overloaded attention span.

Consider the following:

- Imagine you're at the Washington Monument when a young couple with a camera approaches and kindly asks if you'll take their picture. They seem nice enough, so you agree to take a photo of them. As you're lining up the shot, the gentleman explains it's the newest model, he got it for only $400, and it does this, that, and the other. Cool. You take the picture, return the camera, and walk away. It's nice to help people.

- The New York bar is crowded, with a line of people three deep. Just as you manage to flag the bartender's attention, a neighboring patron tries to latch onto your good luck. "Say, buddy, I see you're about to order a couple of drinks," your neighbor says. "If I give you a 10-spot, could you get me a Peach Royale?" The request seems harmless. Why not?

- A colorful cardboard box plastered with a well-known logo of a certain computer maker sits in the lobby of your building for several days. Not only does the trademark get noticed, but residents may also assume a neighbor has made the purchase. So the computer company gets a warm association in the minds of certain consumers.

All perfectly reasonable and innocent everyday occurrences, right? But how would you feel if the couple at the Washington Monument raving about their new camera was really a pair of actors planted in targeted locations to praise the virtues of digital cameras to an unsuspecting public? Your innocent neighbor in the bar was actually performing a "lean-over"—a paid commercial for Peach Royale. And the computer box was left in the lobby of your building deliberately at the minimal cost of a "contribution" to the building's doorman.

So now you get really paranoid. You've heard of product placement, where movies offer lingering shots on specific products (funny how the actors always drink Coke or Heineken beer; and didn't Halle Berry look great in that coral-colored Ford Thunderbird in the James Bond movie *Die Another Day*—did you know you could buy a Thunderbird in that exact color?). But what if that group of commuters on your morning train discussing a new movie or TV show or book was planted there deliberately? What if the friendly woman with the cute 6-year-old at the playground who was talking about how her son loves his new video game was also an actress?

Such tactics take the concept of target marketing to a whole new level. Advertisers plant seemingly average folks in the middle of a demographically desirable crowd and begin to sing the praises of a new product or service while conveniently failing to mention that they have been hired to do so, and may have never even heard of the product or service before they took the gig.

1. Is this unethical marketing? Explain why or why not.

2. Critics argue that such campaigns "blur the lines between consumerism and con artistry." Is that a fair assessment? Why or why not?

3. How would you feel if you were involved in such an ambush?

4. If the majority of consumers are already skeptical about most advertising they are exposed to, how do you think the general public would feel about such marketing campaigns?

5. Supporters of these campaigns argue that our economy is built on consumerism and that if you don't find more effective ways to reach consumers, the entire economy will suffer. Does that make the practice OK? Should we just accept it as a nuisance and a necessary evil like solicitation calls during dinner?

6. Would your opinion change if the advertisers were more obvious in their campaigns—such as admitting after each skit that the raving fans were really actors?

Sources: First and second items are adapted from Neil McOstrich, "Crossing the Line," *Marketing Magazine* 107, no. 45 (November 11, 2002), p. 24; and the third from Brian Steinberg, "Undercover Marketing Is Gaining Ground—Some Promoters Are Doing It—Others Question Its Ethics," *The Wall Street Journal* (eastern edition), December 18, 2000, p. B17D.

Internet Exercises

1. Visit the U.S. government recall website www.recalls.gov, select a product recall event from the past three years, and answer the following questions:

   a. What information would you consider to be evidence of an ethical transgression in this product recall?

b. Other than recalling the product, what other actions did the company take to address the situation?

c. What steps would you suggest that the company should have taken to restore that reputation?

2. Locate the websites for the American Marketing Association (AMA) and the American Institute of Certified Public Accountants (AICPA). One has a "Professional Code of Conduct," and the other has a "Statement of Ethics." Does the terminology make a difference? Why or why not?

a. Compare and contrast the components of each approach.

b. Since the AMA offers certification as a "Professional Certified Marketer," would the organization benefit from promoting a professional code of conduct like the AICPA? Why or why not?

[Team Exercises]

1. **Is it ethical to ambush?**
   Divide into two teams. One team must prepare a presentation advocating the use of the ambush marketing tactics described in the Review Exercises. The other team must prepare a presentation explaining the ethical dilemmas those tactics present.

2. **In search of an ethical department.**
   Divide into groups of three or four. Each group must select one of the organizational departments featured in this chapter (HR, R&D, marketing, sales, and finance) and document the potential areas for unethical behavior in that department. Prepare a presentation outlining an example of an ethical dilemma in that department and proposing a solution for resolving it.

3. **An isolated incident?**
   Divide into two groups, and prepare arguments *for* and *against* the following behavior: *You are the regional production manager for a tire company that has invested many millions of dollars in a new retreading process that will allow you to purchase used tires, replace the tread, and sell them at a significantly lower cost (with a very healthy profit margin for your company). Initial product testing has gone well, and expectations for this very lucrative new project are very high. Promotion prospects for those managers associated with the project are also very good. The company chose to go with a "soft" launch of the new tires, introducing them into the Malaysian market with little marketing or advertising to draw attention to the new product line. Once demand and supply are thoroughly tested, the plan is to launch the new line worldwide with a big media blitz. Sales so far have been very strong based on the low price. However, this morning, your local contact in Malaysia sent news of a bus accident in which two schoolchildren were killed. The cause of the accident was the front left tire on the bus, which lost its tread at high speed and caused the bus to roll over. You are only three days away from your next progress report meeting and only two weeks from the big worldwide launch. You decide to categorize the accident as an isolated incident and move forward with your plans for the introduction of your discount retread tires to the world market.*

4. **The sole remaining supplier.**
   Divide into two groups, and prepare arguments *for* and *against* the following behavior: *In the mid-1970s heart pacemakers ran on transistors before advances in technology replaced them with the silicon computer chips we are all familiar with today. Your company has found itself in a situation where it is the last remaining supplier of a particular transistor for the current models of heart pacemakers on the market. Your competitors have all chosen to get out of the business, claiming that the risks of lawsuits related to malfunctioning pacemakers was simply too great to make the business worthwhile. Your management team has now arrived at the same conclusion. The chief executive officer defends the decision by arguing that as a business-to-business supplier to other manufacturers, you have no say in how the transistors are used, so why should the fact that they are used in life-saving equipment factor into the decision? Your responsibility is to your shareholders, not to the patients who depend on these pacemakers. You are not responsible for all the other manufacturers getting out of the business.*

Thinking Critically

>> BOOSTING YOUR RÉSUMÉ

"Everybody has stretched the truth a little on their résumés at one time or another, right?" That's the question that people who are about to give their own résumés a little boost ask themselves as a way of dealing with the twinge of guilt they are probably feeling as they adjust their job title or make that six months of unemployment magically disappear by claiming a consulting project. In the harsh light of day, résumé inflation is not only unethical, but if you transfer those untruths onto a job application form, which is a legal document, then the act also becomes illegal. Consider the outcomes for these former occupants of high-ranking (and high-paying) positions:

© AP Photo/Joe Raymond

- Marilee Jones, dean of admissions for the Massachusetts Institute of Technology (MIT), claimed to hold degrees in biology from Rensselaer Polytechnic Institute and Albany Medical College and to hold a doctorate degree. She resigned in April 2007 after officials at MIT discovered the truth.

- George O'Leary resigned just five days after being hired as Notre Dame's football coach in 2001 when it was revealed that he did not hold a master's degree in education from "NYU–Stony Brook" (a nonexistent institution), nor had he lettered three times as a football player for the University of New Hampshire (both of which he had claimed on his résumé). O'Leary retired in October 2015 after 12 seasons as the coach of the University of Central Florida Knights. He is contracted to remain as a "special liaison" to UCF through 2020 at a reported salary of $200,000 a year.

- Scott Thompson, the former president of PayPal, was hired as CEO of Yahoo in January 2012. Activist investor Daniel Loeb notified Yahoo's board of directors in May 2012 that Thompson's claim of a degree in accounting and computer science from Stonehill College was an embellishment, and that Thompson's degree was only in accounting. Yahoo initially stood by Thompson, but when further investigation revealed that the same claim had been made on legal statements for PayPal and eBay (PayPal's parent company), he claimed that the search firm that placed him was to blame for the error. Thompson resigned two weeks later and became CEO of online shopping service ShopRunner.

- Ronald Zarrella, former CEO of Bausch & Lomb, the eye care company, was required to give up $1.1 million of a planned $1.65 million bonus when it was discovered that although he had attended New York University's Stern School of Business, he had never earned the MBA that he claimed to have on his résumé. Interestingly, the board of directors of Bausch & Lomb, a company recognized by Standard & Poor's as an example of good corporate governance, chose not to fire Zarrella, claiming that he brought too much value to the company and its shareholders to dismiss him.

If the risks are so high, why do people continue to embellish the details on a document that is supposed to accurately reflect their skills and work experience? Pressure! Getting hired by a company is a competitive process, and you need to make the best sales pitch you can to attract the attention of the HR person assigned to screen the applications for a particular position (or, at least, the applications that make it through the software program that screens résumés for keywords related to the open position). In such a pressured environment, justifying an action on the basis of an assumption that everyone else is probably doing it starts to make sense. So changing dates, job titles, responsibilities, certifications, and/or academic degrees can now be classified as "little white lies," but as you can see from our three examples in this case, those little white lies can come back to haunt you.

QUESTIONS

1. Does the competitive pressure to get hired justify the decision to boost your résumé? Why?

2. Do you think the board of directors of Bausch & Lomb made the right decision in choosing not to fire Zarrella? Why or why not?

3. What steps should companies take during the hiring process to ensure that such bad hires do not happen?

4. Can you polish your résumé without resorting to little white lies? Provide some examples of how you might do that.

5. Your friend has been unemployed for two years. She decides to boost her résumé by claiming to have been a consultant for those two years in order to compete in a very tough job market. She explains that a colleague of

hers did the same thing to cover a six-month period of unemployment. Does the longer period of unemployment make the decision any less unethical? Why or why not?

6. If you discovered that a colleague at work had lied on her résumé, what would you do? .

Sources: R. Weiss, "By George It's Blarney," *New York Daily News,* December 15, 2001; Tom Fornelli, "UCF's George O'Leary Resigns as Coach," www.cbssports.com, October 25, 2015; Steve Berkowitz, "UCF Will Pay George O'Leary $200,000 a Year through 2020," *USA Today,* October 26, 2015; and James B. Stewart, "In the Undoing of a CEO, a Puzzle," *The New York Times,* May 18, 2012.

Thinking Critically `3.2`

>> A LOSS OF PRIVACY

On July 10, 2011, the *News of the World,* a British tabloid newspaper, published its last edition after being in regular publication since 1843. The newspaper's parent company, Rupert Murdoch's News Corp., had succumbed to increasing pressure to shut down the paper in response to a phone-hacking scandal in which journalists from the paper sought the assistance of private investigators in accessing the cell phone voice mail accounts of celebrities and the British royal family and of bribing members of the police force for information in the search for "breaking news."

Further investigation revealed cases of illegal access to voice mails and payments to police officers for information as far back as 2003, but the "phone-hacking scandal," as it became known, wasn't made public until July 2009 when it was revealed that News Group Newspapers (the division of News Corp. that published the *News of the World*) had paid out more than £1 million to settle claims of the alleged involvement of its journalists in phone hacking between 2003 and 2007. Andy Coulson, the editor of the newspaper during that period, admitted to members of Parliament when appearing before the Culture, Media, and Sports Committee, that things went "badly wrong" but insisted that he knew nothing about the alleged phone hacking.

Coulson's public profile after leaving the *News of the World* continued to be a problem for News Corp.—especially when his role as communications chief for the Conservative Party led to his appointment as head of the govern-

© James Hardy/PhotoAlto RF

ment's media operations with the election of David Cameron as prime minister in May 2010. The unrelenting public outcry over the phone-hacking scandal prompted Coulson's resignation in January 2011.

The level of public outcry had escalated when news broke of the alleged hacking of the cell phone of a murdered 13-year-old schoolgirl, Milly Dowler, whose remains had been found in September 2002. In July 2011, lawyers for Dowler's family revealed that police reports stated that Milly's voice mail messages had been hacked, allegedly by an investigator working for the *News of the World,* while the police were searching for her. The lawyers claimed that individual messages had been deleted to make room in her mailbox, which misled police and her family into believing that the young girl was still alive.

When Rupert Murdoch appeared before a parliamentary committee in July 2011, he testified, "This is the most humbling day of my life." He then explained that the newspaper represented less than 1 percent of News Corp.'s holdings, and with over 50,000 people to manage around the world, he couldn't possibly be expected to know every detail of every company. This testimony mirrored the responses of all the senior executives called to appear before the committee. Rebekah Brooks, editor of the *News of the World* from 2000 to 2003, and later the CEO of News International, the operator of all Murdoch's British papers, including *The Sun, The Times,* and *The Sunday Times;* James Murdoch, Rupert

CONTINUED >>

Murdoch's eldest son and deputy chief operating officer of News Corp.; and several former senior editors all claimed to have no direct knowledge of the alleged activities of their journalists, despite being presented with video testimony collected by actor Hugh Grant from a former journalist who outlined in detail how the phone hacking was performed and how the behavior was "expected" and "fully endorsed" by the editorial team.

By September 2012, more than 80 people had been arrested in connection with the multiple cases against News Corp., and the company had taken charges of over $315 million in its financial reporting for legal fees, civil settlements (some as high as $600,000), and the cost of closing the *News of the World.* On February 26, 2012, Murdoch launched *The Sun on Sunday* as a replacement for the *News of the World.*

Coulson was found guilty of conspiring to hack phones and served an 18-month prison sentence. In June 2015, he was acquitted of a more serious charge of perjury while giving evidence, bringing his legal troubles related to the phone hacking scandal to an end. By contrast, Rebekah Brooks, who was cleared of all charges and was reported to have received a $15 million severance package after resigning from News Corp. in 2011, returned to the News Corp. family in September 2015 as chief executive of News UK with a reported annual salary of $5 million.

QUESTIONS

1. Why would newspaper journalists resort to such methods in order to deliver "breaking news"?

2. If the alleged phone hacking and bribery took place as far back as 2003, how is it possible that the story was not made public until 2009?

3. Why would Andy Coulson feel pressure to resign as head of the government's media operations only eight months after being appointed to the position?

4. Do you think that the closure of the *News of the World* represents an appropriate resolution of this scandal? Why or why not?

5. If the phone hacking had been restricted just to the cell phones of celebrities, would the public outcry have been so large? Why or why not?

6. What could Rupert Murdoch have done differently here?

Sources: Indu Chandrasekhar, Murray Wardrop, and Andy Trotman, "Phone Hacking: Timeline of the Scandal," *The Telegraph,* July 23, 2012; Erik Larson, "News Corp. Seeks to Limit Damages in Phone-Hacking Trial," *Bloomberg Businessweek,* September 25, 2012; "News Corporation: Have I Got News for You," *The Economist,* September 29, 2012; "A Report on Phone Hacking: Dial M for Muddle," *The Economist,* May 5, 2012; Martin Evans, "Andy Coulson: The Rise and Fall of the Essex Boy Who Went from Downing Street to Belmarsh Prison," *The Telegraph,* June 3, 2015; and Mark Sweney and Roy Greenslade, "Rebekah Brooks' Return Confirmed," *The Guardian,* September 2, 2015.

Thinking Critically 3.3

>> JOHNSON & JOHNSON AND THE TYLENOL POISONINGS

A bottle of Tylenol is a common feature of any medicine cabinet as a safe and reliable painkiller, but in the fall of 1982, this household brand was driven to the point of near extinction along with the fortunes of parent company Johnson & Johnson as a result of a product-tampering case that has never been solved. On September 29, 1982, seven people in the Chicago area died after taking Extra-Strength Tylenol capsules that had been laced with cyanide. Investigators later determined that the bottles of Tylenol had been purchased or shoplifted from seven or eight drugstores and supermarkets and then replaced on shelves after the capsules in the bottle had been removed, emptied of their acetaminophen powder, and filled with cyanide.

The motive for the killings was never established, although a grudge against Johnson & Johnson or the retail chains selling the brand was suspected. A man called James Lewis attempted to profit from the event by sending an extortion letter to Johnson & Johnson, presumably inspired by the $100,000 reward the company had posted, but the police dismissed him as a serious suspect. He was jailed for 13 years for the extortion but never charged with the murders.

The response of Johnson & Johnson to the potential destruction of its most profitable product line has since become business legend and is taught today as a classic case study in crisis management at universities all over the world.

Company Chairman James E. Burke and other senior executives were initially advised to pull bottles only from the Midwest region surrounding the Chicago area where the deaths had occurred. The decision they made was to order the immediate removal and destruction of more than 31 million bottles of the product nationwide, at an estimated cost to the company of more than $100 million. At the time, Tylenol held a 35 percent share of the painkiller market. This attack on the brand quickly reduced that share to less than 7 percent.

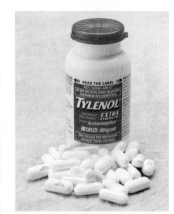

© McGraw-Hill Education/Eric Misko, Elite Images Photography

Why would the company make such an expensive decision when there were cheaper and more acceptable options open to it? To answer that question, we need to look at the company's Credo—the corporate philosophy statement that has guided the company since its founder, General Robert Wood Johnson, wrote the first version in 1943.

The opening line of the Credo explains why the decision to incur such a large cost in responding to the Tylenol deaths was such an obvious one for the company to make: "We believe our first responsibility is to the doctors, nurses and patients, to mothers and fathers, and all others who use our products and services." That responsibility prompted the company to invest millions in developing tamper-proof bottles for its No. 1 brand and a further $100 million to win back the confidence of its customers.

The actions appeared to pay off. In less than a year, Tylenol had regained a market share of more than 28 percent. Whether that dramatic recovery was due to savvy marketing or the selfless response of company executives in attempting to do "the right thing" for their customers remains a topic of debate more than a quarter of a century later.

QUESTIONS

1. Although Johnson & Johnson took a massive short-term loss as a result of its actions, it was cushioned by the relative wealth of the company. Should it have acted the same way if the survival of the firm were at stake?

2. James E. Burke reportedly said that he felt that there was no other decision he could have made. Do you agree? Could he, for example, have recalled Tylenol only in the Midwest? Was there a moral imperative to recall all Tylenol?

3. What was the moral minimum required of the company in this case? Would it favor some stakeholders more than others? How would you defend balancing the interests of some stakeholders more than others?

4. Imagine that a developing country volunteers to take the recalled product. Its representatives make assurances that all the tablets will be visually inspected and random samples taken before distribution. Would that be appropriate in these circumstances? Would it have been a better solution than destroying all remaining Tylenol capsules?

5. Apparently no relatives of any of the victims sued Johnson & Johnson. Would they have had a moral case if they had? Should the company have foreseen a risk and done something about it?

6. How well do you think a general credo works in guiding action? Would you prefer a typical mission statement or a clear set of policy outlines, for example? Do you see any way in which the Johnson & Johnson Credo could be improved or modified?

Sources: S. Tifft and L. Griggs, "Poison Madness in the Midwest," *Time,* October 11, 1982; I. Molotsky, "Tylenol Maker Hopeful on Solving Poisoning Case," *The New York Times,* February 20, 1986; B. Rudolph, "Coping with Catastrophe," *Time,* February 24, 1986; and Johnson & Johnson Credo, www.jnj.com/connect/about-jnj/jnj-credo/.

[References]

1. P. Kotler, "Is Marketing Ethics an Oxymoron?" *Marketing Management,* November–December 2004, pp. 30–35.

2. Adapted from A. Pomery, "The Ethics Squeeze," *HR Magazine,* March 2006.

3. M. R. Vickers, "Business Ethics and the HR Role: Past, Present, and Future," *Human Resource Planning* 28, no. 1 (2005).

4. The Institute of Internal Auditors, www.theiia.org.

5. Curtis C. Verschoor, "Ethical Culture: Most Important Barrier to Ethical Misconduct," *Strategic Finance* 87, no. 6 (December 2005), p. 19.

Source: U.S. Coast Guard photo by Petty Officer 3rd Class Patrick Kelley

CORPORATE SOCIAL
RESPONSIBILITY

After studying this chapter, you should be able to:

4-1 Describe and explain *corporate social responsibility (CSR)*.

4-2 Distinguish between *instrumental* and *social contract* approaches to CSR.

4-3 Explain the business argument for "doing well by doing good."

4-4 Summarize the five driving forces behind CSR.

4-5 Explain the *triple bottom-line* approach to corporate performance measurement.

4-6 Discuss the relative merits of carbon-offset trading.

FRONTLINE FOCUS
An Improved Reputation

Claire was recently promoted to the newly created position of CSR manager for a regional oil distribution company. Not long ago the company had received negative media coverage as a result of a small oil leak in one of its storage tanks. Fortunately, the oil didn't leak into the water supply, but the Environmental Protection Agency (EPA) is still testing the soil to verify if any of the leaked oil reached groundwater levels.

The owner of the company, Mr. Jones, promoted Claire from the marketing department so that the company could polish its brand with a "new environmentally friendly message."

Claire considers herself to be very environmentally responsible. She recycles everything she can; she drives an electric car; she participates in neighborhood cleanup events; and she only buys from companies with strong CSR reputations.

In her first meeting with Mr. Jones, Claire receives very clear instructions:

"We took a double whammy here Claire. The cleanup for the leak will cost a ton of money, and even though oil prices are at historic lows, we're losing customers because of the leak story. I need some quick ideas to turn our reputation around without spending any money, and I need them yesterday."

QUESTIONS

1. What type of CSR approach is Mr. Jones looking to adopt here? Read the definitions in the following sections for more details.
2. Would you say that Mr. Jones' statement represents a sincere commitment to CSR practices at the oil company? Why or why not?
3. What should Claire do now? Research the CSR initiatives of some regional oil companies for ideas.

> Years ago William Jennings Bryan once described big business as "nothing but a collection of organized appetites."
>
> **Daniel Patrick Moynihan, 1986**

>> Corporate Social Responsibility

Consider that age-old icon of childhood endeavors: the lemonade stand. Within a corporate social responsibility context, it's as if today's thirsty public wants much more than a cool, refreshing drink for a quarter. They're demanding said beverage be made of juice squeezed from lemons not sprayed with insecticides toxic to the environment and prepared by persons of appropriate age in kitchen conditions that pose no hazard to those workers. It must be offered in biodegradable paper cups and sold at a price that generates a fair, livable wage to the workers—who, some might argue, are far too young to be toiling away making lemonade for profit anyway. It's enough to drive young entrepreneurs straight back to the sandbox.[1]

Corporate social responsibility (CSR)—also referred to as *corporate citizenship* or *corporate conscience*—may be defined as the actions of an organization that are targeted toward achieving a social benefit over and above maximizing profits for its shareholders and meeting all its legal obligations.

> **Corporate Social Responsibility (CSR)** The actions of an organization that are targeted toward achieving a social benefit over and above maximizing profits for its shareholders and meeting all its legal obligations. Also known as *corporate citizenship* and *corporate conscience*.

This definition assumes that the corporation is operating in a competitive environment and that the managers of the corporation are committed to an aggressive growth strategy while complying with all federal, state, and local legal obligations. These obligations include payment of all taxes related to the profitable operation of the business, payment of all employer contributions for its workforce, and compliance with all legal industry standards in operating a safe working environment for its employees and delivering safe products to its customers.

However, the definition only scratches the surface of a complex and often elusive topic that has gained increased attention in the aftermath of corporate scandals that have presented many organizations as being the image of unchecked greed. While CSR may be growing in prominence, much of that prominence has come at the expense of organizations that found themselves facing boycotts and focused media attention on issues that previously were not considered as part of a traditional strategic plan. As Porter and Kramer point out:[2]

Many companies awoke to [CSR] only after being surprised by public responses to issues they had not previously thought were part of their business responsibilities. Nike, for example, faced an extensive consumer boycott after *The New York Times* and other media outlets reported abusive labor practices at some of its Indonesian suppliers in the early 1990s. Shell Oil's decision to sink the Brent Spar, an obsolete oil rig, in the North Sea led to Greenpeace protests in 1995 and to international headlines. Pharmaceutical companies discovered that they were expected to respond to the AIDS pandemic in Africa even though it was far removed from their primary product lines and markets. Fast-food and packaged food companies are now being held responsible for obesity and poor nutrition.

Activists of all kinds . . . have grown much more aggressive and effective in bringing public pressure to bear on corporations. Activists may target the most visible or successful companies merely to draw attention to an issue, even if those corporations actually have had little impact on the problem at hand. Nestlé, for example, the world's largest purveyor of bottled water, has become a major target in the global debate about access to fresh water, despite the fact that Nestlé's bottled water sales consume just 0.0008 percent of the world's fresh water supply. The inefficiency of agricultural irrigation, which uses 70 percent of the world's supply annually, is a far more pressing issue, but it offers no equally convenient multinational corporation to target.

Whether the organization's discovery of the significance of CSR was intentional or as a result of unexpected media attention, once CSR becomes part of its strategic plan, choices have to be made as to how the company will address this new element of corporate management.

PROGRESS ✔ QUESTIONS

1. Define *corporate social responsibility.*
2. Name two other terms that may be used for socially aware corporate behavior.
3. Give four examples of a corporation's legal obligations.
4. Do investors always invest money in companies to make a profit?

>> Management without Conscience

Many take an **instrumental approach** to CSR and argue that the only obligation of a corporation is to make profits for its shareholders in providing goods and services that meet the needs of its customers. The most famous advocate of this "classical" model is the Nobel Prize-winning economist Milton Friedman, who argued:[3]

> The view has been gaining widespread acceptance that corporate officials . . . have a social responsibility that goes beyond serving the interests of their stockholders. . . . This view shows a fundamental misconception of the character and nature of a free economy. In such an economy, there is one and only one social responsibility of business—to use its resources and engage in activities designed to increase its profits so long as it stays within the rules of the game, which is to say, engages in open and free competition, without deception or fraud. . . . Few trends could so thoroughly undermine the very foundations of our free society as the acceptance by corporate officials of a social responsibility other than to make as much money for their stockholders as possible.

From an ethical perspective, Friedman argues that it would be unethical for a corporation to do anything other than deliver the profits for which its investors have entrusted it with their funds in the purchase of shares in the corporation. He also stipulates that those profits should be earned "without deception or fraud." In addition, Friedman argues that, as an employee of the corporation, the manager has an ethical obligation to fulfill his role in delivering on the expectations of his employers:[4]

> In a free-enterprise, private-property system, a corporate executive is an employee of the owners of the business. He has direct responsibility to his employers. That responsibility is to conduct the business in accordance with their desires, which generally will be to make as much money as possible while conforming to the basic rules of the society, both those embodied in law and those embodied in ethical custom. . . . The key point is that, in his capacity as a corporate executive, the manager is the agent of the individuals who own the corporation . . . and his primary responsibility is to them.

© Andrey Armyagov/Shutterstock RF

Is McDonald's more culpable for childhood obesity than a local burger joint since it sells to a much wider audience? Should your local restaurants be held to similar standards?

Friedman's view of the corporate world supports the rights of individuals to make money with their investments (provided it is done honestly), and it recognizes the clear legality of the employment contract—as a manager, you work for me, the owner (or us, the shareholders), and you are expected to make as much profit as possible to make our investment in the company a success. This position does not prevent the organization from demonstrating some form of social conscience—donating to local charities or sponsoring a local Little League team, for example—but it restricts such charitable acts to the discretion of the owners (presumably in good times rather than bad), rather than recognizing any formal obligation on the part of the corporation and its management team.

This very simplistic model focuses on the internal world of the corporation itself and assumes that there are no external consequences to the actions of the

> **Instrumental Approach** The perspective that the only obligation of a corporation is to maximize profits for its shareholders in providing goods and services that meet the needs of its customers.

Social Contract Approach The perspective that a corporation has an obligation to society over and above the expectations of its shareholders.

corporation and its managers. Once we acknowledge that there is a world outside that is affected by the actions of the corporation, we can consider the **social contract approach** to corporate management.

In recent years, the notion of a social contract between corporations and society has undergone a subtle shift. Originally, the primary focus of the social contract was an economic one, assuming that continued economic growth would bring an equal advancement in quality of life. However, the rapid growth of U.S. businesses in size and power in the 1960s, 1970s, and 1980s changed that focus. Continued corporate growth was not matched by an improved quality of life. Growth at the expense of rising costs, wages growing at a lower rate than inflation, and the increasing presence of substantial layoffs to control costs were seen as evidence that the old social contract was no longer working.

Key Point

How does your company approach the issue of corporate social responsibility? Does it take an instrumental or social contract approach? Provide an example to support your answer.

The growing realization that corporate actions had the potential to impact tens of thousands of citizens led to a clear opinion shift. Fueled by special interest groups including environmentalists and consumer advocates, consumers began to question some fundamental corporate assumptions: Do we really need 200 types of breakfast cereal or 50 types of laundry soap just so we can deliver aggressive earnings growth to investors? What is this constant growth really costing us?

The modern social contract approach argues that because the corporation depends on society for its existence and continued growth, the corporation has an obligation to meet the demands of that society rather than just the demands of a targeted group of customers. As such, corporations should be recognized as social institutions as well as economic enterprises. By recognizing all their stakeholders (customers, employees, shareholders, vendor partners, and their community partners) rather than just their shareholders, corporations, it is argued, must maintain a longer-term perspective than just the delivery of quarterly earnings numbers.

PROGRESS ✓ QUESTIONS

5. What is the instrumental model of corporate management?
6. What is the social contract model of corporate management?
7. Research Friedman's article—what are the assumptions of his argument?
8. Do you agree or disagree with the social contract model? Why?

>> Management by Inclusion

Corporations do not operate in an isolated environment. As far back as 1969, Henry Ford II recognized that fact:[5]

> The terms of the contract between industry and society are changing. . . . Now we are being asked to serve a wider range of human values and to accept an obligation to members of the public with whom we have no commercial transactions.

Their actions impact their customers, their employees, their suppliers, and the communities in which they produce and deliver their goods and services. Depending on the actions taken by the corporation, some of these groups will be positively affected and others will be negatively affected. For example, if a corporation is operating unprofitably in a very competitive market, it is unlikely that it could raise prices to increase profits. Therefore, the logical choice would be to lower costs—most commonly by laying off its employees, since giving an employee a pink slip takes him or her off the payroll immediately.

While those laid-off employees are obviously hardest hit by this decision, it also has other far-reaching consequences. The communities in which those employees reside have now lost the spending power of those employees, who, presumably, no longer have as much money to spend in the local market until they find alternative employment. If the corporation chooses to shut down a factory, the community also loses property tax revenue from that factory, which negatively impacts the services it can provide to its residents—schools, roads, police force, and so forth. In addition, those local suppliers who made deliveries to that factory also have lost business and may have to make their own tough choices as a result.

What about the corporation's customers and shareholders? Presumably the layoffs will help the corporation remain competitive and continue to offer low prices to its customers, and the more cost-effective operation will hopefully improve the profitability of the corporation. So there are, at least on paper, winners and losers in such situations.

Recognizing the interrelationship of all these groups leads us far beyond the world of the almighty bottom line, and those organizations that do demonstrate a "conscience" that goes beyond generating profit inevitably attract a lot of attention. As Jim Roberts, professor of marketing at the Hankamer School of Business, points out:[6]

> I like to think of corporate social responsibility as doing well by doing good. Doing what's in the best long-term interest of the customer is ultimately doing what's best for the company. Doing good for the customer is just good business.

Look at the tobacco industry. Serving only the short-term desires of its customers has led to government intervention and a multibillion-dollar lawsuit against the industry because of the industry's denial of the consequences of smoking. On the other hand, alcohol manufacturers realized that by at least showing an interest in their consumers' well-being ("Don't drink and drive," "Drink responsibly," "Choose a designated driver"), they have been able to escape much of the wrath felt by the tobacco industry. It pays to take a long-term perspective.

"Doing well by doing good" seems, on the face of it, to be an easy policy to adopt, and many organizations have started down that road by making charitable donations, underwriting projects in their local communities, sponsoring local events, and engaging in productive conversations with special interest groups about earth-friendly

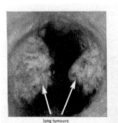

WARNING:
CIGARETTES CAUSE LUNG CANCER

85% of lung cancers are caused by smoking. 80% of lung cancer victims die within 3 years.

Health Canada

Source: U.S. Department of Agriculture

In Canada, cigarette packaging is required to have a graphic label that details the potential health risks of smoking. The same requirement will soon be introduced in the United States. How do you think American consumers will respond to the government's decision?

Real World Applications

Theresa works the drive-through station at her local fast-food restaurant. Lately the company has been aggressively promoting its "healthy options" kids' menu that includes apple slices instead of french fries and chocolate or plain milk instead of sodas. For the first couple of weeks, Theresa is instructed to clarify with each customer whether the person wanted fries or apple slices and soda or milk. However, her manager quickly realizes that the extra questions increased the average order time and contributed to longer lines at the drive-through. Now she has been told to assume that the order is regular (fries and a soda) unless the customer specifies otherwise. What responsibility (CSR) does the fast-food restaurant have to the consumer in this situation? What would you do if you were Theresa?

packaging materials and the use of more recyclable materials. However, mistrust and cynicism remain among their customers and citizens of their local communities. Many still see these initiatives as public relations exercises with no real evidence of dramatic changes in the core operating philosophies of these companies.

>> The Driving Forces behind Corporate Social Responsibility

Joseph F. Keefe of NewCircle Communications asserts that there are five major trends behind the CSR phenomenon:[7]

1. *Transparency:* We live in an information-driven economy where business practices have become increasingly transparent. Companies can no longer

 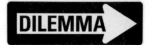

Jon Bennett had always lamented that his grandfather's prospecting skills in the far reaches of rural Texas had succeeded in completely missing any lucrative oil deposits. The land was basically worthless scrub that barely supported a small cattle operation that made so little money that Bennett was forced to work a second job as a mechanic at the only gas station in the one stoplight town at the eastern border of his land. Now, however, if that nerdy little engineer from Global Resources was to be believed, all that was about to change.

Bennett had been hearing about ranchers in Colorado and Wyoming getting big checks for natural gas drilling rights on their land, and now it seemed that while his grandfather's land had no oil, it had enough natural gas deposits in a type of rock called shale to interest one of the largest natural gas producers in the country. He and his neighboring landowners had attended a very slick presentation in the town hall, where engineers from Global had laid out how much natural gas they thought was in the area, and how they would go about getting it out of the ground. They had kicked off the presentation with a video that outlined how "socially responsible" Global was, how the company was committed to "transparency" (a big word for "full disclosure"), and how it made every effort to protect the environment and the communities in which it operated. One of the engineers had stated, "We believe there's enough natural gas here to keep our wells busy for decades, but when we're done, I promise you we'll leave the place exactly as we found it—you'll never be able to tell we were even here."

Since the town was centrally located to several large ranches in the area, Global was planning, they said, to invest a considerable amount of money in expanding the infrastructure of the area. Bennett wasn't exactly sure what that meant, but he heard the words: more roads, more jobs, new storage facilities, bigger schools. That was enough to get his attention.

The town hall meeting had been for invited landowners only, but Bennett had been surprised to see people picketing outside the hall. They carried signs proclaiming that "Fracking Is Toxic!" and "Global Lies!" and they were yelling slogans including: "Don't be tempted by the money!" "Don't Believe Them!" and "Fracking will kill our land!"

Bennett hadn't heard the word *fracking* before, but when he fired up his old laptop and started searching the web, the information he found did give him cause for concern. The injection of pressurized fluids (meaning

© Glow Images RF

water and other chemicals) to break up (or "fracture") the shale rock to release the natural gas was either perfectly safe or dangerously toxic. Critics argued that the research on the chemicals being used was too new to fully understand the consequences to the local water supplies and soil. Advocates of the process argued that it was no different from the pumping of mud into oil wells to replace the oil being drilled out of the ground. That had seemed reasonable to Bennett, but the video of a man in Pennsylvania lighting a match at his kitchen sink and watching the water coming out of his faucet catch fire was disconcerting.

Bennett was even more confused after the leasing specialist from Global visited him at his ranch. "Mr. Bennett," he began, "based on our study of your acreage, we are prepared to offer you an initial payment of $500,000 for drilling rights, and I can confidently forecast an annual payment to you of at least $250,000 for the next 10 years."

QUESTIONS

1. If Global is paying a fair market price for drilling rights, are there any ethical violations here? Why or why not?
2. Are the Global engineers as committed to "full disclosure" as they claim to be?
3. Is Global Resources Corp. being socially responsible, or are its local initiatives just window dressing?
4. What would you do if you were in Bennett's shoes? Why?

GLOBAL RESOURCES

sweep things under the rug—whatever they do (for good or ill) will be known, almost immediately, around the world.

2. *Knowledge:* The transition to an information-based economy also means that consumers and investors have more information at their disposal than at any time in history. They can be more discerning, and can wield more influence. Consumers visiting a clothing store can now choose one brand over another based upon those companies' respective environmental records or involvement in sweatshop practices overseas.

3. *Sustainability:* The earth's natural systems are in serious and accelerating decline, while global population is rising precipitously. In the last 30 years alone, one-third of the planet's resources—the earth's "natural wealth"—have been consumed. . . . We are fast approaching or have already crossed the sustainable yield thresholds of many natural systems (fresh water, oceanic fisheries, forests, rangelands), which cannot keep pace with projected population growth. . . . As a result, corporations are under increasing pressure from diverse stakeholder constituencies to demonstrate that business plans and strategies are environmentally sound and contribute to sustainable development.

4. *Globalization:* The greatest periods of reform in U.S. history . . . produced child labor laws, the minimum wage, the eight-hour day, workers' compensation laws, unemployment insurance, antitrust and securities regulations, Social Security, Medicare, the Community Reinvestment Act, Clean Air Act, Clean Water Act, Environmental Protection Agency, and so forth. All of these reforms constituted governmental efforts to intervene in the economy in order to [improve] the worst excesses of market capitalism. Globalization represents a new stage of capitalist development, this time without . . . public institutions [in place] to protect society by balancing private corporate interests against broader public interests.

5. *The Failure of the Public Sector:* Many if not most developing countries are governed by dysfunctional regimes ranging from the [unfortunate] and disorganized to the brutal and corrupt. Yet it is not developing countries alone that suffer from [dilapidated] public sectors. In the United States and other developed nations, citizens arguably expect less of government than they used to, having lost confidence in the public sector as the best or most appropriate venue for addressing a growing list of social problems.

Even with these major trends driving CSR, many organizations have found it difficult to make the transition from CSR as a theoretical concept to CSR as an operational policy. Ironically, it's not the ethical action itself that causes the problem; it's how to promote those acts to your stakeholders as proof of your new corporate conscience without appearing to be manipulative or scheming to generate press coverage for policies that could easily be dismissed as feel-good initiatives that are simply chasing customer favor.

In addition, many CSR initiatives do not generate immediate financial gains to the organization. Cynical customers may decide to wait and see if this is real or just a temporary project to win new customers in a tough economic climate. This delayed response tests the commitment of those organizations that are inclined to dispense with experimental initiatives when the going gets tough.

Corporations that choose to experiment with CSR initiatives run the risk of creating adverse results and ending up worse off than when they started:

- Employees feel that they are working for an insincere, uncaring organization.
- The public sees little more than a token action concerned with publicity rather than community.
- The organization does not perceive much benefit from CSR and so sees no need to develop the concept.

PROGRESS ✓ QUESTIONS

9. List the five major trends driving CSR.
10. Which one do you think is the most important? Why?
11. Explain why organizations are struggling to adopt CSR initiatives.
12. Why would customers be cynical of CSR initiatives?

BANNING THE REAL THING

In 1999, following a campaign by a student group known as Students Organizing for Labor and Economic Equality (SOLE), the University of Michigan instituted a Vendor Code of Conduct that specified key performance criteria from all university vendors. The code included the following:

General Principles

The University of Michigan has a long-standing commitment to sound, ethical, and socially responsible practices. In aligning its purchasing policies with its core values and practices, the University seeks to recognize and promote basic human rights, appropriate labor standards for employees, and a safe, healthful, and sustainable environment for workers and the general public. . . . In addition, the University shall make every reasonable effort to contract only with vendors meeting the primary standards prescribed by this Code of Conduct.

Primary Standards

- Nondiscrimination
- Affirmative Action
- Freedom of Association and Collective Bargaining
- Labor Standards: Wages, Hours, Leaves, and Child Labor
- Health and Safety
- Forced Labor
- Harassment or Abuse

Preferential Standards

- Living Wage
- International Human Rights
- Environmental Protection
- Foreign Law

Compliance Procedures

University-Vendor Partnership. The ideal University-vendor relationship is in the nature of a partnership, seeking mutually agreeable and important goals. Recognizing our mutual interdependence, it is in the best interest of the University to find a resolution when responding to charges or questions about a vendor's compliance with the provisions of the Code.

On November 30, 2004, SOLE submitted formal complaints against one specific university vendor—the Coca-Cola Co.—with which the university held 12 direct and indirect contracts totaling just under $1.3 million in fiscal year 2004. The complaints against Coca-Cola were as follows:

- Biosolid waste disposal in India. The complaint alleged that bottling plant sludge containing cadmium and other contaminants has been distributed to local farmers as fertilizer.
- Use of groundwater in India. The complaint alleged that Coca-Cola is drawing down the water table/aquifer by using deep-bore wells; water quality has declined; shallow wells used by local farmers have gone dry; and poor crop harvests near bottling plants have resulted from lack of sufficient irrigation water.

© McGraw-Hill Education/
Mark Dierker, photographer

- Pesticides in the product in India. Studies have found that pesticides have been detected in Coca-Cola products in India that are in excess of local and international standards.
- Labor practices in Colombia. Data showing a steep decline in Sinaltrainal, a Colombian bottler's union (from approximately 2,300 to 650 members in the past decade); SOLE claims repeated incidents with paramilitary groups threatening and harming union leaders and potential members, including allegations of kidnapping and murder. SOLE is also concerned about working conditions within the bottling plants.

The Vendor Code of Conduct Dispute Review Board met in June 2005 to review the complaints and recommended that Coca-Cola agree in writing no later than September 30, 2005, to a third-party independent audit to review the complaints. An independent auditor satisfactory to both parties had to be selected by December 31, 2005. The audit had to be completed by March 2006, with the findings to be received by the university no later than April 30, 2006. Coca-Cola would then be expected to put a corrective action plan in place by May 31, 2006. Since one of the 12 contracts was scheduled to expire on June 30, 2005, with another seven expiring between July and November 2005, Coca-Cola was formally placed on probation until August 2006 pending further investigation of the SOLE complaints. The board also recommended that the university not enter into new contracts or renew any expiring contracts during this period and that it agree only to short-term conditional extensions with reassessment at each of the established deadlines to determine if Coca-Cola has made satisfactory progress toward demonstrating its compliance with the Vendor Code of Conduct.

The situation got progressively worse for Coca-Cola. By December 2005, at least a dozen institutions worldwide had divested from the Coca-Cola Co. on the grounds of alleged human rights violations in Asia and South America. On December 8, New York University began pulling all Coke products from its campus after Coca-Cola refused to submit to an independent investigation by that day's deadline.

On December 30, 2005, the University of Michigan suspended sales of Coke products on its three campuses beginning January 1, 2006, affecting vending machines, residence halls, cafeterias, and campus restaurants. Kari Bjorhus, a spokesperson for the Coca-Cola Co., told *The Detroit News,* "The University of Michigan is an important school, and I respect the way they worked with us on this issue. We are continuing to try hard to work with the university to address concerns and assure them about our business practices."

QUESTIONS

1. Which ethical standards are being violated here?
2. Is the university being unreasonable in the high standards demanded in its Vendor Code of Conduct?
3. Do you think the university would have developed the Vendor Code of Conduct without the aggressive campaign put forward by SOLE?
4. How should Coca-Cola respond in order to keep the University of Michigan contracts?

Sources: University of Michigan, www.umich.edu; Associated Press, December 30, 2005; *The Michigan Daily,* September 29, 2005; and University of Michigan News Service, June 17, 2005.

>> The Triple Bottom Line

Organizations pursue operational efficiency through detailed monitoring of their bottom line—that is, how much money is left after all the bills have been paid from the revenue generated from the sale of their product or service. As a testament to how seriously companies are now taking CSR, many have adapted their annual reports to reflect a triple bottom-line approach, for which they provide social and environmental updates alongside their primary bottom-line financial performance. The phrase has been attributed to John Elkington, cofounder of the business consultancy SustainAbility, in his 1998 book *Cannibals with Forks: The Triple Bottom Line of 21st Century Business.* As further evidence that this notion has hit the business mainstream, there is a trendy acronym, *3BL,* for you to use to prove, supposedly, that you are on the "cutting edge" of this trend.

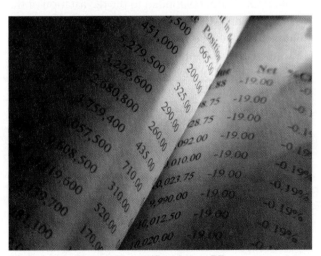

© Don Carstens/Brand X Pictures/Getty Images RF

To some degree, 3BL is like the children's story, "The Emperor's New Clothes." While it may be easy to support the idea of organizations pursuing social and environmental goals in addition to their financial goals, there has been no real evidence of how to measure such achievements, and no one has yet volunteered to play the part of the little boy who tells the emperor he is naked. If you subscribe to the old management saying that "if you can't measure it, you can't manage it," the challenges of delivering on any 3BL goals become apparent. Norman and MacDonald present the following scenario:[8]

Imagine a firm reporting that:

(a) 20 percent of its directors were women,

(b) 7 percent of its senior management were members of "visible" minorities,

(c) It donated 1.2 percent of its profits to charity,

(d) The annual turnover rate among its hourly workers was 4%, and

(e) It had been fined twice this year for toxic emissions.

Now, out of context (e.g., without knowing how large the firm is, where it is operating, and what the averages are in its industrial sector) it is difficult to say how good or bad these figures are. Of course, in the case of each indicator we often have a sense of whether a higher or lower number would generally be better, from the perspective of social/ethical performance. The conceptual point, however, is that these are quite simply not the sort of data that can be fed into an income-statement-like calculation to produce a final net sum.

So if you can't measure it, can you really arrive at a "bottom line" for it? It would appear that many organizations are taking a fairly opportunistic approach in adopting the terminology without following through on the delivery of a consistent methodology. Could the feel-good terminology associated with 3BL help you make a convincing case if you are seeking to make amends for prior transgressions? Consider the following from Coca-Cola's "2004 Citizenship Report":[9]

> Our Company has always endeavored to conduct business responsibly and ethically. We have long been committed to enriching the workplace, preserving and protecting the environment, and strengthening the communities where we operate. These objectives are all consistent with—indeed essential to—our principal goal of refreshing the marketplace with high-quality beverages.

If we compare this commitment to the accusations made by students at the University of Michigan in the ethical dilemma "Banning the Real Thing," we can see how challenging CSR can be. It may be easy to make a public commitment to CSR, but actually delivering on that commitment to the satisfaction of your customers can be much harder to achieve.

JUMPING ON THE CSR BANDWAGON

Just as we have a triple bottom line, organizations have jumped on the CSR bandwagon by adopting three distinct types of CSR—ethical, altruistic, and strategic—for their own purposes.

Ethical CSR represents the purest or most legitimate type of CSR in which organizations pursue a clearly defined sense of social conscience in managing their financial responsibilities to shareholders, their legal responsibilities to their local community and society as a whole, and their ethical responsibilities to do the right thing for all their stakeholders.

Organizations in this category have typically incorporated their beliefs into their core operating philosophies. Companies such as The Body Shop, Ben & Jerry's Homemade Ice Cream, and Tom's of Maine were founded on the belief that the relationship between companies and their consumers did not have to be an adversarial one and that corporations should honor a social contract with the communities in which they operate and the citizens they serve.

Altruistic CSR takes a philanthropic approach by underwriting specific initiatives to give back to the company's local community or to designated national or international programs. In ethical terms, this giving back is done with funds that rightly belong to shareholders (but it is unlikely that McDonald's shareholders, for example, would file a motion at the next annual general meeting for the return of the funds that McDonald's gives to the support of its Ronald McDonald Houses).

Of greater concern is that the choice of charitable giving is at the discretion of the corporation, which places the individual shareholders in the awkward position of unwittingly supporting causes they may not support on their own, such as the antiabortion or gun control movements. Critics have argued that, from an ethical perspective, this type of CSR is immoral since it represents a violation of shareholder rights if they are not given the opportunity to vote on the initiatives launched in the name of corporate social responsibility.

The relative legitimacy of altruistic CSR is based on the argument that the philanthropic initiatives are authorized without concern for the corporation's overall profitability. Arguing in *utilitarian* terms, corporations are merely doing the greatest good for the greatest number.

Examples of altruistic CSR often occur during crises or situations of widespread need. Consider the following:

- Southwest Airlines supports the Ronald McDonald Houses with donations of both dollars and employee-donated volunteer hours. The company considers giving back to the communities in which it operates an appropriate part of its mission.
- Shell Oil Corp. responded to the devastation of the tsunami disaster in Asia in December 2004 with donations of fuel for rescue transportation and water tanks for relief aid, in addition to financial commitments of several million dollars for disaster relief. Shell employees matched many of the company's donations.
- In September 2005, the home improvement retail giant Home Depot announced a direct cash donation of $1.5 million to support the relief and rebuilding efforts in areas devastated by Hurricane Katrina. In addition, the company announced a corporate month of service, donating 300,000 volunteer hours to communities across the country and over $200,000 in materials to support the activities

Ethical CSR Purest or most legitmate type of CSR in which organizations pursue a clearly defined sense of social conscience in managing their financial responsibilities to shareholders, their legal responsibilities to their local community and society as a whole, and their ethical responsibilities to do the right thing for all their stakeholders.

Altruistic CSR Philanthropic approach to CSR in which organizations underwrite specific initiatives to give back to the company's local community or to designated national or international programs.

© Jocelyn Augustino/FEMA

Volunteer work as corporate policy is not limited to major corporations. What are some smaller-scale examples of altruistic efforts that companies can engage in?

of 90 stores in recovery, cleanup, and rebuilding efforts in their local communities.

- Since 1974, Xerox has supported multiple programs for social responsibility under the heading of its Community Involvement Program. In 2013, more than $1.3 million was earmarked to facilitate the participation of 13,000 employees in community-focused causes.

Strategic CSR runs the greatest risk of being perceived as self-serving behavior on the part of the organization. This type of philanthropic activity targets programs that will generate the most positive publicity or goodwill for the organization. By supporting these programs, companies achieve the best of both worlds: They can claim to be doing the right thing, and, on the assumption that good publicity brings more sales, they also can meet their fiduciary obligations to their shareholders.

Compared to the alleged immorality of altruistic CSR, critics can argue that strategic CSR is ethically commendable because these initiatives benefit stakeholders while meeting fiduciary obligations to the company's shareholders. However, the question remains: Without a win–win payoff, would such CSR initiatives be authorized?

The danger in this case lies in how actions are perceived. Consider, for example, two initiatives launched by Ford Motor Co.:

- Ford spent millions on an ad campaign to raise awareness of the need for booster seats for children over 40 pounds and under 4 feet 9 inches (most four- to eight-year-olds) and gave away almost a million seats as part of the campaign.
- During the PR battle with Firestone Tires over who was to blame for the rollover problems with the Ford Explorer, Ford's CEO at the time, Jacques Nasser, made a public commitment to spend up to $3 billion to replace 13 million Firestone Wilderness AT tires for free on Ford Explorers because he saw them as an "unacceptable risk to our customers."

> **Strategic CSR** Philanthropic approach to CSR in which organizations target programs that will generate the most positive publicity or goodwill for the organization but that run the greatest risk of being perceived as self-serving behavior on the part of the organization.

If we attribute motive to each campaign, the booster seat campaign could be interpreted as a way to position Ford as the auto manufacturer that cares about the safety of its passengers as much as its drivers. The tire exchange could be interpreted the same way, but given the design flaws with the Ford Explorer alleged by Firestone, couldn't it also be seen as a diversionary tactic?

One of the newest and increasingly questionable practices in the world of CSR is the notion of making your operations "carbon neutral" in such a way as to offset whatever damage you are doing to the environment through your greenhouse gas emissions by purchasing credits from "carbon-positive" projects to balance out your emissions. Initially developed as a solution for those industries that face significant challenges in reducing their emissions (airlines or automobile companies, for example), the concept has quickly spawned a diverse collection of vendors that can assist you in achieving carbon neutrality, along with a few markets in which emissions credits can now be bought and sold.

Key Point !

Should it matter if a company is being opportunistic in adopting CSR practices? As long as there is a positive outcome, doesn't everyone benefit in the long run? Why or why not?

PROGRESS ✓ QUESTIONS

13. Explain the term *triple bottom line.*

14. Explain the term *ethical CSR.*

15. Explain the term *altruistic CSR.*

16. Explain the term *strategic CSR.*

>> Being socially responsible

Consider how important your beliefs about corporate social responsibility and sustainability are in your daily life. Do you spend your hard-earned money at stores that promote environmental awareness and "green" capitalism? Or does your budget force you to find the best prices and not think about the damage done to achieve the lowest possible cost?

How will those beliefs impact your life choices in the future? Will you focus your employment search on companies with good CSR records? Or will the need to pay the bills outweigh that element and force you to take the highest-paying job you can find? It is important to remember that the paycheck may not be enough to address a poor cultural fit or a direct conflict between your values and those of your employer. It's better to extend your search for a while, if necessary, to find a company that you are proud to work for rather than taking the first opportunity that comes along only to find yourself at odds with many of the company's policies and philosophies.

>> Buying Your Way to CSR

Do you know what your carbon footprint is? At http://www.carbonfootprint.com/calculator1.html, you can calculate the carbon dioxide emissions from your home, your car, and any air travel you do, and then calculate your total emissions on an annual basis. The result is your "footprint." You can then purchase credits to offset your emissions and render yourself "carbon neutral." If you have sufficient funds, you can purchase more credits than you need to achieve neutrality and then join the enviable ranks of carbon-positive people who actually take more carbon dioxide out of the cycle than they produce. That, of course, is a technicality since you aren't driving less or driving a hybrid, nor are you being more energy conscious in how you heat or cool your home. You are doing nothing more than buying credits from other projects around the world, such as tree planting in indigenous forests, wind farms, or even outfitting African farmers with energy-efficient stoves, and using those positive emissions to counterbalance your negative ones. Companies such as Dell Computer, British Airways, Expedia Travel, and BP have experimented with programs where customers can pay a fee to offset the emissions spent in manufacturing their products or using their services.

If this sounds just a little strange, consider that this issue of offsetting is serious enough to have been ratified by the Kyoto Protocol—an agreement between 160 countries that became effective in 2005 (and which the United States has yet to sign). The protocol requires developed nations to reduce their greenhouse gas emissions not only by modifying their domestic industries (coal, steel, automobiles, etc.) but also by funding projects in developing countries in return for carbon credits. It didn't take long for an entire infrastructure to develop in order to facilitate the trading of these credits so that organizations with high emissions (and consequently a larger demand for offset credits) could purchase credits in greater volumes than most individual projects would provide. In the first nine months of 2006, the United Nations estimated that over $22 billion of carbon was traded.

As with any frontier (read: unregulated) market, the early results for this new industry have been questionable to say the least. Examples of unethical practices include:

- Inflated market prices for credits—priced per ton of carbon dioxide—varying from $3.50 to $27 a ton, which explains why some traders are able to generate profit margins of 50 percent.
- The sale of credits from projects that don't even exist.

- Selling the same credits from one project over and over again to different buyers who are unable to verify the effectiveness of the project since they are typically set up in remote geographic areas.
- Claiming carbon-offset credits on projects that are profitable in their own right.

As these questionable practices gain more media attention, some of the larger players in this new industry—companies such as JPMorgan Chase and Deutsche Bank, which have multibillion-dollar investments in the credit trading arena—are demanding that commonly accepted codes of conduct be established in order to clean up the market and offer greater incentives for customers to trade their credits. In November 2006, Deutsche Bank teamed up with more than a dozen investment banks and five carbon-trading organizations in Europe to create the European Carbon Investors and Services Association (ECIS) to promote the standardization of carbon trading on a global scale. In 2003, the Chicago Climate Exchange (CCX) was launched with 13 charter members and today remains the only trading system for all six greenhouse gases (carbon dioxide, methane, nitrous oxide, hydrofluorocarbons, perfluorocarbons, and sulfur hexafluoride) in North America. In 2005, CCX launched the European Climate Exchange (ECX) and the Chicago Climate Futures Exchange (CCFE), which offers options and futures contracts on emissions credits. Membership of CCX has now reached almost 300 members.

>> Conclusion

So if there is nothing ethically wrong in "doing well by doing good," why isn't everyone doing it? The key concern here must be customer perception. If an organization commits to CSR initiatives, then they must be real commitments rather than short-term experiments. You may be able to gamble on the short-term memory of your customers, but the majority will expect you to deliver on your commitment and to provide progress reports on those initiatives that you publicized so widely.

But what about some of the more well-known CSR players? When we consider Ben & Jerry's Homemade Ice Cream or The Body Shop, for example, both organizations made the concept of a corporate social conscience a part of their core philosophies before CSR was ever anointed as a management buzzword. As such, their good intent garnered vast amounts of goodwill: Investors admired their financial performance, and customers felt good about shopping there. However, if the quality of their products had not lived up to customer expectations, would they have prospered over the long term? Would customers have continued to shop there if they didn't like the products? "Doing well by doing good" will only get you so far.

In this context, it is unfair to accuse companies with CSR initiatives of abandoning their moral responsibilities to their stakeholders. Even if you are leveraging the maximum possible publicity from your efforts, that will only get the people in the door. If the product or service doesn't live up to expectations, they won't be back. Customers will not settle for second-rate service or product quality just because a charitable cause is involved. Therefore, your product or service must meet and ideally exceed the expectations of your customers, and if you continue to do that for the long term (assuming you have a reasonably competent management team), the needs of your stakeholders should be well taken care of.

What remains to be seen, however, is just how broadly or, more specifically, how quickly the notion of 3BL will become part of standard business practice and reach some common terminology that will allow consumers and investors to accurately assess the extent of a company's social responsibility. As long as annual reports simply present glossy pictures of the company's good deeds around the world, it will be difficult for any stakeholder to determine whether a change has taken place in that company's core business philosophy, or whether it's just another example of opportunistic targeted marketing.

Without a doubt, the financial incentive (or threat, depending on how you look at it) is now very real, and has the potential to significantly impact an organization's financial future. Consider these two examples:

- In April 2003, the California Public Employees Retirement System (CalPERS), which manages almost $750 million for 1.5 million current and retired employees of California, publicly urged pharmaceutical company GlaxoSmithKline to review its policy of charging for AIDS drugs in developing countries. In March 2008, CalPERS went even further and listed five American companies on its 2008 Focus List to highlight the

CONTINUED >>

pension fund's concerns about stock and financial underperformance and corporate governance practices (which we'll learn more about in Chapter 5). The companies listed were the Cheesecake Factory, Hilb Rogal & Hobbs (an insurance brokerage firm), Ivacare (a health care equipment provider), La-Z-Boy, and Standard Pacific (a home-building company).

- In June 2006, the government of Norway, which manages a more than $200 billion pension fund from oil revenues for its citizens notified Walmart and Freeport (a U.S.-based mining company) that they were being excluded as investments for the pension fund on the grounds that the companies have been responsible for either environmental damage or the violation of human rights in their business practices.

With such financial clout now being put behind CSR issues, the question of adoption of some form of social responsibility plan for a corporation should no longer be *if* but *when*.

FRONTLINE FOCUS
An Improved Reputation—Claire Makes a Decision

After reading all of the negative media coverage about the leak, Claire realized that, with no money available for big budget projects, the best she could do in the short term would be to emphasize that the company cared about the community it served.

The leak was an accident—the EPA found no evidence of shoddy maintenance practices—but the community had been directly impacted. Employees who lived in the community were embarrassed when confronted in the street by angry residents. They took pride in their work and took the loss of customers very personally. Falling sales also brought the threat of job cuts that damaged morale even more.

Claire chose to present a two-step plan to turn around the company's reputation:

1. A commitment to transparent communication. Mr. Jones would write an open letter to the media acknowledging the errors of the leak and making a public commitment to working with the EPA inspectors and implementing whatever changes they want the company

to make. Mr. Jones would also write a second letter to employees acknowledging the issue and addressing their concerns about their community and their job security.

2. At the next shareholder's meeting (in three months), Mr. Jones would, with Claire's help, propose a more proactive CSR strategy with a planned rollout of capital investments. The projects would be small at first—sponsoring highway cleanup outside the head office, allowing employees to spend one day per month volunteering in the community, and sponsoring a local community event. Over time, larger projects could be introduced, such as switching to hybrid or electric cars for the sales fleet or solar power for the office.

QUESTIONS
1. Did Claire do the right thing here?
2. Do you think that customers will be convinced? Why or why not?
3. What do you think Mr. Jones's reaction will be?

[For Review]

1. **Describe and explain *corporate social responsibility (CSR)*.**

   Corporate social responsibility—also referred to as corporate citizenship or corporate conscience—may be defined as the actions of an organization that are targeted toward achieving a social benefit over and above maximizing profits for its shareholders and meeting all its legal obligations. Typically, that "benefit" is targeted toward environmental issues, such as reducing pollution levels or recycling materials instead of dumping them in a landfill. For global organizations, CSR can also involve the demonstration of care and concern for local communities and indigenous populations.

2. **Distinguish between *instrumental* and *social contract* approaches to CSR.**

   An instrumental approach to CSR takes the perspective that the only obligation of a corporation is to make profits for its shareholders in providing goods and services that meet the needs of its customers. Corporations argue that they meet their social obligations through the payment of federal and state taxes, and they should not, therefore, be expected to contribute anything beyond that.

   Critics of the instrumental approach argue that it takes a simplistic view of the internal processes of a corporation in isolation, with no reference to the external consequences of the actions of the corporation and its managers. The social contract approach acknowledges that there is a world outside that is impacted by the actions of the corporation, and since the corporation depends on society for its existence and continued growth, there is an obligation for the corporation to meet the demands of that society rather than just the demands of a targeted group of customers.

3. **Explain the business argument for "doing well by doing good."**

   Rather than waiting for the media or their customers to force them into better CSR practices, many organizations are realizing that incorporating the interests of all their stakeholders (customers, employees, shareholders, vendor partners, and their community partners), instead of just their shareholders, can generate positive media coverage, improved revenues, and higher profit margins. "Doing well by doing good" seems, on the face of it, to be an easy policy to adopt, and many organizations have started down that road by making charitable donations, underwriting projects in their local communities, sponsoring local events, and engaging in productive conversations with special interest groups about earth-friendly packaging materials and the use of more recyclable materials.

4. **Summarize the five driving forces behind CSR.**

   Joseph F. Keefe of NewCircle Communications asserts that there are five major trends behind the CSR phenomenon. Each of the trends is linked with the greater availability and dispersal of information via the World Wide Web using websites, blogs, and social media mechanisms such as Twitter:

   - Transparency: *Companies can no longer sweep things under the rug—whatever they do (for good or ill) will be known, almost immediately, around the world.*
   - Knowledge: *The transition to an information-based economy also means that consumers and investors have more information at their disposal than at any time in history. They can be more discerning, and can wield more influence. Consumers visiting a clothing store can now choose one brand over another based upon those companies' respective environmental records or involvement in sweatshop practices overseas.*
   - Sustainability: *We are fast approaching or have already crossed the sustainable yield thresholds of many natural systems (fresh water, oceanic fisheries, forests, rangelands), which cannot keep pace with projected population growth. . . . As a result, corporations are*

   under increasing pressure from diverse stakeholder constituencies to demonstrate that business plans and strategies are environmentally sound and contribute to sustainable development.

   - Globalization: *Globalization represents a new stage of capitalist development, this time without . . . public institutions [in place] to protect society by balancing private corporate interests against broader public interests.*
   - The Failure of the Public Sector: *In the United States and other developed nations, citizens arguably expect less of government than they used to, having lost confidence in the public sector as the best or most appropriate venue for addressing a growing list of social problems. This, in turn, has increased pressure on corporations to take responsibility for the social impact of their actions rather than expecting the public sector to do so.*

5. **Explain the *triple bottom-line* approach to corporate performance measurement.**

   Documenting corporate performance using a triple bottom-line (3BL) approach involves recording social and environmental performance in addition to the more traditional financial bottom-line performance. As corporations understand the value of promoting their CSR activities, annual reports start to feature community investment projects, recycling initiatives, and pollution-reduction commitments. However, while financial reports are standardized according to generally accepted accounting principles (GAAP), social and environmental performance reports currently do not offer the same standardized approach.

6. **Discuss the relative merits of carbon-offset trading.**

   The Kyoto Protocol—an agreement between 160 countries that became effective in 2005 (and which the United States has yet to sign)—required developed nations to reduce their greenhouse gas emissions either by modifying their own domestic industries or funding projects in developing nations in return for "carbon credits." This has spawned a thriving (and currently unregulated) business in trading credits for cold hard cash. On the one hand, those funds can be used to develop infrastructures in poorer communities, but critics argue that the offset credit option allows corporations to buy their way into compliance rather than being forced to change their operational practices.

[Key Terms]

Altruistic CSR **78**

Corporate Social Responsibility (CSR) **70**

Ethical CSR **78**

Instrumental Approach **71**

Social Contract Approach **72**

Strategic CSR **79**

[Review Questions]

1. Would organizations really be paying attention to CSR if customers and federal and state agencies weren't forcing them to? Why or why not?

2. Would the CSR policies of an organization influence your decision to use its products or services? Why or why not?

3. Which is more ethical: altruistic CSR or strategic CSR? Provide examples to explain your answer.

4. How would you measure your carbon footprint?

5. If a carbon-offset project is already profitable, is it ethical to provide credits over and above those profits? Why or why not?

6. Consider the company you currently work for (or one you have worked for in the past). What initiatives could it start to be more socially responsible? How would you propose such changes?

[Review Exercises]

Payatas Power. On July 1, 2000, a mountain of garbage at the Payatas landfill on the outskirts of Quezon City In the Philippines fell on the surrounding slum community killing nearly 300 people and destroying the homes of hundreds of families who foraged the dump site. In 2007, Pangea Green Energy Philippines Inc. (PGEP), a subsidiary of Italian utility company Pangea Green Energy, announced an ambitious plan to drill 33 gas wells on the landfill to harvest methane gas from the bottom of the waste pile. An initial U.S.$4 million investment built a 200-kilowatt power plant to be fueled by the harvested methane. The power generated makes the landfill self-sufficient and allows excess power to be sold to the city power grid.

However, the real payoff will come from carbon-offset credits. Methane gas is 21 times more polluting than carbon dioxide as a greenhouse gas. Capturing and burning methane releases carbon dioxide and therefore has 21 times less emission impact—a reduction that can be captured as an offset credit. PGEP will arrange trading of those carbon credits in return for a donation of an estimated U.S.$300,000 to the Quezon City community—funds that will be used to develop the local infrastructure and build schools and medical centers for the Payatas community. The landfill has now been renamed Quezon City Controlled Disposal Facility.

1. The PGEP-Payatas project is being promoted as a win–win project for all parties involved. Is that an accurate assessment? Why or why not?

2. The Payatas project is estimated to generate 100,000 carbon credits per year. At an average market value of $30 per credit (prices vary according to the source of the credit), PGEP will receive an estimated $3 million from the project. On those terms, is the $300,000 donation to the Payatas community a fair one?

3. How could Quezon City officials ensure that there is a more equitable distribution of wealth?

Sources: Melody M. Aguiba, "Payatas: From Waste to Energy," www.newsbreak.com, September 24, 2007; and www.quezoncity.gov.ph.

[Internet Exercises]

1. Review the CSR policies of a Fortune 100 company of your choice. Would you classify its policies as ethical, altruistic, strategic, or a combination of all three? Provide examples to support your answer.

2. Review the annual report of a Fortune 100 company of your choice. What evidence can you find of triple bottom-line reporting in the report? Provide examples to support your answer.

[Team Exercises]

1. **Instrumental or social contract?**
   Divide into two teams. One team must prepare a presentation advocating for the instrumental model of corporate management. The other team must prepare a presentation arguing for the social contract model of corporate management.

2. **Ethical, altruistic, or strategic?**
   Divide into three groups. Each group must select one of the following types of CSR: ethical CSR, altruistic CSR, or strategic CSR. Prepare a presentation arguing for the respective merits of each approach, and offer examples of initiatives that your company could engage in to adopt this strategy.

3. **Closing a factory.**
   Divide into two groups, and prepare arguments *for* and *against* the following behavior: *Your company is managing to maintain a good profit margin on the computer parts you manufacture in a very tough economy. Recently, an opportunity has come along to move your production capacity overseas. The move will reduce manufacturing costs significantly as a result of tax incentives and lower labor costs, resulting in an anticipated 15 percent increase in profits for the company. However, the costs associated with shutting down your U.S.-based operations would mean that you wouldn't see those increased profits for a minimum of three years. Your U.S. factory is the largest employer in the surrounding town, and shutting it down will result in the loss of over 800 jobs. The loss of those jobs is expected to devastate the economy of the local community.*

4. **A limited campaign.**
   Divide into two groups and prepare arguments *for* and *against* the following behavior: *You work in the marketing department of a large dairy products company. The company has launched a "revolutionary" yogurt product with ingredients that promote healthy digestion. As a promotion to launch the new product, the company is offering to donate 10 cents to the American Heart Association (AHA) for every foil top from the yogurt pots that is returned to the manufacturer. To support this campaign, the company has invested millions of dollars in a broad "media spend" on television, radio, web, and print outlets, as well as the product packaging itself. In very small print on the packaging and advertising is a clarification sentence that specifies that the maximum donation for the campaign will be $10,000. Your marketing analyst colleagues have forecast that first-year sales of this new product will reach 10 million units, with an anticipated participation of 2 million units in the pot-top return campaign (a potential donation of $200,000 without the $10,000 limit). Focus groups that were tested about the new product indicated clearly that participants in the pot-top return campaign attach positive feelings about their purchase to the added bonus of the donation to the AHA.*

Thinking Critically

>> SUSTAINABLE CAPITALISM

Whether you subscribe to the notion of "people, planet, profits" or the less media-friendly "triple bottom line" of financial, environmental, and social performance, critics of corporate social responsibility (CSR) argue that the concept

Former U.S. Vice President Al Gore
© McGraw-Hill Education/Jill Braaten, photographer

has served its purpose but no longer pushes the message of environmental and social awareness far enough. Glossy annual reports and photogenic websites illustrating the wonderful work of corporate-funded nonprofit organizations around the world may be very reassuring to stakeholders who want to see evidence of more conscious capitalism than the pursuit of profit at any cost. However, this project-based approach, it is argued, facilitates the development of "window-dressing" strategies where the high visibility of PR-friendly projects may be used to divert attention from the lack of fundamental change in the way most corporations conduct business.

In February 2012, the nonprofit arm of Generation Investment Management, LLP (GenerationIM), a hedge-fund company started in 2004 by former U.S. Vice President Al Gore and ex-Goldman Sachs partner David Blood, issued a call-to-action manifesto for what the company calls "sustainable capitalism" (https://www. genfound.org/media/pdf-generation-sustainable-capitalism-v1.

pdf). With a core mission closely aligned to Gore's long-established advocacy of climate change and resource scarcity awareness, GenerationIM pursues an investment approach based on:

the idea that sustainability factors—economic, environmental, social and governance criteria—will drive a company's returns over the long term. By integrating sustainability issues with traditional analysis, we seek to provide superior investment returns.

The manifesto proposes several changes to the way the capitalist system currently works (or, from GenerationIM's perspective, fails to work), along with a call to action to achieve sustainable capitalism by 2020. The first of five specific actions is to "identify and incorporate risks from stranded assets," which would require corporations to more accurately value items, such as carbon emissions, water usage, or local labor costs, where any significant changes in price (due either to market forces or federal legislation) would have a dramatically negative impact on bottom-line profitability. This, the manifesto contends, would reveal many companies to be in a more financially precarious position than their current financial reporting might suggest.

The second action item is the requirement of "integrated reporting" of environmental, social, and governance (ESG) performance alongside mandated financial returns. This proposal has generated significant pushback from several large corporations, which argue that it assumes a level of maturity in ESG data that isn't in place yet. As an alternative, advocates point to a requirement in South Africa for companies to either publish such an integrated report or to publish an explanation as to why they couldn't.

The third action item is to "end the default practice of issuing quarterly earnings guidance." This is by no means a new proposal, but there is growing evidence of a willingness to give it serious consideration. In 2009, Paul Polman, the chief executive of Unilever (an Anglo-Dutch consumer goods company with brands ranging from Q-tips to Ben & Jerry's Homemade Ice Cream), stopped his company from publishing full financial results every quarter. Value investor Warren Buffet has also adamantly refused to provide quarterly guidance at Berkshire Hathaway. Broader acceptance of this practice, however, will require a dramatic change in the inflexible expectations of Wall Street analysts who persist in offering their prognostications on a quarterly basis.

The fourth and fifth action items address the perceived problem of short-term management at the expense of longer-term sustainable value creation. If corporations were to "align compensation structures with long-term sustainable performance," it is argued, there would be greater accountability for decisions made in the interests of stock price over corporate value. If a senior executive's compensation package includes stock options, the executive may be tempted to pay more attention to the price of that stock than the long-term ramifications of the strategic decisions made in support of that stock price. Financial rewards, the manifesto argues, should be paid out over the period during which the results are realized. This position has gained broad acceptance, but it also represents something of a conflict of interest for Al Gore, who exercised stock options for 59,000 shares as an Apple director in January 2013 at a strike price of $7.475 a share ($441,025) for stock worth over $29 million.

The fifth action item is to "encourage long-term investing with loyalty-driven securities." With the average time period that investors hold a stock on the New York Stock Exchange falling from eight years in 1960 to as little as four months in 2010, this issue of "short-termism" is seen as a major handicap to sustainable capitalism, with companies demonstrating a willingness to sacrifice research and development and capital reinvestment in favor of piling short-term results on top of more short-term results to keep the share price stable. However, there is clear evidence of corporate support for the fifth item. Cosmetics company L'Oreal and Air Liquide have both offered shareholder bonuses for holding shares longer than a specified period of time. Technology companies, such as Zynga, LinkedIn, and Google, have taken a different approach by adopting dual-class voting shares that allow company founders to operate without the pressure to produce short-term results.

Critics argue that these action items represent nothing more than an attempt to burden an efficient capitalist model with political correctness. GenerationIM's decision to go beyond the more familiar "green" or "ethical" investment fund model, and commit to these specific issues in its investment selection criteria, means that we may have to wait much longer for the promised larger returns of sustainable capitalism.

QUESTIONS

1. Why is "people, planet, profits" a more media-friendly message than a triple bottom-line approach to CSR?
2. On what grounds could the CSR initiatives of a corporation be dismissed as window dressing?
3. What is meant by the term *sustainable capitalism?*
4. Based on the information in this case and a review of GenerationIM's manifesto document, is there any correlation of its proposal to the commonly accepted tenets of CSR?
5. What challenges do you foresee in the broader acceptance of sustainable capitalism around the world?
6. How would you go about introducing sustainable capitalism in your company?

Sources: "Blood, Gore and Capitalism," *The Economist,* February 16, 2012; "Taking the Long View," *The Economist,* November 24, 2012; General Investment Management, LLP, "Sustainable Capitalism," www.generationim.com/sustainability/report/, February 15, 2012; and *Environmental Leader,* "On Sustainable Capitalism," January 9, 2013.

Thinking Critically 4.2

>> CORPORATE SOCIAL IRRESPONSIBILITY

Despite PR posturing, corporate philanthropy is down from 25 years ago. To be taken seriously, companies should pledge 1 percent of pretax earnings, say Leo Hindery Jr. and Curt Weeden.

When companies forsake their broadly defined social responsibilities or use spin to construct a deliberately overinflated image of their corporate citizenship, the end result is a private sector and a civil society out of balance.

Too prevalent today are heavily promoted, self-generated snippets designed to show how businesses are meeting their obligations to society. Paid advertisements that wave banners about how companies address global warming, curb health care costs, or improve public education often are smoke screens to hide a troubling trend: the significant falloff in corporate charitable contributions.

CONTINUED >>

ANEMIC GENEROSITY

© PhotoDisc/Getty Images RF

Twenty-five years ago, businesses allocated about 2 percent, on average, of their pretax profits for gifts and grants, according to a report by the Giving USA Foundation and the Indiana University Center on Philanthropy. Today, companies are only about one-third as generous. Based on a recent analysis of IRS tax returns—which are, of course, devoid of hype—business charitable deductions now average only about 0.7 percent of pretax earnings. (These figures don't take into account employee volunteer hours, as the IRS does not allow deductions for employee volunteer time, even if it is time off with pay.)

Granted, measuring overall corporate responsibility requires more than just analyzing a company's philanthropic donations. Fair treatment of employees, making or selling safe products, paying taxes, and complying with environmental standards are all ingredients that should be in the social responsibility mix. However important these things are, though, they are not more important than a corporationwide commitment to use an appropriate percentage of a company's pretax resources to address critical issues that affect employees, communities, the nation, and the planet.

Badly needed is a meaningful voluntary commitment by the business community to "ante up" a minimum budget for corporate philanthropy. A reasonable requirement for any company that wants to call itself a good corporate citizen ought to be to spend at least 1 percent of its previous year's pretax profit for philanthropic purposes.

NONFINANCIAL RETURNS

Convincing senior management to increase rather than cut back a company's philanthropy budget may seem a daunting, if not impossible, task, particularly at a time when the overall corporate profit picture has become so cloudy. But if executives understand that an effectively managed contribution program can deliver strong returns to a corporation, then 1 percent of pretax earnings should take on the look and feel of an investment, not a handout.

Rather than a self-imposed tax, a contribution can actually be managed in a way that makes it a powerful business tool. That happens when, to the extent practicable, company donations are directed to nonprofit groups closely aligned with the interests of the corporation's employees, communities, and business objectives. At the same time, a corporate contribution shouldn't be solely about advancing the interests of the company. If contributions are designed only to bolster the bottom line, if they are used to support pet projects of senior managers or board members, or if they are purely selfish in their intent, we believe they fall short of the definition of what it takes to be considered the proper conduct of a good corporate citizen.

This ante-up proposal is intended to be the bottom rung of the corporate citizenship ladder. Businesses that are "best in class" in the corporate philanthropy field also need to manage contributions strategically that go well beyond the recommended pretax minimum of 1 percent. Some companies are already clearing this higher bar. In Minneapolis–St. Paul, for example, more than 150 companies—including such large corporations as Target and General Mills—are every year donating at least 5 percent of their pretax earnings. (Disclosure: In 1998, the year before Tele-Communications Inc., where [Hindery] was then CEO, merged into AT&T, TCI contributed a bit more than 1 percent of its operating cash flow to charity. Like our counterparts in the cable industry, TCI in those years had substantial pretax losses because of significant depreciation and amortization.)

To reverse the downward trend in corporate giving, we need a cadre of self-motivated and sensitive CEOs to lead the way. We need men and women who will match actions with words by carrying out combined corporate contributions and community-relations initiatives that are supported by adequate resources and time, rather than by more chest-beating ad campaigns and press releases.

1. Why would companies choose to inflate the image of their corporate citizenship?

2. Is it ethical to direct company donations to "nonprofit groups closely aligned with the interests of the corporation's employees, communities, and business objectives"? Why or why not?

3. Is it ethical to direct company donations to support "pet projects of senior managers or board members"? Why or why not?

4. Why would budgeting a fixed percentage of pretax profits for corporate philanthropy be seen as a more convincing commitment to CSR than just funding a variety of projects?

5. The authors of this article claim that "an effectively managed contribution program can deliver strong returns to a corporation." What might those returns be?

6. Does the fact that Target and General Mills donate five times more than the minimum 1 percent make them five times more socially responsible? Why or why not?

Sources: Leo Hindery Jr. and Curt Weeden, "Corporate Social Irresponsibility," *BusinessWeek* Viewpoint, July 8, 2008. Hindery is a contributor to the *BusinessWeek* column Outside Shot. He is a managing partner of InterMedia Partners, former CEO of Tele-Communications Inc., its successor AT&T Broadband, and the YES Network. Curt Weeden is president of Business & Nonprofit Strategies, Inc., and former CEO of the Association of Corporate Contributions Professionals. He is the author of *Corporate Social Investing* (Berrett-Koehler, 1998).

Thinking Critically 4.3

>> MONSANTO'S MYSTERY WHEAT

In May 2013, an Oregon farmer was trying to kill weeds in a 125-acre field he planned to leave fallow for the next growing season. Included in those weeds were some wheat plants that looked to the farmer like traditional soft white wheat.

However, after spraying the field with Roundup, the weed killer manufactured by Monsanto, the $14 billion agricultural conglomerate based in Creve Coeur, Missouri, the wheat stalks did not die.

The farmer sent some samples for testing to a laboratory at Oregon State University, where it was confirmed that the wheat strain was MON71800, also known as "Roundup Ready" wheat, also developed by Monsanto. The wheat strain had earned the name "Roundup Ready" because it had been genetically modified to be resistant to glyphosate, the active ingredient in the Roundup weed killer product, along with strains of soybeans and corn.

Monsanto had developed the strains during field tests from 1998 to 2005 in 16 states, including Oregon. The plan had been to introduce the seeds as companion products to the weed killer, but a negative market reaction to genetically modified (GMO) wheat had led the company to focus on corn, cotton, and oilseeds instead.

© GarethPriceGFX/Getty Images RF

CONTINUED >>

A DETAILED INVESTIGATION

Once the strain of wheat had been identified, the United States Department of Agriculture (USDA) launched an immediate investigation into the source of the GMO wheat strain. Had the seeds simply been blown across from a Monsanto test plot by wind? Had there been a mistake in the mixing of strains at the seed plant? Worse still, had those seeds found their way into wheat exports overseas?

Monsanto's concerns about negative market reaction proved to be well founded. Even though soft white wheat represented only 15 percent of the $8 billion U.S. wheat export business, the response from wheat importers was immediate. Japan, the top buyer of American wheat, suspended all white wheat imports, and South Korea announced the introduction of tests for GMO wheat on all U.S. wheat and wheat flour upon arrival. The European Union advised its 27 member nations to increase testing, prompting a single-day fall of 4 percent in Monsanto's share price and a petition to "Say No to Monsanto," signed by tens of thousands of people.

The Korean tests found no evidence of GMO wheat strains in any of the shipments, and USDA investigators found no further evidence of the MON71800 strain anywhere else on the farm of the original finding or in the entire Pacific Northwest growing region. Japan resumed its importation of U.S. wheat after a two-month delay.

Unfortunately, this lack of evidence did nothing to calm the rumor mill. Monsanto's chief technology officer, Robert Fraley, added a conspiracy element to the case by suggesting that anti-GMO activists could have stolen the seeds, held on to them for a decade after the original seed trials, and deliberately planted them in the field to disrupt wheat exports. Members of the Oregon Wheat Commission were more inclined to lay the blame on human error of a mislabeled or misplaced bag of seeds.

A LEGAL RESOLUTION

Any disruption in wheat exports can affect the financial stability of more than 160,000 American farms, and so the resulting lawsuits against Monsanto came as no surprise. Even with a stated mission of "producing more, conserving more, improving lives," Monsanto's reputation on corporate responsibility was less than stellar. As a manufacturer of Agent Orange, the toxic defoliant used during the Vietnam War, Monsanto's current conduct continued to be haunted by its corporate history. Aggressive litigation against farmers to enforce patents in cases of inadvertent cross-pollination of Monsanto seeds (a case that went all the way to the Supreme Court in 2011) had also created a very combative relationship between the company and its agricultural customers.

In a November 2014 settlement, Monsanto agreed to pay a total of $2.375 million to resolve litigation in relation to the mystery of MON71800 with no admission of liability. The amount was divided into a contribution of $250,000 to four wheat growers associations and $2.125 million into a settlement fund for Pacific Northwest farmers who grew soft white wheat strains between May and November 2013. Given that there was no further evidence found of MON71800 beyond the original samples, the settlement was seen as reimbursement for disruption and loss of revenue.

With no resolution of the source of the GMO strain of wheat, and no admission of liability, Monsanto was under no obligation to modify its internal processes in any way. With no subsequent claim of responsibility by anti-GMO activists, as proposed by the company's chief technology officer, the incident remains a mystery.

QUESTIONS

1. Did Monsanto violate any ethical standards in developing genetically modified wheat and planning to sell it as a companion product to Roundup?

2. What should it have done differently?

3. Was it ethical for Monsanto to settle the litigation with no admission of responsibility or commitment to change any internal practices? Why or why not?

4. Did Japan make the right decision when it banned all imports of U.S. soft wheat?

5. Food scientists argue that Mother Nature has been genetically modifying plant species for thousands of years, and that technology now gives them the opportunity to do the same for the welfare of a global population. Explain the ethical position of this argument.

6. Anti-GMO protesters warn of the creation of "frankenfoods" that have the potential to harm our bodies in ways that we do not yet understand. Explain the ethical position of this argument.

Sources: Alison Rice, "Monsanto, Soft-White Wheat Farmers Announce $2.375 Million Settlement," agweb.com, November 12, 2014; Bill Donahue, "The Search for Monsanto's Rogue GMO Wheat," *Bloomberg,* June 21, 2013; Dan Charles, "In Oregon, The GMO Wheat Mystery Deepens," *NPR,* July 18, 2013; "Taking Root: The Developing World Embraces a Controversial Technology," *The Economist,* February 25, 2010; and Paul Klein, "Monsanto's Genetically Engineered Wheat Scandal Is No Surprise," *Forbes,* June 5, 2013.

[References]

1. Melanie Merrifield, "Corporate America's Latest Act: Juggling Corporate Social Responsibility," *Baylor Business Review* 2, no. 1 (Fall 2003).

2. Michael E. Porter and Mark R. Kramer, "Strategy and Society: The Link between Competitive Advantage and Corporate Social Responsibility," *Harvard Business Review*, December 2006.

3. Milton Friedman, *Capitalism and Freedom* (Chicago: University of Chicago Press, 1962), p. 133.

4. Ibid.

5. R. C. Chewning, J. W. Eby, and S. J. Roels, *Business through the Eyes of Faith* (San Francisco: Harper & Row, 1990), p. 207.

6. Melanie Merrifield, "Corporate America's Latest Act: Juggling Corporate Social Responsibility," *Baylor Business Review* 2, no. 1 (Fall 2003).

7. Ibid.

8. Wayne Norman and Chris MacDonald, "Getting to the Bottom of Triple Bottom Line," *Business Ethics Quarterly,* March 2003.

9. "The Coca-Cola Company 2004 Citizenship Report," www.thecoca-colacompany.com/ourcompany/pdf/2004_citizenship_report.pdf.

© Abel Mitja Varela/Getty Images RF

CHAPTER 5

CORPORATE GOVERNANCE

After studying this chapter, you should be able to:

5-1 Explain the term *corporate governance*.

5-2 Understand the responsibilities of the board of directors and the major governance committees.

5-3 Explain the significance of the "King I" and "King II" reports.

5-4 Explain the differences between the following two governance methodologies: "comply or explain" and "comply or else."

5-5 Identify an appropriate corporate governance model for an organization.

FRONTLINE FOCUS
"Incriminating Evidence"

Marco is a paralegal for a large regional law firm. His company has just landed a new and very important client—Chemco Industries, one of the largest employers in the area.

Marco's prospects with his firm appear to have taken a major leap, as he has been assigned to support one of the senior partners of the law firm, David Collins, as he prepares to defend Chemco in a lawsuit brought by a group of Chemco shareholders.

The lawsuit claims that the senior management of Chemco knew that the firm's financial performance for the second quarter of the year was way below Wall Street expectations. It also knew that the likely reaction to that news would be a dramatic reduction in the price of Chemco shares. In addition, the lawsuit claims that since the stock price would most likely go below the price of the stock options that the board of directors had granted to senior management, those options would be worthless. So rather than let that happen, the Chemco shareholders argued, executives in senior management "massaged the numbers" on the company's true financial performance while selling their own shares in the company, and they kept massaging the numbers until they were able to exercise all their stock options.

Marco is well aware of the significance of this case and is excited at the prospect of working with David Collins. His first assignment is to review all the correspondence relating to stock transactions by senior executives in order to document exactly when they exercised their stock options and sold their stock. The review is expected to take several days of intensive work.

On the third day, Marco comes across a paper copy of an e-mail from David Collins to the CEO of Chemco. Since this would have no relevance to the sale of stock, Marco assumes that the e-mail was misfiled and starts to place the sheet of paper in a separate pile for refiling later. As he does so, one word that is boldface and underlined in the e-mail catches his eye—"problematic." As he reads the e-mail in full, Marco realizes that David Collins is advising the CEO to "ensure that any e-mails or written documentation that could be 'problematic' for their case be removed immediately."

QUESTIONS

1. Which committee would have granted stock options to the senior management of Chemco Industries? Review Figure 5.1 for more information on this.
2. The e-mail suggests that the CEO was well aware of what was going on at Chemco Industries. Do you think the board of directors was aware of the activities of senior management? Which committee would be responsible for monitoring ethical practices at Chemco?
3. What should Marco do now?

> Earnings can be as pliable as putty when a charlatan heads the company reporting them.
>
> **Warren Buffett**

>> Corporate Governance

The business world has seen an increasing number of scandals in recent years, and numerous organizations have been exposed for poor management practices and fraudulent financial reporting. When we review those scandals, several questions come to mind:

- Who was minding the store?
- How were these senior executives allowed to get away with this?
- Aren't companies supposed to have a system of checks and balances to prevent such behavior?
- When did the CEO of an organization suddenly become answerable to no one?

In seeking answers to these questions, we come to the issue of who really carries the authority in an organization—that is, who has the final say? In other words, are corporations governed in the same manner as our society? And if they're not, are these examples of unethical corporate behavior evidence that they should be?

Corporate governance is the process by which organizations are directed and controlled. However, when we examine who is controlling the corporation, and for whom, the situation gets a little more complicated. Before the development of large corporations, which are separate legal entities, managers and owners of organizations were the same people. As the organizations grew, wealthy owners started to hire professional managers to run the businesses on their behalf, which raised interesting questions:

- Could the managers be trusted to run the businesses in the best interests of the owners?
- How would they be held accountable for their actions?
- How would absentee owners keep control over these managers?

The development of a separate corporate entity allowed organizations to raise funds from individual shareholders to enlarge their operations. The involvement of individual shareholders diluted the ownership

Corporate Governance The system by which business corporations are directed and controlled.

Board of Directors A group of individuals who oversee governance of an organization. Elected by vote of the shareholders at the annual general meeting (AGM), the true power of the board can vary from institution to institution from a powerful unit that closely monitors the management of the organization to a body that merely rubber-stamps the decisions of the chief executive officer (CEO) and executive team.

of the original owners and also brought in a new group to which the managers of the business would now be accountable. As the corporations grew in size, and pension funds and other institutional investors purchased larger blocks of shares, the potential impact of the individual shareholder was greatly diminished, and the managers were presented with a far more powerful "owner" to whom they were now accountable.

As we discussed in Chapter 4, some argue that in addition to the interests of the company owners, managers are accountable to the public interest—or, more specifically, to their stakeholders: their customers, their vendor partners, state and local entities, and the communities in which they conduct their business operations.

So corporate governance is concerned with how well organizations meet their obligations to all these people. Ideally, mechanisms are in place to hold them accountable for that performance and to introduce corrective action if they fail to live up to that performance expectation.[1]

Corporate governance is about the way in which boards oversee the running of a company by its managers, and how board members are, in turn, accountable to shareholders and the company. This has implications for company behavior toward employees, shareholders, customers, and banks. Good corporate governance plays a vital role in underpinning the integrity and efficiency of financial markets. Poor corporate governance weakens a company's potential and at worst can pave the way for financial difficulties and even fraud. If companies are well governed, they will usually outperform other companies and will be able to attract investors whose support can finance further growth.

>> What Does Corporate Governance Look Like?

The owners of the corporation (at the top of Figure 5.1) supply equity or risk capital to the company by purchasing shares in the corporation. They are typically a fragmented group, including individual public shareholders, large blocks of private holders, private and public institutional investors, employees, managers, and other companies.

The **board of directors**, in theory, is elected by the owners to represent their interests in the effective running of the corporation. Elections take place at annual shareholders' meetings, and directors are appointed to serve for specific periods of time. The board is typically made up of inside and outside members—inside members hold management positions in the company, whereas outside members do not. The term *outside director* can be misleading because some outside members may have direct connections to the company as creditors, suppliers, customers, or professional consultants.

© Photodisc Collection/Getty Images RF

The **audit committee** is staffed by members of the board of directors plus independent or outside directors. The primary responsibilities of the audit committee are to oversee the financial reporting process, monitor internal controls (such as how much spending authority an executive has), monitor the choice of accounting policies and procedures, and oversee the hiring and performance of external auditors in producing the company's financial statements.

The **compensation committee** is also staffed by members of the board of directors plus independent or outside directors. The primary responsibility of the compensation committee is to oversee compensation packages for the senior executives of the corporation (such as salaries, bonuses, stock options, and other benefits such as, in extreme cases, personal use of company jets). Compensation policies for the employees of the corporation are left to the management team to oversee.

Audit Committee An operating committee staffed by members of the board of directors plus independent or outside directors. The committee is responsible for monitoring the financial policies and procedures of the organization—specifically the accounting policies, internal controls, and the hiring of external auditors.

Compensation Committee An operating committee staffed by members of the board of directors plus independent or outside directors. The committee is responsible for setting the compensation for the CEO and other senior executives. Typically, this compensation will consist of a base salary, performance bonus, stock options, and other perks.

FIG. 5.1 Governance of the Modern Corporation

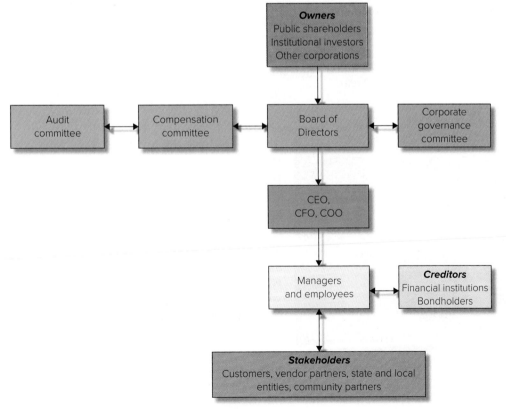

Source: Adapted from Fred R. Kaen, *A Blueprint for Corporate Governance* (New York: AMACOM, 2003).

The **corporate governance committee** represents a more public demonstration of the organization's commitment to ethical business practices. The committee (staffed by board members and specialists) monitors the ethical performance of the corporation and oversees compliance with the company's internal code of ethics as well as any federal and state regulations on corporate conduct.

>> In Pursuit of Corporate Governance

Corporate Governance Committee Committee (staffed by board members and specialists) that monitors the ethical performance of the corporation and oversees compliance with the company's internal code of ethics as well as any federal and state regulations on corporate conduct.

While the issue of corporate governance has reached new heights of media attention in the wake of corporate scandals, the topic itself has been receiving increasing attention for more than a decade.

In 1992 Sir Adrian Cadbury led a committee in Great Britain to address *financial*

© Simon Dawson/Bloomberg via Getty Images

As governor of the Bank of England, Mervyn King's name was attached to a 1994 report calling for a code of corporate practices that consider the larger community.

aspects of corporate governance in response to public concerns over directors' compensation at several high-profile companies in Great Britain. The subsequent financial scandals surrounding the Bank of Credit and Commerce International (BCCI) and the activities of publishing magnate Sir Robert Maxwell generated more attention for the committee's report than was originally anticipated. In the executive summary of the report, Cadbury outlined the committee's position on the newly topical issue of corporate governance:[2]

> At the heart of the Committee's recommendations is a Code of Best Practice designed to achieve the necessary high standards of corporate behaviour. . . . By adhering to the Code, listed companies will strengthen both their control over their businesses and their public accountability. In so doing they will be striking the right balance between meeting the standards of corporate governance now expected of them and retaining the essential spirit of enterprise.

Two years after the release of the Cadbury report, attention shifted to South Africa, where Mervyn King, a corporate lawyer, former High Court judge, and the governor of the Bank of England at the time, led a committee that published the "King Report on Corporate Governance" in 1994. In contrast to Cadbury's focus on internal governance, the King report "incorporated a code of corporate practices and conduct that looked beyond the corporation itself, taking into account its impact on the larger community."[3]

"King I," as the 1994 report became known, went beyond the financial and regulatory accountability upon which the Cadbury report had focused and took a more integrated approach to the topic of corporate governance, recognizing the involvement of all the corporation's stakeholders—the shareholders, customers, employees, vendor partners, and the community in which the corporation operates—in the efficient and appropriate operation of the organization.[4]

Even though King I was widely recognized as advocating the highest standards for corporate governance, the committee released a second report eight years later, referred to as "King II," which formally recognized the need to move the stakeholder model forward and consider a triple bottom line as opposed to the traditional single bottom line of profitability. The triple bottom line recognizes the economic, environmental, and social aspects of a company's activities. In the words of the King II report, companies must "comply or explain" or "comply or else."[5]

According to King II,

> . . . successful governance in the world in the 21st century requires companies to adopt an inclusive and not exclusive approach. The company must be open to institutional activism and there must be greater emphasis on the sustainable or non-financial aspects of its performance. Boards must apply the tests of fairness, accountability, responsibility, and transparency to all acts or omissions and be accountable to the company but also responsive and responsible towards the company's identified stakeholders. The correct balance between conformance with governance principles and performance in an entrepreneurial market economy must be found, but this will be specific to each company.[6]

>> Two Governance Methodologies: "Comply or Explain" or "Comply or Else"?

The Cadbury report argued for a guideline of **comply or explain**, which gave companies the flexibility to comply with governance standards or explain why they do not in their corporate documents (annual reports, for example). The vagueness of what would constitute an acceptable explanation for not complying, combined with the ease with which such explanations could be buried in the footnotes of an annual report (if they were even there at all), raised concerns that comply or explain really wouldn't do much for corporate governance.

The string of financial scandals that followed the report led many critics to argue that comply or explain obviously offered no real deterrent to corporations. The answer, they argued, was to move to a

PROGRESS ✔ QUESTIONS

5. Which two scandals greatly increased the attention paid to the 1992 Cadbury report?
6. Explain the "right balance" that Cadbury encourages companies to pursue.
7. Explain the difference between the King I and King II reports.
8. Explain the difference between "comply or explain" and "comply or else."

more aggressive approach of **comply or else**, where failure to comply results in stiff financial penalties. The Sarbanes-Oxley Act of 2002 (see Chapter 6) incorporates this approach.

"IN THE KNOW" OR "IN THE DARK"?

With the exception, perhaps, of corporate governance committees, each of the corporations that have faced charges for corporate misconduct in recent years used the governance model shown in Figure 5.1. When questioned, the boards of these corporations all shared similar stories of being "ambushed" or kept in the dark about the massive frauds the senior executives of their corporations allegedly carried out.

What does this mean for investors seeking to put their retirement funds in dependable companies that are well run? What about employees seeking reassurance that those senior corporate officers in the executive suites can be counted on to steer the company to a promising future rather than run it aground?

If all these companies had a governance model in place, where was the oversight? Is it the model that's at fault or the people filling the assigned roles in that model? Consider the different interpretations of just how much authority rests with these official overseers illustrated in the two ethical dilemmas of this chapter, "20/20 Hindsight" and "A Spectacular Downfall."

> **"Comply or Explain"** Guidelines that require companies to abide by a set of operating standards or explain why they choose not to.
>
> **"Comply or Else"** Guidelines that require companies to abide by a set of operating standards or face stiff financial penalties.

THE CHAIRMAN AND THE CEO

If the model of corporate structure shown at the beginning of this chapter is followed, the stockholders of a corporation should elect members of the board of directors. In turn, that board of directors should elect a chairperson. For the vast majority of corporations, however, the model is typically ignored.

The first step in a policy of disregarding the corporate governance model is the decision to merge the roles of chief executive officer (CEO) and chairperson of the board into one individual. In this situation, the oversight that the board of directors is supposed to

> **Key Point** !
>
> The King II report stated that successful governance requires an "inclusive" rather than an "exclusive" approach. What would be the difference between those two approaches?

Sir Allen Stanford, a Texas-born citizen of the Caribbean island of Antigua, seemed to have the life that dreams are made of. As the founder and majority shareholder of the Stanford Financial Group (SFG), based in Houston, Texas, Stanford led a complex network of interlinked financial companies that claimed to manage over $50 billion in assets. Later analysis reduced that figure significantly, but Stanford continued to claim an estimated personal net worth of over $2 billion. He loved the English game of cricket and invested millions of dollars in supporting West Indian teams, including building a state-of-the-art cricket ground in Antigua and underwriting the "Stanford Twenty20 tournament" that offered a $20 million winner-take-all prize in a championship of 20 cricket matches.

Stanford's business skills seemed to know no limits. His business interests included two major banks, a trust company, a real estate development company, a newspaper, a cricket ground, two restaurants, and large tracts of land—and that was just in Antigua. The jewel of his portfolio was reputed to be the Stanford International Bank (SIB) of Antigua. As an "offshore bank," SIB operated outside of U.S. banking regulations. With a reputed $8.5 billion in assets, the bank took money from depositors by an unusual route. No loans were ever made by the bank, although it did claim to have a traditional stock and bond trading department. Clients deposited funds by purchasing certificates of deposits (CDs) that offered above-average interest rates in return for reduced liquidity—in other words, once deposited with SIB, customer funds took 60 days to be returned. The above-average interest rates proved irresistible to investors in the United States and Latin America—over $8 billion was invested in SIB CDs by more than 20,000 investors, which inevitably brought the bank to the attention of the Securities and Exchange Commission (SEC).

Stanford's lifestyle has been referenced in the past tense, because in June 2009, following insider tips from brokers in Stanford's SIB network, he was arrested and charged by U.S. securities regulators over a "massive investment fraud" through SIB. Investigations by SEC personnel uncovered interesting information about Stanford's operations:

- Over $8 billion of the CD funds invested in SIB were, it is alleged, used to fund Stanford's lavish lifestyle and other investment vehicles in a complex Ponzi scheme (refer to Thinking Critically 6.1 for more information on Ponzi schemes). The reduced liquidity of the CDs gave Stanford time to move money around if any investors elected to cash in their investments. Some $6 billion is still claimed to be "unaccounted for."
- Other companies in SFG claimed investment funds that far exceeded their actual deposits. For example, Stanford Financial Co. (SFC), a registered broker and asset management business, had only about $147 million of assets as the wealth management division of a $50 billion company. Further investigation revealed that SFC served only as an "introductory broker" to

© Aaron M. Sprecher/epa/EPA/Corbis

other investment companies such as Bear Stearns and, ironically, Bernard Madoff.
- When stock markets around the world began crashing in 2008, SFG reported a year-end loss of only 1.3 percent after a decade of consistent double-digit growth that has been described as "suspiciously smooth."
- Stanford's heavily marketed knighthood came not from the Queen of England, but from the governor general of Antigua. This might have been connected to Stanford's $87 million in loans to the Antiguan government.

The biggest red flag of Stanford's operation was the governance structure of his multiple and complex corporations. The chief financial officer (CFO) of SIB, James Davis (who chose to cooperate with SEC investigators in return for a reduced sentence), was Stanford's college roommate. The chief investment officer of SFG, Laura Pendergest-Holt, had no financial services or securities experience, and claimed to have limited knowledge of "the whereabouts of the vast majority of the bank's multi-billion investment portfolio," according to the SEC. Other senior corporate officers included Stanford family members, friends, and business associates with cattle ranching and car sales companies in Texas. Of the three key individuals, Pendergest-Holt was the only one to be charged criminally with obstruction of justice. The indictment contended that she misled SEC investigators on several occasions and failed to disclose that she had

ETHICAL DILEMMA

20/20 HINDSIGHT

several preparatory meetings with other SFG executives before meeting with SEC investigators. In June 2012, she agreed to plead guilty to one charge of obstruction and to serve three years in prison for her role in the fraud.

Stanford continued to profess his innocence by claiming that he was wrong to trust the integrity of his CFO, James Davis. "The investment and risk committee reported to Jim Davis, not to me," he said. As for the collapse of his financial empire and his inability to repay investors, Stanford blamed the SEC for using him as a "scapegoat" after failing to catch Bernard Madoff, and for the "ripple effect" of its indictment that prompted regulatory agencies around the world to freeze the assets of his multiple investment companies. "I don't think there is any money missing," Stanford said. "There never was a Ponzi scheme, and there never was an attempt to defraud anybody."

Stanford's time in prison was particularly eventful. He was severely beaten by fellow prisoners; he was hospitalized for heart problems; and he developed an alleged addiction to antianxiety medication and was declared incompetent to stand trial. After receiving treatment for the addiction, he continued to plead not guilty in the face of mounting evidence against him. In March 2012, he was found guilty on 13 of 14 counts of fraud, money laundering, and obstruction of justice. In June 2012, he was sentenced to 110 years in prison. Prosecutors had asked for the maximum term of 230 years. Stanford's defense team had asked for 44 months, including time served in prison, which would have left him with only 8 months to serve.

In November 2014, Stanford's legal team filed a 299-page appeal motion in the Fifth U.S. Circuit Court of Appeals in New Orleans, making 10 distinct arguments as to why he should be set free. After having retained over a dozen lawyers over the course of his criminal case, Stanford elected to represent himself in the appeal, only to see the court set aside all claims, including that he was not competent to stand trial, that the trial judge was biased in not allowing Stanford to choose his own lawyer, and that the government did not prove its case.

In a January 2016 interview with the British Broadcasting Corp. (BBC), Stanford remained defiant that the SEC never had the authority to intervene in his offshore businesses and that he would continue to "work night and day" to prove his innocence. With the loss of the appeal, Stanford's original sentence of 110 years will remain in effect.

QUESTIONS

1. How did SIB's status as an "offshore bank" facilitate Stanford's alleged fraud?
2. Why would investors be willing to sacrifice immediate access to the funds they deposited with SIB?
3. What elements were missing from the governance structure of Stanford Financial Group?
4. What was the basis of Stanford's defense?

Sources: Sam Jones, "Fraud Probe at Labyrinth of SFG Companies," *Financial Times,* February 18, 2009; "Howzat! Shocking Allegations against Stanford Group," *The Economist,* February 19, 2009; Joanna Chung, Tracey Alloway, and Jeremy Lemer, "The Stanford Scandal: Why Were Red Flags Ignored?" *The Financial Times,* February 19, 2009; Clifford Krauss, "Chief Investment Officer at Stanford Group Indicted," *The New York Times,* May 13, 2009; Clifford Krauss, "Stanford Points Fingers in Fraud Case," *The New York Times,* April 21, 2009; "Ex-Tycoon R. Allen Stanford Sentenced to 110 Years," *Associated Press,* June 14, 2012; Michael E. Lindenberger and Murray Wass, "Allen Stanford Files 299-Page Appeal of His 110-Year Sentence," *The Dallas Morning News,* October 4, 2014; Jonathan Stempel, "Allen Stanford Loses Appeal of Ponzi Scheme Conviction," *Reuters,* October 29, 2015; and Dan Roan and Patrick Nathanson, "Defiant US Fraudster Allen Stanford Vows to Clear His Name," *BBC News,* January 11, 2016.

provide has been lost, and the operational focus of the company has switched from long term (to the extent that board members serve a two-year contract) to short term, where the CEO is focusing on the numbers for the next quarter.

The argument in favor of merging the two roles is one of efficiency—by putting the leadership of the board of directors and the senior management team in the hands of the same person, the potential for conflict is minimized, and, it is argued, the board is given the benefit of leadership from someone who is in touch with the inner workings of the organization rather than an outsider who needs time to get up to speed.

The argument against merging the two roles is an ethical one. Governance of the corporation is now in the hands of one person, which eliminates the checks and balances process that the board was created for in the first place. As time passes, as we have seen with the Stanford example in "20/20 Hindsight," the CEO slowly populates the board with friends who are less critical of the CEO's policies and more willing to vote larger and larger salary and benefits packages. With a rubber-stamp board in place to authorize every wish, the CEO now becomes a law unto himself or herself. The independence of the board is compromised,

PROGRESS ✔ QUESTIONS

9. What is the argument in favor of merging the roles of chairperson and CEO?
10. What is the argument against merging the roles of chairperson and CEO?
11. Explain the difference between a short-term and long-term view in the governance of a corporation.
12. Is it unethical to populate your board of directors with friends and business acquaintances? Why or why not?

and the power of the stockholders is minimized. The CEO can pursue policies that are focused on maintaining a high share price in the short term (to maximize the price he will get when he cashes in all the share options that his friends on the board gave him in the last contract) without any concern for the long-term stability of the organization—after all, there will probably be another CEO by then.

>> Effective Corporate Governance

When corporations reach out to consultants, or are approached by consultants with new solutions to maximize the effectiveness of their corporate governance, the issues of finding an accepted benchmark and a comparative measure of one company's corporate governance versus another's inevitably arise. Acronyms typically feature prominently in these measurement frameworks. For example, INSEAD, the European business school, offers the "CRAFTED" principles of governance: "Good corporate governance is a culture and a climate of **C**onsistency, **R**esponsibility, **A**ccountability, **F**airness, **T**ransparency, and **E**ffectiveness that is **D**eployed throughout the organization."[7] However, the application of a commonly accepted numerical scoring template remains frustratingly elusive.

The CRAFTED principles appear to be fairly self-explanatory, and, when questioned, most boards of directors would no doubt offer their wholehearted support for them. So where does the oversight process break down?

If the board is to serve its purpose in setting the operational tone for the organization, it should be composed of members who represent professional conduct in their own organizations. Proper authority should be granted, so that the board members can fulfill their responsibilities of oversight, guidance, and approval to the best of their abilities.

Unfortunately, the CRAFTED principle of transparency is often forgone in favor of tightly managed information flow by the executive leadership of the organization; and the appointments to the board more often reflect the trading of professional favors and quid pro quo agreements than the utilization of the best available skills and experience.

CEOs may feel challenged and a little threatened by dissent from their board, but if all they really want is a rubber stamp of every decision presented to the board members, then those CEOs are failing in their fiscal responsibility to their stakeholders and overlooking a tremendous resource of experience that remains available to them.

Real World Applications

You are a sales executive for a national equipment manufacturer. You joined the company straight out of college and have always been proud to work for the organization. Lately, however, you have become increasingly concerned about the office politics that have been going on at the corporate headquarters. Several senior executives have left, some very suddenly, and a lot of the changes can be traced back to the appointment of the CEO, Bill Thompson. Yesterday it was announced that Alex Dale, the chairman of the company (and the grandson of the founder), would be retiring at the end of the month (only two weeks away). The e-mail announcement also clarified that Bill Thompson would be assuming the position of chairman in addition to his role as CEO. You think back to your college ethics course and wonder whether this is really a good thing for the company as a whole. Would combining both roles raise any concerns for stakeholders over effective corporate governance? Why or why not?

By the same token, the board must be willing to work with the executive leadership to provide feedback and guidance in a detailed and timely manner. Electing to take strategic projects "under advisement" for extended periods of time may serve to reinforce the power of the board of directors, but that gets achieved at the risk of lost opportunities.

Running a company of any size requires constant evaluation of risk-versus-reward scenarios. The corporate governance model assumes that the board of directors and executive leadership work together in making those evaluations. CEOs who try to populate their boards with friends and colleagues—cronyism—may well be putting their egos ahead of the needs of the business.

22 QUESTIONS FOR DIAGNOSING YOUR BOARD

Walter Salmon, a longtime director with over 30 years of boardroom experience, took this prescriptive approach even further in a 1993 *Harvard Business Review* article by recommending a checklist of 22 questions to assess the quality of your board. If you answer yes to all 22 questions, you have an exemplary board.[8]

1. Are there three or more outside directors for every insider?
2. Are the insiders limited to the CEO, the COO, and the CFO?
3. Do your directors routinely speak to senior managers who are not represented on the board?
4. Is your board the right size (8 to 15 members)?
5. Does your audit committee, not management, have the authority to approve the partner in charge of auditing the company?
6. Does your audit committee routinely review high-exposure areas?
7. Do compensation consultants report to your compensation committee rather than to the company's human resource officers?
8. Has your compensation committee shown the courage to establish formulas for CEO compensation based on long-term results—even if formulas differ from industry norms?
9. Are the activities of your executive committee sufficiently contained to prevent the emergence of a two-tier board?
10. Do outside directors annually review succession plans for senior management?
11. Do outside directors formally evaluate your CEO's strengths, weaknesses, objectives, personal plans, and performance every year?
12. Does your nominating committee rather than the CEO direct the search for new board members and invite candidates to stand for election?
13. Is there a way for outside directors to alter the meeting agenda set by your CEO?
14. Does the company help directors prepare for meetings by sending relevant routine information, as well as analyses of key agendas ahead of time?
15. Is there sufficient meeting time for thoughtful discussion in addition to management monologues?
16. Do the outside directors meet without management on a regular basis?
17. Is your board actively involved in formulating long-range business strategy from the start of the planning cycle?
18. Does your board, rather than the incumbent CEO, select the new chief executive—in fact as well as in theory?
19. Is at least some of the director's pay linked to corporate performance?
20. Is the performance of each of your directors periodically reviewed?
21. Are directors who are no longer pulling their weight discouraged from standing for reelection?
22. Do you take the right measures to build trust among directors?

> **Key Point !**
>
> In what ways would "a culture of open dissent" among board members improve the corporate governance of an organization?

Even with a board that passes all the tests and meets all the established criteria, ethical misconduct can still come down to the individual personalities involved. Consider the media storm surrounding the conduct of Sepp Blatter, the former president of FIFA (Fédération Internationale de Football Association).

A SPECTACULAR DOWNFALL

The sport of soccer, known as football outside of North America, was tarnished by evidence of bribery and corruption at FIFA, football's global governing body. In particular, the culture created under FIFA's defiant president, Joseph "Sepp" Blatter, appeared to endorse greed on a spectacular scale as votes from FIFA delegates were allegedly made available for sale as countries sought to win the rights to host the World Cup every four years.

When 14 FIFA officials were arrested in their Zurich, Switzerland, hotel rooms on May 27, 2015, on the eve of a congress meeting, the world of soccer was taken by surprise, especially since those arrests were made at the request of the U.S. Department of Justice (DOJ).

By December 2015, a total of 16 officials had received a 92-count indictment on criminal charges including racketeering, money laundering, and wire fraud amounting to more than $150 million over the past 24 years.

The money was allegedly received from national sports associations seeking to influence the appointment of host cities for World Cup championships, and from companies with commercial connections to FIFA seeking "lucrative media and marketing rights" to FIFA tournaments. The scheduled World Cup championships in Russia (2018) and Qatar (2022) came under particular scrutiny, with the award to Qatar raising the most suspicions, since football would be a very difficult sport to play

CONTINUED >>

in the average 100- to 115-degree heat and stifling humidity of a Qatari summer.

© Michael Buholzer/Stringer/Getty Images

THE BLATTER REIGN

While the DOJ arrests prompted worldwide media coverage, sports media journalists and officials were less surprised. Blatter's 17-year reign as FIFA's eighth president had been marred by frequent allegations of corruption from the day he won the office in 1998 after serving 17 years as the top deputy to the retiring president, Joao Havelange. The vote against his Swedish rival, Lennart Johansson, was very close, leading to bribery allegations that were never proven.

Toward the end of his first term in office, Blatter was implicated in the bankruptcy of FIFA's marketing partner, International Sports and Leisure (ISL), that collapsed with debts of more than $100 million. While investigations verified kickbacks to FIFA executives amounting to tens of millions of dollars, Blatter walked away with an assessment of "clumsy" conduct but no evidence of criminal or unethical behavior.

Over the next decade, Blatter was connected to numerous scandals related to bribes, financial mismanagement, and highly questionable tactics during reelection campaigns, but emerged unscathed. In 2011, FIFA convened an independent panel to propose governance reforms in the face of increasing criticism over the conduct of Blatter and his team of senior executives. Recommendations of fixed terms, age limits, and increased transparency of association finances were ignored. Those that sought to challenge Blatter in elections or in the proposal of policy changes were rewarded with a swift departure from the organization.

It is a testament to Blatter's apparent control over FIFA that he was reelected for a fifth term as president immediately following the May 27, 2015, arrests. He responded to the actions of the DOJ and British media in covering the story by saying: "I forgive but I don't forget." However, when the extent of the alleged malfeasance was made public, Blatter announced his resignation from the presidency four days later, declaring that: "FIFA needs a profound restructuring."

The beginning of the end for Blatter came on September 25, 2015, when Swiss investigators issued criminal proceedings against him in relation to the assignment of valuable World Cup television rights to former FIFA official Jack Warner for a fraction of their true value. The contract dated back to 2005 when the Caribbean broadcast rights for the 2010 and 2014 World Cups were sold to Warner for a mere $600,000. He then sold those rights to a Jamaica-based cable television station for an alleged $15 million to $20 million profit.

THE END OF A DARK ERA

In the face of mounting allegations against Blatter, longtime FIFA sponsors, including McDonald's, Visa, Coca-Cola, and Anheuser-Busch InBev, began calling for Blatter to sever all ties with FIFA, labeling him as an obstacle to reform. Blatter remained defiant, even in the face of a formal suspension by the organization's ethics committee for 90 days. On December 21, 2015, Blatter and Michel Platini, the president of UEFA, European football's governing body, were found guilty of ethics violations by FIFA's ethics committee and barred from the sport for eight years. Both men appealed the decision to the Court of Arbitration for Sport, and their ban was reduced to only six years.

On February 25, 2016, 45-year-old Gianni Infantino, the former general secretary of UEFA, was appointed as Blatter's successor as the ninth president of FIFA on a platform that committed to restoring "the image of FIFA and the respect of FIFA." Blatter, who turned 80 in March 2016, announced: "With the adoption of [reforms], expectations on him will be even higher. But I am convinced that my successor will put them in place . . . I had this burden on me. And now it is finished."

QUESTIONS

1. Which stakeholders were impacted by Blatter's leadership at FIFA?
2. Where were the failures in corporate governance in this case?
3. Is there any evidence of good corporate governance in this case?
4. What steps should the new president of FIFA take to restore corporate governance?

Sources: "Timeline: Sepp Blatter's Reign at FIFA," *The Economist,* June 2, 2015; Owen Gibson, "Sepp Blatter Under Pressure over World Cup TV Rights Links to Jack Warner," *The Guardian,* September 13, 2015; Evan Perez and Shimon Prokupecz, "U.S. Charges 16 FIFA Officials in Widening Probe," *CNN,* December 3, 2015; Kevin Rawlinson, "Sepp Blatter's Reign as Head of FIFA Marked by Scandal from the Outset," *The Guardian,* December 21, 2015; "The Rise and Fall of Sepp Blatter," *The New York Times,* December 21, 2015; and "Sepp Blatter Free of FIFA 'Presidency Burden,'" *Al Jazeera,* February 27, 2016.

>> Governing your career

In this chapter we review the importance of organizational oversight through a corporate governance structure. Give some thought to the oversight of your career in the future. As you have read, an organization's board of directors is designed to be both an advisory group and a governing body. Do you have a team of people you can count on for advice or guidance? Do you work with a mentor who is willing to share his or her experience and advice with you to help you make important decisions in your life?

Many successful businesspeople acknowledge that developing a dream team of advisers has been critical to their business and personal success in life. Being willing to reach out to others and seek their advice and guidance on a regular basis, they believe, has helped them prepare for important decisions and plan for long-term career choices. Making those decisions is ultimately your responsibility, but the more insight and information you have available to you, the more confident you may be in the final choice that you make.

Why would people agree to serve on your dream team? Perhaps they want to give something back in recognition of the success they have earned or to share in the joy of watching someone they regard as having tremendous potential move on to bigger and better career opportunities. Then as you progress in your business career, you, in turn, can give something back by agreeing to mentor a young student with strong potential or to serve on the dream team of several promising students to help them succeed in their lives.

THE DANGERS OF A CORPORATE GOVERNANCE CHECKLIST

There is more to effective corporate governance than simply maintaining a checklist of items to be monitored on a regular basis. Simply having the mechanisms in place will not, in itself, guarantee good governance. Enron, for example, had all its governance boxes checked:[9]

- Enron separated the roles of chairman (Kenneth Lay) and chief executive officer (Jeffrey Skilling)—at least until Skilling's surprise resignation.
- The company maintained a roster of independent directors with flawless résumés.
- It maintained an audit committee consisting exclusively of nonexecutives.

However, once you scratched beneath the surface of this model exterior, the true picture was a lot less appealing:

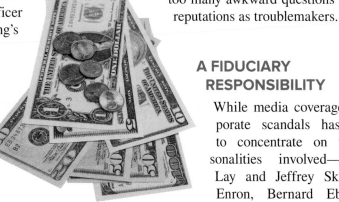

© Tetra Images/Punchstock RF

- Many of the so-called independent directors were affiliated with organizations that benefited directly from Enron's operations.
- The directors enjoyed substantial "benefits" that continued to grow as Enron's fortunes grew.
- Their role as directors of Enron, a Wall Street darling, guaranteed them positions as directors for other companies—a career package that would be jeopardized if they chose to ask too many awkward questions and gain reputations as troublemakers.

A FIDUCIARY RESPONSIBILITY

While media coverage of corporate scandals has tended to concentrate on the personalities involved—Kenneth Lay and Jeffrey Skilling at Enron, Bernard Ebbers at WorldCom, Richard Scrushy at HealthSouth, John Rigas at Adelphia Cable, and Dennis Kozlowski at Tyco—we cannot lose sight of the fact that corporate governance is about managers fulfilling a fiduciary responsibility to the owners of their companies. A *fiduciary responsibility* is ultimately based on trust, which is a difficult trait to test when you are hiring a manager or to enforce once that manager is in place. Enforcement only becomes an option when that trust has been broken. In the meantime, organizations must depend on oversight and the development of processes and mechanisms to support that oversight—the famous checks and balances.

The payoff for such diligence is that "a commitment to good corporate governance . . . make[s] a company both more attractive to investors and lenders, and more profitable. Simply put, it pays to promote good corporate governance."[10] Consider the following examples:

- A Deutsche Bank study of Standard & Poor's 500 firms showed that companies with strong or improving corporate governance outperformed those with poor or deteriorating governance practices by about 19 percent over a two-year period.
- A Harvard-Wharton study showed that if an investor purchased shares in U.S. firms with the strongest shareholder rights and sold shares in the ones with the weakest shareholder rights, the

investor would have earned above average returns of 8.5 percent per year.

- The same study also found that U.S.-based firms with better governance have faster sales growth and were more profitable than their peers.
- In a 2002 McKinsey survey, institutional investors said they would pay premiums to own well-governed companies. Premiums averaged 30 percent in Eastern Europe and Africa and 22 percent in Asia and Latin America.

>> Conclusion

Having the right model in place will not take you far if that model is eventually overrun by a corporate culture of greed and success at all costs. Even organizations that have been publicly exposed for their lack of corporate governance still appear to have lessons to learn. Tyco, for example, made a very public commitment to clean house under the direction of Edward Breen, "but it has refused to replace the audit firm that failed to uncover massive abuses by its former chief executive or to give up its Bermuda domicile [formal offshore residence for tax purposes], which insulates it from shareholder litigation and so genuine accountability." In addition, "at WorldCom

(now part of Verizon), where Michael Capellas was brought in to clean up the mess left by Bernie Ebbers, the bankruptcy court vetoed his proposed compensation package as "grossly excessive."[11]

No system of corporate governance can completely defend against fraud or incompetence. The test is how far such aberrations can be discouraged and how quickly they can be brought to light. The risks can be reduced by making the participants in the governance process as effectively accountable as possible. The key safeguards are properly constituted boards, separation of the functions of chairperson and of chief executive, audit committees, vigilant shareholders, and financial reporting and auditing systems that provide full and timely disclosure.[12]

FRONTLINE FOCUS
"Incriminating Evidence"—Marco Makes a Decision

Marco broke into a cold sweat as soon as he finished reading the e-mail. He realized that if it were made public, it would mean the end for the CEO of Chemco, the senior managers, David Collins, and probably anyone assigned to the Chemco case. What the heck was he supposed to do now? Tell David Collins? Pretend he hadn't found it and shred it? Should he go public with it or send it anonymously to the lawyers for the Chemco shareholders?

He started imagining the consequences for each of those actions and decided that anything that involved him looking for a new paralegal position wasn't a good choice. He also thought about the Enron case and how long it had taken to get the two senior officers, Ken Lay and Jeff Skilling,

into court, with no money left at the end of it all to return to shareholders who had lost their life savings when the company collapsed.

"It's just not worth it," Marco thought. "And anyway, who would pay attention to a rookie paralegal?" With that, he took the piece of paper and placed it into the shredder.

QUESTIONS

1. What could Marco have done differently?
2. What do you think will happen now?
3. What will be the consequences for Marco, David Collins, and Chemco Industries?

[For Review]

1. **Explain the term _corporate governance_.**

   Corporate governance is the process by which organizations are directed and controlled. Using a series of boards and committees, corporate governance is designed to oversee the running of a company by its managers and to ensure that the interests of all the stakeholders (customers, employees, vendor partners, state and local entities, and the communities in which the company operates) are fairly represented and treated.

2. **Understand the responsibilities of the board of directors and the major governance committees.**

   A board of directors is a group of senior experienced executives who oversee governance of an organization. Elected by shareholder vote at the annual general meeting, the true power of the board can vary from a powerful unit that closely monitors the management of the organization, to a body that merely rubber-stamps the decisions of the chief executive officer (CEO) and executive team.

   Effective corporate governance models typically include three major oversight committees, staffed by members of the board of directors and appropriately qualified specialists:

   - _The audit committee, which oversees the financial reporting process, monitors internal controls over corporate expenditure, monitors accounting policies and procedures, and oversees the hiring and performance of external auditors in producing the company's financial statements._

   - _The compensation committee, which oversees compensation packages for the senior executives of the corporation (such as salaries, bonuses, stock options, and other benefits such as, in extreme cases,_ personal use of company jets). In these days of highly compensated executives (such as Sepp Blatter in the Ethical Dilemma, "A Spectacular Downfall"), such discussions often involve extensive negotiations with a designated "agent" for the executive in question. Compensation policies for the employees of the corporation are usually left to the management team to oversee.

   - _As corporations come under increasing pressure to publicly demonstrate their commitment to ethical business practices, many are choosing to establish separate corporate governance committees to monitor the ethical performance of the corporation and oversee compliance with the company's internal code of ethics as well as any federal and state regulations on corporate conduct._

3. **Explain the significance of the "King I" and "King II" reports.**

   Published as the "King Report on Corporate Governance" in 1994, Mervyn King's report changed the emphasis on corporate governance from internal governance of corporate operations to practices that looked beyond the corporation itself and included its impact on the community at large. A second report released eight years later ("King II") formally recognized the need to incorporate all stakeholders and consider a triple bottom-line (3BL) approach to corporate performance and profitability.

4. **Explain the differences between the following two governance methodologies: "comply or explain" and "comply or else."**

   The requirement to "comply or explain" demands that organizations must demonstrate that they are abiding by a set of rules or clearly explain why they are choosing not to. By comparison, "comply or else" imposes financial penalties for organizations that choose not to abide by that set of rules.

5. **Identify an appropriate corporate governance model for an organization.**

   The European business school INSEAD emphasizes corporate governance as an organizational culture issue, with a goal of maintaining a climate through its CRAFTED principles of " **C**onsistency, **R**esponsibility, **A**ccountability, **F**airness, **T**ransparency, and **E**ffectiveness that is **D**eployed throughout the organization."[13] However, while the acronym may set an appropriate tone, it does not offer any specific guidance on setting performance benchmarks or comparative measures of effective governance as compared to other organizations.

[Key Terms]

Audit Committee 95

Board of Directors 94

Compensation Committee 95

"Comply or Else" 97

"Comply or Explain" 97

Corporate Governance 94

Corporate Governance Committee 96

[Review Questions]

1. Why do corporations need a board of directors?

2. What is the value of adding "outside directors" to your board?

3. Which is more important to effective corporate governance: an audit committee or a compensation committee? Why?

4. Many experienced senior business executives serve on multiple corporate boards. Is this a good thing? Explain your answer.

5. Many of Enron's "independent" directors were affiliated with organizations that benefited directly from Enron's operations. How would you address this clear conflict of interest?

6. Outline the corporate governance structure of the company you work for (or one you have worked for in the past).

[Review Exercises]

GlobalMutual was, by all accounts, a model insurance company. Profits were strong and had been for several years in a row. The company carried the highest ratings in its industry, and it had recently been voted one of the top 100 companies to work for in the United States in recognition of its very employee-focused work environment. GlobalMutual offered very generous benefits: free lunches in the cafeteria, onsite day care facilities, and even free Starbucks coffee in the employee break rooms. In an industry that was still struggling with the massive claims after a succession of hurricanes in the United States, GlobalMutual was financially stable and positioned to become one of the major insurance companies in the nation.

So why were the CEO, William Brown; the CFO, Anne Johnson; and the COO, Peter Brooking, all fired on the same day with no explanation other than that the terminations were related to issues of conduct?

1. Who would most likely have intervened to terminate the senior team over issues of conduct?

2. Give some examples of the kind of ethical misconduct that could have led to the termination of the entire senior leadership of GlobalMutual.

3. Was it a good idea to fire them all at the same time with no detailed explanation?

4. How are the stakeholders of GlobalMutual likely to react to this news? Explain your answer.

Source: Adapted from George O'Brien, "A Matter of Ethics," *BusinessWest* 22, no. 4 (June 13, 2005), p. 9.

[Internet Exercises]

1. Review the website of the International Corporate Governance Network (ICGN) at www.icgn.org.

   a. What is the ICGN's stated mission?

   b. How can this organization affect corporate governance in the business world?

   c. The ICGN offers "policy" guidance in several areas. Select one, and summarize how that guidance contributes to the general discussion on corporate governance.

2. Review the annual report of a Fortune 100 company of your choice. Who serves on the board of directors for the company? Are there any designated "outside" directors? On how many other boards do those outside directors serve? What does the company gain from having these outside directors on the board?

[Team Exercises]

1. **Chairperson and/or CEO.**
   Divide into two teams. One team must prepare a presentation advocating for the separation of the roles of chairperson and CEO. The other team must prepare a presentation arguing for the continued practice of allowing one corporate executive to be both chairperson and CEO.

2. **Compensation.**
   You serve on your organization's compensation committee, and you are meeting to negotiate the retirement package for your CEO who is retiring after a very successful 40-year career with your organization—the last 20 as CEO, during which time the company's revenues grew more than fourfold and gross profits increased by over 300 percent. Divide into two teams, arguing *for* and *against* the following compensation package being proposed by the CEO's representative:

   - Unlimited access to the company's New York apartment.
   - Unlimited use of the corporate jet and company limousine service.
   - Courtside tickets to New York Knicks games.
   - Box seats at Yankee Stadium.
   - VIP seats at the French Open, U.S. Open, and Wimbledon tennis tournaments.
   - A lucrative annual consulting contract of $80,000 for the first five days and an additional $17,500 per day thereafter.
   - Reimbursement for all professional services—legal, financial, secretarial, and IT support.
   - Stock options amounting to $200 million.

3. **An appropriate response.**
   You sit on the board of directors of a major airline that just experienced a horrendous customer service event. A severe snowstorm stranded several of your planes and caused a ripple effect throughout your flight schedule, stranding thousands of passengers at airports across the country and keeping dozens of passengers as virtual hostages on planes for several hours as they waited for departure slots at their airport. The press has covered this fiasco at length and is already calling for a passenger bill of rights that will be based primarily on all the things your airline didn't do to take care of its passengers in this situation. Your CEO is the founder of the airline, and he has been featured in many of your commercials raving about the high level of customer service you deliver. The board is meeting to review his continued employment with the company. Divide into two teams and argue the case *for* and *against* terminating his employment as a first step in restoring the reputation of your airline.

4. **Ideal corporate governance.**
   Divide into groups of three or four. Each group must map out its ideal model for corporate governance of an organization—for example, the number of people on the board of directors, separate roles of chairperson and CEO, inside and outside directors, and employee representation on the board. Prepare a presentation arguing for the respective merits of each model and offer evidence of how each model represents the best interests of all the organization's stakeholders.

Thinking Critically

>> TESCO'S VANISHING PROFITS

On September 22, 2014, Tesco, the largest supermarket chain in Britain and second-largest retailer in the world after Walmart, announced the company had overstated profits for the first half of its financial year by an estimated

© Apidech Ninkhlai / 123RF

£250 million (about $420 million). The error arose as a result of the "accelerated recognition of commercial income and delayed accrual of costs." In layman's terms, Tesco had been paying suppliers later and recognizing promotional revenues from them sooner than it should have.

The announcement surprised financial markets, adding further damage to a stock price that was already reeling from a profit warning three weeks earlier that had stated that first-half profits would be £1.1 billion as compared to an expected £1.6 billion. The resulting 8 percent drop in share price erased £1.5 billion from Tesco's market value, making a total reduction of £6 billion lost since the company's chief executive, Phil Clark, had been removed in July.

Dave Lewis, who had replaced Clark in September after a 27-year career at Unilever, shared as part of the profit overstatement announcement that:

- Four senior executives from Tesco UK—the managing director, finance director, commercial director, and group-sourcing executive—had been removed from their positions.
- The accounting firm Deloitte had been brought in to perform an independent review of the accounts previously audited by PriceWaterhouseCoopers (PwC).
- Legal advisers Freshfields had been contracted to scrutinize the UK food business that was responsible for the overestimation.
- The Financial Conduct Authority (FCA), the UK's chief financial regulator, had been contacted in relation to the overstatement of profits.

Tesco had been losing revenue and market share to both upscale and discount competitors in recent years, prompting the departure of Clark after declining financial performance. The company's reputation for quality had suffered after traces of horsemeat were found in some of its beef products, and German discount competitors, Aldi and Lidl, had gained an 8 percent market share in the UK, primarily at Tesco's expense.

On October 23, 2014, the company restated its first-half figures as a result of the initial investigation into the accounting errors. The estimated figure of £250 million was increased to a final figure of £263 million and was accompanied by the announcement of the resignation of the company chairman, Sir Richard Broadbent. In response to an admission that the practices that led to the overstatement had been going on for over a year, CEO Lewis said, "Three immediate priorities are clear: to recover our competitiveness in the UK, to protect and strengthen our balance sheet and to begin the long journey back to building trust and transparency into our business and brand."

A statement within Tesco's results for its Annual General Meeting in May 2015 summarized the industrywide implications for the accounting scandal. The disclosure of the overstatement of profits in 2014 had prompted the departure of PwC as Tesco's auditor; an ongoing investigation by the FCA as to whether the company broke rules on accurate financial disclosure; an ongoing investigation by the Serious Fraud Office (SFO) and an investigation by the Groceries Code Adjudicator, the supermarket industry regulator in the UK, into Tesco's treatment of suppliers.

The involvement of the SFO leaves Tesco exposed to fines of an estimated £350 million (1 percent of its UK grocery sales), in addition to potential repayments of hundreds of millions of pounds to suppliers if any evidence of inappropriate conduct through "arbitrary unjustified cash payments" is uncovered.

Concerns over complex supplier arrangements between retailers and food, drink, and consumer goods manufacturers prompted the Financial Reporting Council (FRC), the UK's auditing and accountancy watchdog organization, to announce that such arrangements would be getting special attention in the 2015/2016 financial year. The retail audits will be separate from previously announced investigations into PwC's audits going as far back as 2012.

For Tesco, there is some hope that in return for its full cooperation with the SFO, it may be able to negotiate a "deferred prosecution agreement" (DPA)—a deal that requires high court approval—to avoid criminal prosecution. A DPA deal would not protect individuals who might still face criminal charges as a result of their actions within their roles in the company.

In September 2016, the SFO announced that charges for fraud would be brought against three Tesco directors—Christopher Bush, managing director of Tesco UK, Carl Rogberg, UK finance director, and John Scouler, food director. Each was charged with fraud by abuse of position and fraud by false accounting which could result in prison sentences of up to ten years and seven years respectively.

QUESTIONS

1. In what way does this scandal demonstrate a lack of corporate governance on Tesco's part?
2. Were the actions taken by newly appointed chief executive Dave Lewis sufficient to address that lack of governance? Explain.
3. Does the fact that the actions that led to the overstatement of profits had been going on for over a year make the lack of governance any worse? Why or why not?
4. Does PwC bear some responsibility here? Why or why not?
5. Lewis identified three immediate priorities in turning the Tesco situation around. What are they and will they be enough? Explain.
6. What else should Tesco do to restore investor confidence in their business ethics?

Sources: "Tesco: Very Little Helps," *The Economist*, April 25, 2015; Sean Farrell, "Tesco Suspends Senior Staff and Starts Investigation into Overstated Profits," *The Guardian,* September 22, 2014; Sean Farrell, "Tesco to Be Investigated by FCA over Accounting Scandal," *The Guardian,* October 1, 2014; Geoffrey Smith, "Tesco Chairman Resigns after $420 Million Accounting Scandal," *Fortune,* October 23, 2014; Sarah Butler, "Accountancy Watchdog to Focus on Suppliers after Tesco Profit Scandal," *The Guardian,* May 28, 2015; Graham Ruddick, "Tesco Could Be Fined £500m over Accounting Scandal, Say Analysts," *The Guardian,* January 25, 2016; and Ashley Armstrong, "Former Tesco bosses face 10 years in jail if found guilty of SFO fraud charges," *The Telegraph,* September 9, 2016.

Thinking Critically 5.2

>> SOCGEN

In 1995, Barings Bank PLC, which proudly boasted of its position as banker to the Queen of England, collapsed after announcing trading losses of £827 million. The majority of those losses (greater than $1 billion) were attributed to one trader, Nick Leeson, who had been promoted from a back-office clerical role to a position as a futures trader. Leeson had used his knowledge of back-office procedures to hide the size of the trades he was placing on the Japanese stock market. The reward for his efforts was a six-year jail sentence. Fortunately, Barings clients were in no danger because the losses involved only Barings' own trading accounts. The Dutch bank Internationale Nederland Groep NV (ING) subsequently purchased the assets of the collapsed bank.

In January 2008, history repeated itself on a much grander scale when Société Générale (SocGen), one of France's largest banks, revealed that a rogue trader, Jérôme Kerviel, had placed a series of bad bets on European futures to the tune of a €4.9 billion ($6.9 billion) loss for SocGen.

© Photodisc/Getty Images RF

CONTINUED >>

Kerviel's activities sent a shock wave through world financial markets that were already reeling from large trading losses from the U.S. mortgage crisis, not only because of the sheer size of SocGen's losses that were allegedly attributable to one trader but also because of the apparent lack of controls in place over transactions amounting to billions of dollars.

Investigations into the exact methods by which Kerviel was able to conceal his activities revealed significant gaps in both SocGen's risk management systems (the extent to which the bank is exposed to risky trades) and financial controls (the functional department responsible for ensuring that all trades—purchases and sales—are balanced at the end of a trading period):

- How could an inexperienced midlevel trader earning a modest €100,000 a year (a low salary by the standards of his fellow traders) be allowed to run up a trading position with a risk exposure to the bank of as much as €50 billion?
- Investigations revealed that Kerviel had been engaging in unauthorized trades since 2005 and that the European exchange on which he placed those trades had raised concerns about his activities in November 2007. Some suggested that the profits Kerviel's trading activity for that year earned—€55 million ($81 million)—factored into SocGen's decision not to investigate Kerviel's activities in any detail.
- Kerviel's profits in 2007 appeared to convince him that he had discovered a new and highly lucrative system for futures trading. Investigators could find no other motive for his actions than simply a desire to increase his remuneration at the bank through a year-end bonus for strong financial performance. They found no evidence of any intent to embezzle funds, and they noted an apparently naive belief in his trading skills.
- While there were changes in personnel in the aftermath of the disastrous trading activities, including the head of the equity futures division and the head of information technology, the board of directors of SocGen refused to accept the resignation of CEO Daniel Bouton, and he, in turn, declined to accept the resignation of Jean-Pierre Mustier, the chief executive of SocGen's corporate and investment banking division.
- Critics of SocGen's leadership team argued that a takeover of the bank would be the inevitable outcome of this event. One analyst was quoted as stating: "The management has lost its credibility and that is the first barrier to any takeover bid. There is likely to be a lot of interest from around Europe."
- Kerviel was arrested at the end of January and charged with breach of trust, falsifying and using falsified documents, and breaching IT control access codes.
- In contrast, Kerviel has also become something of an Internet celebrity, with many French sites hailing him as a modern-day Robin Hood or the Che Guevara of finance. One enterprising web merchant quickly produced a range of T-shirts in support of Kerviel, including one that reads "Jérôme Kerviel's girlfriend," and another that reads, "Jérôme Kerviel, €4,900,000,000, Respect."
- SocGen's biggest rival in France, BNP Paribas, had tried unsuccessfully to acquire SocGen in 1999 in a hostile takeover bid. The rival was, therefore, the most logical choice to come after SocGen in such an obvious moment of defenselessness. However, after considering the option of another takeover bid, BNP chose not to pursue the opportunity. SocGen avoided the same fate as Barings Bank by raising an $8 billion rescue fund from private equity investors.

SocGen's clear lack of risk management and financial controls inevitably caught the attention of France's finance minister, Christine Lagarde. Her initial report on the incident, produced within eight days of the event while many simultaneous investigations were still ongoing, raised several key questions including the ease with which Kerviel appeared to avoid detection, even though his trades amounted to billions of dollars, the extent to which the losses caused broader market problems, and what needed to be done to ensure the event never happened again. Her report ended with a call on the French government to give more power to punish those who fail to follow established best practices.

On October 5, 2010, a French court found Kerviel guilty of all charges and sentenced him to five years in jail (with two years of the sentence suspended for time already served). Kerviel was also ordered to repay the €4.9 billion ($6.9 billion) he lost for SocGen. While the company clarified that it had no intention of pursuing Kerviel for the money, the repayment order served a dual purpose—to repudiate Kerviel's defense that SocGen knew about his activities and "looked the other way" as long as those trades were profitable and, more importantly, to strengthen SocGen's defense against future shareholder lawsuits questioning SocGen's governance practices. Kerviel appealed the court's decision.

In October 2012, after a four-week trial in June 2012, a Paris court dismissed his appeal and reiterated that "Jerome Kerviel was the sole creator, inventor, and user of a fraudulent system that caused these damages to Société Générale."

In March 2014, Kerviel lost his final appeal against his three-year sentence. After embarking on a long-distance walk from Paris to Rome and back again, including a meeting with Pope Francis at the Vatican, Kerviel announced that the journey was helping him, "to come to terms with his past and his future." However, while the French High Court upheld the sentence, it did order a review of the damage settlement of €4.9 billion ($6.3 billion) that Kerviel had been ordered to pay, arguing that the lower court had not taken into account SocGen's own responsibility in the case.

Kerviel was released from jail in September 2014 to serve the rest of his sentence under house arrest through the use of an ankle monitor. In June 2016, a French tribunal awarded Kerviel €450,000 for unfair dismissal from his position at SocGen. While the criminal case against him may be over, the new civil trial ordered by the High Court to revisit the damages amount is still ongoing.

QUESTIONS

1. Who are the stakeholders in this case?
2. What did Jérôme Kerviel do wrong?
3. What did SocGen do wrong?
4. Identify the ethical violations that occurred in this case.
5. Would the outcome have been different if Kerviel's trades in European futures had worked out?
6. What actions could SocGen have taken to prevent such large losses?

Sources: "Nick Leeson and Barings Bank," *BBC,* http://news.bbc.co.uk/2/hi/asia-pacific/385021.stm; Marcus W. Brauchli, Nicholas Bray, and Michael R. Sesit, "Barings PLC Officials May Have Been Aware of Trader's Position," *The Wall Street Journal,* March 6, 1995, pp. A1, A6; Nicholas Bray and Michael R. Sesit, "Barings Was Warned Controls Were Lax but Didn't Make Reforms in Singapore," *The Wall Street Journal,* March 2, 1995, p. A3; Paula Dwyer, William Glasgall, Dean Foust, and Greg Burns, "The Lessons from Barings' Straits," *BusinessWeek,* March 13, 1995, pp. 30–33; Alexander MacLeod, "Youthful Trader Sinks Britain's Oldest Bank," *The Christian Science Monitor,* February 28, 1995, pp. 1, 8; Peter Thal Larsen, "SocGen Rogue Trade: Six Sleepless Nights Reveal the Full Impact of Scandal," *Financial Times,* January 25, 2008, pp. 16–17; Martin Arnold and Lina Saigol, "Doubts Cast on Bouton's Position," *Financial Times,* January 25, 2008, p. 17; Pan Kwan Luk, "From 'le Rogue' to the Che of Our Times," *Financial Times,* January 31, 2008, p. 19; Peggy Hollinger, "Hard-Hitting Lagarde Points up SocGen's Lack of Control," *Financial Times,* February 5, 2008, p. 6; "All His Fault," *The Economist,* October 7, 2010; Henry Samuel, "Societe Generale Rogue Trader Jerome Kerviel Appeal Dismissed," *The Telegraph,* October 24, 2012; "French Rogue Trader Jerome Kerviel to Go to Jail," *BBC,* March 19, 2014; "Rogue Trader Jerome Kerviel Leaves French Jail," *BBC,* September 9, 2014; and Angelique Chrisafis, "Former trader Jérôme Kerviel wins unfair dismissal case," *The Guardian,* June 7, 2016.

Thinking Critically   `5.3`

>> VALEANT: THE PHARMACEUTICAL ENRON

The story arc of Valeant Pharmaceuticals will sound familiar to students of "boom and bust" business cases. Once a Wall Street darling, Valeant's shares traded as high as $262 per share in August 2015 as the company pursued an aggressive strategy of growth by acquisition, bringing new drugs into the fold without the often profit-draining expense of research and development (R&D). Company Chief Executive Michael Pearson became a star, and the doors to top-tier investors such as hedge fund big shot Bill Ackman of Pershing Square Capital Management and Robert Goldfarb of the Sequoia Fund were soon opened.

By March 18, 2016, Valeant shares were trading at only $27 with every expectation that they would fall even lower amid allegations of predatory pricing of its drugs to boost revenue, and improper accounting procedures that were used to artificially inflate the financial stability of the company. How did everything go so wrong, so quickly, under the oversight of such experienced investors?

CAUGHT IN THE CROSSFIRE

When Turing Pharmaceuticals CEO and former hedge-fund manager Martin Shkreli announced that the company would be raising the price of its Daraprim drug by over 5,000 percent less than one month after being acquired, media attention toward pharmacy pricing models took center stage. Valeant, which had acquired two commonly used heart drugs, Isuprel and Nitropress, in 2015 and proceeded to raise their prices by 525 percent and 212 percent, respectively, was quickly caught up in that media circus. A study by Deutsche Bank, released less than a week later, revealed that Valeant had actually raised prices on 54 other medications in 2015 alone by an average of 66 percent, which was far higher than the rest of the industry.

CONTINUED >>

© Bloomberg/Getty Images

Bill Ackman, Howard Schiller, and Mike Pearson swear in to a Senate Special Committee on Aging hearing on Valeant Pharmaceuticals.

This followed an equally aggressive strategy in 2014 of raising prices on 62 drugs by an average of 50 percent. The biggest increase in 2015 was for Glumetza that rose from $896 for 90 tablets in January 2013 to $10,020 for the same 90 tablets on July 31, 2015, an increase of over 1,100 percent.

Bill Ackman from Pershing Square Capital Management defended Valeant's strategy, arguing that the increased revenues would support future R&D, but his support did nothing to prevent Valeant from receiving a federal subpoena to explain its drug pricing strategy. In a conference call with Wall Street analysts later in October 2015, CEO Pearson stated that the company would adjust its clearly unpopular strategy of buying companies solely to leverage underpriced drugs in their portfolio.

PHILIDOR

The declining share prices of pharmaceutical companies in response to increased federal scrutiny over their pricing models had by now drawn the attention of short-sellers (investors who speculate that the share prices of targeted companies will continue to fall). Bronte Capital, a hedge fund managed by Australian John Hempton, catalyzed interest in Valeant's shares with a cryptic post featuring a clip from the Mike Nichols' movie *The Graduate* in which the star, Dustin Hoffman, is given advice about his future with one word: plastics. In the Bronte Capital post, that one word was Philidor. No other explanation was offered.

Less than a week later, a report from the Southern Investigative Reporting Foundation revealed that R&O Pharmacy, a specialty pharmacy, was suing Valeant in relation to a $69.8 million demand for "invoiced amounts" from Valeant's general counsel, Robert Chai-Onn. Since R&O had never done business with Valeant, nor ever received an erroneous invoice from the company, the owners of R&O filed suit for a determination that they owed nothing to Valeant. Further due diligence revealed that R&O was doing business with a company called Philidor, based outside of Philadelphia, that was listed as a "pharmacy administrator" with Valeant as its only client. While Philidor appeared to be controlled by Valeant through numerous ownership structures, it had never been mentioned in Valeant's financial disclosures beyond a notation that 40 percent of its revenues were generated through "specialty pharmacies" that managed the filling, shipping, and insurance approval for many of the more complex drugs that Valeant manufactured.

With limited access to corporate information, and a highly convoluted ownership structure for Philidor, R&O's lawsuit raised the concern that Valeant was either the target of fraudulent action from Philidor, or was actively participating in that fraud. A follow-up report by Citron Research, run by short-seller Andrew Left, uncovered more information about Philidor and made a direct accusation of fraud toward Valeant, comparing the company to Enron, referencing the practice of booking revenue before sales had actually been completed. CEO Pearson disclosed in response that Valeant had an option to acquire Philidor but dismissed Left's claims as "erroneous." The subsequent 39 percent fall in Valeant's share price was indicative of the market's lack of confidence in that response.

An October 25, 2015, *Wall Street Journal* article revealed that the operations of Valeant and Philidor were far more intertwined than Pearson was willing to admit, mentioning that Valeant employees used fake aliases from comic book characters, such as Peter Parker, to hide their true identities. In addition rumors began to surface that Philidor was involved in changing prescriptions from generics to Valeant's higher-priced drugs. The company denied the allegations but announced that the pharmacy would shut down immediately.

Bill Ackman came to Valeant's defense again at the end of October, hosting a four-hour conference call with analysts and Pershing Square investors to reassure them that despite the company's short-term legal problems, the long term remained positive. He predicted a doubling of the share price, but the response from the market was a further 16 percent fall.

News of a 20-year deal with Walgreens Boots Alliance that Valeant claimed would save the U.S. health care system as much as $600 million per year did nothing to change the skepticism of investors, especially when Valeant announced the next day that profits in the fourth quarter of 2015 would be impacted by charges related to Philidor.

Pearson announced at the end of 2015 that he was battling pneumonia and that he would be taking a medical leave of absence. Valeant would be run by a team of executives under an "office of the Chief Executive" created by the board of directors, and led by former Chief Financial Officer Howard Schiller as interim CEO.

CIRCULAR FIRING SQUAD

On February 22, 2016, the company announced that it would be restating its financials for 2014 and 2015, citing the same revenue recognition tactics that Citron Research had used in making the comparison to Enron. In the following week, Valeant announced the return of Pearson from medical leave, the withdrawal of its 2016 financial guidance, and the disclosure that the company was under investigation by the Securities and Exchange Commission (SEC).

Bill Ackman, who had continued to buy shares in Valeant, believing them to be a bargain at such depressed prices, stepped forward yet again to restate his confidence in the company. In an interview with CNBC, he stated: "We expect much of the uncertainty will be resolved in the relative short term, hopefully over the next few weeks." His confidence appeared to last about a week, when he told an investor conference that Valeant would probably need a new management team one day before announcing he would be joining the Valeant board along with two other new directors.

On March 21, 2016, Valeant announced that Michael Pearson, the chief executive who had led the company through $35 billion in acquisition deals, financed mostly with debt, was leaving the company. With a compensation package of $55 million since 2012, an estimated $75 billion loss in shareholder value, and a track record of questionable acquisitions and accounting problems, he is likely to remain a focus of the business media for a while. Ex-CFO Howard Schiller was also asked to resign as part of what some analysts called a "circular firing squad," but he refused, saying that he had done nothing wrong.

Two days later, Robert Goldfarb, longtime leader of the Sequoia Fund, announced he would be stepping down. After allowing an investment in Valeant to grow as high as 30 percent of Sequoia's portfolio, the $5.6 billion fund had lost 10.9 percent in the first quarter of 2016, underperforming 98 percent of its peers. Ironically, shares of Valeant climbed 24 percent on the announcements of both departures, but with multiple federal investigations ahead, the road to recovery will probably be a very long one.

QUESTIONS

1. Identify three examples of poor corporate governance in this case.
2. Why do you think Bill Ackman has remained so supportive of Valeant?
3. Critics have described the Valeant board of directors as weak. Is that a fair assessment? Why or why not?
4. Is the release of negative research information by a company that is actively shorting the shares of that company an unethical business practice? Why or why not?
5. Does the fact that Citron Research was proven right in its accusations about Valeant validate its short-selling tactics?
6. How can the newly staffed board of directors begin to restore investor confidence in Valeant?

Sources: Laura Lorenzetti, "Biotech Stocks Dive as Lawmakers Take Aim at Valeant for Drug Price Hikes," *Fortune,* September 28, 2015; Cary Helfand, "Valeant's Price-Hike Strategy Goes Far beyond Two High-Profile Increases," *FiercePharma,* October 5, 2015; Roddy Boyd, "The King's Gambit: Valeant's Big Secret," *Southern Investigative Reporting Foundation,* October 19, 2015; Andrew Left, "Valeant: Could This Be the Pharmaceutical Enron?" *Citron Research,* October 21, 2015; Jonathan D. Rockoff and Jeanne Whalen, "Valeant and Pharmacy More Intertwined Than Thought," *The Wall Street Journal,* October 25, 2015; Lucinda Shen, "Bill Ackman Says Valeant Will Be Fine," *Fortune,* March 1, 2016; "He Who Would Valeant Be: Lessons from a Drug Firm's Disaster," *The Economist,* March 19, 2016; Stephen Gandel, "What Caused Valeant's Epic 90% Plunge," *Fortune,* March 20, 2016; Cynthia Koons, "Valeant's 'Circular Firing Squad' Claims CEO Pearson," *Bloomberg,* March 21, 2016; and Sarah Krouse and Daisy Maxey, "Leader of Valeant Investor Sequoia Resigns," *The Wall Street Journal,* March 23, 2016.

[References]

1. Organization for Economic Co-operation and Development (OECD) Principles of Corporate Governance, 2004, www.oecd.org/daf/corporate/principles.

2. Cadbury Report, "The Financial Aspects of Corporate Governance," December 1992.

3. Michael Barrier, internal auditor, "Principles, not Rules," August 2003, www.theiia.org.

4. Tricia Bisoux, "In Pursuit of Good Governance," and "What IS Good Governance?" *BizEd,* March–April 2004.

5. Cliffe Dekker, 2003, "King Report on Corporate Governance for South Africa 2002: What It Means to You," www.cliffedekker-hofmeyr.com/.

6. Ibid.

7. Yilmaz Argüden, "Measuring the Effectiveness of Corporate Governance," *INSEAD Knowledge,* April 16, 2010.

8. Walter J. Salmon, "Crisis Prevention: How to Gear Up Your Board," *Harvard Business Review,* January–February 1993.

9. International Finance Corp., World Bank Group, "The Irresistible Case for Corporate Governance," September 2005, www.gcgf.org/.

10. Ronald Berenbeim, "Giving Ethics Operational Meaning in Corporate Governance," *Executive Speeches* 19, no. 5 (April–May 2005), p. 19.

11. "Corporate Governance Mom: Nell Minow," *The Economist,* April 10, 2003.

12. Cadbury Report, "The Financial Aspects of Corporate Governance," December 1992.

13. Yilmaz Argüden, "Measuring the Effectiveness of Corporate Governance," INSEAD Knowledge, April 16, 2010.

CHAPTER 6

© John Atkins/Corbis RF

THE ROLE OF
GOVERNMENT

After studying this chapter, you should be able to:

6-1 Identify the five key pieces of U.S. legislation designed to discourage, if not prevent, illegal conduct within organizations.

6-2 Understand the purpose and significance of the Foreign Corrupt Practices Act (FCPA).

6-3 Calculate monetary fines under the three-step process of the U.S. Federal Sentencing Guidelines for Organizations (FSGO).

6-4 Compare and contrast the relative advantages and disadvantages of the Sarbanes-Oxley Act (SOX).

6-5 Explain the key provisions of the Dodd-Frank Wall Street Reform and Consumer Protection Act.

FRONTLINE FOCUS

Too Much Trouble

Susan is a junior accounting assistant with one of the largest auditing firms in the Midwest. Since the Enron fraud case and the passing of the Sarbanes-Oxley Act, her company has been very busy—in fact, it has so much business, it is starting to turn clients down.

For Susan, so much business means great opportunities. Each completed audit takes her one step closer to running her own auditing team and finally to leading her own audit. The work is hard and the hours are often long, but Susan loves the attention to detail and the excitement of discovering errors and then getting them corrected. Also, knowing that the clients are releasing financial reports that are clean and accurate makes her feel that she is doing her part to restore the reputation of the financial markets one client at a time.

One morning, her boss, Steven Thompson, comes into her office carrying a thick manila folder. "Hi, Susan, what are you working on right now?" he asks.

Typical Thompson, Susan thinks. *Straight to the point with no time for small talk.*

"We should be finished with the Jones audit by the end of the day. Why?" Susan replied.

"I need a small favor," Steven continued. "We've had this new small-business client show up out of the blue after being dropped by his previous auditor. It really couldn't have happened at a worse time. We've got so many large audits in the pipeline that I can't spare anyone to work on this, but I don't want to start turning business away in case word gets out that we're not keeping up with a growing client base—who knows when the next big fish will come along?"

"I'm not sure I follow you, Steven," answered Susan, confused.

"I don't want to turn this guy away, but we don't want his business either—too small to be a real moneymaker. So just take a quick look at his file, and then quote him a price for our services—and here's where I need the favor. Make the quote high enough that he will want to go somewhere else. Can you do that?"

QUESTIONS

1. The Sarbanes-Oxley Act created an oversight board for all auditing firms. Look at the outline of the act, presented later in the chapter, for more information on the Public Company Accounting Oversight Board (PCAOB). Would the PCAOB endorse trying to dump a prospective client in this manner?
2. Is being too busy with other clients a justification for deliberately driving this customer away?
3. What should Susan do now?

> People who enjoy eating sausage and obey the law should not watch either being made.
>
> **Otto von Bismarck (1815–1898), chancellor of Germany**

>> Key Legislation

For those organizations that have demonstrated they are unable to keep their own house in order by maintaining a strong ethical culture, the last line of defense has been a legal and regulatory framework that offers financial incentives to promote ethical behavior and imposes penalties for those that choose not to adopt such behavior. Since the 1970s, there have been several attempts at behavior modification to discourage, if not prevent, illegal conduct within organizations:

- The Foreign Corrupt Practices Act (1977).
- The U.S. Federal Sentencing Guidelines for Organizations (1991).
- The Sarbanes-Oxley Act (2002).
- The Revised Federal Sentencing Guidelines for Organizations (2004).
- The Dodd-Frank Wall Street Reform and Consumer Protection Act (2010).

>> The Foreign Corrupt Practices Act (1977)

Foreign Corrupt Practices Act (FCPA) Legislation introduced to control bribery and other less obvious forms of payment to foreign officials and politicians by American publicly traded companies.

Disclosure (FCPA) The FCPA requirement that corporations fully disclose any and all transactions conducted with foreign officials and politicians.

Prohibition (FCPA) The FCPA inclusion of wording from the Bank Secrecy Act and the Mail Fraud Act to prevent the movement of funds overseas for the express purpose of conducting a fraudulent scheme.

Facilitation Payments (FCPA) Payments that are acceptable (legal) provided they expedite or secure the performance of a routine governmental action.

Routine Governmental Action (FCPA) Any regular administrative process or procedure, excluding any action taken by a foreign official in the decision to award new or continuing business.

The **Foreign Corrupt Practices Act (FCPA)** was introduced to more effectively control bribery and other less obvious forms of payment to foreign officials and politicians by American publicly traded companies as they pursued international growth. Before passage of this law, the illegality of this behavior was punishable only through "secondary" sources of legislation:

1. The Securities and Exchange Commission (SEC) could fine companies for failing to disclose such payments under its securities rules.
2. The Bank Secrecy Act also required full disclosure of funds that were taken out of or brought into the United States.

3. The Mail Fraud Act made the use of the U.S. mail or wire communications to transact a fraudulent scheme illegal.

By passing the FCPA, Congress was attempting to send a clear message that the competitiveness of U.S. corporations in overseas markets should be based on price and product quality rather than the extent to which companies had paid off foreign officials and political leaders. To give the legislation some weight, the U.S. Department of Justice (DOJ) and the SEC jointly enforce the FCPA.

The act encompasses all the secondary measures that were currently in use to prohibit such behavior by focusing on two distinct areas:

- **Disclosure:** The act requires corporations to fully disclose any and all transactions conducted with foreign officials and politicians, in line with the SEC provisions.
- **Prohibition:** The act includes wording from the Bank Secrecy Act and the Mail Fraud Act to prevent the movement of funds overseas for the express purpose of conducting a fraudulent scheme.

A BARK WORSE THAN ITS BITE

Even with the apparent success of consolidating three pieces of secondary legislation into one primary tool for the prohibition of bribery, the FCPA was still criticized for lacking any real teeth because of its formal recognition of **facilitation payments**, which would otherwise be acknowledged as bribes. The FCPA finds these payments acceptable provided they expedite or secure the performance of a **routine governmental action**.

Examples of routine governmental actions include:

- Providing permits, licenses, or other official documents to qualify a person to do business in a foreign country.
- Processing governmental papers, such as visas and work orders.
- Providing police protection, mail pickup and delivery, or scheduling inspections associated with contract performance or inspections related to transit of goods across a country.
- Providing phone service, power, and water supply; loading and unloading cargo; or protecting perishable products or commodities from deterioration.
- Performing actions of a similar nature.

The key distinction in identifying bribes was the exclusion of any action taken by a foreign official in the decision to award new or continuing business. Such decisions, being the primary target of most questionable payments, were not deemed to be routine governmental action.[1]

FCPA IN ACTION

Alstom According to the December 22, 2014, edition of *The New York Times,* French industrial giant Alstom paid $772 million in criminal penalties to settle bribery charges brought by the U.S. Department of Justice. The company was alleged to have paid more than $75 million from 2000 to 2011 to secure $4 billion in engineering projects around the world that led to profits of over $300 million. While Alstom had agreed to sell most of its engineering business to General Electric (GE) for €12.4 billion in June 2014, the DOJ settlement required that Alstom, and not GE, would have to pay the fine.[2]

BNY Mellon According to the August 18, 2015, *FCPA Blog,* BNY Mellon agreed to pay $14.8 million to settle charges brought by the SEC that the company had violated FCPA rules. Between 2010 and 2011,

© James Hardy/PhotoAlto RF

BNY was alleged to have provided valuable student internships to family members of foreign government officials that were directly linked to a Middle Eastern sovereign wealth fund. The case was settled through an internal administrative order with no admission or denial of liability by BNY Mellon. The settlement amount was calculated based on a $5 million penalty, $1.5 million in interest, and $8.3 million in *disgorgement* (designated repayment of ill-gotten gains).[3]

MAKING SENSE OF FCPA

Figure 6.1 summarizes the fine lines between legality and illegality in some of the prohibited behaviors and approved exceptions in the FCPA provisions.

The Department of Justice can enforce criminal penalties of up to $2 million per violation for corporations and other business entities. Officers, directors, stockholders, employees, and agents are subject to a fine of up to $250,000 per violation and imprisonment for up to five years. The SEC may bring a civil fine of up to $10,000 per violation. Penalties under the books and record-keeping provisions can reach up to $5 million and 20 years' imprisonment for individuals and up to $25 million for organizations.

Key Point

If you pay money to a government official to expedite the processing of permits, licenses, or other official documents over and above the normal processing time, how is that not a bribe? Is the distinction between "normal operations" and "new or continuing business" a valid one?

PROGRESS ✔ QUESTIONS

1. What was the primary purpose of the FCPA?
2. What was the maximum fine for a U.S. corporation under the FCPA?
3. Which two distinct areas did the FCPA focus on?
4. List four examples of routine governmental actions.

FIG.6.1 **Illegal versus Legal Behaviors under the FCPA**

Illegal	Legal
Bribes: • Payments of money or anything else of value to influence or induce any foreign official to act in a manner that would be in violation of his or her lawful duty. • Payments, authorizations, promises, or offers to any other person if there is knowledge that any portion of the payment is to be passed along to a foreign official or foreign political party, official, or candidate for a prohibited purpose under the act. Note that knowledge is defined very broadly and is present when one knows an event is certain or likely to occur; even purposely failing to take note of an event or being willfully blind can constitute knowledge.	Grease payments: • Facilitating payments to foreign officials in order to expedite or secure the performance of a routine governmental action. For example, routine governmental action could include obtaining permits, licenses, or other official documents; expediting lawful customs clearances; obtaining the issuance of entry or exit visas; providing police protection, mail pickup and delivery, and phone service; and performing actions that are wholly unconnected to the award of new business or the continuation of prior business.
Record-keeping and accounting provisions: • Books, records, and accounts must be kept in reasonable detail to accurately and fairly reflect transactions and dispositions of assets. • A system of internal accounting controls is devised to provide reasonable assurances that transactions are executed in accordance with management's authorization.	Marketing expenses: • Payments to foreign officials made in connection with the promotion or demonstration of company products or services (e.g., demonstration or tour of a pharmaceutical plant) or in connection with the execution of a particular contract with a foreign government.
	Payments lawful under foreign laws: • Payments may (very rarely) be made to foreign officials when the payment is "lawful under the written laws of the foreign country."
	Political contributions: • Unlike in the United States, where foreign nationals are prohibited from making political contributions to U.S. political parties and candidates, it may occasionally be appropriate for a U.S. company's overseas operations to make a political contribution on behalf of the company. Contributions not only include checks to political parties or candidates, but also payments for fund-raising dinners and similar events. This would be an example of a payment that could violate the FCPA were it not for written local law. Donations to foreign charities: • U.S. companies may make donations to bona fide charitable organizations provided that the donation will not be used to circumvent the FCPA and that the contribution does not violate local laws, rules, or regulations.

>> The U.S. Federal Sentencing Guidelines for Organizations (1991)

The U.S. Federal Sentencing Commission was established in 1984 by the Comprehensive Crime Control Act and was charged with developing uniform sentencing guidelines for offenders convicted of federal crimes. The guidelines became effective on November 1, 1987. At that time, they consisted of seven chapters and applied only to individuals convicted of federal offenses.

In 1991, an eighth chapter was added to the guidelines. Chapter 8 is more commonly referred to as the **Federal**

Federal Sentencing Guidelines for Organizations (FSGO) Chapter 8 of the guidelines that hold businesses liable for the criminal acts of their employees and agents.

Sentencing Guidelines for Organizations (FSGO). It applies to organizations and holds them liable for the criminal acts of their employees and agents.

FSGO requires that organizations police themselves by preventing and detecting the criminal activity of their employees and agents.

In its mission to promote ethical organizational behavior and increase the costs of unethical behavior, the FSGO establishes a definition of an organization that is so broad as to prompt the assessment that "no business enterprise is exempt." In addition, the FSGO includes such an exhaustive list of covered business crimes that it appears frighteningly easy for an organization to run afoul of federal crime laws and become subject to FSGO penalties.

Penalties under FSGO include monetary fines, organizational probation, and the implementation of an operational program to bring the organization into compliance with FSGO standards.

MONETARY FINES UNDER THE FSGO

If an organization is sentenced under FSGO, a fine is calculated through a three-step process:

Step 1. *Determination of the "Base Fine."* The base fine will normally be the greatest of:

- The monetary gain to the organization from the offense.
- The monetary loss from the offense caused by the organization, to the extent the loss was caused knowingly, intentionally, or recklessly.
- The amount determined by a judge based on an FSGO table.

The table factors in both the nature of the crime and the amount of the loss suffered by the victim. Fraud, for example, is a level-six offense; a fraud causing harm in excess of $5 million is increased by 14 levels to a level-20 offense. Evidence of extensive preplanning to commit the offense can raise that two more levels to level 22. To put these levels in dollar terms, crimes at level six or lower involve a base fine of $5,000; offense levels of 38 or higher involve a base fine of $72.5 million.

Step 2. *The Culpability Score.* Once the base fine has been calculated, the judge will compute a corresponding degree of blame or guilt known as the **culpability score**. This score is simply a multiplier with a maximum of 4, so the worst-case scenario would be a fine of four times the maximum base fine of $72.5 million, for a grand total of $290 million. The culpability score can be increased (or aggravated) or decreased (or mitigated) according to predetermined factors.

Aggravating Factors

- High-level personnel were involved in or tolerated the criminal activity.
- The organization willfully obstructed justice.
- The organization had a prior history of similar misconduct.
- The current offense violated a judicial order, an injunction, or a condition of probation.

Mitigating Factors

- The organization had an effective program to prevent and detect violations of law.
- The organization self-reported the offense to appropriate governmental authorities, fully cooperated in the investigation, and accepted responsibility for the criminal conduct.

Step 3. *Determining the Total Fine Amount.* The base fine multiplied by the culpability score gives the total fine amount. In certain cases, however, the judge has the discretion to impose a so-called **death penalty**, where the fine is set high enough to match all the organization's assets. This is warranted where the organization was operating primarily for a criminal purpose.

> **Culpability Score (FSGO)** The calculation of a degree of blame or guilt that is used as a multiplier of up to four times the base fine. The culpability score can be adjusted according to aggravating or mitigating factors.
>
> **Death Penalty (FSGO)** A fine that is set high enough to match all the organization's assets—and basically put the organization out of business. This is warranted where the organization was operating primarily for a criminal purpose.

ORGANIZATIONAL PROBATION

In addition to monetary fines, organizations also can be sentenced to probation for up to five years. The status of probation can include the following requirements:

- Reporting the business's financial condition to the court on a periodic basis.
- Remaining subject to unannounced examinations of all financial records by a designated probation officer and/or court-appointed experts.
- Reporting progress in the implementation of a compliance program.
- Being subject to unannounced examinations to confirm that the compliance program is in place and is working.

COMPLIANCE PROGRAM

Obviously the best way to minimize your culpability score is to make sure that you have some form of program in place that can effectively detect and prevent violations of law—a compliance program. The FSGO prescribes seven steps for an effective compliance program:

1. *Management oversight.* A high-level official (such as a corporate ethics officer) must be in charge of and accountable for the compliance program.
2. *Corporate policies.* Policies and procedures designed to reduce the likelihood of criminal conduct in the organization must be in place.
3. *Communication of standards and procedures.* These ethics policies must be effectively communicated to every stakeholder of the organization.
4. *Compliance with standards and procedures.* Evidence of active implementation of these policies must be provided through appropriate monitoring and reporting (including a system for employees to

report suspected criminal conduct without fear of retribution).

5. *Delegation of substantial discretionary authority.* No individuals should be granted excessive discretionary authority that would increase the risk of criminal conduct.

6. *Consistent discipline.* The organization must implement penalties for criminal conduct and for failing to address criminal misconduct in a consistent manner.

7. *Response and corrective action.* Criminal offenses, whether actual or suspected, must generate an appropriate response, analysis, and corrective action.

If all of this seems like an enormous administrative burden, consider the following example: A $25,000 bribe has been paid to a city official to ensure an award of a cable television franchise. This is a level-18 offense with a base penalty of a $350,000 fine. Due to a variety of factors (e.g., culpability, multipliers), that penalty is now increased to $1.4 million.

The minimum fine with mitigating circumstances (e.g., the company has a compliance plan and there was no high-level involvement in the bribery) would have placed this fine in the $17,500 to $70,000 range instead of $1.4 million.

If that doesn't discourage you, consider the additional risk of negative publicity to your organization, which could result in a significant loss of sales, additional scrutiny from vendors, and even a drop in your stock price.[4]

PROGRESS ✓ QUESTIONS

5. What are the three steps in calculating financial penalties under FSGO?
6. What is the maximum fine that can be levied?
7. What is the maximum term of organizational probation?
8. What is the "death penalty" under FSGO?

 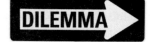

THE BRIBERY GAP

In 1997, 35 countries signed the convention of the Organization for Economic Cooperation and Development (OECD) to make it a crime to bribe foreign officials. In May 1999, the OECD issued a series of six principles (updated in 2004) that have since become the basis of the corporate governance position of the World Bank and the International Monetary Fund (IMF). However, in 2015 alone:

- In February 2015, Goodyear Tire and Rubber Co. agreed to pay $16.2 million to settle charges from the SEC under FCPA for the payment of bribes in Kenya and Angola to increase tire sales. Goodyear subsidiaries were accused of paying more than $3.2 million in bribes to employees of state-owned and private companies between 2007 and 2011.
- In May 2015, BHP Billiton paid $25 million to settle SEC charges in relation to FCPA offenses. BHP had been accused of improperly sponsoring foreign government officials as guests at the 2008 Summer Olympics in Beijing, China. The case was settled through an internal administrative order without going to court.
- In July 2015, New Jersey-based construction management company Louis Berger International paid $17.1 million to resolve FCPA criminal offenses. In the resolution, the company admitted paying bribes to foreign officials in India, Indonesia, Kuwait, and Vietnam in order to win contracts. The settlement included a deferred prosecution agreement that will require a compliance monitor for at least three years.
- In September 2015, Hitachi Ltd. paid $19 million to resolve SEC charges. The case was brought in relation to payments made to South Africa's ruling

© Charles Gullung/zefa/Corbis RF

political party in connection with contracts to build two multimillion-dollar power plants.

American companies operating under increasing federal and regulatory scrutiny face real consequences from trying to do business in a global business environment in which foreign business seems to function on the basis of "gifts" at every stage of the transaction.

- In December 2012, the SEC charged Eli Lilly and Co. with violations of the FCPA for improper payments made by subsidiaries to foreign government officials in Russia, Brazil, China, and Poland; and accepted a settlement in the amount of $29 million for offenses including the following:

  The SEC alleged that the Indianapolis-based pharmaceutical company's subsidiary in Russia used offshore 'marketing agreements' to pay millions of dollars to third parties chosen by government customers or distributors, despite knowing little or nothing about the third parties beyond their offshore address and bank account information.

  Employees at Lilly's subsidiary in China falsified expense reports in order to provide spa treatments, jewelry, and other improper gifts and cash payments to government-employed physicians.

  Lilly's subsidiary in Poland made eight improper payments totaling $39,000 to a small charitable foundation that was founded and administered by the head of one of the regional government health authorities in exchange for the official's support for placing Lilly drugs on the government reimbursement list.

In November 2012, the Department of Justice issued a 120-page "Resource Guide" to the FCPA, including numerous case studies designed to clarify what actions would and would not be considered to be violations of the law. The guide was written as a resource for DOJ attorneys, but attorneys in private practice are encouraging their clients to become familiar with it.

QUESTIONS

1. Is it ethical for U.S. regulations to put U.S. companies at an apparent disadvantage to their foreign competitors? Explain why or why not.
2. If foreign companies pay bribes, does that make it OK for U.S. companies to do the same? Explain why or why not.
3. If you could prove that new jobs, new construction, and valuable tax revenue would come to the United States if the bribe were paid, would that change your position? Explain your answer.
4. It would seem that the playing field will never be level—someone will always be looking for a bribe, and someone will always be willing to pay it if she or he wants the business badly enough. If that's true, why bother to put legislation in place at all?

Sources: Richard L. Cassin, "The 2015 FCPA Enforcement Index," *The FCPA Blog,* January 4, 2016; Erin Fuchs, "Pfizer Admits to Bribing Foreign Officials and Agrees to Fork Over $60 Million," *Businessinsider.com,* August 7, 2012; U.S. Securities and Exchange Commission, Press Release 2012-273, December 20, 2012; and Charlie Savage, "Justice Department Issues Guidance on Overseas Bribes," *The New York Times,* November 14, 2012.

REVISED FEDERAL SENTENCING GUIDELINES FOR ORGANIZATIONS (2004)

In May 2004, the U.S. Sentencing Commission proposed to Congress that there should be modifications to the 1991 guidelines to bring about key changes in corporate compliance programs. The revised guidelines, which Congress formally adopted in November 2004, made three key changes:

- They required companies to periodically evaluate the effectiveness of their compliance programs on the assumption of a substantial risk that any program is capable of failing. They also expected the results of these risk assessments to be incorporated back into the next version of the compliance program.
- The revised guidelines required evidence of actively promoting ethical conduct rather than

just complying with legal obligations. For the first time, the concept of an ethical culture was recognized as a foundational component of an effective compliance program.

- The guidelines defined accountability more clearly. Corporate officers are expected to be knowledgeable about all aspects of the compliance program, and they are required to receive formal training as it relates to their roles and responsibilities within the organization.

> **Key Point !**
>
> The multiplication of a base fine amount by a culpability score under FSGO has the potential to generate fines in the hundreds of millions of dollars. Do you think that knowledge will prompt organizations to reconsider their unethical practices? Why or why not?

PROGRESS ✓ QUESTIONS

9. Explain the seven steps of an effective compliance program.

10. What are *aggravating* and *mitigating* factors?

11. Explain the risk assessments required in the 2004 revised FSGO.

12. What were the three key components of the 2004 revised FSGO?

>> The Sarbanes-Oxley Act (2002)

The **Sarbanes-Oxley Act (SOX)** became law on July 30, 2003.[5] It was a legislative response to a series of corporate accounting scandals that had begun to dominate the financial markets and mass media since 2001.

Sarbanes-Oxley Act (SOX) A legislative response to the corporate accounting scandals of the early 2000s that covers the financial management of businesses.

Public Company Accounting Oversight Board (PCAOB) An independent oversight body for auditing companies.

Launched during a period of extreme investor unrest and agitation, SOX was hailed by some as "one of the most important pieces of legislation governing the behavior of accounting firms and financial markets since [the SEC] legislation in the 1930s."

However, supporters of this law were equally matched by its critics, leaving no doubt that SOX may be regarded as one of the most controversial pieces of corporate legislation in recent history.

The act contains 11 sections, or titles, and almost 70 subsections covering every aspect of the financial management of businesses. Each of the 11 sections can be seen to relate directly to prominent examples of corporate wrongdoing that preceded the establishment of the legislation—the Enron scandal in particular.

TITLE I: PUBLIC COMPANY ACCOUNTING OVERSIGHT BOARD

The series of financial collapses of publicly traded companies that the financial community had previously recommended as "strong buys" or "Wall Street darlings" had the greatest negative impact on investor confidence—especially since the accounts of all these companies had supposedly been audited as accurate by established and highly regarded auditing firms.

The creation of the **Public Company Accounting Oversight Board (PCAOB)** as an independent oversight body was an attempt to reestablish the perceived independence of auditing companies that the conflict of interest in Arthur Andersen's auditing and consulting relationship with Enron had called into question. In addition, as an oversight board, the PCAOB was charged with maintaining compliance with established standards and enforcing rules and disciplinary procedures for those organizations that found themselves out of compliance. Any public accounting firms that audited the records of publicly traded companies were required to register with the board and to abide by operational standards set by that board.

TITLE II: AUDITOR INDEPENDENCE

In addition to establishing the PCAOB, SOX introduced several key directives to further enforce the independence of auditors and hopefully restore public confidence in independent audit reports:

1. Prohibits specific "nonaudit" services of public accounting firms as violations of auditor independence.
2. Prohibits public accounting firms from providing audit services to any company whose senior officers (chief executive officer, chief financial officer, controller) were employed by that accounting firm within the previous 12 months.
3. Requires senior auditors to rotate off an account every five years and junior auditors every seven years.
4. Requires the external auditor to report to the client's audit committee on specific topics.
5. Requires auditors to disclose all other written communications between management and themselves.

TITLES III THROUGH XI

Here are some highlights of Titles III through XI.

Title III: Corporate Responsibility

- Requires audit committees to be independent and undertake specified oversight responsibilities.
- Requires CEOs and CFOs to certify quarterly and annual reports to the SEC, including making representations about the effectiveness of their control systems.
- Provides rules of conduct for companies and their officers regarding pension blackout periods—a direct response to the Enron situation where corporate executives were accused of selling their stock while employees had their company stock locked in their pension accounts.

Title IV: Enhanced Financial Disclosures

- Requires companies to provide enhanced disclosures, including a report on the effectiveness of internal controls and procedures for financial reporting (along with external auditor sign-off on that report), and disclosures covering off-balance sheet transactions—most of the debt Enron hid from analysts and investors was placed in off-balance sheet accounts and hidden in the smallest footnotes in its financial statements.

Title V: Analyst Conflicts of Interest

- Requires the SEC to adopt rules to address conflicts of interest that can arise when securities analysts recommend securities in research reports and public appearances—each of the "rogue's gallery" of companies in the 2001–2002 scandals had been highly promoted as growth stocks by analysts.

Title VI: Commission Resources and Authority

- Provides additional funding and authority to the SEC to follow through on all the new responsibilities outlined in the act.

Title VII: Studies and Reports

- Directs federal regulatory bodies to conduct studies regarding consolidation of accounting firms, credit rating agencies, and certain roles of investment banks and financial advisers.

Title VIII: Corporate and Criminal Fraud Accountability

- Provides tougher criminal penalties for altering documents, defrauding shareholders, and certain other forms of obstruction of justice and securities fraud. Arthur Andersen's activities in shredding Enron documents directly relates to this topic.
- Protects employees who provide evidence of fraud. Enron and WorldCom were both exposed by the actions of individual employees (see Chapter 7, "Blowing the Whistle").

Title IX: White-Collar Crime Penalty Enhancements

- Provides that any person who attempts to commit white-collar crimes will be treated under the law as if the person had committed the crime.
- Requires CEOs and CFOs to certify their periodic reports and imposes penalties for certifying a misleading or fraudulent report.

Title X: Corporate Tax Returns

- Conveys the sense of the Senate that the CEO should sign a company's federal income tax return.

Title XI: Corporate Fraud and Accountability

- Provides additional authority to regulatory bodies and courts to take various actions, including fines or imprisonment, with regard to tampering with records, impeding official proceedings, taking extraordinary payments, retaliating against corporate whistle-blowers, and certain other matters involving corporate fraud.

Section 404 of the Sarbanes-Oxley Act (listed as Title IV in this chapter) is estimated to have generated auditing fees in the hundreds of millions of dollars—all in the hope of enforcing ethical conduct in U.S. organizations. The legislation was swift and wide-ranging and was specifically designed to restore investor confidence in what, for a brief period, appeared to be financial markets that were run with two primary goals: corruption and greed.

The danger with such a rapid response is that key issues have a tendency to be overlooked in the eagerness to demonstrate responsiveness and decisiveness. In this case, the question of whether you can really legislate ethics was never answered.

What SOX delivers is a collection of tools and penalties to punish offenders with enough severity to put others off the idea of bending or breaking the rules in the future, and enough policies and procedures to ensure that any future corporate criminals are going to have to work a lot harder to earn their money than the folks at Enron, WorldCom, and the rest—there are a lot more people watching now.

However, SOX does not help you create an ethical corporate culture or hire an effective and ethical board of directors—you still have to do that for yourself. Just be sure to remember that there are now a lot more penalties and people waiting to catch you if you don't.

PROGRESS ✔ QUESTIONS

13. Explain the role of the PCAOB.
14. Which title requires CEOs and CFOs to certify quarterly and annual reports to the SEC?
15. Which title protects employees who provide evidence of fraud?
16. What are the five key requirements for auditor independence?

FOXES GUARDING THE HENHOUSE?

The Sarbanes-Oxley Act, which the United States enacted in an atmosphere of extraordinary agitation in 2002, is one of the most influential—and controversial—pieces of corporate legislation ever to have hit a statute book. Its original aim, on the face of it, was modest: to improve the accountability of managers to shareholders, and [then] calm the raging crisis of confidence in American capitalism aroused by scandals at Enron, WorldCom, and other companies. The law's methods, however, were anything but modest, and its effects are going to be far-reaching.

The cost of all this [new oversight] is steep. A survey by Financial Executives International, an association of top financial executives, found that companies paid an average of $2.4 million more for their audits [in 2004] than they had anticipated (and far more than the statute's designers had envisaged). . . . This result underlines a notable and unintended consequence of the legislation: It has provided a bonanza for accountants and auditors—a profession thought to be much at fault in the scandals that inspired the law, and which the statute sought to rein in and supervise.

Already reduced in number by consolidation and the demise of Arthur Andersen, the big accounting firms are now known more often as the Final Four than the Big Four, since any further reduction is thought unlikely.

WHO'S LOOKING OUT FOR THE LITTLE GUY?

Smaller companies without access to the internal resources (or funds to pay for external resources) to comply with Sarbanes-Oxley are being particularly hard-hit by the legislation, even though the transgressions that prompted the statute in the first place came from large, publicly traded organizations. This is not to suggest that smaller firms don't face their own ethical problems—it just seems that they are expected to carry an administrative burden that is equal to that of their much larger counterparts.

NOT VERY NEIGHBORLY

Sarbanes-Oxley applies to all companies that issue securities under U.S. federal securities statutes, whether headquartered within the United States or not. Thus, in addition to U.S.-based firms, approximately 1,300 foreign firms from 59 countries fall under the law's jurisdiction.

Reactions to SOX from this quarter were swift. Some foreign companies that had previously contemplated offering securities in the U.S. market reconsidered in light of the conflicts they believe SOX created. For example,

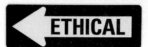 

© PhotoAlto/Punchstock RF

in October 2002, Porsche AG announced it would not list its shares on the New York Stock Exchange. A company press release identified the passage of SOX as the "critical factor" for this decision and singled out CEO and CFO certification of financial statements for criticism. After recounting the process Porsche uses to prepare, review, and approve its financial reports, the release concluded that "any special treatment of the Chairman of the Board of Management [i.e., Porsche's CEO] and the Director of Finance would be illogical because of the intricate network within which the decision-making process exists; it would be irreconcilable with German law."

QUESTIONS

1. SOX has introduced sweeping changes in the name of enforcing corporate ethics. Is it really a "fair" piece of legislation? Explain your answer.
2. Do U.S. ethical problems give us the right to demand ethical controls from international companies based outside the United States?
3. Does the decision to increase auditing requirements seem to be an ethical solution to the problem of questionable audits? Explain your requirements.
4. If there were more than four large accounting firms in the marketplace, would that make the decision more ethical? Explain your answer.

Source: "A Price Worth Paying?" *The Economist,* May 19, 2005.

>> Wall Street Reform

In September and October 2008, financial markets around the world suffered a severe crash as the consequences of aggressive lending to subprime borrowers in a deregulated environment came back to haunt companies that, as recently as a few months earlier, had reported record earnings based on these questionable lending practices. Some companies, such as JPMorgan Chase (which purchased the assets of Bear Stearns and Washington Mutual at fire-sale prices) and Wells Fargo (which purchased Wachovia Bank at an equally discounted price), were able to benefit from this downturn, but two companies in particular came to exemplify a new round of corporate arrogance and questionable ethics that earned them a place in the rogue's gallery previously occupied by such infamous companies as Enron, WorldCom, and HealthSouth.

American Insurance Group (AIG), formerly one of the world's largest insurance companies, received a lifeline loan of $85 billion from the U.S. government in September 2008, followed by an additional $37.8 billion in October 2008. The need for the rescue funding (which AIG was expected to repay by selling pieces of its global business) followed the company's descent into near bankruptcy after it invested extensively in complicated financial contracts used to underwrite mortgage-backed securities.

Intervening to rescue a venerable name in the finance industry could be justified on the basis of a need to restore stability at a time of extreme global instability, but when two senior executives for AIG—Chief Executive Martin J. Sullivan and Chairman Robert Willumstad—appeared before the House Oversight and Government Reform Committee, questions focused less on the company's recovery strategy and more on the lack of oversight and poor financial judgment that got them into the mess in the first place.

The decision to proceed with a celebratory sales meeting in California for the top sales agents of AIG's life insurance subsidiary, with a budget for the event of $440,000, only one week after the government came forward with the $85 billion bailout loan, drew particular criticism from members of the committee. In addition, Sullivan's positive comments, recorded in December 2007, reassuring investors of AIG's financial health only days after receiving warnings from company auditors about the company's exposure to these risky mortgage contracts drew severe criticism from the committee.

In November 2008, the Federal Reserve and the Treasury Department coordinated an even larger deal for AIG that raised the overall cost of the rescue to $152.5 billion, after the company petitioned that the sale of assets to repay the loan would take longer than

© Frank Rumpenhorst/EPA/Corbis

The financial crisis that began in fall 2008 had an impact that will likely affect markets for some time.

originally anticipated. After announcing a $25 billion loss for the third quarter of 2008, AIG was able to negotiate a reduction in the original bailout loan from $85 billion to only $60 billion, along with a reduction in the interest rate on that loan. The additional $37.8 billion loan was replaced by an outright purchase of $40 billion of AIG stock as part of the Treasury's $700 billion bailout package—the so-called Troubled Asset Relief Program (TARP). In addition, the Federal Reserve purchased $22.5 billion of the company's mortgage-backed securities and added an additional $30 billion to underwrite the complicated financial contracts that had led to AIG's near collapse.

Lehman Brothers Holdings, an investment house that had historically been held in the same high regard as AIG, did not fare as well in this financial crisis. For reasons known only to the government, Lehman did not receive a bailout loan like AIG's and collapsed in the summer of 2008. When Chief Executive Richard S. Fuld Jr. appeared before the House Oversight and Government Reform Committee in October 2008, questions focused on the same issue of reassurances of financial health in the face of audited reports indicating extreme risk exposures and, in particular, Fuld's highly lucrative compensation package with Lehman—a total of almost $500 million in salary and bonus payments over the last eight years of his employment with the company.

It is ironic and alarming that the enactment of the Sarbanes-Oxley Act, supposedly to prevent the recurrence of the type of corporate malfeasance that Enron and WorldCom came to exemplify, should be followed so quickly by evidence that the lessons from the days of Enron remained unlearned.

Life Skills

>> Governing your own ethical behavior

Does the fact that we appear to need government legislation to enforce ethical business practices both here and overseas suggest that we are unable to self-govern our individual ethical behavior? Can we be trusted to act in an ethical manner both in our personal and professional lives? Or do we need a regulatory framework and a clearly defined system of punishment to force people to act ethically or face the consequences?

As we discussed in Chapter 1, your personal value system represents the cumulative effect of a series of influences in your life—your upbringing, religious beliefs, community influences, and peer influences from your friends. As such, your ethical standards already represent a framework of influences that have made you the person you are today. However, where you take that value system in the future depends entirely on you. State and federal bodies may put punitive legislation in place to enforce an ideal model of personal and professional behavior, but whether or not you abide by that legislation comes down to the decisions you make on a daily basis. Can you stay true to your personal value system and live your life according to your own ethical standards? Or are you the type of person who is swayed by peer pressure and social norms to the point where you find yourself doing things you wouldn't normally do?

Developing a clear sense of your personal values is as much about knowing what you aren't willing to do as it is about knowing what you are willing to do. Understanding the difference allows you to remain grounded and focused while those around you sway in the wind in search of someone to help them make a decision. It's when someone is not acting in his or her best interests that poor decisions are made and things can start to go wrong.

THE DODD-FRANK WALL STREET REFORM AND CONSUMER PROTECTION ACT (2010)

On July 21, 2010, the U.S. government's plan to ensure that the words "too big to fail" would never be applied to Wall Street again was delivered in the form of the **Dodd-Frank Wall Street Reform and Consumer Protection Act.**[6] Weighing in at an astounding 2,319 pages, Dodd-Frank survived an acrimonious journey through Congress in the face of Republican opposition and aggressive lobbying by Wall Street companies ("Big Finance"), which sought to weaken what was expected to be a tough response to a global financial crisis.

With midterm elections scheduled for November 2010, the expectation from critics was that the final version of the bill would be watered down with a series of compromises as politicians balanced their support for key provisions of the bill without risking any damage to their reelection hopes. As it was, the legislation passed with no Republican support. A final verdict is still up for debate, since many of the provisions had implementation deadlines of several years into the future, and the Republican controlled Congress is still trying to repeal much of the bill, but with Dodd-Frank celebrating its fifth birthday on July 21, 2015, the primary achievements of the legislation can be summarized as follows.

The Consumer Financial Protection Bureau

Applauded as bringing a much-needed consumer focus to regulatory oversight of financial products and services, the creation of the **Consumer Financial Protection Bureau (CFPB)** generated considerable debate over the independence and

Dodd-Frank Wall Street Reform and Consumer Protection Act Legislation that was promoted as the "fix" for the extreme mismanagement of risk in the financial sector that led to a global financial crisis in 2008–2010.

Consumer Financial Protection Bureau (CFPB) A government agency within the Federal Reserve that oversees financial products and services.

power of the bureau—in other words, who would control it, and how much damage could it do. The final version placed the bureau within the Federal Reserve and assigned separate financing and an independent director to minimize the potential for aggressive lobbying practices by financial services companies.

The responsibilities originally granted to the bureau were extensive and included authority to examine and enforce regulations for banks and credit unions with assets over $10 billion; the creation of a new Office of Financial Literacy; the creation of a national consumer complaint hotline; and, most confusingly, the consolidation of all consumer protection responsibilities currently handled by the Office of the Comptroller of the Currency, Office of Thrift Supervision, Federal Deposit Insurance Corporation (FDIC), Federal Reserve, National Credit Union Administration (NCUA), the Department of Housing and Urban Development (HUD), and the Federal Trade Commission (FTC).

Republican opposition to the confirmation of any director included threats of a filibuster (a deliberate attempt to delay a debate or block a vote), forcing the appointment of Richard Cordray as a "recess appointment" by President Obama in July 2013, two years after the legislation was enacted.

The Financial Stability Oversight Council Promoted as the "fix" for "too big to fail," the **Financial Stability Oversight Council (FSOC)** is empowered to act if a bank with more than $50 billion in assets "poses a grave threat to the financial stability of the United States."[7] That action in response to the threat can include limiting the ability of the bank to merge with, acquire, or otherwise become affiliated with another company; restricting the ability to offer financial products or services; terminating one or more activities; imposing conditions on how the company conducts business; and selling or transferring assets to unaffiliated entities to mitigate any perceived risk.

The council is led by the Treasury secretary and is made up of top financial regulators. With over 180 banks with assets above $50 billion, the FSOC can act on not only banks that are too big to fail but also banks that may be deemed to be "too interconnected" with other financial institutions to fail. The warning being given here, at least, is that the riskier the institution is determined to be, the more regulated it will become. Critics have argued that community banks are now suffering as a result of the regulatory paperwork demanded by the FSOC.

The Volcker Rule American economist and past Federal Reserve Chairman Paul Volcker proposed that there should be a key restriction in the legislation to limit the ability of banks to trade on their own accounts (termed *proprietary trading*). The original *Volcker rule* sought to stop the trading of *derivatives* (which are financial instruments based on the performance of other financial instruments, such as mortgage-backed securities) completely, but was scaled back to a compromise that limited the ethically questionable practices of banks taking opposing positions to trades that they are simultaneously promoting to their clients. After tooth-and-nail battles with the banking industry that delayed the implementation of the rule until the fifth anniversary of the original legislation, the final version still leaves too much of what critics refer to as "haziness." Banks are banned from proprietary trading, but they can still hedge investments and take other steps to protect client positions in specific investments. There is already growing evidence of banks simply reclassifying proprietary trades as "hedged investments" to leverage this gray area.[8]

With over 2,300 pages, 1,500 provisions, and about 398 rule-making requirements, the elements of the legislation go far beyond the three items listed above, but these three have been most actively promoted as evidence of a strong response to extreme mismanagement of risk in the financial sector. However, the effectiveness of the legislation remains to be proved, and critics are concerned that there are still too many unknowns for the Dodd-Frank Act to be acknowledged as a success. For example, banker salaries are

> **Financial Stability Oversight Council (FSOC)** A government agency established to prevent banks from failing and otherwise threatening the stability of the U.S. economy.

© Travelwide/Alamy RF

still so high as to warrant Democratic promises to curb the practice, and the largest financial institutions are still "too big to fail." In addition, the simplification of confusing mortgage disclosure forms (which many foreclosed homeowners blamed as contributing to their lack of understanding of the true nature of their adjustable mortgages) that was promised by 2012 was still not accomplished in 2016.[9]

>> Conclusion

With the banking industry aggressively seeking to undermine legislation designed to enforce ethical business conduct, students of business ethics can be forgiven for wondering if corporations can ever be counted on to "do the right thing." Indeed, cynics would argue that the first order of business for the financial institutions directly affected by Dodd-Frank was to assign teams to figure out ways around the new rules and restrictions. However, if, as we discussed in Chapter 5, the internal governance mechanisms of corporations can't always be counted on to prevent unethical behavior, what other options are there to protect consumers?

In the especially complex world of financial services, where individual investors trust their hard-earned savings to mutual fund managers in the hope of providing enough for a secure and comfortable retirement, any evidence of mismanagement of those savings can result in a loss of trust that may prove very difficult to regain.

In the next chapter we consider the actions of employees on the inside of corporations who experience corporate malfeasance directly and find themselves face-to-face with the ethical dilemma of speaking out or looking the other way.

FRONTLINE FOCUS

Too Much Trouble—Susan Makes a Decision

Susan was beginning to realize that the Sarbanes-Oxley Act was a mixed blessing. Greater scrutiny of corporate financial reports was meant to reassure investors, and it was certainly bringing her firm plenty of business, but now she was faced with this "small favor" to her boss. On the face of it, she couldn't really understand why they just didn't tell this guy that they only worked with clients worth a dollar figure that was higher than his company's valuation and be done with it, but her boss was so paranoid about the firm's reputation, and he was convinced that the next big client was always just around the corner.

Susan spent a couple of hours reviewing the file. Steven's assessment had been accurate—this was a simple audit with no real earning potential for the company. If they weren't so busy, they could probably assign a junior team—her team perhaps—and knock this out in a few days, but Steven had bigger fish to fry.

Susan thought for a moment about asking her boss to let her put a small team together to do this one, but then she realized that by not delivering on the small favor he had asked, she could be ruining her chances for getting assigned to some of the bigger audits down the road. So she ran the numbers, multiplied them by four, and submitted the price quotation.

Unfortunately, the quotation was so outrageous that the small-business client complained to the PCAOB, which promptly wrote a letter demanding a full explanation of Susan's company's pricing schedule.

QUESTIONS

1. What could Susan have done differently here?
2. What do you think will happen now?
3. What will be the consequences for Susan, Steven Thompson, and their auditing firm?

[For Review]

1. **Identify the five key pieces of U.S. legislation designed to discourage, if not prevent, illegal conduct within organizations.**

   • *The Foreign Corrupt Practices Act (1977): The act was passed to more effectively control bribery payments to foreign officials and politicians by American publicly traded companies.*

   • *The U.S. Federal Sentencing Guidelines for Organizations (1991): FSGO applies to organizations and holds them liable for the criminal acts of their employees and agents.*

   • *The Sarbanes-Oxley Act (2002):SOX was a legislative response to a series of corporate accounting scandals that had begun to dominate the financial markets in 2001.*

- *The Revised Federal Sentencing Guidelines for Organizations (2004): The revision modified the 1991 guidelines by requiring periodic evaluation of the effectiveness of corporate compliance programs and evidence of active promotion of ethical conduct rather than passive compliance.*
- *The Dodd-Frank Wall Street Reform and Consumer Protection Act (2010): The act introduced a complex list of new rules and restrictions designed to provide greater regulatory oversight of the financial sector, along with improved protection for consumers.*

2. **Understand the purpose and significance of the Foreign Corrupt Practices Act (FCPA).**

   The FCPA represented an attempt to send a clear message that the competitiveness of U.S. corporations in overseas markets should be based on price and product quality rather than the extent to which companies had paid off foreign officials and political leaders. However, the legislation was criticized for lacking any real "teeth" because of its formal recognition of "facilitation payments" for "routine governmental action" such as the provision of permits, licenses, or visas. Critics argued that since the payment of bribes was typically designed to expedite the paperwork on most projects, the recognition of these facilitation payments did nothing more than legalize the payment of bribes.

3. **Calculate monetary fines under the three-step process of the U.S. Federal Sentencing Guidelines for Organizations (FSGO).**

   - *Step 1: Calculate the "base fine" based on the greatest of the monetary gain to the organization from the offense, the monetary loss from the offense caused by the organization, or an amount determined by the judge.*
   - *Step 2: Compute a corresponding degree of blame or guilt known as the "culpability score" that can be increased (or aggravated) or decreased (or mitigated) according to predetermined factors.*
   - *Step 3: Multiply the base fine by the culpability score to arrive at the total fine amount. In certain cases the judge has the discretion to impose a so-called death penalty, where the fine is set high enough to match all the organization's assets.*

4. **Compare and contrast the relative advantages and disadvantages of the Sarbanes-Oxley Act (SOX).**

   The aim of SOX was to improve the accountability of managers to shareholders and to calm the raging crisis of confidence in American capitalism aroused by scandals at Enron, WorldCom, and other companies. The establishment of the PCAOB and the specific changes to auditor independence and corporate responsibility certainly helped achieve that aim. However, critics argue that the rush to restore confidence produced legislation that was too heavy-handed in its application. Smaller companies were directly affected by the additional auditing costs, even though the unethical behavior that SOX was designed to address had occurred in publicly traded companies. In addition, the legislation applied to all companies issuing securities under U.S. federal securities statutes (whether headquartered in the United States or not), which brought 1,300 foreign firms from 59 countries under the law's jurisdiction.

5. **Explain the key provisions of the Dodd-Frank Wall Street Reform and Consumer Protection Act.**

   Passed into law in July 2010, Dodd-Frank was promoted as the "fix" for the extreme mismanagement of risk in the financial sector that led to a global financial crisis in 2008–2010. At over 2,300 pages, the legislation presented a complex list of new rules and restrictions designed to provide greater regulatory oversight of the financial sector, along with improved protection for consumers. The three most actively promoted elements of Dodd-Frank were:

   - *The Consumer Financial Protection Bureau (CFPB): Designed as an independently run entity in the Federal Reserve, the CFPB promises to act on any perceived misconduct by financial institutions in the treatment of their customers.*
   - *The Financial Stability Oversight Council (FSOC): Led by the Treasury secretary and a team of senior financial regulators, the FSOC is empowered to regulate any bank with assets over $50 billion if it determines that the business practices of the bank pose "a grave threat to the financial stability of the United States." As the promised fix for "too big to fail," the FSOC has the power to intervene in any aspect of the bank's management up to and including the termination of business practices.*
   - *The Volcker rule: Proposed by former Federal Reserve Chairman Paul Volcker, this rule limits the ability of banks to trade on their own accounts (i.e., invest their own money) in any way that might threaten the financial stability of the institution (and, by definition, the financial markets as a whole).*

[Key Terms]

Consumer Financial Protection Bureau (CFPB) 128

Culpability Score (FSGO) 121

Death Penalty (FSGO) 121

Disclosure (FCPA) 118

Dodd-Frank Wall Street Reform and Consumer Protection Act 128

Facilitation Payments (FCPA) 118

Federal Sentencing Guidelines for Organizations (FSGO) 120

Financial Stability Oversight Council (FSOC) 129

Foreign Corrupt Practices Act (FCPA) 118

Prohibition (FCPA) 118

Public Company Accounting Oversight Board (PCAOB) 124

Routine Governmental Action (FCPA) 118

Sarbanes-Oxley Act (SOX) 124

[Review Questions]

1. Which is the most effective piece of legislation for enforcing ethical business practices: FCPA, FSGO, SOX, or Dodd-Frank? Explain your answer.

2. "The FCPA has too many exceptions to be an effective deterrent to unethical business practices." Do you agree or disagree with this statement? Explain your answer.

3. What issues prompted the revision of the Federal Sentencing Guidelines for Organizations in 2004?

4. Do you think the requirement that CEOs and CFOs sign off on their company accounts will increase investor confidence in those accounts? Why or why not?

5. Why may the Sarbanes-Oxley Act of 2002 be regarded as one of the most controversial pieces of corporate legislation in recent history?

6. Based on the information in this chapter, can the Dodd-Frank Act of 2010 prevent "too big to fail"? Explain your answer.

[Review Exercises]

Universal Industries is in desperate need of a large contract to boost its declining U.S. revenues. The company doesn't have a lot of international exposure, despite its ambitious name, but its chief operating officer (COO) may be about to change that. By coincidence, at a recent class reunion, he ran into an old classmate who was a high-ranking federal official responsible for a lot of the bidding for large defense contracts. After several rounds of drinks, the classmate began talking about his latest projects.

Universal has done a lot of defense work as a subcontractor for the major players in the industry, and the COO was able to leverage that experience to use his insider information to get Universal added to the list for several requests for proposal (RFPs) on a large expansion of a Middle Eastern military base.

To strengthen its position in the bidding process, several key Universal operatives made unpublicized visits to the towns surrounding the base and, in return for gifts of cash and other favors to local businesspeople and politicians, managed to tie up the exclusive services of several local contractors, making it almost impossible for the other contenders to meet the requirements of the RFPs. The COO was equally generous in his gift to the daughter of his classmate in recognition of his help in getting the inside information.

Unfortunately, even though the new military contracts were going to provide more than enough money to boost Universal's performance numbers, they weren't going to go into effect until the following quarter. After a behind-closed-doors discussion, the senior management team decided that Universal would adjust some of its fourth-quarter expenses in order to hit the price target that the analysts were expecting. The team fully expected that the revenue from the military contracts would allow them to make up for the adjustments in the next financial year.

However, because Universal's annual revenue exceeded $1.4 billion, the CEO and CFO were required to put their signatures on the financial reports confirming their authenticity.

After a couple of sleepless nights, and confident that the military contracts would help them fix all this in the end, they both signed.

1. Identify the ethical transgressions in this example.

2. Which piece of legislation would apply to each transgression?

3. What would be the penalties for each transgression?

4. If Universal could prove that it had a compliance program in place, how would that affect the penalties?

Internet Exercises

1. Locate the website for Berlin-based Transparency International (TI).

   a. What is the stated mission of TI?

   b. Explain the Corruptions Perception Index.

   c. Which are the least and most corrupt countries on the index?

   d. Summarize how the "Together Against Corruption: Transparency International Strategy 2020" report was compiled.

2. Using Internet research, review the involvement of former Harvard law professor, and now Massachusetts senator, Elizabeth Warren in the Consumer Financial Protection Bureau (CFPB).

   a. What was Warren's involvement in the government response to the collapse of the financial markets?

   b. How is she connected to the CFPB?

   c. What were the objections to her involvement with the CFPB?

   d. What was Warren's declared agenda for the CFPB?

Team Exercises

1. **Protecting your people at all costs.**
   Your company is a major fruit processor that maintains long-term contracts with plantation owners in Central America to guarantee supplies of high-quality produce. Many of those plantations are in politically unstable areas and your U.S.-based teams travel to those regions at high personal risk. You have been contacted by a representative from one of the local groups of freedom fighters demanding that you make a "donation" to their cause in return for the guaranteed protection of the plantations with which you do business. The representative makes it very clear that failure to pay the donation could put your team on the ground at risk of being kidnapped and held for ransom. Your company is proud of its compliance with all aspects of the FCPA and the revised FSGO legislation. Divide into two groups, and argue your case *for* and *against* paying this donation.

2. **Budgeting for bribes.**
   You are a midlevel manager for the government of a small African nation that relies heavily on oil revenues to run the country's budget. The recent increase in the price of oil has improved your country's budget significantly, and, as a result, many new infrastructure projects are being funded with those oil dollars— roads, bridges, schools, and hospitals—which are generating lots of construction projects and very lucrative orders for materials and equipment. However, very little of this new wealth has made its way down to the lower levels of your administration. Historically, your government has always budgeted for very low salaries for government workers in recognition of the fact that their paychecks are often supplemented by payments to expedite the processing of applications and licensing paperwork. Your boss feels strongly that there is no need to raise the salaries of the lower-level government workers because the increase in infrastructure contracts will bring a corresponding increase in payments to those workers and, as he pointed out, "companies that want our business will be happy to make those payments." Divide into two groups, and argue *for* and *against* the continuation of this arrangement.

3. **The pros and cons of SOX.**
   Divide into two teams. One team must defend the introduction of Sarbanes-Oxley as a federal deterrent to corporate malfeasance. The other team must criticize the legislation as being ineffective and an administrative burden.

4. **The key components of SOX.**
   Divide into groups of three or four. Distribute the 11 sections of SOX reviewed in this chapter. Each group must prepare a brief presentation outlining the relative importance of its section to the overall impact of SOX and the prohibition of unethical business practices.

Thinking Critically

6.1

>> PONZI SCHEMES

The practice of providing old (or early) investors above-average returns on their investment with funds raised from new (or late) investors in the absence of any real business operation to generate profits is illegal, unethical, and, regrettably, not

© Photodisc/Getty Images RF

a new idea. It used to be referred to as "robbing Peter to pay Paul." In 1899, a New York scam artist named William Miller promised investors returns as high as 520 percent in one year based on his supposed insider information on profitable businesses. He scammed people out of almost $25 million in today's money before being exposed and jailed for 10 years.

In 1920 the practice was given a new name—Ponzi scheme—in "honor" of Charles Ponzi, an Italian immigrant who, after numerous failed business ventures, began to promote the spectacular returns to be made by buying international reply coupons (IRC)—coupons that could be used to purchase stamps in order to reply to a letter, like an international self-addressed envelope—in local currencies, and cashing them in at U.S. currency rates. For example, "a person could buy 66 international reply coupons in Rome for the equivalent of $1. Those same 66 coupons would cost $3.30 in Boston," where Ponzi was based. It is debatable whether or not Ponzi genuinely believed that he had stumbled across a real business opportunity— a simplified version of currency trading in a way—but his response

was immediate, promising investors returns of 50 percent on their original investment in just 90 days. However, the opportunity attracted so much money so quickly—as much as $1 million poured into his office in one day—that Ponzi was either unable or unwilling to actually buy the IRCs. Had he tried to do so, he would have realized that there were not enough IRCs in existence to deliver the kinds of returns he was promising his investors. Instead, Ponzi chose to use the funds coming in from new investors to pay out the promised returns to older investors—robbing Peter to pay Paul.

It was only a matter of time before the funds coming in would be insufficient to meet the demands of older investors with their original capital and their 50 percent return. Ponzi was able to keep the scheme going by encouraging those older investors to keep "rolling over" their investment, but once rumors began to surface about the questionable nature of the Ponzi enterprise, fewer and fewer people opted to roll over, choosing instead to take their money out. At that point the whole system collapsed, and Ponzi's business enterprise was exposed as fraudulent. For his brief encounter with fame and fortune, Charles Ponzi eventually served 12 years in prison, and was deported back to Italy. He later emigrated to Brazil, still presumably in search of fame and fortune. He died in 1949 in the charity ward of a Rio de Janeiro hospital with only enough money to his name to cover his burial expenses. His name, however, lives on—the practice of robbing Peter to pay Paul was forever replaced with the name *Ponzi scheme*.

In subsequent decades, Ponzi has inspired many imitators:

- In January 2009, the Securities and Exchange Commission charged an 82-year-old man, Richard Piccoli, with operating a Ponzi scheme that scammed investors out of $17 million over five years by promising "safe" returns of only 7 percent based on real estate investments that were never made.
- In July 2010, Fort Lauderdale lawyer Scott Rothstein sold stakes in large fictitious legal settlements, scamming investors out of $1.2 billion, and causing considerable embarrassment to Florida Republican politicians who were recipients of large donations from Rothstein's newfound wealth.
- In April 2010, former Minnesota business tycoon Tom Petters was sentenced to 50 years in prison for orchestrating a $3.7 billion scheme to convince investors that they were buying large shipments of electronics that would then be sold to big-box retailers such as Costco and Sam's Club. Victims included retirees, church groups, and Wall Street hedge funds.

134 • *Business Ethics Now*

- In October 2014, a grand jury indicted Paul Burks, founder of penny-bid auction site ZeekRewards, for running an $850 million alleged Ponzi scheme. Investors were promised daily returns of 1.5 percent, but at its collapse, the program would have needed almost $2.8 billion in reserves to meet obligations to an estimated 2 million victims.
- In January 2015, the SEC won a $580 million judgment against Edwin Fujinaga, founder of MRI International, for running an estimated $800 million Ponzi scheme directed at Japanese investors. MRI promised over 8,000 investors that they could receive annual returns of 10 percent or more by funding the purchase of accounts receivables from medical providers at a discount and collecting the full amount from insurance companies.

In December 2008, a formerly highly respected Wall Street money manager, Bernard Madoff, was accused of masterminding a Ponzi scheme on such a grand scale that the practice may well be replaced with the name "Madoff scheme." The amount of money involved in Madoff's alleged scam is staggering—an estimated $65 billion stolen over decades.

As a traditionally low-profile investment professional, former chairman of the NASDAQ stock exchange, and an occasional consultant to the Securities and Exchange Commission on matters of investment regulation, Madoff became a multimillionaire in the early days of computer-based stock trading before he became attracted to the more lucrative business of managing other people's money. He built a reputation of sure and steady returns for his clients, earning the affectionate nickname "T-Bill Bernie" to reflect the same security as investing in government-backed Treasury bills. Madoff's success wasn't based on spectacular returns from year to year (he averaged between 10 and 18 percent per year), but rather on consistent solid performance year after year. He didn't market his services aggressively, preferring instead to allow satisfied clients to bring in family members and friends. He generated an aura of exclusivity, often declining to accept investments, which only served to make those potential investors want to invest with him even more.

This perceived exclusivity and a strategic marketing plan that targeted wealthy investors in places such as Palm Beach, Florida, allowed Madoff to build a solid reputation over decades, attracting high-profile investors and large investments from global banks in the hundreds of millions of dollars along the way. However, the financial meltdown at the end of 2008 prompted investors to start withdrawing their funds to meet other obligations, and when Madoff was faced with withdrawal requests totaling almost $7 billion, the carefully constructed scam fell apart in a matter of hours.

In the early emotional days of this exposed and still alleged scandal, one of the primary concerns is the appointment of blame. Who knew what, when, and could this have been prevented? The SEC has come under considerable scrutiny for its role in this. Madoff's operation was examined on four separate occasions since 1999, with two detailed investigations launched in 2002 and 2006. No evidence of fraud was uncovered, and Madoff received only a mild reprimand for irregularities in paperwork. Now that $65 billion appears to have disappeared, with no trading records available to track the money, there are many questions to be answered. What is known for sure is that Madoff was sentenced to 150 years in jail (the maximum sentence allowed) in June 2009. Given Madoff's age of 71, the district judge for the case, Denny Chin, acknowledged that the sentence was designed to be symbolic and to reflect the severity of the crime and the damage done to so many individual investors.

Boston-based money manager Harry Markopoulos had written an 18-page letter to the SEC in 2005 identifying 29 different red flags about Madoff's operation, basically questioning the mathematical improbability of such solid returns year after year and suggesting that the only way to achieve those returns was to either trade on insider information or create a totally fictitious trading record.

Supposedly "sophisticated" investors, who gave Madoff large sums to invest from pension funds, family trusts, and endowments, were wiped out. Even worse, many individual investors, who entrusted their savings to other money managers who then invested that money with Madoff, also lost substantial amounts in an investment they never even knew they had.

Much will be written about Madoff's psychological state of mind in allegedly masterminding such a complex scam over decades and, more importantly, fooling so many of the elite of Wall Street and the regulatory mechanisms that are supposed to be in place to prevent such a scam from happening. It remains to be seen whether this information will produce any dramatic changes in the regulatory framework of the financial markets to ensure that a Ponzi scheme on such a staggering scale never occurs again.

CONTINUED >>

QUESTIONS

1. Charles Ponzi was a working-class Italian immigrant who was eager to find success in America. Bernard Madoff was already a multimillionaire before he started his scheme. Does that make one more unethical than the other? Why or why not?

2. Explain how a Ponzi scheme works.

3. Does the SEC bear any responsibility in the extent of the Madoff scheme? If so, in what way?

4. Does the fact that Madoff offered less outrageous returns (10 to 18 percent per year) on investments compared to Ponzi's promise of a 50 percent return in only 90 days make Madoff any less unethical? Why or why not?

5. Can the investors who put their money in Madoff's funds without any due diligence, often on the basis of a tip from a friend or a "friend of a friend," really be considered victims in this case? Why or why not?

6. What should investors with Bernard Madoff have done differently?

Sources: A. Altman, "Ponzi Schemes," *Time.com,* December 15, 2008; J. Gapper, "Wall Street Insiders and Fools' Gold," *Financial Times,* December 17, 2008; A. Sloan, "Commentary: The Real Lesson of the Madoff Case," CNN.com, January 9, 2009; M. Zuckoff, "What Madoff Could Learn from Ponzi," money.CNN.com, January 13, 2009; R. Chew, "Bernie Madoff's Victims: Why Some Have No Recourse," Time.com, January 12, 2009; and www.ponzitracker.com.

Thinking Critically 6.2

>> INDIA'S ENRON

In December 2008, one of the largest players in India's outsourcing and information technology sectors, Satyam Computer Services, fell from grace with such force and speed that the reverberations were felt around the globe. Ironically, the name *Satyam* means "truth" in Sanskrit, but the company, founded by brothers Ramalinga and Ramu Raju, now has a new nickname: India's Enron.

Founded in 1987, Satyam was positioned to take full advantage of the capabilities of satellite-based broadband communications, allowing it to serve clients across the globe from its offices in Hyderabad. The rising demand for computer programmers to fix code in software programs in advance of Y2K (the year 2000 problem) fueled an aggressive growth plan for the company. It was listed on the Bombay Stock Exchange in 1991, and achieved a listing on the New York Stock Exchange in May 2001. By 2006, Satyam had about 23,000 employees and was reporting annual revenues of $1 billion. Growth continued as the company served expanding needs for outsourced services from U.S. companies looking to control and preferably reduce operating costs. By 2008, Satyam was reporting over $2 billion in revenue with 53,000 employees in 63 countries worldwide.

© Photodisc/Getty Images RF

This made the company the fourth-largest software services provider alongside such competitors as WiPro Technologies, Infosys, and HCL. It was serving almost 700 clients, including 185 Fortune 500 companies, generating more than half of its revenue from the United States. Satyam's client roster included such names as General Electric, Cisco, Ford Motor Co., Nestlé, and the U.S. government.

Prominence in the software services sector brought with it increased attention and a growing reputation. In 2007, Ramalinga Raju was the recipient of Ernst & Young's Entrepreneur of the Year award. In September 2008 the company received the Golden Peacock Award for Corporate Governance from the World Council for Corporate Governance, which endorsed Satyam as a leader in ethical management practices.

Signs that there were problems at Satyam first appeared in October 2008 when it was revealed that the World Bank had banned the company from pursuing any service contracts after evidence was uncovered that Satyam employees had offered "improper benefits to bank staff" and "failed to account for all fees charged" to the World Bank. WiPro Technologies had also been banned by the World Bank in 2007 for "offering shares of its 2000 initial public offering to World Bank employees," so Satyam appeared to have some company in the arena of questionable business practices in the software solutions sector.

However, the situation escalated in December 2008 after Satyam's board voted against a proposed deal for Satyam to buy two construction companies for $1.6 billion. The Raju brothers held ownership stakes in both companies, and they were run by Ramalinga Raju's sons. Four directors resigned in response to the proposed deal, and Satyam stock was punished by investors, forcing the brothers to sell their own stock as the falling share price sparked margin calls on their investment accounts. The dire financial situation prompted Ramalinga Raju to confess in a four-and-a-half-page letter to the board of Satyam Computer Services that the company had been overstating profits for several years and that $1.6 billion in assets simply did not exist. It did not take long for investors to piece the information together that the proposed $1.6 billion purchase of the construction companies would have, conveniently, filled the $1.6 billion hole in Satyam's accounts.

In his confession, Raju attempted to address accusations of a premeditated fraud by stating: "What started as a marginal gap between actual operating profit and the one reflected in the books of accounts continued to grow over the years. It has attained unmanageable proportions as the size of the company operations grew." He wrote, "It was like riding a tiger, not knowing how to get off without being eaten."

The analogy of being eaten by a tiger certainly seems appropriate. The scandal has had repercussions for the software services sector as a whole, casting shadows on Satyam's competitors and also on India's corporate governance framework. As with Enron's collapse, attention immediately turned to the role of the accounting company responsible for auditing Satyam's accounts and, allegedly, failing to notice that $1.6 billion in assets did not exist. For Enron it was Arthur Andersen, and the accounting firm did not survive. For Satyam it was PricewaterhouseCoopers, which had certified that Satyam had $1.1 billion in cash in its accounts, when the company really had only $78 million.

The response of Indian authorities was immediate—jail for the founders of Satyam, and the swift appointment of an interim board of more reputable businesspeople as the country scrambled to restore its reputation and reassure investors and customers alike that Satyam was a regrettable exception rather than a common example of unethical business practices in the face of competitive pressures in a global market.

In January 2009, the Securities and Exchange Board of India made it mandatory for the controlling shareholders of companies to disclose when they were pledging shares as collateral to lenders—a direct response to the Satyam scandal. In April 2009, Tech Mahindra, the technology arm of Indian conglomerate Mahindra Group, won an auction to buy the operations of Satyam at a price of less than one-third of the company's stock value before the confession of Ramalinga Raju. The justification for the bargain price lay in the loss of 46 customers, including Nissan, Sony, the United Nations, and State Farm Insurance, in the aftermath of the scandal. Analysts commented in response to the sale that the situation could have been much worse for Satyam were it not for the timing of the global recession. With so many other priorities to address, many customers elected to avoid the headaches of switching IT suppliers (with all the software and hardware changes that might entail) and give Satyam the opportunity to figure things out.

In March 2012, Tech Mahindra and Mahindra Satyam announced plans to merge, creating a new entity worth combined annual revenues of $2.4 billion. With a stated profit of $61 million in the fourth quarter of 2011, analysts appeared willing to accept that Satyam had turned the corner and put the scandal behind them. By 2015, Tech Mahindra had continued to grow with an aggressive program of acquisitions. Targeting $5 billion in annual revenue by the end of the 2015–2016 fiscal year, the company's acquisition of Lightbridge Communications Corp. (LCC)—its sixth acquisition since 2012—showed clear signs of meeting that goal.

CONTINUED >>

In April 2015, Ramalinga Raju and nine other coconspirators were sentenced to seven years in jail for the Satyam fraud. That sentence was suspended by an Indian appeals court in May 2015 on the basis they had already served 35 months in jail, a substantial part of their sentence, and they were granted bail to further appeal their convictions. If the appeals are unsuccessful, the original sentences will be reapplied.

QUESTIONS

1. Does Ramalinga Raju's assertion that this fraud only "started as a marginal gap" change the ethical question here? Would the situation be different if there was evidence that there had been a deliberate intent to deceive investors from the beginning?

2. Why do you think Satyam's board of directors refused to support the proposed purchase of the construction companies?

3. Outline the similarities between the Enron scandal and Satyam Computer Services' situation.

4. PricewaterhouseCoopers (PWC) made a public commitment to cooperate with investigators. Did the Satyam situation represent the same threat for PWC as Enron did for Arthur Andersen? Why or why not?

5. Will the response of the Securities and Exchange Board of India be enough to prevent another scandal like Satyam? Explain.

6. What benefits do Tech Mahindra and Mahindra Satyam hope to achieve with the announced merger? Explain.

Sources: H. Timmons, "Financial Scandal at Outsourcing Company Rattles a Developing Country," *The New York Times,* January 8, 2009; E. Corcoran, "The Seeds of the Satyam Scandal," *Forbes,* January 8, 2009; S. V. Balachandran, "The Satyam Scandal," *Forbes,* January 7, 2009; J. Kahn, H. Timmons, and B. Wassener, "Board Tries to Chart Path for Outsourcer Hit by Scandal," *The New York Times,* January 13, 2009; "Salvaging the Truth," *The Economist,* April 16, 2009; "Mahindra Satyam and Tech Mahindra Approve Merger Plan," *BBC Business News,* March 21, 2012; "Satyam Computers: Indian Court Suspends B. Ramalinga Raju Sentence," *BBC India News,* May 12, 2015; and Shivani Shinde Nadhe, "Tech Mahindra Comes a Step Closer to 2015 Goal,' *Business Standard,* December 16, 2015.

Thinking Critically 6.3

>> "OFF-LABEL" MARKETING

In corporate governance researched by industry, the pharmaceutical industry features very prominently, with multiple examples of questionable corporate conduct. Consider the following cases of settlements between pharmaceutical companies and the Department of Justice (DOJ) for illegal marketing activities:

- In May 2012, the DOJ announced it had reached a settlement totaling $1.5 billion with Abbott Laboratories for unlawful promotion of the drug Depakote. Abbott had promoted the drug to control agitation and aggression in elderly dementia patients, and also to treat schizophrenia, when the U.S. Food and Drug Administration (FDA) had approved its use only in the treatment of epileptic seizures, bipolar mania, and migraines.

- In July 2012, the DOJ announced that GlaxoSmithKline (GSK) had agreed to pay $3 billion to resolve multiple cases regarding "unlawful promotion of certain prescription drugs, its failure to report certain safety data, and its civil liability for alleged false price reporting practices." The settlement was touted as the largest health care fraud settlement in U.S. history at the time. Two specific examples of this "off-label" promotion were marketing Paxil as a treatment for pediatric depression and marketing Wellbutrin for weight loss, sexual dysfunction, substance addiction, and attention deficit hyperactivity disorder (ADHD). In neither case was FDA approval granted for these treatments.

- In November 2013, the DOJ announced that global health care giant Johnson & Johnson (J&J) had agreed to pay more than $2.2 billion to settle civil and criminal liabilities in relation to off-label marketing and kickbacks. The settlement included $485 million in criminal fines and $1.72 billion in civil penalties with the federal government and states in relation to the prescription drugs Risperdal, Invega, and Natrecor.

Each of these settlements lacked any admission of liability on the part of the drug companies, nor were there any specific commitments to improve internal processes to prevent these activities from occurring again (other than promising to remain compliant to existing legislation). While the Justice Department may be publicly committed to stamping out illegal marketing activities as part of a larger commitment to minimizing health care fraud, the questions remain as to whether these monetary settlements are large enough to be truly punitive, and whether or not they achieve any effective conduct modification on the part of the pharmaceutical companies themselves.

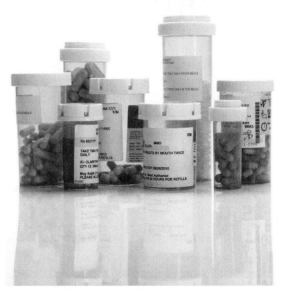

© Jeffrey Coolidge/Getty Images RF

For the FDA, approving a drug for a specific treatment includes prohibition of promotion for any other uses, even if those alternative use statements are true. In 2015, Amarin Pharma, a small drug manufacturer, challenged this position by claiming that limiting marketing promotions for Vascepa, its cardiovascular health drug, violated the company's First Amendment rights to free speech. Judge Paul A. Engelmayer of the federal district court in Manhattan, sided with Amarin Pharma, arguing that the FDA's allowance for physicians to prescribe medications for nonapproved uses (the FDA does not regulate physicians, the states do) represented sufficient incongruity to support the argument that the FDA approach to off-label marketing was restrictive.

The judge's decision granted a preliminary injunction that prevented the FDA from bringing any further action against Amarin Pharma, and the FDA was considering its options at the time this case was written. In September 2015, Pacira Pharmaceuticals filed a similar lawsuit against the FDA in the U.S. District Court for the Southern District of New York, seeking a similar injunction to protect its product, Exparel. It remains to be seen if other companies will follow suit.

QUESTIONS

1. Why would illegal marketing activities feature so frequently in the pharmaceutical industry? At what point would they be considered endemic?

2. Why would pharmaceutical companies choose to continue such practices even when it is made clear that they are illegal?

3. What should the respective boards of directors be doing here? How should they be held accountable?

4. Critics argue that fines are too affordable. In other words, a $1 billion fine for activities that generate several billions of dollars in illegal sales simply becomes a cost of doing business. Should fines be more punitive? How much would be enough?

5. Is the payment of a monetary fine sufficient restitution for these offenses? Why or why not?

6. If the FDA elects to change its position on off-label marketing, would this be a good thing for consumers? Why or why not?

Sources: "GlaxoSmithKline to Plead Guilty and Pay $3 Billion to Resolve Fraud Allegations and Failure to Report Safety Data," *Department of Justice, Office of Public Affairs,* July 2, 2012, and "Johnson & Johnson to Pay More Than $2.2 Billion to Resolve Criminal and Civil Investigations," *Department of Justice, Office of Public Affairs,* November 4, 2013; Peter J. Henning, "FDA's 'Off-Label' Drug Policy Leads to Free-Speech Fight," *The New York Times,* August 10, 2015; and Jann Bellamy, "The Amarin Case: Off-Label Promotion and a Double Standard for Prescription Drugs vs. Dietary Supplements," *Science-Based Medicine,* October 15, 2015.

[References]

1. Adapted from Procopio, Cory, Hargreaves, and Savitch, LLP, "Summary of the U.S. Foreign Corrupt Practices Act," http://www.procopio.com/uploads/model/Block/4535/pdf/93/summary-of-the-u-s-foreign-corrupt-practices-act-854.pdf

2. Danielle Ivory, "Alstom to Plead Guilty and Pay U.S. a $772 Million Fine in a Bribery Scheme," *The New York Times,* December 22, 2014.

3. Richard L. Cassis, "BNY Mellon Pays $15 Million in FCPA Settlement for Internship Hiring Practices," *The FCPA Blog,* August 18, 2015.

4. W. M. Rexroad, T. J. F. Bishop, J. A. Ostrosky, and L. M. Leinicke, "The Federal Sentencing Guidelines for Organizations: Self-Policing Is Central to Minimizing Liability Risk," *The CPA Journal* 69, no. 2 (February 1999); D. R. Dalton, M. B. Metzger, and J. W. Hill, "The New U.S. Sentencing Commission Guidelines: A Wake-Up Call for Corporate America," *The Academy of Management Executive* 8, no. 1 (February 1994), p. 7.

5. "The Sarbanes-Oxley Act of 2002: Strategies for Meeting New Internal Control Reporting Challenges—A White Paper," copyright 2002 Pricewaterhouse-Coopers, as used in L. P. Hartman, *Perspectives in Ethics,* 3rd ed. (New York: McGraw-Hill, 2005), pp. 681–683.

6. U.S. Senate Committee on Banking, Housing, and Urban Affairs, http://banking.senate.gov/public/.

7. "The Dodd-Frank Bill Up Close," in DealBook, ed. Andrew Ross Sorkin, *The New York Times,* June 28, 2010, http://dealbook.blogs.nytimes.com/2010/06/28/the-dodd-frank-bill-up-close/.

8. Kevin, McCoy, "Dodd-Frank Act: After 3 Years, a Long To-Do List," *USA Today,* June 3, 2013.

9. Brady Dennis, "Congress Passes Financial Reform Bill," *The Washington Post,* July 16, 2010.

© John Lund/Drew Kelly/Blend Images LLC RF

BLOWING THE
WHISTLE

After studying this chapter, you should be able to:

7-1 Explain the term *whistle-blower,* and distinguish between internal and external whistle-blowing.

7-2 Understand the different motivations of a whistle-blower.

7-3 Evaluate the possible consequences of ignoring the concerns of a whistle-blower.

7-4 Recommend how to build internal policies to address the needs of whistle-blowers.

7-5 Analyze the possible risks involved in becoming a whistle-blower.

FRONTLINE FOCUS
Good Money

Ben is a sales team leader at a large chain of tire stores. The company is aggressive and is opening new stores every month. Ben is very ambitious and sees plenty of opportunities to move up in the organization—especially if he is able to make a name for himself as a star salesman.

As with any retail organization, Ben's company is driven by sales, and it is constantly experimenting with new sales campaigns and incentive programs for its salespeople. Ben didn't expect this morning's sales meeting to be any different—a new incentive tied to a new campaign, supported by a big media campaign in the local area.

Ben's boss, John, didn't waste any time in getting to the point of the meeting:

"OK guys, I have some big news. Rather than simply negotiating short-term incentives on specific brands to generate sales, the company has signed an exclusive contract with Benfield Tires to take every tire produced in the new Voyager line. That exclusive contract comes with a huge discount based on serious volume. In other words, the more tires we sell, the more money we'll make—and I'm talking about good money for the company and very good bonus money for you—so put everybody into these tires. If we do well in this first contract with Benfield, there could be other exclusives down the road. This could be the beginning of something big for us."

John then laid out the details on the sales incentive and showed Ben and his fellow team leaders how they could earn thousands of dollars in bonuses over the next couple of months if they pushed the new Benfield Voyagers.

Ben could certainly use the money, but he was concerned about pushing a new tire model so aggressively when it was an unknown in the marketplace. He decided to talk to their most experienced tire mechanic, Rick. Rick had worked for the company for over 25 years—so long that many of the younger guys joked that he either had tire rubber in his veins or had apprenticed on Henry Ford's Model T.

"So, Rick, what do you think about these new Benfield Voyagers?" asked Ben. "Are they really such a good deal for our customers, or are they just a moneymaker for us?"

Rick was very direct in his response: "I took a look at some of the specs on them, and they don't look good. I think Benfield is sacrificing quality to cut costs. By the standards of some of our other suppliers, these tires would qualify as 'seconds'—and pretty bad ones too. You couldn't pay me to put them on my car—they're good for 15,000 miles at the most. We're taking a big risk promoting these tires as our top model."

QUESTIONS

1. If Ben decides to raise concerns about the product quality of the Benfield Voyagers, he will become a whistle-blower. The difference between internal and external whistle-blowing is discussed later in the chapter. Which approach should Ben follow if he does decide to raise his concerns?

2. The five conditions that must exist for whistle-blowing to be ethical are outlined later in the chapter. Has Rick given Ben enough information to be concerned about the Benfield Voyagers?

3. What should Ben do now?

> The word *whistle-blower* suggests that you're a tattletale or that you're somehow disloyal. . . . But I wasn't disloyal in the least bit. People were dying. I was loyal to a higher order of ethical responsibility.

Dr. Jeffrey Wigand, *The Insider*

>> What Is Whistle-Blowing?

When an employee discovers evidence of malpractice or misconduct in an organization, he or she faces an ethical dilemma. On the one hand, the employee must consider the "rightness" of his or her actions in raising concerns about this misconduct and the extent to which such actions will benefit both the organization and the public good. On the other hand, the employee must balance a public duty with a corresponding duty to his or her employer to honor the trust and loyalty placed in him or her by the organization.

So some serious choices have to be made. First, the employee can choose to "let it slide" or "turn a blind eye"—a choice that will relate directly to the corporate culture under which the organization operates. An open and trusting culture would encourage employees to speak out for the greater good of the company and fellow employees. A closed and autocratic culture, on the other hand, would lead employees to believe that it would be wiser not to draw attention to themselves, to simply keep their mouths shut. However, if an employee's personal value system prompts him or her to speak out on the misconduct, the employee immediately takes on the role of a **whistle-blower**.

The employee then faces a second and equally important choice. One option is to bring the misconduct to the attention of a manager or supervisor and take the complaint through appropriate channels within the organization. We refer to this option as **internal whistle-blowing**. If the employee chooses to go outside the organization and bring the misconduct to the attention of law enforcement officials or the media, we refer to this decision as **external whistle-blowing**.

Whistle-Blower An employee who discovers corporate misconduct and chooses to bring it to the attention of others.

Internal Whistle-Blowing An employee discovering corporate misconduct and bringing it to the attention of his or her supervisor, who then follows established procedures to address the misconduct within the organization.

External Whistle-Blowing An employee discovering corporate misconduct and choosing to bring it to the attention of law enforcement agencies and/or the media.

PROGRESS ✔ QUESTIONS

1. What is a whistle-blower?
2. What is internal whistle-blowing?
3. What is external whistle-blowing?
4. Is whistle-blowing a good thing?

>> The Ethics of Whistle-Blowing

It may be argued that whistle-blowers provide an invaluable service to their organizations and the general public. The discovery of illegal activities before the situation is revealed in the media could potentially save organizations millions of dollars in fines and lost revenue from the inevitable damage to their corporate reputations. The discovery of potential harm to consumers (from pollution or product-safety issues, for example) offers immeasurable benefit to the general public. From this perspective, it is easy to see why the media often applaud whistle-blowers as models of honor and integrity at a time when integrity in the business world seems to be in very short supply.

However, in contrast to the general perception that whistle-blowers are brave men and women putting their careers and personal lives at risk to do the right thing, some argue that such actions are not brave at all—they are, it is argued, actions motivated by money or by the personal egos of "loose cannons" and "troublemakers" who challenge the policies and practices of their employers while claiming to act as the corporate conscience. In addition, rather than being viewed as performing a praiseworthy act, whistle-blowers are often severely criticized as informers, "sneaks," spies, or "squealers" who have in some way breached the trust and loyalty they owe to their employers.

© Radlund & Associates/Getty Images RF

WHEN IS WHISTLE-BLOWING ETHICAL?

Whistle-blowing is appropriate—ethical—under five conditions:[1]

1. When the company, through a product or decision, will cause serious and considerable harm to the public (as consumers or bystanders) or break existing laws, the employee should report the organization.
2. When the employee identifies a serious threat of harm, he or she should report it and state his or her moral concern.
3. When the employee's immediate supervisor does not act, the employee should exhaust the internal procedures and chain of command to the board of directors.

4. The employee must have documented evidence that is convincing to a reasonable, impartial observer that his or her view of the situation is accurate, and evidence that the firm's practice, product, or policy seriously threatens and puts in danger the public or product user.

5. The employee must have valid reasons to believe that revealing the wrongdoing to the public will result in the changes necessary to remedy the situation. The chance of succeeding must be equal to the risk and danger the employee takes to blow the whistle.

WHEN IS WHISTLE-BLOWING UNETHICAL?

If there is evidence that the employee is motivated by the opportunity for financial gain or media attention or that the employee is carrying out an individual vendetta against the company, then the legitimacy of the act of whistle-blowing must be questioned.

The potential for financial gain in some areas of corporate whistle-blowing can be considerable:

- On November 30, 2005, New York City's Beth Israel Hospital agreed to pay $72.9 million to resolve allegations from a former hospital executive that it falsified Medicare cost reports from 1992 to 2001. The case stemmed from a 2001 whistle-blower lawsuit filed in the U.S. District Court in New York City by a former Beth Israel vice president of financial services, Najmuddin Pervez. Pervez was expected to receive 20 percent of the recovery amount, around $15 million.[2]

- In June 2010, Northrop Grumman Corp. agreed to pay the federal government $12.5 million to settle allegations that the company caused false claims to be submitted to the government. Allegedly, Northrop Grumman's Navigation Systems Division failed to test electronic components it supplied for military airplane, helicopter, and submarine navigation systems to ensure that the parts would function at the extreme temperatures required for military and space uses. This case was filed under the *qui tam* provisions of the federal False Claims Act by whistle-blower Allen Davis, a former quality assurance manager at Northrop Grumman's Navigation Systems Division facility in Salt Lake City. Davis will receive $2.4 million out of the settlement.[3]

- Douglas Durand, former vice president of sales for TAP Pharmaceutical Products, received a $126 million settlement from the U.S. government after filing suit against his employer and a TAP rival, the former Zeneca, Inc., accusing both companies of overcharging the federal government's Medicare program by tens of millions of dollars.[4]

Under the federal Civil False Claims Act, also known as "Lincoln's Law," whistle-blowers (referred to as "relators") who expose fraudulent behavior against the government are entitled to between 10 and 30 percent of the amount recovered. Originally enacted during the Civil War in 1863 to protect the government against fraudulent defense contractors, the act was strengthened as recently as 1986 to make it easier and safer for whistle-blowers to come forward. The lawsuits brought under the act are referred to as *qui tam,* which is an abbreviation for a longer Latin phrase that establishes the whistle-blower as a deputized petitioner for the government in the case. Since 1986, more than 2,400 *qui tam* lawsuits have been filed, recovering over $2 billion for the government and enriching whistle-blowers by more than $350 million.

> *Qui Tam* Lawsuit A lawsuit brought on behalf of the federal government by a whistle-blower under the False Claims Act of 1863.

Whether the motivation to speak out and reveal the questionable behavior comes from a personal ethical decision or the potential for a substantial financial windfall will probably never be completely verified, but the threat of losing your job or becoming alienated from colleagues by speaking out against your employer must be diminished by the knowledge that some financial security will likely result. Whether the choice is based on ethical or financial considerations, you had better be very sure of your facts and your evidence had better be irrefutable before crossing that line.

> ### Key Point !
>
> The large payouts to whistle-blowers in *qui tam* lawsuits are a direct result of the way the legislation is written. Is it fair to question the motives of those whistle-blowers simply because the corporate conduct they are revealing affects the U.S. government? On the other hand, do you think the potential for that payout influences that person's decision to become a whistle-blower?

5. List five conditions for whistle-blowing to be considered ethical.

6. Under what condition could whistle-blowing be considered unethical?

7. If you blow the whistle on a company for a personal vendetta against another employee but receive no financial reward, is that more or less ethical than doing it just for the money?

8. Would the lack of any financial reward make you more or less willing to consider being a whistle-blower? Why?

THE YEAR OF THE WHISTLE-BLOWER

Since examples of internal whistle-blowing rarely receive media attention, it is impossible to track the history of such actions. However, external whistle-blowing is a 20th-century phenomenon. One of the first instances of the use of the term *whistle-blower* occurred in 1963 when Otto Otopeka was dismissed from the U.S. State Department after giving classified documents on security risks to the chief counsel of the Senate Subcommittee on Internal Security. In the 1970s, the Watergate scandal broke after former Marine commander Daniel Ellsberg leaked over 7,000 pages of confidential Pentagon documents on government misconduct in the Vietnam conflict to the press, risking life imprisonment to do so; and an anonymous source named Deep Throat (only recently revealed to be Mark Felt, former assistant director of the FBI during the Nixon administration) helped *Washington Post* journalists Bob Woodward and Carl Bernstein expose the extent of government misconduct in attempting to track down Ellsberg.

Public awareness of whistle-blowers reached a peak in 2002 when *Time* magazine awarded its Person of the Year award to three women "of ordinary demeanor but exceptional guts and sense":[5]

- *Sherron Watkins,* the vice president at Enron Corp., who, in the summer of 2001, wrote two key e-mails warning Enron Chairman Ken Lay that it was only a matter of time before the company's creative "accounting treatment" would be discovered and bring the entire organization down.

- *Coleen Rowley,* an FBI staff attorney, who rose to public prominence in May 2002 when she made public a memo to Director Robert Mueller about the frustration and dismissive behavior she faced from the FBI when her Minneapolis, Minnesota, field office argued for the investigation of a suspected terrorist, Zacarias Moussaoui, who was later indicted as a co-conspirator in the September 11, 2001, attacks.

- *Cynthia Cooper,* whose internal auditing team first uncovered questionable accounting practices at WorldCom. Her team's initial estimates placed the discrepancy at $3.8 billion; the final balance was nearer to $11 billion.

>> The Duty to Respond

Whether you believe whistle-blowers to be heroes who face considerable personal hardship to bring the harsh light of media attention to unethical behavior, or you take the opposing view that they are breaking the oath of loyalty to their employer, the fact remains that employees are becoming increasingly willing to respond to any questionable behavior they observe in the workplace. The choice for an employer is to ignore them and face public embarrassment and potentially ruinous financial penalties, or to create an internal system that allows whistle-blowers to be heard and

© Christian Simonpietri/ Sygma/Corbis

© Mark Peterson/Corbis

Karen Silkwood

In the 1983 film Silkwood, *Meryl Streep portrayed Karen Silkwood, a nuclear plant employee who blew the whistle on unsafe practices. The real Karen Silkwood died in an auto accident under mysterious circumstances.*

With their classic portrayals of good guys against the corporate bad guys, movie depictions of whistle-blowers are by no means a new idea. Films such as *The China Syndrome, Silkwood,* and *The Insider* have documented the risks and challenges whistle-blowers face in bringing the information they uncover to the general public.

The movie *The Insider* documents the case of Dr. Jeffrey Wigand and his decision to go public with information alleging that his employer, the tobacco company Brown & Williamson (B&W), was actively manipulating the nicotine content of its cigarettes. Wigand was portrayed by Russell Crowe, and the part of Lowell Bergman, the CBS *60 Minutes* producer who helped Wigand go public, was played by Al Pacino.

The movie captures several key issues that are common to many whistle-blower cases:

 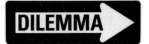

© Photodisc/Getty Images RF

- Wigand was initially reticent to speak out about the information—partly out of fear of the impact on his family if he lost his severance package and health benefits under the terms of his confidentiality agreement with B&W, and partly because of his strong sense of integrity in honoring any contracts he had signed. It was only after B&W had chosen to modify the confidentiality agreement after firing Wigand (allegedly for "poor communication skills") that Wigand, angered by B&W's apparent belief that he wouldn't honor the confidentiality agreement he had signed, chose to go public.
- B&W's response was immediate and aggressive. It won a restraining (or "gag") order against Wigand to prevent him from giving evidence as an expert witness in a case against tobacco companies brought by the state of Mississippi, but he testified anyway. B&W then proceeded to undertake a detailed disclosure of Wigand's background in order to undermine his reputation, eventually releasing a thick report titled "The Misconduct of Jeffrey S. Wigand Available in the Public Record." The extent to which the findings of this investigation were exaggerated was later documented in a *New York Times* newspaper article. The movie portrays Bergman as providing the material for a *New York Times* journalist to refute the B&W claims against Wigand.
- Wigand's testimony was extremely damaging for B&W. He not only accused the CEO of B&W, Thomas Sanderfur, of misrepresentation in stating before congressional hearings in 1994 that he believed that nicotine was not addictive, but Wigand also claimed that cigarettes were merely "a delivery system for nicotine."
- Even though Wigand's credibility as a witness had been verified, CBS initially chose not to run Wigand's interview with CBS reporter Mike Wallace in fear of a lawsuit from B&W for "tortious interference" (which is defined as action by a third party in coming between two parties in a contractual relationship—that is, CBS would be held liable for intervening between Wigand

and B&W in the confidentiality agreement Wigand had signed). The fact that CBS's parent company was in the final stages of negotiations to sell CBS to the Westinghouse Corp. was seen as evidence of CBS's highly questionable motivation in avoiding the danger of tortious interference. In reality, the fear of litigation was probably well founded. After ABC had run an equally controversial segment on its *Day One* show accusing Philip Morris of raising nicotine levels in its cigarettes, Philip Morris, along with another tobacco company, R. J. Reynolds, launched a $10 billion lawsuit against ABC, which was forced to apologize and pay the tobacco companies' legal fees (estimated at over $15 million).

- In November 1998, B&W subsequently joined with three other tobacco giants—Philip Morris, R. J. Reynolds, and Lorillard—in signing the Tobacco Master Settlement Agreement (MSA), settling state lawsuits against them in 46 states for recovery of the medical costs of treating smoking-related illnesses. The settlement totaled $206 billion and included provisions that forbade marketing directly or indirectly to children and banned or restricted the use of cartoons, billboards, product placement, or event sponsorship in the marketing of tobacco products.
- As vice president for research and development for B&W, Wigand was a corporate officer for the company and, therefore, the highest-ranking insider ever to turn whistle-blower at the time. His reward for speaking out was that he never reached the $300,000 salary level he held at B&W again. At the time his story went public, he had found employment as a teacher in Louisville, Kentucky, teaching chemistry and Japanese for $30,000 a year. His marriage didn't survive the intense media scrutiny and B&W's attempts to discredit him.
- Six years later, Wigand was interviewed by *Fast Company* magazine, and he shared his unhappiness with the title of whistle-blower: "The word whistle-blower suggests that you're a tattletale or that you're somehow disloyal," he says. "But I wasn't disloyal in

CONTINUED >>

THE INSIDER

the least bit. People were dying. I was loyal to a higher order of ethical responsibility."

QUESTIONS

1. Wigand was initially unwilling to go public with his information. What caused him to change his mind?
2. Did CBS pursue Wigand's story because it was the right thing to do, or because it was a good story?

3. Since CBS played such a large part in bringing Wigand's story to the public, do you think the network also had an obligation to support him once the story broke? Explain why or why not.
4. Was CBS's decision not to run the interview driven by any ethical concerns?

Sources: Elizabeth Gleick, "Where There's Smoke," *Time,* February 12, 1996, p. 54; Ron Scherer, "One Man's Crusade against Tobacco Firms," *Christian Science Monitor,* November 30, 1995, p. 3; and "Jeffrey Wigand: The Whistle-Blower," *Fast Company,* March 2002.

responded to *before* the issue escalates to an external whistle-blowing case. Obviously, responding to whistle-blowers in this context means addressing their concerns, and not, as many employers have decided, firing them.

Before 2002, legal protection for whistle-blowers existed only through legislation that encouraged the moral behavior of employees who felt themselves compelled to speak out, without offering any safeguards against retaliation aimed at them. As far back as the False Claims Act of 1863, designed to prevent profiteering from the Civil War, the government has been willing to split up to 30 percent of the recovered amount with the person filing the petition—a potentially lucrative bargain—but it offered no specific prohibitions against retaliatory behavior.

The Whistleblower Protection Act of 1989 finally addressed the issue of retaliation against federal employees who bring accusations of unethical

behavior. The act imposed specific performance deadlines in processing whistle-blower complaints and guaranteed the anonymity of the whistle-blower unless revealing the name would prevent criminal activity or protect public safety. The act also required prompt payment of any portion of the settlement to which the whistle-blower would be entitled, even if the case were still working its way through the appeals process.

The Whistleblower Protection Act of 1989 applied only to federal employees. Not until the Sarbanes-Oxley Act of 2002 (also known as the Corporate and Criminal Fraud Accountability Act, and most commonly abbreviated to SOX) did Congress take an integrated approach to the matter of whistle-blowing by both prohibiting retaliation against whistle-blowers and encouraging the act of whistle-blowing itself.[6]

The Dodd-Frank Wall Street Reform and Consumer Protection Act of 2010 introduced a new reward program for whistle-blowers who report securities law violations to the Securities and Exchange Commission (SEC) or the Commodity Futures Trading Commission (CFTC). The legislation stipulates that if more than $1 million is collected, the whistle-blower is entitled to between 10 and 30 percent of the monies collected, in addition to a clear entitlement to job and confidentiality protection. The SEC's new Office of the Whistleblower was created in August 2011 and received 2,700 tips in its first year.

> **Key Point**
>
> The language on a whistle-blower's entitlement to "all compensatory damages to make the employee whole" is not clear in the SOX legislation. Considering the cases you have read in this chapter, what would you need to be made "whole"?

PROGRESS ✓ QUESTIONS

9. If an employee blows the whistle on an organization on the basis of a rumor, is that ethical?
10. If that information turns out to be false, should the employee be liable for damages? Explain your answer.
11. Compensation under Dodd-Frank isn't as clear as the percentage of the funds recovered for a government whistle-blower. Does that make it less likely that we'll see more whistle-blowing under Dodd-Frank?
12. Under SOX, complaining to the media isn't recognized as whistle-blowing. Is that ethical?

>> Addressing the Needs of Whistle-Blowers

Given this new legal environment surrounding whistle-blowers, all employers would be wise to put the following mechanisms in place:

1. A well-defined process to document how such complaints are handled—a nominated contact person, clearly identified authority to respond to the complaints, firm assurances of confidentiality, and nonretaliation against the employee.
2. An employee hotline to file such complaints, again with firm assurances of confidentiality and nonretaliation to the employee.

3. A prompt and thorough investigation of all complaints.
4. A detailed report of all investigations, documenting all corporate officers involved and all action taken.

Above all, employers must have a commitment to follow through on any and all reports whether or not those reports end up being substantiated. For a **whistle-blower hotline** to work, trust must be established between employees and their employer—trust that the information can be given anonymously and without fear of retaliation, even if the identity of the whistle-blower is ultimately revealed during the investigation.

The organization can make all the promises in the world, but until that first report is investigated through to a full conclusion, the hotline may never ring again. If the investigation is perceived to be half-hearted, or there is even the remotest suggestion of a cover-up, then the hotline will definitely never ring again.

> **Whistle-Blower Hotline**
> A telephone line by which employees can leave messages to alert a company of suspected misconduct without revealing their identity.

A HOTLINE CALL

Real World Applications

Pat is the newest member of a three-person crew for the local franchise of a national moving company. The team leader is Gene, who has been with the company for a couple of years now. Pat has serious concerns about some of Gene's business practices—he has asked Pat to do some "private" cash-only moves (off the books but using the company's equipment) and has negotiated very low prices for "friends" with, Pat suspects, an agreement to receive cash under the table in return for the low price bid. Pat thinks that Gene's tactics are damaging the company's reputation and putting Pat's job security in jeopardy. The company has a hotline number for employees to share such concerns, and the company guarantees anonymity for all callers. However, with only three people on the crew, if something happens to Gene, Pat is concerned that it won't take Gene too long to figure out who placed the call. What should Pat do?

PROGRESS ✔ QUESTIONS

13. How should managers or supervisors respond to an employee who brings evidence of questionable behavior to their attention?
14. Should that employee be given any reassurances of protection for making the tough decision to come forward?
15. Do you think a hotline that guarantees the anonymity of the caller will encourage more employees to come forward?
16. Does your company have a whistle-blower hotline? How did you find out that there is (or isn't) one?

>> Conclusion: Whistle-Blowing as a Last Resort

The perceived bravery and honor in doing the right thing by speaking out against corporate wrongdoing at personal risk to your own career and financial stability adds a gloss to the act of whistle-blowing that is

The media's attention to Jeffrey Wigand, Sherron Watkins, Coleen Rowley, and Cynthia Cooper could lead you to believe that doing the right thing and speaking out against the perceived wrongdoings of your employer will guarantee you public support as an honorable and ethical person, putting the needs of your fellow human beings before your own. In reality, the majority of whistle-blowers face the opposite situation. They are branded as traitors, shunned by their former colleagues, and often singled out to the extent that they never find work in their respective industries again. Consider the cases of the following two individuals who made the same tough ethical choices as their more famous counterparts with markedly different outcomes.

Khaled Assadi, an American employee of GE Energy, was temporarily assigned to the company's Amman, Jordan, operations, where he was responsible for coordinating with Iraq's governing bodies to secure and manage energy service contracts. In 2011 Assadi reported to both his supervisors and the GE ombudsperson that the company could be in violation of the Foreign Corrupt Practices Act (FCPA) for actions taken in relation to a joint venture agreement with the Iraqi minister of electricity. Assadi alleged that, during the negotiations, the company agreed to hire Iman Mahmood, a woman "closely associated" with the senior deputy minister for electricity, at the specific request of that minister. Assadi was later fired from the company.

In a subsequent lawsuit alleging that his termination represented illegal retaliation for his disclosures of alleged bribery, Assadi stated that he received a negative performance review immediately after reporting his concerns about the hiring of Iman Mahmood, and that GE began "constant and aggressive severance negotiations" to force him to leave the company until it finally "abruptly ended all discussions and terminated" him.

Assadi sought protection under the Dodd-Frank whistle-blower provisions, but in June 2012, the U.S. Court for the Southern District of Texas dismissed the lawsuit on the grounds that the antiretaliation provision did not apply in cases of "extraterritoriality" (where the petitioner was assigned overseas at the time of the alleged event).

Kyle Lagow, a former home appraiser, will receive $14.5 million as part of a whistle-blower lawsuit that accused subprime lender Countrywide Financial (a Bank of America subsidiary) of inflating appraisal values on government-insured loans. Lagow lost his job after raising concerns about appraisal practices at his company, and his inability to find similar employment after the termination placed his family in severe financial hardship.

© U. Baumgarten/Getty Images

His complaint was brought under the *qui tam* provision, and his lawsuit was one of five whistle-blower complaints that were folded into a larger $25 billion national mortgage settlement that five banks—Ally Bank (formerly GMAC), Bank of America, Citicorp, JPMorgan Chase, and Wells Fargo—reached with state and federal officials in February 2012.

QUESTIONS

1. Who took the greater risk here: Khaled Assadi or Kyle Lagow? Why?
2. Was the alleged behavior at GE Energy more or less unethical than the behavior at Countrywide Financial? Explain your answer.
3. Do you think Assadi and Lagow regret their decisions to go public with their information? Why or why not?
4. Do you think their behavior changed anything at either company?

Sources: "Dodd-Frank Whistleblower Provisions not Extended to American Working Abroad," *SEC Whistleblower Blog,* July 6, 2012; and Rick Rothacker, "Bank of America Whistleblower Receives $14.5 Million in Mortgage Case" *Reuters,* May 29, 2012.

THE COLD, HARD REALITY

undeserved. The fact that an employee is left with no option but to go public with information should be seen as evidence that the organization has failed to address the situation internally for the long-term improvement of the corporation and all its stakeholders. Becoming a whistle-blower and taking your story public should be seen as the last resort rather than the first. The fall-out of unceasing media attention and the often terminal damage to the reputation and long-term economic viability of the organization should be enough of a threat to force even the most stubborn executive team to the table with a commitment to fix whatever has been broken. Regrettably, the majority of executives appear to be unwilling to fix the problem internally and, where necessary, notify the appropriate authorities of the problem—they choose to either bury the information and hire the biggest legal gunslinger they can find to discredit the evidence or, as in the case of Jeffrey Wigand, tie their employees in such restrictive confidentiality agreements that speaking out exposes the employee to extreme financial risk, which managers no doubt hope will prompt the employee to "keep his mouth shut."

As Peter Rost explains:[7]

A study of 233 whistle-blowers by Donald Soeken of St. Elizabeth's Hospital in Washington, DC, found that the average whistle-blower was a man in his forties with a strong conscience and high moral values.

After blowing the whistle on fraud, 90 percent of the whistle-blowers were fired or demoted, 27 percent faced lawsuits, 26 percent had to seek psychiatric or physical care, 25 percent suffered alcohol abuse, 17 percent lost their homes, 15 percent got divorced, 10 percent attempted suicide, and 8 percent were bankrupted. But in spite of all this, only 16 percent said they wouldn't blow the whistle again.

Life Skills

>> Making difficult decisions

In Chapter 1, "Understanding Ethics," we talked about using your personal value system to live your life according to your own ethical standards. As you have seen in this chapter, people like Jeffrey Wigand, Sherron Watkins, Coleen Rowley, and Christine Casey may come across situations in their business lives where the behavior they observe is in direct conflict to their ethical standards, and they find themselves unable to simply look the other way.

Ask yourself what you would do in such a situation. Would you ignore it? Could you live with that decision? If you chose to speak out, either as an internal or external whistle-blower, could you live with the consequences of that decision? What if there was a negative impact on the company as a result of your actions and people lost their jobs, as they did at Enron or WorldCom? Could you live with that responsibility?

Speaking out in response to your own ethical standards is only one part of the decision. The consequences for you, your immediate family, your co-workers, and all the other stakeholders in the organization represent an equally important part of that decision. You can see why whistle-blowers face such emotional turmoil before, during, and after what is probably one of the toughest decisions of their lives.

If you find yourself in such a situation, don't make the decision alone. Talk to people you can trust, and let them help you review all the issues and all the potential consequences of the decision you are about to make.

FRONTLINE FOCUS
Good Money—Ben Makes a Decision

Ben lost a lot of sleep that night. He trusted Rick as his most experienced tire mechanic, but he had never seen him be so negative about one particular tire model—and it wasn't as if he had anything to gain by trashing the reputation of a tire that the company wanted to sell so aggressively.

The company had sold seconds before—heck, they even sold "used" tires for those customers looking to save a few bucks. How was this any different? Plus, Rick didn't have to deal with the sales pressure that John placed on his team leaders—you had to hit your quota every week or else—and if the company was pushing Benfield Voyagers, then John expected to see him sell Benfield Voyagers by the dozen.

But what if Rick was right? What if Benfield had cut corners to save on costs? They could end up with another Firestone disaster on their hands. What was Ben supposed to do with this information? If Rick was so concerned, why wasn't he speaking up? The company advertised its hotline for employees to use if they had concerns about any business practices. Why was it Ben's job to say something? He needed this job. He had bills to pay just like the other guys in the store—in fact, the bills were getting pretty high and that bonus money would really help right now.

Ben tossed and turned for a few more hours before reaching a decision. Rick might be right to be concerned, but he was only one guy. The guys at corporate looked at the same specs as Rick did, and if they could live with them, then so could Ben. He wasn't going to put his neck on the block just on the basis of Rick's concerns. If the company was putting its faith in Benfield Voyagers, then Ben was going to sell more of them than anyone else in the company.

Two weeks later, there was a fatal crash involving a minivan with three passengers—a husband and wife and their young son. The minivan had been fitted with Benfield Voyagers at Ben's tire store just one week earlier.

QUESTIONS

1. What do you think will happen now?
2. What will be the consequences for Ben, Rick, their tire store, and Benfield?
3. Should Ben have spoken out against the Voyager tires?

[For Review]

1. **Explain the term *whistle-blower*, and distinguish between internal and external whistle-blowing.**

   When an employee discovers evidence of corporate misconduct and chooses to bring that evidence to the attention of others, he or she becomes a whistle-blower. If that employee chooses to bring the evidence to the attention of executives within the organization through appropriate channels, that option is referred to as internal whistle-blowing. If, on the other hand, the employee chooses to go outside the organization and contact law enforcement officials or the media, that option is referred to as external whistle-blowing.

2. **Understand the different motivations of a whistle-blower.**

   Whistle-blowers are generally considered to be models of honor and integrity at a time when integrity in the business world seems to be in very short supply. However, such actions can also be motivated by the desire for revenge, when an ex-employee feels maligned and tries to create trouble for her former employer. In addition, the potential for financial gain through the settlement of qui tam lawsuits can be seen to bring the true intent of the whistle-blower into question.

3. **Evaluate the possible consequences of ignoring the concerns of a whistle-blower.**

   The opportunity to address illegal or unethical activities before the situation is revealed in the media could potentially save an organization's corporate reputation, prevent a punitive fall in the company's stock price, and, as we saw in Chapter 6, help to minimize federal fines. Choosing to dismiss the concerns of a whistle-blower, as organizations seem to do with disheartening frequency, merely serves to escalate an already volatile situation and place the organization in an even deeper hole when the situation is made public.

4. **Recommend how to build internal policies to address the needs of whistle-blowers.**

   The greatest fear of any whistle-blower is retaliation, both within the organization and within that employee's profession. Addressing that fear requires a guarantee of anonymity in coming forward with whatever evidence has been uncovered. For that guarantee to have any credibility, there must be trust between employees and their employer. Critics argue that expecting such trust to be present in an environment where illegal/unethical behavior is taking place is unrealistic. Nevertheless, the organization can encourage whistle-blowers to come forward with a series of clearly defined initiatives:

- A well-defined process to document how such complaints are handled—a nominated contact person, clearly identified authority to respond to the complaints, firm assurances of confidentiality, and nonretaliation against the employee.
- An employee hotline to file such complaints, again with firm assurances of confidentiality and nonretaliation to the employee.
- A prompt and thorough investigation of all complaints.
- A detailed report of all investigations, documenting all corporate officers involved and all action taken.

5. **Analyze the possible risks involved in becoming a whistle-blower.**

   The media attention given to whistle-blowers as guardians of corporate conscience adds a gloss to the act of whistle-blowing that is undeserved. Jeffrey Wigand's decision cost him his marriage and his career. The media attention can be intrusive and unceasing, with harmful effects on every member of your family. Potentially lucrative settlements may offer some compensation, but those settlements can often take years to materialize and may offer little consolation to family members who have been uprooted and moved cross-country to start new lives away from the media spotlight. We may analyze the actions of a whistle-blower as a personal choice, but ultimately that choice affects many people.

[Key Terms]

External Whistle-Blowing 144

Internal Whistle-Blowing 144

Qui Tam Lawsuit 145

Whistle-Blower 144

Whistle-Blower Hotline 149

[Review Questions]

1. Why are whistle-blowers regarded as models of honor and integrity?

2. Which whistle-blowing option is better for an organization: internal or external? Why?

3. Why would an organization decide to ignore evidence presented by a whistle-blower?

4. Is it reasonable for a whistle-blower to expect a guarantee of anonymity?

5. Why would a whistle-blower be concerned about retaliation?

6. Why is trust such an important issue in whistle-blowing?

[Review Exercises]

How would you act in the following situations?

1. You work for a meatpacking company. You have discovered credible evidence that your company's delivery drivers have been stealing cuts of meat and replacing them with ice to ensure that the delivery meets the stated weight on the delivery invoice. The company has 12 drivers, and, as far as you can tell, they are *all* in on this scheme. Your company has a well-advertised whistle-blower hotline. What do you do?

2. What would you do if your company did *not* have a whistle-blower policy?

3. You later discover that one of the drivers was not a part of the scheme but was fired anyway when the information was made public. What do you do?

4. Should the driver get his job back? Why or why not?

[Internet Exercises]

1. Visit the Government Accountability Project (GAP) at www.whistleblower.org.

   a. What is the mission of GAP?

   b. How is GAP funded?

   c. What kind of assistance is available through GAP for someone thinking about becoming a whistle-blower?

2. Visit the National Whistleblower Center at www.whistleblowers.org.

   a. Select the biography of one whistle-blower (not already mentioned in this book) and briefly summarize the details of the case.

   b. Which publication is recommended for information pertaining to your rights as a whistle-blower?

3. There are now two whistle-blowing websites separated by only one letter: Summarize their differences, and propose which one offers the greatest assistance to a potential whistle-blower.

[Team Exercises]

1. **Guilt by omission.**

   Divide into two groups, and prepare arguments *for* and *against* the following behavior: *You work for a large retail clothing company that spends a large amount of its advertising budget emphasizing that its clothes are "Made in America." You discover that only 15 percent of its garments are actually "made" in America. The other 85 percent are actually either cut from patterns overseas and assembled here in the United States or cut and assembled overseas and imported as completed garments. Your hometown depends on this clothing company as the largest local employer. Several of your friends and family work at the local garment assembly factory. Should you go public with this information?*

2. **"Tortious interference."**

   Divide into two groups, and prepare arguments *for* and *against* the following behavior: *In the case of Dr. Jeffrey Wigand and the Brown & Williamson Tobacco Company, the CBS Broadcasting Company chose not to air Dr. Wigand's 60 Minutes interview with Mike Wallace under threat of legal action for "tortious interference" between B&W and Dr. Wigand. There were suspicions that CBS was more concerned about avoiding any potential legal action that could derail its pending sale to the Westinghouse Corporation. Was CBS behaving ethically in putting the welfare of its stakeholders in the Westinghouse deal ahead of its obligation to support Dr. Wigand?*

3. **A new approach to freshness.**

   Divide into two groups, and prepare arguments *for* and *against* the following behavior: *You work in the meat department of store 2795 of a large retail grocery chain. The company recently announced a change in the meat-handling protocols from the primary supplier. Starting in January, the meat will be gassed with carbon monoxide before packaging. This retains a brighter color for the meat and delays the discoloration that usually occurs as the meat begins to spoil. You understand from the memo that there will be no information on the product label to indicate this protocol change and that the company has no plans to notify customers of this new process. Should you speak out about the procedure?*

4. **California organic.**

   Divide into two groups and prepare arguments *for* and *against* the following behavior: *You work in the accounting department of a family owned mushroom grower based in California that sells premium organic mushrooms to local restaurants and high-end retail grocery stores. The company's product range includes both fresh and dried mushrooms. Your organic certification allows you to charge top dollar for your product, but you notice from invoices that operating costs are increasing significantly without any increase in revenues. The market won't absorb a price increase, so the company has to absorb the higher costs and accept lower profits. One day you notice invoices for the purchase of dried mushrooms from a Japanese supplier. The dried mushrooms are not listed as being organic, but they are apparently being added to your company's dried mushrooms, which are labeled organic and California-grown. Should you speak out about this?*

Thinking Critically

>> QUESTIONABLE MOTIVES

Bradley Birkenfeld was born in the Boston area but spent the last decade of his professional banking career in Geneva, Switzerland, as a personal banker for wealthy American clients of Swiss banking giant UBS. He has achieved notoriety in the financial services industry as the whistle-blower of the largest tax fraud case in history. As a result of evidence he provided, his former employer, UBS, paid a $780 million fine, agreed to modify its international banking practices, and turned over the account records of 4,450 American account holders who, the IRS believed, were actively seeking to evade their U.S. tax obligations.

© Stockbyte/PunchStock

Birkenfeld was an average midlevel banking executive, and his motives in becoming the first banker to ever provide evidence on Swiss banking practices were initially perceived as altruistic. He offered to wear a wire transmitter to record conversations with high-level UBS executives and to provide documentation on almost 19,000 UBS accounts. In return, he asked for immunity for his past actions as a UBS employee. When we consider the nature of his work, his request for immunity appears to be a very smart move.

Birkenfeld's duties—he was a personal banker—included providing concierge-level service, under the protection of highly secretive Swiss banking laws, helping clients invest, spend, and move their money around the world. Such personal service included, for one wealthy client, the purchase of loose diamonds in Geneva and then personal delivery of those diamonds to the United States, carried through customs in a toothpaste tube. Despite a statement from Birkenfeld that the value of the diamonds was "less than $10,000" (which meant that they did not need to be declared at U.S. Customs), the choice of packaging raises questions about his desire to not draw attention to himself while traveling to the United States. Indeed, it was this practice of low-key, "under the radar" visits from UBS bankers to the United States on trips recorded in their business calendars as "vacations" that drew the attention of the FBI.

Evidence provided by Birkenfeld revealed that these "vacations" were, in fact, carefully planned trips to service UBS's wealthy American clients at luxury yacht races and art shows where, conveniently, UBS bankers could also mingle, network, and solicit new clients. Unfortunately, since those bankers were not licensed to conduct business in the United States, their actions amounted to a clear violation of U.S. banking regulations.

With such a strong case, the U.S. government was able to negotiate, for the first time, the delivery of 4,500 client records of U.S. citizens who were using UBS accounts to evade their domestic tax obligations. Even though UBS sought the intervention of the Swiss government to help its case, it came down to pragmatic reality. With 30,000 employees and a large financial services business in the United States, the bank could not risk losing access to such a large market if it was to remain a global banking institution. In 2009, the bank agreed to pay a fine of $780 million to settle the U.S. government's case.

For Birkenfeld, the immediate outcome was not so positive. Despite his request for immunity for past actions as a UBS banker, he elected not to fully disclose his relationship with California real estate billionaire Igor Olenicoff, who was indicted for trying to evade U.S. taxes on $200 million hidden in Swiss and Lichtenstein bank accounts. Birkenfeld was charged with helping Olenicoff by referring him to a UBS specialist in the creation of offshore "shell" corporations designed to hide the true ownership of UBS accounts. Olenicoff cooperated with the investigation and paid $52 million in fines and back taxes. As a result of his cooperation, Olenicoff served no jail time.

Birkenfeld, on the other hand, was charged with conspiracy to commit tax fraud, pleaded guilty, and received a sentence of 40 months in prison, beginning in January 2010. While he did not dispute his relationship with Olenicoff,

CONTINUED >>

Birkenfeld maintained that his involvement was only as a referral to another UBS specialist. As such, he felt strongly that his jail time was unjust given his altruistic services to the U.S. government in providing evidence against UBS. The Department of Justice officials who indicted Birkenfeld stated that if he had fully disclosed the nature of his relationship with Olenicoff, it's unlikely that he would have been prosecuted, which brings us back to the question of Birkenfeld's true motives in coming forward as a whistle-blower—was it really altruism, or was he looking for a way to handle the mess that the Olenicoff case had created for him?

In either event, there was a definite silver lining in Birkenfeld's cloud. As a key figure in the *qui tam* lawsuit between the U.S. government and UBS, he was eligible for up to 30 percent of the money recovered from UBS. On September 11, 2012, the IRS announced that he would receive $104 million for his assistance in the UBS case. Birkenfeld was unable to be present at the press conference announcing the award since he was under house arrest until November 2012. One last ironic fact in Birkenfeld's battle with his former employer and the U.S. government—his award was fully taxable as regular income.

In an April 2015 interview with CNBC, Birkenfeld appeared to be enjoying the fruits of his labors in his private luxury box at TD Gardens, home of his beloved Boston Bruins hockey team. And yet, Birkenfeld made it clear that he wasn't finished with the Department of Justice. He remains committed to the pursuit of explanations as to why 50,000 people were allowed tax amnesty when the DOJ could have pressed the Swiss banks for the names of all Americans who held secret accounts.

Before you admire his altruism, there is an agenda at work here. "Mr. 30 percent," as he became known during his two-and-a-half years in prison, isn't satisfied with his $104 million share of the $780 million UBS settlement. Since those 50,000 people who took advantage of the IRS amnesty program poured an estimated $7 billion into IRS accounts, Birkenfeld and his lawyers are pursuing the same percentage of that larger amount.

QUESTIONS

1. Birkenfeld was adamant that his prison sentence was unfair when compared to the fact that no one else (e.g., Olenicoff or UBS bankers) went to jail. Did he have a point?

2. Why did UBS elect to settle with the U.S. government?

3. Given that there was an immunity agreement in place, what did the Department of Justice gain from prosecuting Birkenfeld?

4. Critics are concerned that even with the large *qui tam* award, Birkenfeld's prison sentence will discourage other tax whistle-blowers from coming forward. Is that a valid concern? Why or why not?

Sources: Janet Novack, "Banker Charged with Helping Billionaire Dodge Taxes," *Forbes,* May 13, 2008; Ken Stier, "Why Is the UBS Whistle-Blower Headed to Prison?" *Time,* October 6, 2009; Stephen M. Kohn, "Whistleblowing: A Get-Rich-Quick Scheme?" *Forbes,* December 4, 2009; Haig Simonian, "The Price of a Whistleblower," *Financial Times,* February 9, 2010; Ken Stier, "U.S. vs. Swiss Tax Cheats: A Whistleblower Ignored," *Time,* February 13, 2010; David Voreacos, "Banker Who Blew Whistle over Tax Cheats Seeks Pardon," *Bloomberg,* June 24, 2010; CBS, "A Crack in the Swiss Vault," *60 Minutes,* August 15, 2010; "The UBS Whistleblower Bradley's Winnings," *The Economist,* September 15, 2012; and Eamon Javors, "Why Did the US Pay This Former Banker $104M?" *CNBC,* April 30, 2015.

Thinking Critically `7.2`

>> OLYMPUS: PAYING A PRICE FOR DOING WHAT'S RIGHT?

Movies like *Silkwood* and *The Insider* have portrayed whistle-blowers as lone heroes on the front line or in middle management, working against corrupt organizations at great personal risk to their own well-being. At Olympus Corp., the Japanese camera and medical equipment manufacturer, the story was dramatically different. The whistle-blower in this case was recently appointed Chief Executive Officer Michael Woodford.

As the former head of both UK and U.S. operations for Olympus, Woodford's appointment as CEO in February 2011 was recognized as both the summation of a meteoric rise of a talented young executive and as a sign that the insular corporate culture of "Japan Inc." was finally changing. Woodford had benefited greatly from the tutelage and mentorship of Olympus Chairman Tsuyoshi Kikukawa, which made the story of Woodford's first few months at the helm even more distressing.

As part of a regular review of Tokyo operations, Woodford began analyzing four separate acquisitions that Olympus had made between 2006 and 2009. Three of the four—a recycling company, a cosmetics company, and a food container company—had cost Olympus $1 billion, but their assets had already been written down to just a fraction of that on the balance sheet, indicating that they were considered to be of no real value to the corporation. Further investigation revealed that all three companies were registered in the Caribbean tax haven Cayman Islands. In addition, all three companies were dissolved and closed shortly after being acquired by Olympus.

The fourth company—a UK-based medical instruments company called Gyrus—was acquired for $2.2 billion in 2008. The purchase included a $687 million "transaction

© McGraw-Hill Education/Christopher Kerrigan, photographer

fee" to two investment bankers, with the funds going into a Cayman Islands account that was also closed shortly after the deal was concluded. Given that investment-banking fees typically amount to only 1 percent of the transaction, a fee of almost 33 percent was suspicious enough to warrant an independent audit, which the Olympus board had authorized in October 2009. The audit report subsequently declared that the company's directors had done nothing wrong.

In an October 11, 2011, memo to Kikukawa, Woodford expressed his suspicions that a series of clear accounting irregularities had destroyed $1.3 billion of shareholder value in what he described as "a catalogue of calamitous errors and exceptionally poor judgment." The memo concluded with a call for Kikukawa to resign as chairman of Olympus Corp. Three days later, Kikukawa and his board of directors responded by firing Woodford from his position as CEO.

Woodford's personal account of the days that followed his termination reads like a spy novel. Fearing for his life on the basis of a personal belief that the accounting scandal involved members of the *yakuza*—the Japanese mafia—Woodford left Japan for the United Kingdom very shortly afterward. It was later reported that Woodford was able to provide sufficient evidence to warrant investigation into his claims by the FBI, Scotland Yard's Serious Crime Unit, and Tokyo's Securities and Exchange Surveillance Commission.

After weeks of denials—and a disconcerting silence among Japan's regulators and mainstream media—the company was forced to concede in the face of incontrovertible evidence that it had misappropriated funds in order to hide investment losses dating back to the 1990s. Public promises were made to introduce a new Corporate Governance Committee and to release five years' worth of revised financial accounts. Kikukawa finally admitted to fraud and stepped down as chairman of Olympus. He along with two other Olympus executives, former executive vice president Hisashi Mori and former auditing officer Hideo Yamada, faced up to 10 years in jail for their roles in the scandal.

In June 2012, Olympus announced that its board of directors had approved a settlement offer with Woodford of 1.2 billion yen ($15.4 million) for unfair dismissal, but the financial impact of the scandal was far from over. The stock price had plummeted by as much as 80 percent in the immediate post-scandal period, and in November 2012, the company announced that 48 mostly foreign institutional investors and pension funds had filed a lawsuit seeking 19.1 billion yen ($240 million) in compensation for investment losses resulting from the revelation of accounting irregularities.

In July 2013, all three former executives were given suspended sentences, serving no jail time for their roles in the accounting scandal. Kikukawa and Yamada were given three-year sentences, and Mori a two-and-a-half-year sentence. Olympus Corp. was ordered to pay $7 million in fines for its role.

Olympus showed early signs of recovering quickly from the scandal. By the time it announced a joint venture with electronics giant Sony to capture a larger share of the global medical equipment market, profits were rising and the share price had recovered most of the earlier losses. However, the recovery appeared to be short-lived.

Just two years after the alliance, Sony agreed to sell half its stake in Olympus to JPMorgan Chase for $600 million, booking an estimated $300 million profit from the investment. The funds were to be used "to strengthen our financial base and for growth investments."

In March 2016, Olympus agreed to pay $646 million to resolve FCPA charges that kickbacks were paid to U.S. doctors in the purchase of medical devices. A further $22.8 million was paid to resolve a DOJ criminal case involving bribes to health care providers in Latin America.

CONTINUED >>

1. What accounting irregularities did Michael Woodford uncover at Olympus?

2. How did the executive leadership respond to Woodford's revelations?

3. Critics argue that Woodford could have been more effective if he had taken a longer-term approach to addressing the accounting scandal, rather than the "showdown" approach he took with Kikukawa. Is that a fair assessment? Why or why not?

4. After the 2012 accounting scandal, Olympus Corp. committed to a major overhaul of its accounting practices. What do the 2016 settlements convey about that overhaul?

Sources: "The Olympus Scandal: Paying a Price for Doing What's Right," *The Economist,* November 24, 2012; Bill Powell, "A Rotten Picture at Olympus," *Time,* December 12, 2012, and "Scandal at Olympus: The CEO Who Knew Too Much," *Time,* October 28, 2011; Michael Woodford, *Exposure: Inside the Olympus Scandal: How I Went from CEO to Whistleblower* (London: Portfolio, November 2012); Yuri Kageyama, "Olympus Whistleblower Wins Millions in Settlement," *Bloomberg Businessweek,* June 8, 2012; "Olympus Investors Seek $240 Million Compensation," *Associated Press,* November 13, 2012; "Olympus Scandal: Former Executives Sentenced," *BBC Business News,* July 3, 2013; Pavel Alpeyev and Grace Huang, "Sony Agrees to Halve Its Olympus Stake with Sale to JPMorgan," *Bloomberg News,* April 1, 2015; and David Voreacos and John Tozzi, "Olympus Will Pay $646 Million to End Kickback, Bribe Probes," *Bloomberg News,* March 1, 2016.

Thinking Critically   7.3

>> THE OLIVIERI CASE

In April 1993, Dr. Nancy Olivieri, head of the hemoglobinopathy program at the Hospital for Sick Children (HSC), the teaching hospital for the University of Toronto in Canada, signed an agreement with the Canadian drug company Apotex to

© Royalty-Free/Corbis RF

undertake clinical trials on a drug called deferiprone (referred to as L1 during the study). The drug was designed to help children with thalassemia, an inherited blood disorder that can cause the fatal buildup of iron in the blood. The agreement that Olivieri signed with Apotex included a clause (later referred to as a "gag clause") that specifically prevented the unauthorized release of any findings in the trial for a period of three years:

> As you now [sic], paragraph 7 of the LA-02 Contract provides that all information whether written or not, obtained or generated by you during the term of the LA-02 Contract and for a period of three years thereafter, shall be and remain secret and confidential and shall not be disclosed in any manner to any third party except with the prior written consent of Apotex. Please be aware that Apotex will take all possible steps to ensure that these obligations of confidentiality are met and will vigorously pursue all legal remedies in the event that there is any breach of these obligations.

The existence of this clause was to prove significant to the relationship between Olivieri and Apotex. After reporting some initial positive findings in the trial in April 1995, Olivieri reported in December 1996 that long-term use of the drug appeared to result in the toxic buildup of iron in the liver of a large number of her pediatric patients—a condition known as *hepatic fibrosis.* When she reported the findings to Apotex, the company determined that her interpretation of the data was incorrect. Olivieri then contacted the hospital's Research Ethics Board (REB), which instructed her to change the consent form for participation in the trial to ensure that patients were made aware of the risks of long-term use of the drug.

After copying Apotex on the revised form, the company notified Olivieri that the Toronto trials were being terminated effective immediately and that she was being removed as chair of the steering committee of the global trial that included patients in Philadelphia and Italy. When Olivieri notified Apotex that she and her research partners, including Dr. Gary Brittenham of Case Western Reserve University in Cleveland, were planning to publish their findings in the August 1998 issue of the *New England Journal of Medicine,* Apotex Vice President Michael Spino threatened legal action for breaching the confidentiality clause in her agreement with the company.

Olivieri then asked the HSC administration for legal support in her forthcoming battle with Apotex. The administrators declined. She then approached the University of Toronto, where the dean of the Faculty of Medicine declined to get involved on the grounds that her contract with Apotex had been signed without university oversight and that the university would never have agreed to the confidentiality clause in the first place.

Olivieri forged ahead with the publication despite this [lack of support] and instantly became celebrated as a courageous whistle-blower in the face of corporate greed.

The situation was further clouded by reports that the University of Toronto and HSC were, at the time, in the process of negotiating a $20 million donation from Bernard Sherman, the CEO and founder of Apotex.

The bitter relationship with her employers was to continue for several years, during which time she was referred to the Canadian College of Physicians and Surgeons for research misconduct and dismissed from her post at HSC, only to be reinstated following the aggressive support of several of her academic colleagues, including Dr. Brenda Gallie of the Division of Immunology and Cancer at HSC, who led a petition drive that succeeded in garnering 140 signatures in support of a formal enquiry into Dr. Olivieri's case.

That enquiry was undertaken by both the Canadian College of Physicians and Surgeons, which found her conduct to be "exemplary," and by the Canadian Association of University Teachers, whose 540-page report concluded that Dr. Olivieri's academic freedom had been violated when Apotex stopped the trials and threatened legal action against her.

The two-and-a-half-year battle ended in January 1999 when an agreement was brokered between the university, HSC, and Olivieri thanks to the efforts of two world-renowned experts in blood disorders—Dr. David Nathan of Harvard and Dr. David Weatherall of Oxford who intervened on the basis of the international importance of Dr. Olivieri's research. Working with the president of the University of Toronto, Robert Pritchard, and lawyers for both parties, a compromise settlement was reached that reinstated Olivieri as head of the hemoglobinopathy program at HSC, covered her legal expenses up to $150,000, and withdrew all letters and written complaints about her from her employment file.

As part of the agreement, a joint working group appointed by the University of Toronto and the university's Faculty Association was chartered with the task of making "recommendations on changes to university policies on the dissemination of research publications and conflict of interest and the relationship of these issues to academic freedom."

QUESTIONS

1. Was it ethical for Apotex to include a three-year gag clause in the agreement with Dr. Olivieri?

2. Even though Dr. Olivieri later admitted that she should never have signed the agreement with Apotex that included a confidentiality clause, does the fact that she *did* sign it have any bearing on her actions here? Why or why not?

3. Was Olivieri's decision to publish her findings about the trial an example of universalism or utilitarianism? Explain your answer.

4. If we identify the key players in this case as Dr. Olivieri, Apotex, the Hospital for Sick Children, and the University of Toronto, what are the conflicts of interest between them all?

5. What do you think would have happened if Dr. Olivieri's fellow academics had not supported her in her fight?

6. How could this situation have been handled differently to avoid such a lengthy and bitter battle?

Sources: Robert A. Phillips and John Hoey, "Constraints of Interest: Lessons at the Hospital for Sick Children," *Canadian Medical Association Journal* 159 (October 20, 1998), p. 8; John Hoey and Anne Marie Todkill, "The Olivieri Story, Take Three," *Canadian Medical Association Journal* 173 (October 11, 2005), p. 8; and David Hodges, "Dr. Olivieri, Sick Kids, U of T Resolve Disputes," *Medical Post* 38, no. 43 (November 26, 2002), p. 4.

[References]

1. Richard T. DeGeorge, *Business Ethics,* 5th ed. (Upper Saddle River, N.J: Prentice-Hall, 1999).

2. Mark Taylor, "$73 Million . . . and Counting?" *Modern Healthcare* 49 (December 5, 2005), p. 18.

3. "Your Source for Whistleblower Information," www.quitamhelp.com/index.php?/weblog/2010/06/.

4. Neil Weinberg, "The Dark Side of Whistleblowing," *Forbes* 175, no. 5 (March 14, 2005), p. 90.

5. "What's a Whistle-Blower?" *Maclean's* 118, no. 26 (June 27, 2005); "Persons of the Year," *Time,* December 30, 2002–January 6, 2003, p. 32; Richard C. Warren, "Whistleblowing: Subversion or Corporate Citizenship?" (review), *Journal of Occupational and Organizational Psychology* 71, no. 4 (December 1998), p. 372; Ann Hayes Peterson, "Inside the WorldCom Fraud," *Credit Union Magazine* 71, no. 8 (August 2005), p. 15.

6. Laura M. Franze, "Corporate Compliance: The Whistleblower Provisions of the Sarbanes-Oxley Act of 2002," *Insights: The Corporate & Securities Law Advisor* 16 (December 2002), p. 12.

7. Peter Rost, *The Whistleblower: Confessions of a Healthcare Hitman* (Brooklyn, NY: Soft Skull Press, 2006).

8

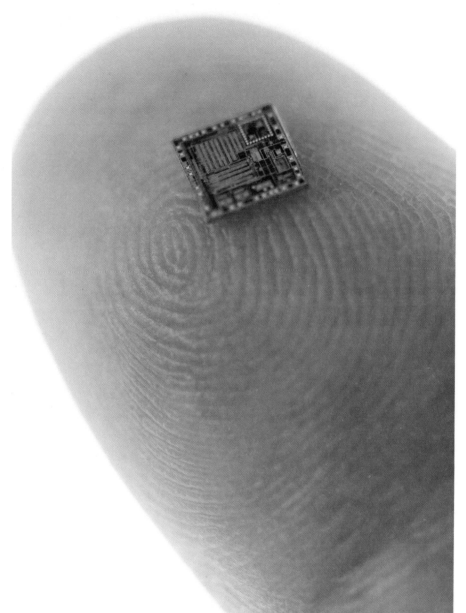

ETHICS AND TECHNOLOGY

After studying this chapter, you should be able to:

8-1 Evaluate the ethical ramifications of recent technological advances.

8-2 Explain the opposing employer and employee views of privacy at work.

8-3 Distinguish between thin and thick consent.

8-4 Evaluate the concept of vicarious liability.

8-5 Analyze an organization's employee-surveillance capabilities.

FRONTLINE FOCUS
Problems at ComputerWorld

Steve has just been hired as a computer repair technician (CRT) for ComputerWorld, a large retail computer store. As a recent graduate from the local technical college, Steve is eager to put his new diploma to good use and make a name for himself at ComputerWorld. "Who knows," he thinks to himself, "in a couple of years I could be running the whole department!" Steve is working with Larry, who's been a CRT at this location for five years. Larry seems nice enough and has promised to "show him the ropes."

Their first customer of the day is Mr. Johnson, who admits to not being "very PC savvy." Larry hooks up the laptop and announces that the hard drive has crashed and needs to be replaced. "The good news," he tells Mr. Johnson, "is that your repair is under warranty so we can switch that hard drive out for you—no problem—leave it with us, and it'll be ready tomorrow morning." Steve is suitably impressed with Larry's quick diagnosis and his firm commitment to Mr. Johnson that his laptop will be ready in the morning. Mr. Johnson, however, doesn't seem so pleased. "What about the old hard drive?" he asks. "There's a lot of personal information on there—can I have it back when you put in the new one?"

"Sorry, no can do," says Larry. "We have to return warranty-replaced parts to the manufacturer—company policy—but don't worry, its technicians will erase all the data on it before it's recycled—we're very careful about that."

Mr. Johnson thinks for a few moments and then decides that he can live with that and leaves the store. Larry quickly replaces the hard drive and throws the old one into a box that Steve notices is labeled "Flea Market" under Larry's workstation.

"What are you doing?" asks Steve. "I thought we had to send that back to the manufacturer for a warranty repair?" "Are you crazy?" laughs Larry. "We just tell the customers that—all the manufacturer needs is a serial number and the paperwork. That's a perfectly good hard drive—all he had was a file conflict. I've already fixed it—but since it's under warranty, he gets a nice new hard drive for free, we get a nice warranty contract, and I get a slightly used hard drive that I can sell at the flea market this weekend."

"But what about all his personal information on the hard drive?" asks Steve. "Aren't you going to erase it?"

"If I have time," laughs Larry.

QUESTIONS

1. The Computer Ethics Institute developed "10 Commandments of Computer Ethics," listed in Figure 8.1. How many of those commandments are being broken here?
2. Larry seems pretty happy with the prospect of selling those slightly used hard drives at the flea market, but what happens if the information on them doesn't get erased? Would ComputerWorld be liable here? Read the section "Vicarious Liability" later in the chapter to find out more.
3. What should Steve do now?

>> Big Brother is watching you.

George Orwell, *1984*, Part 1, Chapter 1

>> Introduction: Ethics and Technology

Technological advances often deliver new and improved functional capabilities before we have had the chance to fully consider the implications of those improvements. Consider the dramatic changes in workplace technology over the last two decades—specifically desktop computing, the Internet, and the growth of e-mail and instant messaging (IM). These technological advances arrived with the promise of "ease of access," "ease of use," and the ever-popular "increased worker productivity."

There is some truth to this assessment of the advantages of technology in the workplace. Consider the following:

Intranet A company's internal website, containing information for employee access only.

Extranet A private piece of a company's Internet network that is made available to customers and/or vendor partners on the basis of secured access by unique password.

- Companies are now able to make vast amounts of information available to employees and customers on their Internet, **intranet**, and **extranet** sites. Information previously distributed in hardcopy format—handbooks, guidebooks, catalogs, and policy manuals—can now be posted to a site and made available to employees and/or customers anywhere in the world in a matter of minutes, and updating that material can be accomplished in hours rather than weeks.
- JetBlue Airways was able to achieve significant cost savings by avoiding the expensive overhead of developing call centers for its reservations department. Using available call-routing technology with a desktop computer and dedicated phone line, JetBlue was able to hire 700 part-time workers in the Salt Lake City area to become its reservations department, working from the comfort of their dens, dining rooms, or spare bedrooms with no costly buildings to staff and maintain, and a much more flexible and satisfied workforce that can log on at a time that's convenient for them with no commute or office dress code.

However, now that these tools have become part of our everyday work environment, many of those wonderful promises have been overshadowed by concerns over loss of privacy in two key areas:

1. Customers must be aware that companies now have the technical capability to send their personal data to any part of the world to take advantage of lower labor costs.
2. As an employee, you must be aware that employers now have the capability of monitoring every e-mail you send and website you visit in order to make sure that you really are delivering on the promise of increased worker productivity.

>> Do You Know Where Your Personal Information Is?

With the availability of a network of fiber-optic cable that spans the globe and an increasingly educated global workforce that is fluent in English, the potential cost savings for American corporations in shipping work overseas to countries with lower labor costs is becoming increasingly attractive. Technically, anything that can be digitized can be sent over a fiber-optic cable.

The first wave of this technological advance came with the establishment of call centers in other parts of the world (predominantly India) to answer, for example, your customer service calls to your credit card company or for tech support on your computer. Very polite young people with suitably American names but with a definite accent can now answer your call as if you were calling an office park in the Midwest. This is just the beginning, as Thomas L. Friedman points out in *The World Is Flat:*[1]

A few weeks after I spoke with [Jaithirth "Jerry"] Rao, the following e-mail arrived from Bill Brody, the president of Johns Hopkins University, whom I had just interviewed for this book:

Dear Tom, I am speaking at a Hopkins continuing education medical meeting for radiologists (I used to be a radiologist). . . . I came upon a very fascinating situation that I thought might interest you. I have just learned that in many small and some

© BananaStock/Jupiterimages RF

medium-size hospitals in the US, radiologists are outsourcing reading of CAT scans to doctors in India and Australia!!! Most of this evidently occurs at night (and maybe weekends) when the radiologists do not have sufficient staffing to provide in-hospital coverage. While some radiology groups will use teleradiology to ship images from the hospital to their home (or to Vail or Cape Cod, I suppose) so that they can interpret images and provide a diagnosis 24/7, apparently the smaller hospitals are shipping CAT images to radiologists abroad. The advantage is that it is daytime in Australia or India when it is nighttime here—so after-hours coverage becomes more readily done by shipping the images across the globe. Since CAT (and MRI) images are already in digital format and available on a network with a standardized protocol, it is no problem to view the images anywhere in the world. . . . I assume that the radiologists on the other end . . . must have trained in [the] US and acquired the appropriate licenses and credentials. . . . The groups abroad that provide these after-hours readings are called "Nighthawks" by the American radiologists that employ them.

The ethical obligations of this new technical capability are just being realized. Should the customer be notified where the call center is based? Should the customer be notified that the person answering the call who introduces himself as "Ray" is really Rajesh from Mumbai? If you are referred to a radiologist for treatment, are you entitled to know that your CAT scan is being beamed across the globe for another radiologist on the opposite side of the world to read? Advocates argue that assigning patient ID numbers rather than full names or personal information can guarantee patient confidentiality, but once the information is in digital format on a network, what guarantees are there that someone else isn't tapping into that network?

>> The Promise of Increased Worker Productivity

Computers, e-mail, instant messaging, and the World Wide Web have changed our work environments beyond recognition over the last two decades, but with those changes have come a new world of ethical dilemmas. With a simple click, you can check the news on CNN, e-mail a joke to a friend, check the weather forecast for your trip next weekend, check in with that friend you've been meaning to call, and spread some juicy "dirt" that you just overheard in the break room—but the question is, Should you? We can identify two distinct viewpoints on this issue: the *employer view* and the *employee view*.

THE EMPLOYER POSITION

As an employee of the organization, your productivity during your time at work represents the performance portion of the pay-for-performance contract you entered into with the company when you were hired. Therefore, your actions during that time—your allotted shift or normal work period—are at the discretion of the company. Other than lunch and any scheduled breaks, all your activity should be work-related, and any monitoring of that activity should not be regarded as an infringement of your privacy. If you want to do something in private, don't do it at work.

The organization has an obligation to its stakeholders to operate as efficiently as possible, and to do so, it must ensure that company resources are not being misused or stolen and that company data and proprietary information are being closely guarded.

THE EMPLOYEE POSITION

As an employee of the company, I recognize that my time at work represents the productivity for which I

PROGRESS ✓ QUESTIONS

1. How would you feel if you found out that someone halfway around the world from your doctor's office was reading your CAT scan?

2. Would your opinion change if you knew the cost savings from outsourcing were putting American radiologists out of a job? What if they were being read this way because there was a shortage of qualified medical personnel here? Would that change your opinion?

3. Should your doctor be obligated to tell you where your tests are being read? Why or why not?

4. Storing private information in digital format simplifies the storage and transfer of that information and offers cost savings that are (hopefully) passed on to customers. Does using ID numbers instead of names meet the company's obligation to maintain your privacy in this new digital world?

receive an agreed amount of compensation—either an hourly rate or an annual salary. However, that agreement should not intrude upon my civil rights as an individual— I am an employee, not a servant. As such, I should be notified of any electronic surveillance and the purpose of that surveillance. The actions of a small number of employees in breaking company rules should not be used as a justification to take away everyone's civil rights. Just because the guy in the cube next to me surfs the web all day doesn't mean that we all do. Electronic monitoring implies that we can't be trusted to do our jobs—and if you can't trust us, why are you employing us in the first place?

Arriving at a satisfactory resolution of these opposing arguments has proved to be difficult for two reasons. First, the availability of ongoing technological advancements has made it increasingly difficult to determine precisely where work ends and personal life begins. Second, the willingness to negotiate or compromise has risen and fallen in direct relation to the prevailing job market.

>> When Are You "at Work"?

The argument over privacy at work has traditionally centered on the amount of time that employees were on-site—in the office or at the factory or store or hospital or call center, and so on. With the advances in computer technology and the new capability of **telecommuting**, which allows you to work from home (or anywhere) and log in to your company's network remotely, the concept of "at work" has become blurred.

With the availability of technology has come the expectation that you can check e-mails at home or finish a presentation the night before the big meeting. The arrival of the BlackBerry (affectionately known as the "crackberry" by many users and their partners) has made many employees available to their boss at all times of the day and night—24/7 unless they turn off the message notification function!

! Key Point

Is there any common ground between the employer and employee positions on the use of technology at work? What resolution would you propose?

A FAILURE TO DISCLOSE

My name is Sally Jones, and I am the office manager for Chuck Wilson, CPA, a small accounting firm in the Midwest. Life is good—it's a healthy business with a good mix of small business and individual returns, and Chuck has been a great guy to work for. He's well respected in our community as an active member of the local chamber of commerce; he does pro bono work for several local nonprofit organizations; and he's built up a loyal customer base over the years. The problem is Chuck Junior. It's always been Chuck's plan that Junior would take over the business, and with Junior having just passed his CPA exams, that time would seem to be now. The number of boating and fishing magazines that have suddenly appeared on Chuck's desk make me believe that he is thinking more seriously about retirement than ever before.

I don't begrudge Chuck his retirement—he's earned it. My job here is secure. I have done good work for Chuck, and his customers like me. However, Chuck Junior is already looking to put his mark on the business. I wouldn't be surprised if he's having some "Under New Management" signs prepared for the day when he does take over the practice. Junior likes to think of himself as "on the cutting edge of new technology" and "ready to take it to the streets" to take on the local H&R Block and Jackson Hewitt

← ETHICAL   DILEMMA →

© INSADCO/Photography/Alamy Stock Photo

offices that handle such a large portion of the individual tax returns every year. He's all excited about an article he read in one of his business magazines that he thinks will give us an advantage over the big guys—and he's already been in contact with the company that was featured in the article.

His plan is to send all our individual tax returns to a company in India that will guarantee the return will be prepared in less than 48 hours by accountants in its offices who are U.S.-licensed CPAs. The term for this is *outsourcing*. This, says Junior, will allow us to go after the more labor-intensive but profitable corporate returns at tax time instead of having all our time taken up with the individual returns. It will also save us from hiring any additional staff for the season. He's even figured out that, with the cost of each return this company will charge us, we can undercut the big guys and take away some of their business. He's already planning a big advertising campaign in the local papers and radio stations.

I'm happy to give him the benefit of the doubt on this idea, but here's my concern—he's not planning to tell anyone how we're going to do this. He's not going to

mention that someone else (whom he's never met) will be preparing the tax return or that the customers' personal information will be e-mailed to India to complete the return. He says that the customers won't care as long as the return is quick, accurate, and cheaper than the other guys. With all those ads for "immediate refunds," I can see his point, but his failure to disclose just doesn't sit right with me.

QUESTIONS

1. Is Sally right to be concerned about Chuck's plan? Explain why or why not.
2. Chuck Junior is obviously focusing on the money to be saved (and made) with this plan. What are the issues he is not considering?
3. Do you think Chuck Senior has signed off on this plan? If not, should Sally tell him? Explain why or why not.
4. Would the plan still succeed if Chuck Junior disclosed all the details?

Source: Inspired by Steven Mintz, "The Ethical Dilemmas of Outsourcing," *The CPA Journal* 74 (March 2004), p. 3.

In this new environment, the concept of being at work has become far more flexible. Availability has now become defined by accessibility. If I can reach you by phone or e-mail, I can ask you a question or assign you a task. The time of day or the day of the week is of secondary importance—it's a competitive world out there, and only the truly committed team players get ahead.

Employees, in return, have begun to expect the same flexibility in taking care of personal needs during working hours. If I stay up late working on a presentation for an important meeting the next day, shouldn't I then be allowed to call my dentist and make an appointment during my workday? What happens if I forget to send my mother some flowers for Mother's Day? If I order them online during my workday, am I still technically goofing off and therefore failing to meet my boss's expectations as a dedicated and productive employee?

If employee rights were recognized in this argument, then for those rights to have any validity, it would follow that employees should give their consent to be monitored by all this technology. However, as Adam Moore points out, the state of the job market will inevitably create a distinction between two types of consent: **thin** and **thick**.[2]

THIN CONSENT

If an employee receives formal notification that the company will be monitoring all e-mail and web activity—either at the time of hire or during employment—and it is made clear in that notification that his or her continued employment with the company will be dependent on the employee's agreement to abide by that monitoring, then the employee may be said to have given thin consent. In other words, there are two options: agree to the monitoring or pursue other employment opportunities. You could argue that the employee has at least been notified of the policy, but the notification is based on the assumption that jobs are hard to come by and the employee is not in a position to quit on principle and risk temporary unemployment while seeking a position with another company.

Thin Consent Consent in which the employee has little choice. For example, when an employee receives formal notification that the company will be monitoring all e-mail and web activity—either at the time of hire or during employment—and it is made clear in that notification that his or her continued employment with the company will be dependent on the employee's agreement to abide by that monitoring.

Thick Consent Consent in which the employee has an alternative to unacceptable monitoring. For example, if jobs are plentiful and the employee would have no difficulty in finding another position, then the employee has a realistic alternative for avoiding an unacceptable policy.

THICK CONSENT

If employment conditions are at the other end of the scale—that is, jobs are plentiful and the employee would have no difficulty in finding another position—then consent to the monitoring policy could be classified as thick since the employee has a realistic alternative if he or she finds the policy to be unacceptable.

PROGRESS ✓ QUESTIONS

5. Define the term *telecommuting*.

6. Summarize the employer position on privacy at work.

7. Summarize the employee position on privacy at work.

8. Explain the difference between *thin* and *thick* *consent*.

Abstract notions of notification and consent are idealistic at best. Consider the following account of life in a call center in the United Kingdom documented by "Jamie":[3]

Back in October, I started work at a call centre for a very large UK company. There were about 1,000 staff there, split into teams which would compete with each other on sales volumes. Winning teams might get a case of wine to share, or something like that. There was also a personal bonus scheme driven by sales.

I was an "outbound telesales agent." This means we phoned customers at home with the aim of selling the company's services. I knew that most customers don't like to be phoned while at home, and if any customer clearly didn't want the call, I would end it, and flag their account for "no future correspondence," though we were specifically told only to do this in extreme cases.

The bonus scheme encouraged some of my colleagues (mostly students) to sell aggressively—selling products that customers didn't want—for the bonus. These staff would usually have left the company by the time there were any repercussions.

A lot of customers imagine telesales agents as being spotty idiots trawling phonebooks ringing people as they go through the book. But the company's call system is quite complex. A database of all customers is kept (obviously!) and the computers dial these customers (depending on flags set on their accounts).

As soon as someone picks the phone up, the computer transfers it to the next available agent. The agent has no physical control over the call, the headphones beep, and there's a customer on the other end saying "Hello?" and that's it. The agent then performs the spiel.

There would probably be about 30 seconds between coming off a call, and the next one coming in (when I started, I was told there was about 90 seconds) and this continues throughout the shift.

The call centre is a pretty stressful place, with most of the agents getting as stressed or more stressed than the customers.

Increasingly higher sales targets started coming in, and more products were being introduced. Unfortunately, the training to go with these products was pretty poor, being in the form of glossy—but shallow—PowerPoint presentations. We knew the basics of the products, but we could not answer all questions, and this didn't go down well with some of the more knowledgeable customers. If it was something we might have an idea on, then I'm afraid we would sometimes bullsh*t.

I think telesales calls were targeted not to exceed about six minutes.

One day, they decided to open an inbound sales channel. The idea was to try to sell products to customers who were calling in to us. I signed up, thinking maybe things would be a bit easier. What a surprise to come onto the sales floor and take incessant customer complaint calls, having completed three weeks of training for inbound sales!

© Tony Baker/Brand X/Corbis

We were expected to take all manner of calls. We had to use different systems for logging orders and calls, and those systems were very difficult to use—with DOS-like command-line interfaces.

There would be a command to look up a customer's address/general details. Another command would look up an order on a customer's account. Instead of having a mouse and clicking things, we had to use commands and order codes to issue products on customers' accounts. We would then have to use a different command if we wanted to enter the customer's delivery address details. Another command later, and we would then be able to confirm the dates for the order. And after another command, the order would be confirmed.

So, the customer would be waiting impatiently on the phone, thinking the agent was a slow typist. The agent may then get stressed, because they cannot find a particular order code for a certain product, or cannot remember a certain command, or might make a typing error—that sort of thing.

This all had to be done within nine minutes.

After dealing with the complaint, we then had to try to sell them extra products using our inbound sales training. And this is far from easy—nothing like ringing up a company to complain and having one of their agents try to flog you more products!

I started to question my manager as to whether there was any point in this, but got nowhere. Managers, in general, seemed uninterested in what we were doing, beyond telling us of the new products we were to try to sell, or relaying irrelevant upper-management news. The general level of management skill seemed low to me.

Eventually, I resigned and was escorted off the premises by security.

PROGRESS ✓ QUESTIONS

9. How would you describe the atmosphere in this call center?

10. Jamie's calls were monitored at all times by a call center supervisor. Is that ethical? Why or why not?

11. What would you say is the worst part of working in this call center?

12. When Jamie resigned, she was escorted from the building by security. Is that ethical? Why or why not?

>> The Dangers of Leaving a Paper Trail

We may resent the availability of technology that allows employers to monitor every keystroke on our computers, but it is often the documents written on the machines that do the most harm. Consider the following recent events:

- In September 2010, Facebook CEO and cofounder Mark Zuckerberg faced the embarrassment of seeing internal instant messages (IMs) that he had written made public. The IMs revealed Zuckerberg bragging about how much information he had obtained about people based on their Facebook submissions. He admitted publicly that he wrote the IMs and stated that he "absolutely" regretted writing them.[4]

- In November 2010, the Dublin, Ireland, office of accountancy firm PricewaterhouseCoopers was forced to launch an internal investigation after an e-mail ranking the "Top 10" of the new young female associates was circulated among 17 male staff members in the office. The e-mail was quickly forwarded to other businesses and proceeded to "go viral," spreading across the Internet.[5]

- In November 2012, four-star general and CIA Director David Petraeus resigned in the face of an e-mail scandal that revealed an extramarital affair with his biographer, Paula Broadwell. The scandal also entangled the career of the top U.S. commander in Afghanistan, General John Allen, whose "flirtatious" e-mails with Tampa, Florida, socialite Jill Kelley were revealed in the Petraeus investigation. Allen was later exonerated.[6]

- In May 2014, an employee of the Riverside Community College District (RCCD) decided to work around the file-size limit of their internal database by sending a file containing personal information on over 35,000 students to an external researcher from a personal e-mail account. The e-mail address of the intended recipient was mistyped, resulting in the data going to a complete stranger. RCCD claimed there was no evidence that the erroneous e-mail account was active.[7]

- In June 2014, a contractor working for Goldman Sachs mailed confidential data to a stranger's e-mail address, apparently confusing "gs.com" (Goldman's in-house account) with "gmail.com." The data was so confidential that Goldman was forced to pursue a court order to force Google to delete the e-mail from the recipient's account after there had been no response from the account holder. Google later confirmed that the account had not been accessed since the confidential data had been sent.[8]

Life Skills

>> The Mixed Blessing of Technology

Take a moment and think about how many benefits we are able to derive from the Internet, personal computers, and smartphones. Without them, you could still call someone on a landline, but for a long-distance friend you would probably write a letter and send it by snail mail. To do research for a homework assignment, you would go to the library to use an encyclopedia rather than Google or Wikipedia and then type your paper on a typewriter!

The world of instant access—e-mails, IM, texting on your Galaxy, HTC, or iPhone—has certainly made communication faster and easier, but have you ever stopped to consider the downside of that instantaneous access? You may pride yourself on your ability to multitask and do homework, e-mails, texts, shop online, and check out YouTube videos, all at the same time, but how often do you turn everything off and really focus on the subject you are working on?

In the work environment, instant access goes both ways. To your boss, you are just an e-mail, phone call, or text message away—so what if you are at home eating dinner? She needs that information now or needs that report on her desk by 9 a.m., so why shouldn't she call you?

Recent technological advances have blurred the lines between work and home life, and while being a team player can help your long-term career prospects, you're no good to your company if you are a burned-out shell who never finds downtime to rest and recharge your batteries. So find the time to switch off, unplug, and, as the saying goes, just chill!

Vicarious Liability A legal concept that means a party may be held responsible for injury or damage even when he or she was not actively involved in an incident.

Cyberliability A legal concept that employers can be held liable for the actions of their employees in their Internet communications to the same degree as if those employers had written those communications on company letterhead.

With the immediate nature of Internet communication and the potential damage that evidence gathered from the electronic trail of e-mails can do, it's easy to see why organizations have become so concerned about the activities of their employees. If the negative effect on your corporate brand and reputation weren't enough of a reason to be concerned, then the legal concept of vicarious liability should grab any employer's attention.

VICARIOUS LIABILITY

Vicarious liability is a legal concept that means a party may be held responsible for injury or damage

even when he or she was not actively involved in an incident. Parties that may be charged with vicarious liability are generally in a supervisory role over the person or parties personally responsible for the injury or damage. The implications of vicarious liability are that the party charged is responsible for the actions of his or her subordinates.

There are a variety of situations in which a party may be charged with vicarious liability. Contractors may face charged [sic] of vicarious liability if their subcontractors fail to complete a job, perform the job incorrectly, or are found guilty of other contract violations. Parents have been charged with vicarious liability when the actions of their children cause harm or damage. Employers can face a number of situations involving vicarious liability issues, including sexual harassment of one employee by another, discriminatory behavior by an employee against fellow employees or customers, or any other action in which one of their employees personally causes harm, even if that employee acts against the policies of the employer.[9]

So as an employer, you could be held liable for the actions of your employees through Internet communications to the same degree as if they had written those communications on company letterhead. The new term for this is **cyberliability**, which applies the existing legal concept of liability to a new world—computers. The extent of this new liability can be seen in the top categories of litigation recorded by Elron Software:[10]

- Discrimination
- Harassment
  - Obscenity and pornography
  - Defamation and libel
  - Information leaks
  - Spam

If we acknowledge the liabilities employers face that are a direct result of the actions of their employees, does that justify employee monitoring to control (and hopefully prevent) any action that might place the company at risk? Or are employees entitled to some degree of privacy at work?

TELECOMMUTING 24/7

Real-World Applications

When Sue's husband Jeff got a promotion, his new job required an 800-mile move. Sue really liked her job and didn't want to leave the company, so she negotiated a change in her position that allowed her to work from her new home and visit the office twice a month. The technology in her home office means she can telecommute with no problems. However, her boss seems to think that not having to commute to work every day means that Sue is available on call, and Sue is starting to get concerned about the number of early morning and late evening calls and e-mails for work that needs to be done ASAP. What should she do?

TOP 20 BLONDE JOKES

Bill Davis was really torn about the complaint that had just landed on his desk from a female employee in the accounting department. As HR director for Midland Pharmaceuticals, it was his job to address any complaints about employee behavior. Over the years, the company had invested a lot of money in training employees on the biggest employee behavior issues—sexual harassment and discrimination—probably, Bill suspected, because of the real danger of lawsuits that could cost the company tens if not hundreds of thousands of dollars to settle. However, this complaint had Bill stumped.

Midland was a midsize regional company of about 180 employees. Its rural location provided a good quality of life for its employees—no commuting headaches, good schools, and salaries that were competitive with its more metropolitan competitors. Turnover was not an issue—in fact, the last employee newsletter had featured eight members of the same family working for Midland, and the next edition would feature one family with

© Radius Images/Corbis

three generations working for the company. This was a good company to work for, and Bill enjoyed his job as HR director.

CONTINUED >>

Jane Williams was a new employee in accounting. She had moved here as part of her husband's relocation to the area with another company about three months ago. Bill's conversation with her manager had revealed that she was a model employee—punctual, reliable, and very productive. Then Steve Collins in the warehouse had decided to brighten everyone's Friday by forwarding an e-mail that one of his buddies had sent to him. The title of the e-mail was "Top 20 Blonde Jokes." Steve had used the corporate e-mail directory to send the e-mail to everyone with a simple "Happy Friday!" message, so Bill had opened it and, he confessed to himself, laughed at a couple of the jokes. He had then moved on to the quarterly report he was working on and thought nothing more of it.

Jane, who was blonde ("a natural blonde," as she had pointed out in her e-mail), did not find the e-mail funny at all—in fact, she took such offense to it that she filed a formal grievance against Steve, claiming that the e-mail created "a hostile working environment" for her (one of the key phrases the lawyers had emphasized in the harassment training). Bill had also been told that Jane was trying to get some of the other women in the department on her side by complaining that since the blonde jokes were always about females, they were discriminatory to women.

Bill had interviewed Jane personally when she was hired, and she didn't strike him as the type of employee who would try to hold the company for ransom over such a thing, so he suspected that the "hostile work environment" comment was meant more as an indication of her emotional response to the e-mail than a serious threat of legal action. However, her complaint was a formal one, and he needed to act on it. Unfortunately, Midland's policies on e-mail communication had always been fairly informal. It had never been raised as an issue before now. People were always sending jokes and silly stories, and Midland had relied upon the common sense of its employees not to send anything offensive or derogatory.

The IT folks took all the necessary precautions for network and data security, but as a family-owned company, the thought of monitoring employee e-mails had never been considered. Now, Bill feared, the issue would have to be addressed.

QUESTIONS

1. Was Steve Collins wrong to send the e-mail? Why?
2. Is Jane Williams overreacting in filing her formal complaint? Explain why or why not.
3. What impact do you think any change in the employee privacy policies would have at Midland?
4. What are Bill Davis's options here?

It was terribly dangerous to let your thoughts wander when you were in any public place or within range of a telescreen. The smallest thing could give you away. A nervous tic, an unconscious look of anxiety, a habit of muttering to yourself—anything that carried with it the suggestion of abnormality, of having something to hide. In any case, to wear an improper expression on your face . . . was itself a punishable offense. There was even a word for it in Newspeak: facecrime.

George Orwell, *1984*, Book 1, Chapter 5

THE RIGHT TO PRIVACY—BIG BROTHER IS IN THE HOUSE

Listen for this generic statement the next time you call a company and navigate through the voice-mail menu—this is usually the last thing you hear before you are (hopefully) connected to a live person:

Calls may be monitored for quality control and training purposes.

In his novel *1984,* George Orwell created a dark and bleak world where "Big Brother" monitored everything you did and controlled every piece of information to which you were given access. Many supporters of employee privacy rights argue that we have reached that state now that employers have the technology to monitor every keystroke on your computer, track every website you visit, and record every call you make. The vicarious liability argument is presented to justify these actions as being in the best interests of shareholders, but what is in the best interests of the employees?

The liability argument and the recent availability of capable technology may be driving this move toward an Orwellian work environment, but what are the

FIG.8.1

10 Commandments of Computer Ethics

1. Thou shalt not use a computer to harm other people.

2. Thou shalt not interfere with other people's computer work.

3. Thou shalt not snoop around in other people's computer files.

4. Thou shalt not use a computer to steal.

5. Thou shalt not use a computer to bear false witness.

6. Thou shalt not copy or use proprietary software for which you have not paid.

7. Thou shalt not use other people's computer resources without authorization or proper compensation.

8. Thou shalt not appropriate other people's intellectual output.

9. Thou shalt think about the social consequences of the program you are writing or the system you are designing.

10. Thou shalt always use a computer in ways that ensure consideration and respect for your fellow humans.

Source: Computer Ethics Institute, "Ten Commandments of Computer Ethics," *Computer Professionals for Social Responsibility,* http://cpsr.org/issues/ethics/cei.

PROGRESS ✔ QUESTIONS

13. Which of the "10 Commandments of Computer Ethics," in Figure 8.1, carries the strongest ethical message? Why?

14. Define the term *vicarious liability.*

15. List four of the top categories of litigation related to Internet communications.

16. Define the term *cyberliability.*

long-term effects likely to be? Employee turnover costs organizations thousands of dollars in recruitment costs, training, and lost productivity. Creating a "locked-down" place to work may protect your liability, but it may also drive away those employees who really aren't comfortable being treated like lab rats.

Key Point

Critics argue that constant employee surveillance only serves to escalate the stress of an already pressure-filled work environment. What do you think?

>> Conclusion

The Computer Ethics Institute offers simple guidelines on the appropriate use of technology, but the debate over whether all this technology demands a new techno-friendly school of ethics is likely to continue. However, addressing the issue in real time requires us to consider how many of the issues have really changed from the variables we have been discussing in the previous seven chapters of this book. We are still talking about the same stakeholders, conducting the same business transactions in the same fiercely competitive markets. What have changed are the platforms on which those transactions can now take place and, more importantly, the speed with which they occur.

Should the same rules that apply to recording telephone calls apply to e-mails in the same way, or should there be a different set of rules? The reality is that our working lives have changed dramatically since the arrival of all this technology. We all spend a lot more time at work, and the availability of instant access to our work means that the line between work life and private life is now much less clearly defined. This change should mean that the employer's ability to intrude on our personal lives

CONTINUED >>

with an urgent request would be balanced by an equal flexibility in our time at work—but does that really happen where you work? If you think this debate is being overhyped in the media, consider the following summary of employee surveillance capabilities.[11]

Remarkably invasive tools exist to monitor employees at the workplace. These include:

- Packet-sniffing software can intercept, analyze, and archive all communications on a network, including employee e-mail, chat sessions, file sharing, and Internet browsing. Employees who use the workplace network to access personal e-mail accounts not provided by the company are not protected. Their private accounts, as long as they are accessed on workplace network or phone lines, can be monitored.
- Keystroke loggers can be employed to capture every key pressed on a computer keyboard. These systems will even record information that is typed and then deleted.

- Phone monitoring is pervasive in the American workplace. Some companies employ systems that automatically monitor call content and breaks between receiving calls.
- Video surveillance is widely deployed in the American workplace. In a number of cases, video surveillance has been used in employee bathrooms, rest areas, and changing areas. Video surveillance, under federal law, is acceptable where the camera focuses on publicly accessible areas. However, installment in areas where employees or customers have a legitimate expectation of privacy, such as inside bathroom stalls, can give the employee a cause of action under tort law.
- "Smart" ID cards can track an employee's location while he or she moves through the workplace. By using location tracking, an employer can monitor whether employees spend enough time in front of the bathroom sink to wash their hands. New employee ID cards can even determine the direction the worker is facing at any given time.

FRONTLINE FOCUS
Problems at ComputerWorld—Steve Makes a Decision

Steve thought long and hard about what he should do now. As a new employee, he really didn't want to get a reputation as a troublemaker, and he liked working with Larry most of the time. Anyway, there was no harm done. Mr. Johnson got a new hard drive under his warranty, ComputerWorld got the replacement contract (keeping Larry and him employed!), and Larry got his perk of a slightly used hard drive to sell at the flea market next weekend. As far as ComputerWorld was concerned, the drives were destroyed—its employee manual instructed them to drill holes through the drives and recycle them. What else was the manufacturer going to do with them? Break them up and recycle them for scrap? That seemed like a waste of a perfectly good hard drive.

Larry's a reliable guy, thought Steve. *I'm sure he'll remember to erase those drives before he sells them.*

Before he knew it, Steve was "one of the guys." Larry taught him all the "tricks of the trade," and between them they built a lucrative side business

of used computer parts repaired under warranty, listed as "destroyed," and then sold at the flea market on the weekends.

Unfortunately, two months later, Mr. Johnson received a telephone call from someone who had bought a used hard drive at the flea market. The seller had told him that the drive had been erased, but when he installed it, he found all Mr. Johnson's personal information still on the hard drive.

QUESTIONS
1. What could Steve have done differently here?
2. What do you think will happen now?
3. What will be the consequences for Steve, Larry, Mr. Johnson, and ComputerWorld?

[For Review]

1. **Evaluate the ethical ramifications of recent technological advances.**

   Technological advances often deliver new and improved functionality before we have had the chance to fully

   consider the ethical ramifications of those improvements. Having a computer at every employee's workstation enables rapid communication, but it also allows employers to monitor every e-mail sent and website visited. Consumers who register on a company's website often provide personal data with no clear understanding of what the company will do with that data or how securely they will be stored.

2. Explain the opposing employer and employee views of privacy at work.

The employer view begins with the premise that other than lunch and any scheduled breaks, all your activity should be work-related. Any nonwork-related web surfing or personal e-mails represent a misuse of company property. Using monitoring software to track such activity is not an infringement of privacy but a standard monitoring procedure of company property.

In contrast, the employee view resents the intrusion of monitoring practices as a clear infringement of civil rights. With the constant connectivity of laptops and smartphones now blurring the line between work hours and home life, employees argue that greater flexibility is warranted. In addition, from a trust perspective, employees raise the question that if you feel the need to monitor them constantly, why did you hire them in the first place?

3. Distinguish between thin and thick consent.

In an economic climate of high unemployment, any formal notification of corporate monitoring of e-mail and web activity, with a clear "take it or leave" message, represents thin consent, since the employees have limited options available to them if they object to the monitoring practices.

If employees do have options available to them, such as when jobs are plentiful or their skills are highly marketable, then consent to the monitoring practices would be considered thick, since those employees would have realistic alternatives if they found the practices unacceptable.

4. Evaluate the concept of vicarious liability.

Vicarious liability is a legal concept that means a party may be held responsible for injury or damage even when he or she was not actively involved in an incident. The implications of vicarious liability are that the party charged

is responsible for the actions of his or her subordinates. In this case, the "party" would be the corporation, and the "subordinates" would be the employees of that corporation. However, companies have always been liable for the actions of their employees in the performance of their designated work responsibilities. What has changed is the notion of cyberliability, where an employee's Internet activity (web surfing and e-mails) can be treated in the same manner as letters written on company letterhead. Therefore, anything inappropriate, offensive, unethical, or illegal that an employee does while "on the clock" can expose the company to vicarious liability. On that basis, monitoring software is just allowing companies to do something they have always wanted to do but never had the capability until now.

5. Analyze an organization's employee-surveillance capabilities.

In chronological order of arrival in our work environment, phone monitoring has been employed for decades. Before the technology existed to record calls automatically, human beings (operators or supervisors) could be called upon to "listen in" to conversations. Video surveillance has slowly expanded from the secure protection of key access points to an office or factory to a more widespread monitoring of every area of the company's physical plant. The rapid advancement of computer technology (and the perceived increase in cyberliability) has led to the development of keystroke-logging software to capture every key pressed on a computer keyboard. Similarly, "packet-sniffing" software (named after the practice of breaking up blocks of information into packets for distribution over the Internet) can intercept, analyze, and store all communications on a network. The most recent advance has been the "smart" ID card that can track an employee's location while he or she moves through the workplace. In the same manner as GPS monitoring of delivery vehicles, the company now knows where you are at all times.

[Key Terms]

Cyberliability 171

Extranet 164

Intranet 164

Telecommuting 166

Thick Consent 167

Thin Consent 167

Vicarious Liability 170

[Review Questions]

1. Should you be allowed to surf the web at work? Why or why not?

2. Are your telephone calls monitored where you work? If they are, how does that make you feel? If they aren't monitored, how would you feel if that policy were introduced?

3. What would you do if someone sent you an e-mail at work that you found offensive? Would you just delete it or say something to that person?

4. If you had the chance to work from home and telecommute, would you take it? If the opportunity meant that you had to allow your company to monitor every call on your phone and every keystroke on your computer, would you still take it? Explain why or why not.

5. You have just been issued a new company iPhone (to make sure you never miss an important e-mail or phone call!). Are you now obligated to answer those calls and e-mails at any time, day or night? Why or why not?

6. Would you use that new iPhone for personal calls and e-mails? Why or why not?

[Review Exercises]

Removing temptation. I'm the customer service director for Matrix Technologies, a manufacturer of design software. We've recently upgraded our customer service extranet service to allow our clients to download software updates (including any patches or "bug fixes") directly from our extranet site. The initial response from the majority of our customers has been very positive—the new process is convenient, quick, and reliable—they love it. Everyone, that is, except for our large local government client. The new service doesn't help it at all—and the reason for that really has me stumped. Earlier this year, this client made the decision to remove access to the Internet from all its desktop computers, so no access to the Internet means no access to our customer service site to download our upgrades. When I asked the IT director if he was pulling my leg, he got mad at me. Apparently its IT personnel installed some monitoring software on the system and found that employees were spending almost 40 percent of their time surfing the web—mostly to news and entertainment sites, but sometimes to places that would make you blush! Its response was swift and effective. The employees came in one morning and found that they no longer had access to the web from their desktops. Now we have to come up with a plan to mail upgrade CDs to 24 regional offices.

1. How well did Matrix's client handle this situation?

2. What kind of message does this send to the employees of Matrix's client?

3. What other options were available here?

4. On the assumption that the downloadable software patches can greatly improve updates for its client, does Matrix have an ethical obligation to get involved here? Explain your answer.

[Internet Exercises]

1. Visit the website for the RAND Center for Corporate Ethics and Governance (CCEG) at www.rand.org/jie/centers/corporate-ethics.html.

   a. What does the CCEG do?

   b. What are the stated comparative advantages of the CCEG?

   c. Select and summarize a current CCEG research project.

2. Visit the website for the Electronic Frontier Foundation (EFF) at www.eff.org.

   a. What does the EFF do?

   b. What is the EFF "Bloggers' Rights" project?

   c. What is the "Open Wireless Movement"?

[Team Exercises]

1. **When are you "at work"?**

   Divide into two teams. One team must defend the *employer* position on employee monitoring. The other team must defend the *employee* position. Draw on the policies and experiences you have gathered from your own jobs.

2. **A new billing system.**

   A new system that bills corporate clients is under development, and there is a discussion over how much to invest in error checking and control. One option has been put forward so far, and initial estimates suggest it would add about 40 percent to the overall cost of the project but would vastly improve the quality of the data in the database and the accuracy of client billing. Not spending the money would increase the risk of overcharging some midsize clients. Divide into two groups and prepare arguments *for* and *against* spending the extra money on error checking and control. Remember to include in your argument how stakeholders would be affected and how you would deal with any unhappy customers.

3. **E-mail privacy.**

   Divide into two groups and prepare arguments *for* and *against* the following behavior: *Your company has a clearly stated employee surveillance policy that stipulates that anything an employee does on a company-owned computer is subject to monitoring. You manage a regional office of 24 brokers for a company that offers lump-sum payments to people receiving installment payments—from lottery winnings or personal injury settlements—who would rather have a large amount of money now than small monthly checks for the next 5, 10, or 20 years.*

   You have just terminated one of your brokers for failing to meet his monthly targets for three consecutive months. He was extremely angry about the news, and when he went back to his cube, he was observed typing feverishly on his computer in the 10 minutes before building security arrived to escort him from the premises. When your IT specialist arrives to shut down the broker's computer, he notices that it is still open and logged in to his Gmail account and that there is evidence that several e-mails with large attachments had been sent from his company e-mail address to his Gmail address shortly after the time he was notified that he was being fired. The e-mails had been deleted from the folder of sent items in his company account. The IT specialist suggests that you take a look at the e-mails and specifically the information attached to those e-mails. Should you?

4. **Software piracy.**

   Divide into two groups and prepare arguments *for* and *against* the following behavior: *You run your own graphic design company as a one-person show, doing primarily small business projects and subcontracting work for larger graphic design agencies. You have just been hired as an adjunct instructor at the local community college to teach a graphic design course. You decide that it's easier to use your own laptop rather than worry about having the right software loaded on the classroom machines, and so the college IT department loads the most current version of your graphic design software on your machine. Business has been a little slow for you, and you haven't spent the money to update your own software. The version that the IT department loads is three editions ahead of your version with lots of new functionality.*

   You enjoy teaching the class, although the position doesn't pay very well. One added bonus, however, is that you can be far more productive on your company projects using the most current version of the software on your laptop, and since you use some of that work as examples in your class, you're not really doing anything unethical, right?

Thinking Critically

>> INSTAGRAM: THE DANGERS IN CHANGING YOUR TERMS OF SERVICE

In April 2012, social media giant Facebook purchased the popular photo-sharing service Instagram for $1 billion. Wall Street analysts applauded the deal as a "match made in heaven." Instagram (with a customer-base in the tens of millions) was getting access to Facebook's billion-plus users. Facebook was adding a new service in the hope of attracting even more users. However, within a few short months of the deal, the real agenda behind the transaction was made apparent. At the time of the purchase, Instagram, while developing a very passionate and loyal user base, had yet to figure out how to generate revenue from its business model. The solution appeared in a brief block of text added to the Instagram "terms of service" (TOS) agreement— the same boring, legalese that most users agree to without even reading it. The language of the change read as follows:

> To help us deliver interesting paid or sponsored content or promotions, you agree that a business or other entity may pay us to display your username, likeness, photos (along with any associated meta-data), and/or actions you take, in connection with paid or sponsored content or promotions without any compensation to you.

In other words, the company appeared to be staking claim to the right to sell the photos and username information of all the content uploaded to the site, without any permission or compensation to the user. With over 1 billion photos already uploaded to the service, the likelihood of finding material worthy of financial remuneration seemed highly likely, but the company seriously underestimated the degree of personal attachment between its users and their respective photographs and personal information. They responded with a fervor that appeared to catch the company completely by surprise. Individual users closed their accounts in droves with accompanying angry tweets and Facebook posts condemning the company's actions. Several celebrity and commercial users, such as the National Geographic organization and Mark Zuckerberg's wedding photographer, deleted photographs and suspended their accounts shortly afterward.

© Lionel Bonaventure/AFP/Getty Images

Cofounder Kevin Systrom responded quickly via the company's blog on its website and tried to downplay the issue as a misunderstanding, and declared the possibility of Instagram selling users' photos and personal information as an "interpretation" that was inconsistent with the company's intent: "To be clear: It is not our intention to sell your photos. We are working on updated language in the terms to make sure this is clear."

While Systrom may be given credit for the promptness of his response, the question remained that if Instagram had no intention of selling users' photographs or personal information, what was the plan that required the company to make such an explicit change in its TOS agreement?

For that, we must look to Instagram's new parent company, Facebook, whose initial public offering (IPO) had garnered mixed reviews for a list price that seemed to promise highly inflated revenue performance. The change in the TOS, critics argued, was designed to give Facebook access to user metadata that would allow it to offer detailed profile information on its users to prospective advertisers.

To put this in operational terms, Instagram would be happy to host multiple photos of your dog or cat, but it now reserved the right to make that information available to advertisers of pet-related products or services. As such, while critics and confused users were free to object, based on their interpretation of the modified language of the TOS, one question remains—how did they think the service was going to remain free to use?

Critics of Instagram's actions used the case to send a bigger message about the dangers of accepting modified TOS agreements without reading them first. However, given that they are usually presented in convoluted legal terminology; are often several pages in length; and are usually presented as the last hurdle before restoring the service you are seeking to use, or the purchase you are trying to make, the likelihood of a positive customer response to such appeals is limited. Nevertheless, the case brought positive attention to a new service site called "Docracy," that acts as a consumer watchdog by tracking changes in thousands of TOS agreements across the web. It remains to be seen as to how quickly the service will uncover another poorly executed TOS change.

In March 2016, Instagram announced changes to its feed algorithm that would modify how users would receive notifications and the order in which they would see images. The change was designed to align the algorithm with that of parent company Facebook, but the outcry from users was predictably negative, even though the changes weren't expected to take effect for several months.

QUESTIONS

1. What prompted Instagram to change the terms of service (TOS) agreement?
2. Critics and many Instagram customers reacted very strongly to the TOS change. Was there an error of judgment on the company's part? Why or why not?
3. Was Instagram's response to the PR crisis over the change in the TOS appropriate? Why or why not?
4. How could Instagram handle these situations differently? Do you think the changes to the algorithm will be sufficient to resolve the issue? Why or why not?

Sources: Sam Gustin, "Lessons from Facebook's Instagram Photo Flap," *Time.com,* December 19, 2012; Will Oremus, "Everyone Is Ignoring the Much Bigger Problems with Instagram's New Privacy Policy," *Slate.com,* December 19, 2010; "After Instagram Controversy, a Watchdog Site Tracks Shifting Terms of Service," *The Verge,* February 6, 2013; and Daniel Victor, "Instagram Is Changing Its Feed But (Calm Down) Not Yet," *The New York Times,* March 30, 2016.

Thinking Critically 8.2

>> VOLKSWAGEN • "DEFEAT DEVICES"

For a company that made such an explicit commitment to environmental awareness and sustainability, the accusation by the U.S. Environmental Protection Agency (EPA) in September 2015 that Volkswagen (VW) had installed sophisticated software on 500,000 U.S. vehicles to cheat on emissions tests was the beginning of a true corporate catastrophe.

In VW's 2014 Sustainability Report, reviewed by consulting firm PricewaterhouseCoopers, the word *environment* was mentioned 335 times over 156 glossy pages—an average of twice per page. VW, the world's largest automaker, had built its reputation on cleaner-burning diesel engines that were allegedly better for the long-term sustainability of the planet, attracting tens of thousands of environmentally conscious customers in the process.

© Vytautas Kielaitis/Shutterstock RF

The initial estimate of 500,000 cars quickly proved to be far removed from the truth, when VW admitted to "discrepancies" affecting 11 million vehicles worldwide. Chief Executive Martin Winterkorn resigned in the wake of the growing scandal, and VW announced that it would be setting aside over $7 billion to manage the situation, warning that the final figure could be much higher.

The software, as VW admitted, was designed specifically for the Type EA 189 diesel engines installed in four-cylinder versions of the VW Jetta, Beetle, Golf, Passat, and Audi A3, vehicles that accounted for over 25 percent of the company's

CONTINUED >>

global sales. Its purpose was to trick regulators into believing that the engines complied with all current emissions standards while, as was soon discovered, actually emitting harmful pollutants, specifically nitrogen oxide, at rates of over 40 times the required standards.

As the case progressed and further evidence was discovered, any potential defense argument of a "miscalculation" or "computer error" was quickly dismissed in the face of hard data that the software was purpose-built for the task. While VW continued to refer to the issue as "discrepancies" and "deviations" in their frequent communications to stakeholders and the media, the U.S. Department of Justice (DOJ) announced that it was opening a criminal probe into VW's actions related to what the DOJ termed "defeat devices." The potential criminal penalties, over and above anticipated EPA fines of up to $37,500 per vehicle—a maximum fine of $18 billion—made the announcement of a $7 billion set-aside seem naively optimistic at best.

The response from financial markets was swift and severe, with a stunning 17 percent drop in share price for VW on the day of the announcement, wiping out almost $15 billion in corporate value in one day. The prompt departure of Martin Winterkorn was followed by the immediate appointment of Matthias Müller, the chief executive of Porsche, who promised "maximum transparency" during the upcoming investigations and stated: "My most urgent task is to win back trust."

By January 2016, less than four months after the scandal broke, the sincerity of Müller's commitment was already being questioned by DOJ investigators. While VW claimed to be actively complying with German regulators under the confines of strict German privacy laws, the company was citing the same privacy laws for its inability to comply with information requests from U.S. regulators. Citing Germany's Federal Data Protection Act, which limits access to data, particularly outside the European Union, VW took the position that it was still committed to "maximum transparency" but was obligated to abide by the laws of its home country.

VW's most vocal critics argue that while Müller may be concerned about winning back the trust of VW customers, the company's actions will have far-reaching consequences for sustainability and corporate social responsibility. British Petroleum, for example, made an explicit commitment to changing "BP" to mean "Beyond Petroleum' before the reputation of the company was irreparably damaged by the Deepwater Horizon oil spill in the Gulf of Mexico. It is argued that VW's deliberate actions to hide emissions of a pollutant that has an impact on atmospheric warming of 300 times that of carbon dioxide will make it much harder for investors and consumers to believe any company that states it is committed to environmental sustainability.

In the six months following the EPA announcement, the situation had not improved for VW. Since the "defeat device" was designed to beat emissions tests while maintaining the fuel efficiency that VW marketed so aggressively, there is no software solution to the problem. The vehicles do not meet emission standards, which means that buyers will have to be compensated for an outcome that has yet to be decided. Should buyers receive financial compensation or a replacement vehicle? What about EPA fines and DOJ penalties? All of that remains to be resolved in what will most likely be a lengthy series of lawsuits.

In March 2016, VW failed to meet a court deadline to present a plan to resolve the scandal. The presiding judge gave the company an extension until late April, but expectations among all interested parties were that the extension would be missed, leading to a civil trial.

QUESTIONS

1. Why did VW develop the software in the "defeat devices"?
2. Has Müller's commitment to "maximum transparency" helped or hindered the situation? Explain your answer.
3. Would you buy a VW car based on the information in this case? Why or why not?
4. What should VW be doing to recover from this scandal?

Sources: Jo Confino "Volkswagen Just Nuked the Public's Trust in Companies Trying to Save the Planet," *The Huffington Post,* September 21, 2015; Frank Jordans and Pan Pylas, "VW Rocked by Emissions Scandal as Prosecutors Come Calling," *Associated Press,* September 22, 2015; Nathan Bomey, "Volkswagen Emission Scandal Widens: 11 Million Cars Affected," *USA Today,* September 22, 2015; Danny Hakim and Jack Ewing, "VW Refuses to Give U.S. States Documents in Emissions Inquiries," *The New York Times,* January 8, 2016; and Jack Ewing, "Court Sets Deadline for a Volkswagen Diesel Fix, but Solution Could Prove Elusive," *The New York Times,* March 24, 2016.

Thinking Critically

>> THE HIPAA PRIVACY RULE

On August 21, 1996, Congress enacted the Health Insurance Portability and Accountability Act (HIPAA), a piece of legislation designed to clarify exactly what rights patients have over their own medical information and to specify what procedures are needed to be in place to enforce appropriate sharing of that information within the health care community. According to Richard Sobel of the *Hastings Center Report:* "This law required Congress to pass legislation within three years to govern privacy and confidentiality related to [a patient's] medical record. If that action did not occur, then the Department of Health and Human Services (DHHS) was to identify and publish the appropriate legislation. Because Congress did not pass required legislation, the DHHS developed and publicized a set of rules on medical record privacy and confidentiality" that required compliance from most health care providers by April 14, 2003.

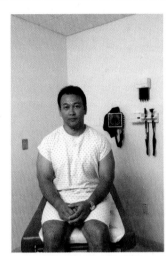

© ColorBlind Images/Blend Images/ Corbis

Since then, the HIPAA legislation has often been referred to as a privacy rule, but in reality it is disclosure legislation that "offers a floor, rather than a ceiling, for health privacy." As such, the true purpose behind the commitment to patient privacy is to control how patient information is collected and by whom, how and where it will be stored safely for future retrieval, and how health care providers and other health care organizations will use it, ideally on a need-to-know basis only.

As Bill Trippe explains the law in an *Econtent* article, "The key . . . is to provide authorized [health care professionals] with precisely the information they need, when they need it—but only the precise information they need so that [patient] privacy is not compromised."

However, while advances in information technology—specifically database technology—appear to offer the promise of functionality to do precisely that, the sheer number of combinations of users and needs in the provision of health care would seem to exceed even those grand promises. Compare, for example, the patient record needs of a doctor prescribing a specific medication, as opposed to those of a doctor giving a full physical examination. The former might need lab results and any relevant research about the medication; the latter would prefer to have the patient's full medical history. It may be possible to retrieve that information from one comprehensive database, but if everyone has different information needs, how do you set up that database to restrict access where appropriate under the banner of need to know or to summarize information where needed to maximize patient privacy?

The logistical challenges of this scenario are further complicated when you consider that the legislation covers not only patient care but also the administrative aspects of the health care system. For example, Sobel comments that HIPAA gave "600,000 'covered entities'—such as health care plans, clearinghouses, and health maintenance organizations—'regulatory permission to use or disclose protected health information for treatment, payment, and health care operations' (known as TPO) without patient consent. Some of these 'routine purposes' for which disclosures are permitted are far removed from treatment. . . . 'Health care operations' (HCO) include most administrative and profit-generating activities, such as auditing, data analyses for plan sponsors, training of non-healthcare professionals, general administrative activities, business planning and development, cost management, payment methods improvement, premium rating, underwriting, and asset sales—all unrelated to patient care."

HIPAA was enacted to address privacy concerns in the face of increasingly sophisticated database technology that can send your most private information to the other side of the globe in a split second. Ironically, however, many

CONTINUED >>

violations of the privacy rule have little connection, if any, with direct patient care and treatment. Consider the following two examples:

1. Patient MW, a victim of domestic abuse, informs [her nurse] that her status as a patient in the hospital must be kept confidential. [The nurse] assures MW that she's safe and that the staff won't share information with anyone who inquires about her. [The nurse] informs the unit clerk not to release any information on MW, but fails to remove MW's name and room number from the assignment board [at the nurses' station]. Later in the shift, MW's husband enters the nurses' station and asks the unit clerk for his wife's number. The unit clerk, following the nurse's instructions, states that she has no information on the person named. The spouse, upon looking around the nurses' station, sees his wife's name and room number. He rushes to the room and physically abuses her. The unit clerk calls hospital security, which promptly arrives and escorts the spouse off the unit. He's subsequently jailed for spousal abuse.

2. A member of the electronic medical record (EMR) staff was conducting a training session for resident physicians and medical students at an outpatient facility. . . . The trainer used fictional patient records specifically created for EMR training purposes for the demonstrations and exercises. During the Q&A session one of the residents stated that just that morning he had had problems prescribing a specific medication in the medication module of the EMR, which had created an inaccurate entry in the patient's electronic chart. The resident asked how he could correct the mistake. Since the trainer knew that many new EMR users had had similar problems with this feature of the EMR, she thought this would be a good "teachable moment." She asked the resident the name of the patient. She then looked up the patient's chart and projected the patient's medication list on the screen for all the class to see. The trainer proceeded to correct the error in the EMR.

While the first example represents a clear violation of the HIPAA legislation, since the patient's room information was publicly accessible simply by visiting the nurses' station, the situation is not so straightforward in the second example. The residents and medical students being trained were employees of a covered entity, and since training falls under the heading of approved health care operations, no violation occurred. Of course, it is debatable as to whether it was appropriate to display the patient's records to the entire group rather than helping the one student after the class, since that choice calls into question the issue of using the minimum information on a need-to-know basis. What is clear, however, is that while the purpose of HIPAA may be clearly stated, the interpretation of the legislation lacks the same degree of clarity.

QUESTIONS

1. Is the term *privacy rule* accurate in describing the HIPAA legislation? Why or why not?

2. Is it ethical for covered entities to be excused from getting patient permission to use their private information for routine purposes? Why or why not?

3. Based on the limited information in this article, do you think the HIPAA legislation achieves its objective of securing patient privacy?

4. How could this issue of patient privacy have been handled in a more ethical manner?

Sources: Judith A. Erlen, "HIPAA-Clinical and Ethical Considerations for Nurses," *Orthopaedic Nursing* 23, no. 6 (November–December 2004); J. Mack, "Beyond HIPAA-Ethics in the e-Health Arena," *Healthcare Executive,* September–October 2004, pp. 32–33; Bill Trippe, "First Do No Harm: Can Privacy and Advanced Information Technology Coexist?" *Econtent* 26, no. 3 (March 2003); Richard Sobel, "The HIPAA Paradox: The Privacy Rule That's Not," *The Hastings Center Report* 37, no. 4 (July–August 2007); Patricia D. Blair, "Make Room for Patient Privacy," *Nursing Management,* June 2003, pp. 28–29; and Bob Brown, "Did They Break the Rules?" *Journal of Health Care Compliance* 10, no. 2 (March–April 2008).

[References]

1. Thomas L. Friedman, *The World Is Flat: A Brief History of the Twenty-First Century* (New York: Farrar, Straus, and Giroux, 2005). Copyright © 2005 by Thomas L. Friedman. Reprinted by permission of Farrar, Straus, and Giroux, LLC.

2. A. Moore, "Employee Monitoring and Computer Technology Evaluative Surveillance v. Privacy," *Business Ethics Quarterly* 10, no. 3 (2000), pp. 697–709.

3. "Life inside a Call Centre," www.letsfixbritain.com/callcentres.htm.

4. Jose Antonio Vargas, "The Face of Facebook," *The New Yorker,* September 20, 2010, www.newyorker.com/reporting/2010/09/20/100920fa_fact_vargas?currentPage=all.

5. Shane Hickey and Fiona Ellis, "Pricewaterhouse-Coopers Staff Brought to Book over Raunchy Emails," *Belfast Telegraph,* November 10, 2010.

6. Scott Shane and Charlie Savage, "Officials Say FBI Knew of Petraeus Affair in the Summer," *The New York Times,* November 11, 2012.

7. Evan Dishevsky, "Email Fails That Will Make You Cringe," *PC Magazine,* August 21, 2014.

8. Ibid.

9. Online Lawyer Source, www.onlinelawyersource.com.

10. "Cyberliability: An Enterprise White Paper," Elron Software, 2001.

11. Electronic Privacy Information Center, www.epic.org/privacy/workplace/.

© Dave and Les Jacobs/Blend Images, LLC

THE FUTURE OF BUSINESS ETHICS

Having examined the challenges involved in developing an ethical culture within an organization, we can now consider what lies ahead for companies as they grow on an international and global scale. Crossing national boundaries to conduct business often involves crossing cultural boundaries at the same time. How do organizations address those cultural differences while staying true to their own ethical principles?

Chapter 9 examines the challenges organizations face in the pursuit of global ethics. While they may prefer to adopt their own policies as a universal standard of ethics, the reality is that the organizations and customers from other countries with whom they conduct business will bring their own moral standards and ethical principles into the relationship. What happens when there is a conflict in those standards?

Chapter 10 examines the big-picture issue of maintaining an ethical culture in the face of all these challenges. This far into the text, we have examined all the issues and the resources available to help organizations and their employees with those issues, but the challenge of maintaining and enforcing a code of ethics must be faced on a daily basis.

© Dave and Les Jacobs/Blend Images, LLC

CHAPTER 9

ETHICS AND GLOBALIZATION

After studying this chapter, you should be able to:

9-1 Understand the ethical issues arising in global business.

9-2 Explain the issue of ethical relativism in a global environment.

9-3 Explain the challenges in developing a global code of ethics.

9-4 Analyze the ramifications of the UN Global Compact.

9-5 Explain the OECD Guidelines for Multinational Enterprises.

FRONTLINE FOCUS
A Matter of Definition

Tom is a copywriter with a regional ad agency that has a very lucrative contract with Smith's national retail chain. He likes working for a smaller agency even though he could probably make more money with a larger national organization. At least here everyone knows each other and works together as a team, and he likes the culture too. The agency does good work for good clients, and it has been known to turn down contracts for campaigns that conflicted with its corporate values. In fact, its decision to turn down a campaign for a local bourbon distillery made the trade press.

Tom has friends at a couple of the national agencies, and they describe the culture as a totally cutthroat one where it's everyone for himself and any business is good business as long as the check clears.

Landing the Smith's account was a big deal for Tom's regional agency, and they all worked hard to make it happen (and celebrated with a party that will probably go down in company history as one of the best ever!). Now the agency has to deliver on everything it promised in its bid for the work. The first big project is the new campaign for the July Fourth sales event coming up. The theme of the event is "Made in America," which the company thinks will tap into a sense of patriotism. Smith's has lined up several very low-priced "loss leaders" to get customers into the store, and it is promoting them heavily as being "made in America."

Tom has been assigned to write the copy for a series of ads about barbecue utensil sets featuring the American flag and red, white, and blue color combinations. As part of his prep kit, Tom receives the product specifications on the items along with the photographs that his copy will support.

As he is reading through the material, Tom notices that his contacts at Smith's included by mistake a copy of the original billing paperwork for the shipment—paperwork showing that the items were actually made in Indonesia by a company named Jakarta Enterprises.

The name seems very familiar to Tom, and he looks the company up on Google. To his dismay, he finds several articles criticizing the business practices of Jakarta Enterprises—specifically in the area of employing young children in sweatshop working conditions.

QUESTIONS

1. Ten guidelines for organizations doing business with developing nations are listed in "The Pursuit of Global Ethics" section. Do you think Smith's is following any of these?
2. Review the UN Global Compact in the "Enforcing Global Ethics" section. How many violations has Smith's incurred by doing business with Jakarta Enterprises?
3. What are Tom's options here?

The world has become small and completely interdependent.

Wendell L. Willkie, Republican presidential nominee defeated by Franklin D. Roosevelt in 1940

>> Ethics and Globalization

Up to now we have focused primarily on a domestic approach to business ethics—how North American organizations get their own house in order and ensure that they have a clearly defined code of ethics that all their stakeholders can relate to and understand.

Once we step outside the domestic environment and conduct business on an international or a global scale, the concept of business ethics changes dramatically. Business transactions in different countries in different languages and different cultures inevitably force North American companies to revisit the ethical principles to which they are committed and to recognize which principles and policies they are willing to negotiate in favor of the client country with which they are looking to do business.

ETHICS IN LESS-DEVELOPED NATIONS

Any discussion of business ethics in this arena must distinguish between the developed and **less-developed nations** of the world. If we follow the traditional stereotypes, companies in the **developed nations** know how the game is played. Business is typically conducted in English, and all international business travelers have read and reread a copy of *Kiss, Bow, or Shake Hands: The Bestselling Guide to Doing Business in More Than 60 Countries.*[1]

These nations are busy playing the game of globalization—everyone is pursuing the same goal of maximum profits with minimum costs, and if individual cultures present some challenges, those can be overcome with translations and cultural adaptations. That, of course, is easier said than done. The assumption that "what works here works there" has managed to get a lot of companies into hot water over the years:[2]

Less-Developed Nation A country that lacks the economic, social, and technological infrastructure of a developed nation.

Developed Nation A country that enjoys a high standard of living as measured by economic, social, and technological criteria.

Utilitarianism Ethical choices that offer the greatest good for the greatest number of people.

- The name Coca-Cola in China was first rendered as *Ke-kou-ke-la*. Unfortunately, The Coca-Cola Co. did not discover until after thousands of signs had been printed that the phrase means, "bite the wax tadpole" or "female horse stuffed with wax," depending on the dialect. Coca-Cola then researched 40,000 Chinese characters and found a close phonetic equivalent, *Ko-kou-ko-le,* which can be loosely translated as "happiness in the mouth" (though a marketing "classic," this story has been denounced as an urban legend).

- In Taiwan, the translation of the Pepsi slogan "Come alive with the Pepsi Generation" came out as "Pepsi will bring your ancestors back from the dead."

- When Parker Pen marketed a ballpoint pen in Mexico, its ads were supposed to say, "It won't leak in your pocket and embarrass you." However, the company mistakenly thought the Spanish word *embarazar* meant "embarrass"; instead, the ads said, "It won't leak in your pocket and make you pregnant."

- An American T-shirt manufacturer in Miami printed shirts for the Spanish market that promoted the pope's visit. But instead of the desired "I Saw the Pope" in Spanish, the shirts proclaimed "I Saw the Potato."

- In Italy, a campaign for Schweppes Tonic Water translated the name into Schweppes *Toilet* Water.

- Bacardi concocted a fruity drink with the name Pavian to suggest French chic, but *Pavian* means *baboon* in German.

- Clairol introduced the Mist Stick, a curling iron, into Germany, only to find out that *mist* is slang for manure.

- When Gerber first started selling baby food in Africa, it used the same packaging as in the United States—jars with pictures of the cute little baby on the label. Only later did it learn that in Africa, companies routinely put pictures on the label that describe what's inside, since most people can't read.

- And, as America's favorite chicken magnate, Frank Perdue, was fond of saying, "It takes a tough man to make a tender chicken." In Spanish, however, his words took on a whole new meaning: "It takes a sexually stimulated man to make a chicken affectionate."

These are all amusing anecdotes, but the economic reality underlying them is far more serious. International markets represent growth, and with profitable growth come happy shareholders and rising stock prices. In addition, international markets represent new customers as well as sources of cheaper materials and cheap labor.

From a business ethics perspective, this constant hunger for growth at any cost presents some challenges. As we recall from our discussion of **utilitarianism** in Chapter 1, any questionable behavior in overseas markets can be explained away by serving the greatest good for the greatest number of people. However, as we discussed in Chapter 1, when you focus on doing the greatest good for the greatest number of people, there is no accountability for individual actions.

So what happens if you simply transplant your "take no prisoners" aggressive business style from the United States to whatever market you happen to be in? Do the same rules apply? Or do you focus on not breaking any local laws and fall back on the old adage, "If it's legal, it must be ethical"? Are American companies bound by their domestic ethical policies when they conduct business overseas, or are they free to adopt (or completely overlook) local ethics? Is this a uniquely American phenomenon, or do French, German, Russian, or Chinese companies adopt similarly flexible attitudes to business ethics when they step outside their national boundaries?

Before we examine these questions in detail, we should clarify some terminology. The term **globalization** has applications in commercial, economic, social, and political environments. For our purposes, we are concerned with globalization as the expansion of international trade to a point where regional trade blocs (Latin America, Europe, Africa) have overtaken national markets, leading eventually to a global marketplace. As these national markets become interdependent, questions arise over the ethical behavior of economically advanced nations toward developing ones.

Operating in this increasingly globalized business world are **multinational corporations (MNCs)**—also referred to as *transnational corporations*—that pursue revenue (and hopefully profit) on the basis of operating strategies that ignore national boundaries as merely bureaucratic obstacles. Economists disagree over the correct definition of an MNC: Some argue that to be truly multinational, an organization must have owners from more than one country (such as Shell's Anglo-Dutch structure);

© Copyright 1997 IMS Communications Ltd/Capstone Design. All Rights Reserved

As a multinational corporation, Shell must reach different markets with different needs. How might this impact local employees at a Shell service station?

others argue that an organization is multinational when it generates products and/or services in multiple countries and when it implements operational policies (marketing, staffing, and production) that go beyond national boundaries.

It is here that the global ethics dilemma becomes apparent: What happens when you go beyond national boundaries? If ethical standards are based on cultural and social norms and customs, what happens when you are operating in an environment that is representative of multiple cultures and societies?

> **Globalization** The expansion of international trade to a point where national markets have been overtaken by regional trade blocs (Latin America, Europe, Africa), leading eventually to a global marketplace.
>
> **Multinational Corporation (MNC)** A company that provides and sells products and services across multiple national borders. Also known as *transnational corporations*.
>
> **Ethical Relativism** Gray area in which your ethical principles are defined by the traditions of your society, your personal opinions, and the circumstances of the present moment.

PROGRESS ✔ QUESTIONS

1. Explain the term *globalization*.
2. What is an MNC?
3. When is "operating in full compliance with local laws and regulations" unethical?
4. Explain the term *utilitarianism*.

Critics have argued that most MNCs have chosen to ignore all ethical standards in the pursuit of the almighty dollar on the basis of the following two arguments:

- If they didn't pursue the business, somebody else would.
- They are operating in full compliance with local laws and regulations, which conveniently happen to be far less restrictive than those they would face in their own country.

>> Ethical Relativism

In such environments, the ideal "black and white" world of ethics must give way to a gray area of **ethical relativism**. Policies and procedures can be hard to follow when your customers don't have comparable policies in their own organizations. In addition, policies that have been outlawed in the United States in an attempt to legally enforce ethical corporate behavior

Galaxy Mining's Indaba copper mine recently experienced its third accident in the three years that the mine has been operating. Several miners were injured but, fortunately, none seriously. However, during the accident repair process (which was accelerated to get the mine up and running as quickly as possible), one of the retaining walls for the mining blade coolant runoff was damaged, allowing several thousand gallons of chemical sludge to seep into the local river. To manage the media response to the accident, Galaxy contracted the services of John "Monty" Montgomery, a self-proclaimed "specialist in local public relations and consulting services." Monty billed Galaxy for $1 million in advance as his standard retainer fee, which was paid without question.

Montgomery took control of the Indaba situation quickly, issuing several authoritative press releases committing Galaxy Mining to prompt and full restitution for any damage done by the leak. Thirty days later a press conference was arranged to announce the construction of a new water treatment facility (funded by Galaxy) that, to quote Montgomery, "will guarantee fresh, clean water for local residents for generations to come." The Indaba leak was never mentioned in the local press again.

When Galaxy's auditors requested more detail on the services provided by Montgomery's organization during a routine audit several months later, he responded with an e-mail confirming that the $1 million was "for services rendered in the management of the Indaba mining

© Comstock/Getty Images RF

incident." No further explanation or documentation was provided.

QUESTIONS

1. Was this an ethical transaction? Explain why or why not.
2. Montgomery "managed" the incident as requested. Is there any evidence to suggest that he did anything unethical?
3. Should the auditors accept his explanation of "services rendered"? Why or why not?
4. What kind of policies should Galaxy Mining put in place to make sure these kinds of "services" aren't utilized again?

Key Point

"Ethical relativism is just smart business. If local customs happen to oppose our code of ethics back home, then we should be flexible and respect those local customs." Is that an ethical approach?

may be standard operating procedure in less-developed nations. Social and political chaos can generate a bureaucracy that bears no relation to a logical reality, leaving companies with the tough decision whether to stand by their Western principles of ethical conduct or submit to the practical reality of the local market and "grease the appropriate palms" to get things done.

>> The Pursuit of Global Ethics

Globalization can be seen to have both an upside and a downside. Supporters of the upside argue that globalization is bringing unprecedented improvements in the wealth and standards of living of citizens in developing nations as they leverage their natural resources or low costs of living to attract foreign investment. For the more economically advanced nations, access to those resources enables lower production costs that equate to lower prices and higher income standards for their customers.

Advocates for the downside of globalization argue that it is merely promoting the dark side of capitalism onto the global stage—developing countries are ravaged for their raw materials with no concern for the longer-term economic viability of their national economies; workers are exploited; and corporations are free to take full advantage of less restrictive legal environments.

So how do you take advantage of the upside of globalization while maintaining your ethical standards and avoiding the downside?

As we have seen in previous chapters, any organization that commits itself to establishing and sticking with a clearly defined code of ethics will face considerable challenges, and its commitment will be tested when the quarterly numbers fall a little short of the forecast. However, moving that ethical commitment to a global stage requires a great deal more planning than simply increasing the scale of the policies and procedures. Just because it was developed here does not mean it can be applied in the same manner elsewhere in the world, and it's likely that the ethical policy will require a lot more refinement than simply translating it into the local language.

Critics have argued that the moral temptations of global expansion have simply been too strong for MNCs to ignore. Faced with constant pressure to increase revenue, cut costs, maximize profitability, and grow market share—ideally all in the next 90 days—companies find themselves tempted to take maximum advantage of the less stringent laws and regulations of local markets and (in what critics consider to be the worst transgression), if there are no clear local ethical standards, to operate in the absence of any standards rather than reverting to their own domestic ethical policies.

So what is the answer here? Is the development of a **global code of conduct** a realistic solution to this issue?

Even though we are now seeing the development of larger trading blocs as neighboring countries (such as the European Union) work together to leverage their size and geographic advantage to take a bigger role on the global economic stage, the individual countries within those trading blocs are not disappearing. For this reason, the customs and norms of those individual societies are likely to prevail.

In fact, the financial strength of the Western nations is seen as a threat to equal representation of the developing nations, and as a result, those developing nations hold onto their national identities and cultures, thereby precluding any agreement on a general standard of business practice.

For advocates of global ethics, this means that a *flexible* solution has to be found—one that provides standards of practice to guide managers as they conduct business across national boundaries in the name of global commerce while respecting the individual customs of the countries in which they are operating.

Richard DeGeorge offers the following guidelines for organizations doing business in these situations:[3]

1. Do no intentional harm.
2. Produce more good than harm for the host country.
3. Contribute to the host country's development.
4. Respect the human rights of their employees.
5. Respect the local culture; work with it, not against it.
6. Pay their fair share of taxes.
7. Cooperate with the local government to develop and enforce just background institutions.
8. Majority control of a firm includes the ethical responsibility of attending to the actions and failures of the firm.

9. Multinationals that build hazardous plants are obliged to ensure that the plants are safe and operated safely.
10. Multinationals are responsible for redesigning the transfer of hazardous technologies so that such technologies can be safely administered in host countries.

DeGeorge's guidelines present something of an ethical ideal that can at best provide a conceptual foundation, but at worst they overlook some of the most severe transgressions that have brought such negative attention to the ethical behavior of MNCs.

> **Global Code of Conduct** A general standard of business practice that can be applied equally to all countries over and above their local customs and social norms.

© Ingrid Publishing/Alamy RF

Are there differences in the ethical issues employees face at a multinational company versus a locally owned company? Which environment do you think you would prefer?

PROGRESS ✔ QUESTIONS

5. Why would a global code of conduct be unrealistic?
6. Select your top five from DeGeorge's guidelines for organizations doing business in less-developed countries, and defend your selections.
7. Can you think of any reasons international organizations wouldn't follow these guidelines? Provide three examples.
8. Do you think DeGeorge's guidelines represent a sufficiently "flexible" solution? Why or why not?

In the pursuit of profit and continued expansion, MNCs have been found guilty of bribery, pollution, false advertising, questionable product quality, and, most prominently, the abuse of human rights in the utilization of "sweatshop" production facilities that fail to meet even the minimum health and safety standards of their home countries and that utilize child labor, often at wage levels that are incomprehensible to Western consumers.

The situation becomes even more complicated when we acknowledge that many global companies have reached such a size that they have a dramatic impact on trade levels just with their own internal transactions. As William Greider observed in *One World, Ready or Not:*[4]

The growth of transnational corporate investments, the steady dispersal of production elements across many nations, has nearly obliterated the traditional understanding of trade. Though many of them know better, economists and politicians continue to portray

© Spencer Platt/Getty Images

CORPORATE INVERSION: A QUESTIONABLE PRACTICE?

In November 2015, pharmaceutical companies Pfizer and Allergan formally announced a $160 billion merger—the largest medical merger in history—creating a company with a combined stock market valuation of over $300 billion. It was by no means a merger of equals. Pfizer, based in New York with assets of more than $170 billion, produces some of the most well known drugs in the U.S. market, including Lipitor (a cholesterol drug), Zithromax (an antiobiotic), and Celebrex (an anti-inflammatory drug). Allergan, based in Dublin, Ireland, has a valuation of one-third of that of Pfizer, and is most well known for its Botox drug. What, then, made the deal so attractive?

Pfizer had already attempted to buy the British pharmaceutical giant AstraZeneca in 2014 but had been turned away over a disagreement over valuation. The decision to switch to Allergan was a clear indication that the interest was not in any strategic synergy or new drug combinations under development. The deal was about reducing Pfizer's tax bill. By merging with an overseas company, and basically giving up its U.S. citizenship, Pfizer could reduce its tax bill to an estimated 18 percent.

While the combined federal and state corporate income tax rates in the United States can be as high as 35 percent, as compared to an average of 25 percent in Europe, detailed tax strategies usually enable U.S. corporations to reduce their domestic tax bill significantly. Merging with, or buying, an overseas corporation and changing your tax home or "domicile" allows a further reduction in the tax rate. However, this process of "corporate inversion" is even more devious. Being domiciled overseas would allow Pfizer to access global profits that were being kept overseas to avoid payment of U.S. taxes on those earnings. The potential savings of $35 billion explained the company's eagerness to find a willing suitor.

Pfizer was not alone in recognizing the potential savings of such corporate inversions. In 2014, the American fast-food chain Burger King acquired the Canadian coffee and donut chain Tim Horton's, moving its corporate domicile to Ontario with a maximum corporate tax rate of only 26.5 percent.

In April 2016, the U.S. Treasury Department announced a rule change targeted at closing the "corporate inversion" loophole that President Barack Obama had labeled "insidious" and "unpatriotic." Pfizer announced shortly afterward that the planned merger with Allergan would no longer take place, and that the company would book a charge of $150 million to compensate Allergan "for reimbursement of expenses associated with the transaction."

The chief executive of Allergan, Brent Saunders, voiced his frustration with the decision, stating that the U.S. Treasury was "building a wall around the U.S. to keep people in." With several other multibillion-dollar inversion deals still in negotiation from such companies as Coca-Cola Co. and Johnson Controls, it seems likely that there will be aggressive lobbying to change the new rules.

QUESTIONS

1. Does the higher U.S. corporate tax rate provide sufficient justification for these inversion deals? Why or why not?
2. Proponents of such deals claim that they are simply maximizing profits and shareholder value. Does that make them ethical? Explain your answer.
3. Why did the U.S. Treasury introduce a rule change?
4. Do you think the change will hold, or will lobbyists succeed in getting the rule reversed? Explain your answer.

Sources: "Inverted Logic," *The Economist,* August 25, 2015; "Pfizer and Allergan Agree to a $160 Billion Merger," *The Economist,* November 23, 2015; Renae Merle, "Giving up Its U.S. Citizenship Could Save Pfizer $35 Billion in Taxes," *The Washington Post,* February 25, 2015; Nathan Bomey and Kevin McCoy, "$160 Billion Pfizer, Allergan Inversion Scrapped," *USA Today,* April 6, 2016; Renae Merle and Carolyn Y. Johnson, "Pfizer, Allergan Call off $160 Billion Merger after U.S. Moves to Block Inversions," *The Washington Post,* April 6, 2016; and "Pfizer Abandons $160bn Allergan Deal," *BBC News,* April 6, 2016.

the global trading system in terms that the public can understand—that is, as a collection of nations buying and selling things to each other. However, as the volume of world trade has grown, the traditional role of national markets is increasingly eclipsed by an alternative system: trade generated within the multinational companies themselves as they export and import among their own foreign-based subsidiaries.

With such a negative track record to begin with, how do you enforce ethical behavior in an organization that is trading with itself? Do the ethical norms of the parent company dominate the corporation's business practices in complete disregard of local customs and traditions? Or is it simply more expedient to "go with the flow" and take advantage of whatever the local market has to offer? Unfortunately, in this new environment, simply categorizing the "parent company" can prove to be a challenge.

>> Enforcing Global Ethics

While companies may be held accountable for ethical performance within their home countries (America's Federal Sentencing Guidelines for Organizations, for example), enforcing ethical behavior once they cross national boundaries becomes extremely difficult. What happens if the behavior is illegal in the company's home country, but not in the local country in which the alleged transgression took place? Would the enforcement of penalties in their home country automatically prevent any future transgressions? What if the profit margins are high enough to simply pay the fines as a cost of doing business?

Enforcing a global ethical standard would require all parties involved to agree on acceptable standards of behavior and appropriate consequences for failing to abide by those standards. Given the fact that many of the hundreds of nations in the world still experience difficulty governing their own internal politics, it would seem that we are many years away from achieving a truly global standard.

In the meantime, organizations such as the United Nations (UN) and the Organization for Economic Cooperation and Development (OECD) have approached the issue of standardizing global ethical conduct by promoting behavior guidelines that MNCs can publicly support and endorse as a strong message to their stakeholders that they are committed to ethical corporate conduct wherever they do business in the world.

THE UN GLOBAL COMPACT

Launched in a speech to the World Economic Forum on January 31, 1999, by UN Secretary-General Kofi Annan, the **UN Global Compact** became operational in July 2000. It represents a commitment on the part of its members to promote good corporate citizenship with a focus on four key areas of concern: the environment, anticorruption, the welfare of workers around the world, and global human rights.

The Global Compact is not a regulatory instrument—it does not "police," enforce, or measure the behavior or actions of companies. Rather, the Global Compact relies on public accountability, transparency, and the enlightened self-interest of companies, labor, and civil society to initiate and share substantive action in pursuing the principles on which the Global Compact is based.

With over 2,000 companies in more than 80 countries making a voluntary commitment to this corporate citizenship initiative, the Global Compact is widely recognized as the world's largest initiative of its kind. By endorsing and actively promoting the message of the Global Compact, companies make public commitments to a set of core values that are captured in 10 key principles that address the four areas of concern:[5]

> **UN Global Compact** A voluntary corporate citizenship initiative endorsing 10 key principles that focus on four key areas of concern: the environment, anticorruption, the welfare of workers around the world, and global human rights.

Human Rights

1. Businesses should support and respect the protection of internationally proclaimed human rights.
2. Businesses should make sure they are not complicit in human rights abuses.

Labor Standards

3. Businesses should uphold the freedom of association and the effective recognition of the right to collective bargaining.
4. Businesses should uphold the elimination of all forms of forced and compulsory labor.
5. Businesses should uphold the effective abolition of child labor.
6. Businesses should uphold the elimination of discrimination in employment and occupation.

Environment

7. Businesses should support a precautionary approach to environmental challenges.

OECD Guidelines for Multinational Enterprises Guidelines that promote principles and standards of behavior in the following areas: human rights, information disclosure, anticorruption, taxation, labor relations, environment, competition, and consumer protection; a governmental initiative endorsed by 30 members of the Organization for Economic Cooperation and Development and 9 nonmembers (Argentina, Brazil, Chile, Estonia, Israel, Latvia, Lithuania, Romania, and Slovenia).

© Steve Allen/Brand X Pictures/ Getty Images

Real World Applications

Laurie has been hired as a PR consultant for a multinational pharmaceutical corporation that has just paid a multimillion-dollar settlement under the Foreign Corrupt Practices Act. Laurie advises the company to make a highly public commitment to supporting the UN Global Compact as a sign of its new pledge to ethical conduct in all its operations around the world. Will that make a difference?

8. Businesses should undertake initiatives to promote greater environmental responsibility.
9. Businesses should encourage the development and diffusion of environmentally friendly technologies.

Anticorruption

10. Businesses should work against all forms of corruption, including extortion and bribery.

PROGRESS ✔ QUESTIONS

9. What is the UN Global Compact?
10. When and why was it created?
11. Explain the 10 key principles of the Global Compact.
12. What would a multinational corporation gain from signing the Global Compact?

>> The OECD Guidelines for Multinational Enterprises

Originally adopted as part of the larger Declaration on International Investments and Multinational Enterprises in 1976, the **OECD Guidelines for Multinational Enterprises** represents a more governmental approach to the same issues featured in the UN's nongovernmental Global Compact.

Supporters argue that the government backing adds credibility to the issues being promoted, but the guidelines carry no criminal or civil enforcement and are not regarded as legally binding. What they do offer are principles and standards of behavior that draw on the same core values as the UN Global Compact across a broader series of issues captured in 10 "chapters":[6]

I. **Concepts and Principles:** Sets out the principles that underlie the guidelines, such as their voluntary character, their application worldwide, and the fact that they reflect good practice for all enterprises.
II. **General Policies:** Contains the first specific recommendations, including provisions on human rights, sustainable development, supply chain responsibility, and local capacity building; and, more generally, calls on enterprises to take full

>> A subtle influence

In Chapter 1 we examined the work of Lawrence Kohlberg and his argument that we develop a reasoning process (and our individual ethical standards) over time, moving through six distinct stages as we are exposed to major influences in our lives.

When we consider ethics from a global perspective and begin to recognize the impact of cultural influences on our personal value system, we come to the realization that our individual ethical standards can often be sheltered from a broader global awareness by those cultural influences.

What do you consider to be your primary cultural influences? As the child of immigrant parents, for example, your value system would be directly affected by influences from both the American culture you live in and your parents' native culture—and if your parents happen to be from two different cultures, then things can really get interesting!

Do you think those cultural influences impact your daily behavior? Much of what you learn about the world in terms of education and daily information is subject to the perspective of the country in which you live. Are you open to that, or would you describe yourself as being open to other viewpoints from other countries?

The development of a reasoning process over time allows these influences to work gradually so that you may not be fully aware of their impact until someone criticizes your viewpoint as being blinkered or, even worse, discriminatory. So if you find yourself in a situation where you are making a decision that involves different cultures or employees from different countries, consider your starting point first.

account of established policies in the countries in which they operate.

III. **Disclosure:** Recommends disclosure on all material matters regarding the enterprise such as its performance and ownership, and encourages communication in areas where reporting standards are still emerging such as social, environmental, and risk reporting.

IV. **Employment and Industrial Relations:** Addresses major aspects of corporate behavior in this area including child and forced labor, nondiscrimination and the right to bona fide employee representation, and constructive negotiations.

V. **Environment:** Encourages enterprises to raise their performance in protecting the environment, including performance with respect to health and safety impacts. Features of this chapter include

recommendations concerning environmental management systems and the desirability of precautions where there are threats of serious damage to the environment.

VI. **Combating Bribery:** Covers both public and private bribery and addresses passive and active corruption.

VII. **Consumer Interests:** Recommends that enterprises, when dealing with consumers, act in accordance with fair business, marketing, and advertising practices; respect consumer privacy; and take all reasonable steps to ensure the safety and quality of goods or services provided.

VIII. **Science and Technology:** Aims to promote the diffusion by multinational enterprises of the fruits of research and development activities among the countries where they operate,

> **Key Point**

If an MNC was looking to raise its profile as an ethical organization, would it be better to support the UN Global Compact or the OECD Guidelines? Why?

thereby contributing to the innovative capacities of host countries.

IX. **Competition:** Emphasizes the importance of an open and competitive business climate.

X. **Taxation:** Calls on enterprises to respect both the letter and spirit of tax laws and to cooperate with tax authorities.

PROGRESS ✓ QUESTIONS

13. What are the OECD Guidelines for Multinational Enterprises?

14. How do the guidelines differ from the UN Global Compact?

15. How are they similar to the UN Global Compact?

16. Can you think of a situation in which a multinational corporation would endorse one or the other? Or should they both be endorsed? Explain your answer.

>> Conclusion

If an organization is committed to ethical business conduct, that commitment should remain constant wherever that business is conducted in the world. Unfortunately, the more evidence of ethical misconduct at home, the greater the likelihood that organizations will fall victim to the temptations offered in the less-regulated developing nations.

Carrying a reputation as a good corporate citizen may bring some positive media coverage and win the business of critical consumers who pay close attention to where the products they buy are sourced and manufactured. However, the real test comes when the quarterly numbers aren't looking as good as Wall Street would like and the need to trim costs will mean the difference between a rising stock price and a falling one.

As the Wendell Willkie quote at the beginning of this chapter indicates, the world is now completely interdependent, and that interdependence extends to both *operations* and *information*. You may be able to save money by contracting with vendors that manufacture goods in sweatshop conditions, and you may be able to let contractors handle your hazardous waste without worrying too much about where they

put it, but these will be short-lived savings and conveniences. Once those actions are made public through investigative media agencies or consumer advocacy groups, your status as a "good corporate citizen" may never be regained.

The concept of global ethics remains frustratingly complex. Advocates of a global code of conduct may rally against sweatshops and the employment of children at unspeakably low wages. However, their proposed solutions for the prohibition of these working conditions often fail to address the replacement of family income when the children are no longer allowed to work, which, in turn, can cause financial devastation to the families involved.

It can be argued that true global citizens should remain ethically involved in all their markets, rather than (as the critics maintain) taking advantage of the weak for the betterment of the strong. Supporters of Milton Friedman's *instrumental* contract may argue that corporations carry no moral obligation to the countries in which they operate beyond abiding by their laws, but when we consider the public backlash against Nike's sweatshops and Kathie Lee Gifford's child labor scandal, it would seem that there is a strong enough financial incentive to address these issues whether you accept a moral obligation or not.

FRONTLINE FOCUS
A Matter of Definition—Tom Makes a Decision

Tom considered his options very carefully. If the media found out about these sweatshops, would that negative publicity make it back to his agency? After all, the agency just wrote the ad copy and negotiated the placement of the ads. It didn't order the items, and if Tom hadn't received the billing paperwork by mistake, his agency wouldn't know where the items were made.

"Even so," thought Tom, "manufacturing any goods in sweatshop conditions is wrong, and our agency doesn't do business with customers that subscribe to the abuse of human rights."

Tom lost no time in bringing this new information about the Smith's campaign to his boss, Charles Cooper, the founder and president of their agency:

"Mr. Cooper, this Smith's campaign could be a big problem for us. Its leading sales items weren't 'made in America' at all. This paperwork shows that the items came from a sweatshop in Indonesia. I did some research on the company that manufactures these items, and it has already been fined on several occasions for human rights violations."

Then Tom took a deep breath. "I know this is a big contract for us, Mr. Cooper, but is this the type of work we are going to do now? I didn't think our agency worked on these kinds of campaigns. Little kids working in sweatshops just so we can have cookouts on the Fourth of July doesn't seem right."

Cooper thought for several minutes before responding: "Are you sure this information is accurate, Tom?"

"Yes, sir. This billing paperwork came with the original prep kit directly from Smith's."

"Then let's get our friends at Smith's on the phone. I'm afraid they are going to be looking for a new agency."

QUESTIONS

1. What do you think Charles Cooper will say to his counterpart at Smith's?
2. What do you think Smith's reaction will be?
3. Is there a chance that Tom's company could save its relationship with Smith's?

[For Review]

1. **Understand the ethical issues arising in global business.**

   Managing the business ethics of a domestic corporation can be challenging enough. Once a company moves onto the international or global stage, the different languages, cultures, and business practices force North American companies to decide which of their ethical principles are nonnegotiable and which are open to discussion in favor of the client country with which they are looking to do business.

2. **Explain the issue of ethical relativism in a global environment.**

   As we learned in Chapter 1, ethical relativism can be driven by local circumstances. Ethical business practices in North America may often be enforced by laws that do not apply to other countries. In such situations, domestic corporations are often required to follow the standard operating procedures (SOPs) of the client country even if, in areas of social and political chaos, those SOPs amount to nothing more than a bureaucratic nightmare. In that scenario, business ethics can often deteriorate into "whatever it takes" to get the deal done.

3. **Explain the challenges in developing a global code of ethics.**

   The idea of developing a general standard of business practice that can be applied equally to all countries over

   and above their local customs and social norms is seen as the best hope for stopping the dark side of global capitalism. Western corporations, it is argued, have the financial strength to make extensive capital investments in developing countries, taking the natural resources of those countries as their raw materials for manufacturing plants elsewhere in the world. Without legal enforcement of ethical business practices, those corporations can conduct business without concern for employee welfare and safety. A global code of conduct, to which all international businesses would subscribe, would, it is believed, put a stop to those practices. However, the financial strength of the Western nations is seen as a threat to equal representation of the developing nations, and as a result, those developing nations hold onto their national identities and cultures, thereby precluding any agreement on a general standard of business practice.

4. **Analyze the ramifications of the UN Global Compact.**

   The UN Global Compact represents a voluntary commitment to corporate citizenship by the 2,000 companies that have elected to participate since the compact became operational in July 2000. Since it is not a regulatory instrument (and, by definition, not enforceable with any form of penalties for failing to comply with the standards of the compact), it is, at best, a public endorsement of the focus on the environment, anticorruption, the welfare of workers around the world, and global human rights. The credibility of the entire initiative is dependent on the public accountability, transparency, and enlightened self-interest of the member organizations in making sure that their global business practices align with the key principles of the compact.

5. **Explain the OECD Guidelines for Multinational Enterprises.**

   Originally adopted as part of the larger Declaration on International Investments and Multinational Enterprises in 1976, the Organization for Economic Cooperation and Development (OECD) Guidelines for Multinational Enterprises represents a more governmental approach to the same issues featured in the UN's nongovernmental Global Compact. Supporters argue that the government backing adds credibility to the issues being promoted, but the guidelines carry no criminal or civil enforcement and are not regarded as legally binding. What they do offer are principles and standards of behavior that draw on the same core values as the UN Global Compact across a broader series of issues captured in 10 "chapters."

[Key Terms]

Developed Nation 188

Ethical Relativism 189

Global Code of Conduct 191

Globalization 189

Less-Developed Nation 188

Multinational Corporation (MNC) 189

OECD Guidelines for Multinational Enterprises 194

UN Global Compact 193

Utilitarianism 188

[Review Questions]

1. Do you think global businesses would be willing to subscribe to a global code of conduct? Explain your answer.

2. Would it be easier to just follow the business practices and customs of the country in which you're doing business? Why or why not?

3. Are there more stakeholders for an international or global company than a domestic one? Explain your answer.

4. How would the Foreign Corrupt Practices Act (FCPA) that we reviewed in Chapter 6 come into play here?

5. Which offers greater guidance to international businesses, the UN Global Compact or the OECD Guidelines for Multinational Enterprises? Explain your answer.

6. What is the most ethical way to do business internationally?

[Review Exercises]

Universal Training Solutions. Kathy James was Universal Training Solutions' top trainer. She had delivered client presentations, held one-day open workshops on sales calls, and had led national rollouts for large training implementations. The opportunity to lead the training for Universal's new South African client, National Bank of SA, was simply too good to miss. She had met with Universal's account manager for National Bank and felt that she had a strong grasp of what the client was looking for.

National Bank of SA had recently invested $10 million (about 60 million rand) in upgrading its call center equipment, and its managers were looking for customer service training to ensure that the call center representatives (CCRs) could provide the highest level of service in their market. Market research had shown that South Africans weren't accustomed to good service from their banks, so this initiative was seen as a good way to gain some market share.

Universal's customer service training program—First Class Service (FCS)—had a phenomenal reputation with dozens of Fortune 500 companies and several global implementations to its credit. It was designed to be delivered in three days with average class sizes of 10 to 12 employees. It was a logical choice for National, which was eager to get the program rolling.

Kathy asked to lead the cultural adaptation team, working with a translator in Johannesburg to translate FCS into Afrikaans (although she had been told by the account manager that most of National's employees spoke very good English). She anticipated that most of the group activities within the program would remain the same—that was what National's buyers had seen at the demonstration. She set up the first of what she thought would be several conference calls with the translator and looked forward to another successful project.

However, the first call brought things to a dramatic halt. As Kathy and the translator got to know each other, the translator asked how much Kathy knew about the South African culture. Kathy had been doing some extensive research on the web after she had been assigned to the project, and she did her best to dazzle the translator with her knowledge. Then the translator asked a question that stumped Kathy: "Why are you only translating this into Afrikaans? Did you know there are 11 national languages in South Africa

and that not recognizing those languages is considered to be a social blunder?"

The translator went on to describe how in many formal presentations (such as the training events Universal was planning to roll out in all National's regional offices over the next six months), it was considered rude not to recognize all the nationalities present in the room—particularly in group activities.

Kathy started to panic. How was she supposed to turn an American three-day program into a South African three-day program that allows time to recognize 11 languages and nationalities in the group exercises?

1. What is the right thing to do here?

2. Why shouldn't National just deliver the American version of CFS? If it works here, it should work there.

3. Which stakeholders will be affected by Kathy's decision?

4. What are her options here?

[Internet Exercises]

1. Visit the website for the Institute for Global Ethics (IGE) at www.globalethics.org.

   a. What is IGE's stated purpose?

   b. Which five values does the IGE identify in building a code of ethics?

   c. How could a corporation benefit from the services of the Institute for Global Ethics?

2. Visit the website for Walmart's Global Ethics at http://www.walmartethics.com/Landing.aspx#

   a. Why did Walmart create Global Ethics?

   b. Summarize how Walmart employees can contact Global Ethics.

   c. Locate and download Walmart's most recent "Global Sustainability Report," and provide three examples of projects that the company has undertaken that demonstrate its commitment to global ethics.

[Team Exercises]

1. **Global or local?**
   Divide into two teams. One team must prepare a presentation advocating for the development of a standardized global code of conduct. The other team must prepare a presentation arguing for the development of a more flexible local code of conduct that takes into account the cultural norms of individual nations.

2. **Restoring a reputation.**
   Divide into groups of three or four. Each group must map out its proposal for restoring the ethical reputation of a multinational corporation that has been fined for one of the following transgressions: bribery, pollution, operating sweatshops, or employing child labor. Prepare a presentation outlining your plan for restoring the reputation of the company with its stakeholders.

3. **Tamiflu.**
   Divide into two groups and prepare arguments *for* and *against* the following behavior: *Your American company operates manufacturing plants throughout Asia, with a combined staff of 20,000 employees. In 2003, after Asia was hit with the severe acute respiratory syndrome (SARS) epidemic, your company introduced a policy to stockpile drugs*

in locations where employees don't have access to high-quality health care. In 2005, SARS was replaced by avian influenza—bird flu—as the primary risk for the next pandemic. Your company responded by stockpiling quantities of the drug Tamiflu, the antiviral drug that is regarded as the best treatment for bird flu in humans.

There has been a reported outbreak of bird flu in a remote region of Vietnam, about 100 miles from where you have a manufacturing plant. The government clinic has a small supply of Tamiflu, but aware of your company's stockpile, the clinic has approached your local plant manager to share some of your supply. The plant manager contacted you for help in responding to the request. Your company policy on this is to make sure employees are taken care of first, and so you decline the request for assistance, claiming that you have insufficient quantities of Tamiflu to meet your immediate needs.

4. **Looking the other way.**

   Divide into two groups and prepare arguments *for* and *against* the following behavior: *You have been sent to investigate a fraud claim made against your company by the customs department in one of the countries where you do business. On arrival, an officer explains that your company is being fined for under-declaring the number of safety boots imported into the country. You notice he is wearing a pair of the "missing" boots.*

   In preparation for your trip you verified that all the shipment and customs paperwork was in order, and you are certain that the number of safety boots has not been under-declared. Since your company's strategic plan features high growth expectations from this region, you are tempted to simply pay the fine and get the officer's name and address so you can send him some other samples of your company's products. However, your company's senior management team recently returned from a strategic planning retreat in which they made a clear commitment to enforce the organization's code of ethics in all business transactions, here and abroad, even at the risk of losing short-term business. Your CEO was quoted in the company newsletter as saying: "We should use our higher moral standards as an opportunity to win customers who want to do business with a reputable organization." So you reach into your briefcase for your copies of the customs paperwork and begin to challenge the officer's accusation of under-declaring.

Source: Inspired by Alison Maitland, "A Code to Export Better Practice," *Financial Times*, London (UK), January 26, 1999, p. 14.

Thinking Critically

>> TOMS SHOES: ETHICALLY GLOBAL?

The focus of most of the chapters in this text has been on companies seeking (or in many cases failing) to operate according to clearly established ethical principles that guide how they treat their stakeholders. The concept of "doing the right thing" has been presented as a natural alignment to their central business purpose, whether that's making cars, computers, or providing financial or consulting services. But what about a company that was started specifically to do the right thing? Not a consulting company to advise other companies on ethical business practices, but a company whose core purpose is "conscious capitalism"—delivering a product as a means to another end.

In 2006 Blake Mycoskie was inspired by a visit to Argentina to bring the traditional Argentine *alpargata* slip-on shoe to the U.S. market. Not an unusual decision for a serial entrepreneur like Mycoskie, but what made this idea unique was his purpose for this business. While doing community service work in Argentina, Mycoskie was struck by the country's health and poverty problems—and in particular the large number of children without shoes. His idea was to work with Argentinean shoemakers and vendors to produce shoes with vibrant colors and prints for the U.S. market and to offer those genuine *alpargata* shoes at a price point that would allow his company to give away one pair free for every pair sold.

© jackie ellis/Alamy Stock Photo

Mycoskie originally intended to give 200 pairs of shoes to the children of Los Piletones in Argentina, but the buy-one-give-one-away model proved so successful that the first "shoe drop," as the donation visits have become known, delivered 10,000 pairs of shoes to match 10,000 pairs purchased by customers at such retailers as Bloomingdale's, Nordstrom, and Urban Outfitters.

In the years since Mycoskie's company TOMS was founded, over 38 million pairs of shoes have been donated in 65 countries under the "One for One" program. The Ethiopian shoe drops are especially significant because of a local disease called *podoconiosis,* a form of elephantiasis. Contracted through the soil, the disease causes disfigurement and ulcers in the lower legs, and sufferers are ultimately banished from their villages like lepers. The good news is that the disease is 100 percent preventable by wearing shoes.

An important point to remember when learning about TOMS is that this is a for-profit company. Mycoskie was inspired by the Newman's Own company started by actor Paul Newman and writer A. E. Hotchner in 1982, which has donated over $300 million to community and health-related benefit programs in the past three decades. Newman's Own is also a for-profit company. The pursuit of a favorable tax status as a nonprofit company was never the point; it was the ability to give away the profits to worthy causes—that's why the companies were created in the first place.

In July 2011, the "One for One" program was expanded to include eyewear, with the purchase of a pair of TOMS eyeglasses providing medical treatment, prescription glasses, or sight-saving surgery through a partnership with the Seva Foundation. The program is currently in operation in 13 countries worldwide—Bangladesh, Cambodia, Egypt, Ethiopia, Guatemala, India, Nepal, Pakistan, Paraguay, Tibet, Tanzania, Uganda, and the United States.

In April 2012, the company asked customers to participate in "A Day without Shoes" in which participants would sacrifice wearing shoes for one day, "so kids don't have to." The campaign garnered a lot of support from existing TOMS customers, but also prompted criticism of the entire TOMS model. Critics argue that the model falls victim to the mistake of "giving a man a fish" rather than "teaching a man to fish." In addition, the "dumping" of thousands of pairs of free shoes in local markets (however well intentioned), does irreparable harm to local shoe manufacturers and vendors who lose their markets overnight. They acknowledge Mycoskie's entrepreneurial skills in combining "peasant chic" with "social conscience," but argue that the "feel-good purchase" factor offers a short-term buzz at the expense of the longer-term impact that could be achieved if the funds could be deployed in a more effective way.

CONTINUED >>

To help celebrate the company's ninth anniversary in May 2015, Mycoskie used Instagram to underline the company's "B1G1" model by donating a pair of shoes for every Instagram photo of bare feet posted with the hashtag #withoutshoes. Other companies, such as eyewear vendor Warby Parker, have taken a different approach to the B1G1 model. Rather than simply giving eyeglasses away, the company covers the cost of training, parts, and manufacture for a second pair of glasses through social venture partners such as VisionSpring, which then employ sales agents (9,000 in 13 countries) to give basic eye exams and sell eyeglasses at affordable prices in their local communities. The premise is that supporting a sales network reduces the likelihood of making communities dependent upon handouts, or situations where donations were made to children who already had eyeglasses or shoes.

TOMS, meanwhile, has taken some steps to address criticism of its "dumping" model, where shoes manufactured in China are given away in Africa, by supporting local manufacturing options to ensure that residents receive shoes that are best suited to their local climate. This, in turn, provides employment in addition to free footwear.

QUESTIONS

1. Does TOMS buy-one-give-one-away model make it a more ethical company than a traditional manufacturer donating money to a charity? Why?

2. Why would customers pay such a high price for a simple linen shoe or pair of sunglasses?

3. Mycoskie designed the TOMS model from the ground up. Could an established company improve its ethical standards by launching a model like TOMS? How?

4. Is the Warby Parker model more or less effective than the TOMS model? Explain your answer.

Sources: Stacy Perman, "Making a Do-Gooder's Business Model Work," *Bloomberg Businessweek,* January 23, 2009; Laurie Burkitt, "Companies' Good Deeds Resonate with Customers," *Forbes,* May 27, 2010; Blake Mycoskie, "The Way I Work," *Inc.,* June 1, 2010; Kiera Butler, "Do Toms Shoes Really Help People?" *Mother Jones,* May 13, 2012; James Poulos, "Toms Shoes: A Doomed Vanity Project?" *Forbes,* April 11, 2012; Marco della Cava, "Toms Uses Instagram to Give away a Million Shoes," *USA Today,* May 5, 2015; and Sarika Bansal, "Shopping for a Better World," *The New York Times,* May 9, 2012.

Thinking Critically 9.2

>> SUICIDES AT FOXCONN

Foxconn Technology Group is a subsidiary of Taiwan's Hon Hai Precision Industry Co. (reputed to be the world's largest "contract manufacturer"). Even as a subsidiary, Foxconn's numbers are impressive—the company employs about 800,000 people, half of whom work in a huge industrial park in Shenzhen, China, called Foxconn City. With 15 separate multi-story buildings, each dedicated to individual customers such as Apple, Dell, Nintendo, and Hewlett-Packard, Foxconn's promotional material proudly states that the company pays minimum wage (900 yuan, or $130 a month), offers free food and lodging along with extensive recreational facilities to its employees—on the face of it, not your stereotypical "sweatshop" environment.

However, in the first half of 2010, 12 Foxconn employees found the working conditions so oppressive that they elected to kill themselves by jumping from the roofs of those 15-story buildings. According to reports, two other employees were seriously injured in suicide attempts, and another 20 were saved before completing their planned attempt. The sudden spate of suicides drew unwelcome attention to the true state of the working conditions in factories that visitors have described as "grim." Labor activists report annual turnover of 40 percent or more as employees leave rather than face dangerously fast assembly lines, "military-style drills, verbal abuse by superiors . . . as well as occasionally being pressured

© iStock.com/
Eddisonphotos RF

to work as many as 13 consecutive days to complete a big customer order—even when it means sleeping on the factory floor."

Consider the case of 19-year-old Ma Xiangqian, a former migrant worker who leapt to his death January 23, 2010. His family revealed that he hated his job at Foxconn: "11-hour overnight shifts, seven days a week, forging plastic and metal into electronic parts amid fumes and dust." In the month before he died, Ma worked 286 hours, including 112 overtime hours, three times the legal limit.

The negative publicity was swift and targeted. Apple's international release of its iPad in Hong Kong was marred by the ritual burning of pictures of iPhones and calls for a global boycott of all Apple products. The negative press prompted an equally swift response from Foxconn customers seeking to distance themselves from the story. Apple, Dell, and HP all announced investigations of the working conditions at Foxconn's plants, with the implied threat of contract termination.

Foxconn's response was to surround the buildings with nets to prevent any further suicide attempts, to hire counselors for employees experiencing stress from the working conditions, and to assign workers to 50-person groups so that they can keep an eye on each other for signs of emotional stress. The company also announced two separate pay increases more than doubling worker pay to 2,000 yuan a month (although workers must pass a three-month review to qualify for the second pay increase). In addition, a series of "motivational rallies," entitled "Treasure Your Life, Love Your Family, Care for Each Other to Build a Wonderful Future," were scheduled for all Foxconn facilities.

While the immediate response was targeted directly at the media criticism, there are concerns about the longer-term consequences for Foxconn and its customers. Hon Hai's reputation and dominance have been built on top quality with wafer-thin margins—margins that may prove to be too thin to absorb a 100 percent increase in labor costs. As for its customers, they may have given implied threats of contract termination, but with Hon Hai as the world leader, there are limited options for alternative suppliers.

Apple asked the Fair Labor Association (FLA), a nongovernment organization, to conduct an extensive audit of Foxconn's operations. The FLA teams visited Foxconn factories in Shenzhen and Chengdu, and surveyed some 35,000 workers at three facilities that assembled Apple products, including iPhones and iPads. The audit report was released March 29, 2012, and found that during the preceding 12 months, workers typically exceeded the 60 hours of work per week stipulated in Apple's agreement with Foxconn. In addition, the report found that many workers also exceeded China's legal limit of 36 hours of overtime per month. In conclusion, the FLA found that conditions were "no worse than any other factory in China."

Foxconn seems unconcerned by the criticism. In July 2015, the company announced that it would be building up to 12 new factories in India, employing as many as 1 million people by 2020. This was seen as a strategic response to rising wage costs and labor disputes in China.

In March 2016, the company announced a $3.5 billion deal to acquire a 66 percent controlling interest in Japanese screen maker Sharp after weeks of negotiations and numerous setbacks. The deal is expected to give Foxconn more leverage with its dealings with Apple (Sharp provides an estimated 25 percent of Apple's iPhone screens), but with around $3 billion in liabilities, Sharp will require some aggressive action to turn around.

QUESTIONS

1. Was Foxconn's response sufficient to stop any future suicide attempts? Why or why not?
2. If the company has operated on "wafer-thin margins," will the Indian and Japanese deals make it a more ethical company? Why or why not?
3. Would you describe Foxconn's response as an example of proactive or reactive ethics? Why?
4. If Apple is committed to addressing working conditions at Foxconn factories, should "no worse than any other factory in China" be an acceptable benchmark? Why or why not?

Sources: "Suicides at Foxconn: Light and Death," *The Economist,* May 27, 2010; Annie Huang, "Foxconn Raises Worker Pay by 30% after Suicides," *Associated Press,* June 2, 2010; David Barboza, "After Suicides, Scrutiny of China's Grim Factories," *The New York Times,* June 6, 2010; Debby Wu, "iPhone Factory Suicides Spur Corporate Pep Rally," *Associated Press,* August 18, 2010; "iAudit," *The Economist,* March 30, 2012; James Crabtree, "Foxconn to Build up to 12 Factories, Employ 1M in India," *Financial Times,* July 14, 2015; and Paul Mozur, "To Woo Apple, Foxconn Bets $3.5 Billion on Sharp," *The New York Times,* March 30, 2016.

>> THE ETHICS OF OFFSHORING CLINICAL TRIALS

The process of offshoring (outsourcing an organizational function overseas) is being applied to clinical drug trials with the same speed and enthusiasm as the transplanting by major U.S. corporations of their customer service call centers to countries such as Ireland, India, and increasingly farther east locations. In a report released in June 2010 by Daniel R. Levinson, the inspector general of the Department of Health and Human Services, 80 percent of the drugs approved for sale in 2008 had trials in foreign countries, and 78 percent of all subjects who participated in clinical trials were enrolled at foreign sites. Ten medicines approved in 2008 received no domestic testing.

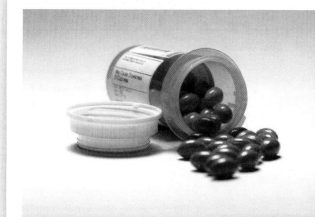
© j4m3z/Getty Images

For U.S.-based pharmaceutical companies, the rush is driven by both attractive options and practical realities:

- Pursuing the same cost advantages as other U.S. corporations, drug companies are now discovering that trials in such regions as Eastern Europe, Asia, Latin America, and Africa can produce the same quality of data at a lower cost and often in a shorter time frame.
- After safety concerns over drugs like the anti-inflammatory Vioxx, which was withdrawn from sale in 2004, regulators such as the Food and Drug Administration (FDA) are now requiring even more data as a prerequisite for the approval of a new drug. That equates to more trials enrolling more people for longer periods of time—sometimes many thousands of patients over 12 months or longer.
- Patients in North America are increasingly unwilling to participate in phase 1 experimental trials, preferring instead to participate in phase 2 or 3 trials where the effectiveness of the drug has already been established and the trials are focused on identifying appropriate dosage levels or potential side effects.
- In contrast, these new overseas trial sites offer "large pools of patients who are 'treatment naive' because the relatively low standard of health care compared with Western countries means they have not had access to the latest and most expensive medicines."
- In North American trials, each doctor may only be able to offer a handful of patients who are willing and able to participate, whereas in populous nations such as India and China, a single doctor may see dozens of patients a day who would be willing trial participants, allowing faster recruitment from a smaller number of sites.

However, pharmaceutical companies don't have everything their own way. Developing countries or not, restrictions are in place either to directly prevent trials or, at the very least, to ensure the professional and ethical management of those trials:

- Many developing countries have laws against "first in person" trials to prevent the treatment of their citizens as guinea pigs in highly experimental drug trials.
- Russia and China have both limited the export of blood and patient tissue samples in recent years, partly out of concern over illegal trafficking in human organs.
- The FDA recently set up an office in China to increase inspections of the rapidly growing number of clinical trials.
- The World Medical Association's 2004 Helsinki declaration called for stringent ethical practices in drug trials, but these remain voluntary practices.

In addition, the rush to take advantage of these cost savings and practical benefits has produced some problems ranging from questionable data to patient deaths:

- In 2003, several patients with AIDS died after an experimental drug trial in Ditan Hospital in Beijing. Viral Genetics, a California biotechnology company, was criticized for failing to explain adequately to participants that they were taking part in a drug trial rather than receiving a proven medicine.
- Further criticism was levied at Viral Genetics for an issue that has become a greater concern for clinical drug trials in general—specifically the use of a sugar pill or placebo as a comparative measure of the efficacy of the drug. In the Ditan trial, questions were raised as to why an antiretroviral treatment—the most effective treatment for AIDS in the West—wasn't used as a comparative treatment.

- The lack of education and lower standards of care in these developing countries also raise questions about patient eligibility for participation in these trials. While they may qualify by diagnosis, do they really understand the concept of informed consent, and, more importantly still, do they realize that once the trial has ended, it may be months or years before they have access to the drug for a prolonged treatment regimen for their condition?

In the end, it is likely that basic economics will win out. Increasingly stringent standards in North America, driven, some would argue, by the litigious nature of our society, will only serve to increase the attractiveness of overseas trials. Without a suitable regulatory framework to oversee these trials and ensure that patients are treated in an ethical manner, the feared picture of uneducated citizens from developing countries being used as guinea pigs in experimental trials that citizens from developed nations are unwilling to participate in will become a reality.

QUESTIONS

1. Identify three factors that are driving pharmaceutical companies to host clinical drug trials overseas.
2. What regulations are in place to oversee the professional and ethical management of these trials?
3. If patients lack the language skills or education to understand the significance of informed consent or the use of a placebo, is it ethical to allow them to participate in the drug trial? Why or why not?
4. What proposals would you offer to make the offshoring of clinical drug trials a more ethical process for all the stakeholders involved?

Sources: "The Next Big Thing," *The Economist,* June 16, 2005; Andrew Jack, "New Lease on Life? The Ethics of Offshoring Clinical Trials," *Financial Times,* January 29, 2008, p. 9; and Gardiner Harris, "Concern over Foreign Trials for Drugs Sold in U.S.," *The New York Times,* June 21, 2010.

[References]

1. Thomas L. Friedman, *The World Is Flat: A Brief History of the Twenty-First Century* (New York: Farrar, Straus, and Giroux, 2005). Copyright © 2005 by Thomas L. Friedman. Reprinted by permission of Farrar, Straus, and Giroux, LLC.

2. "Unfortunate Translations That Harmed Brand Reputations," www.thethinkingblog.com/2007/09/13-unfortunate-translations-that-harmed.html.

3. R. DeGeorge, "Ethics in Personal Business—A Contradiction in Terms?" *Business Credit* 102, no. 8 (1993), pp. 45–46.

4. William Greider, *One World, Ready or Not: The Manic Logic of Global Capitalism* (New York: Touchstone, 1998), p. 22.

5. "Overview of the UN Global Compact," www.unglobalcompact.org/AboutTheGC/index.html.

6. OECD Guidelines for Multinational Enterprises, June 2001, www.oecd.org.

CHAPTER 10

© Stockbyte/Getty Images RF

MAKING IT STICK: DOING WHAT'S RIGHT IN A COMPETITIVE MARKET

After studying this chapter, you should be able to:

10-1 Develop the key components of an ethics policy.

10-2 Analyze the ramifications of becoming a *transparent* organization.

10-3 Understand the difference between *reactive* and *proactive* ethical policies.

10-4 Discuss the challenges of a commitment to *organizational integrity*.

FRONTLINE FOCUS
You Scratch My Back

Adam is a sales rep for a leading pharmaceutical company. His company is in a fierce battle with its largest competitor over the highly lucrative blood pressure medication market. Blood pressure medication is a multibillion-dollar market in the United States, the largest-selling medication after drugs for cholesterol and diabetes. Adam's company has the No. 1 drug and its competitor the No. 2 drug in the market, but like Coke and Pepsi, they are locked in a fierce battle for market share with aggressive marketing campaigns and sales promotions. The company has produced every possible giveaway item with the name of the drug on it, and the trunk and backseat of Adam's company car (not to mention his garage) are crammed with boxes of those items to give away to any doctor who shows an interest in prescribing the medicine.

Today, Adam is visiting a new doctor. The office is actually one he has worked with for a long time, but the partners he knew recently sold their practice and retired, so Adam has a meeting with the new owner of the practice, Dr. Green. As Adam pulls into the parking lot, he has a problem finding a parking space. "This place is busier than ever," he thinks. "I hope old Doc Stevens and his partners got a good price for this practice—it's got to be a gold mine."

In the waiting room, Adam sees all the old familiar faces behind the counter but notices that no one is smiling—all are very serious and focused on paperwork. Jennifer, the office manager, takes him back to Dr. Green's office and leaves him with a word of advice: "Watch yourself, Adam; it's not like the old days."

After 15 minutes, Dr. Green walks in. Adam stands up and introduces himself and politely thanks Dr. Green for making time for him in his busy schedule. Dr. Green doesn't smile or make small talk. He gets straight to the point: "Adam, is it? Well, Adam, let me explain my philosophy in working with pharmaceutical reps. The way I see it, you make as much money on your pills as you can until the patent runs out, and I'd like to see some of that money being spent for the benefit of this practice—lots of free samples for my patients and lots of evidence that your company appreciates my support of their medicines—do you follow me?"

Adam isn't sure what "lots of evidence" meant, but he is pretty sure that Dr. Green was about to explain it to him, so he nods and smiles.

"This practice represents a long-term investment for me, and I paid top dollar for it. Old man Stevens built a good base of patients, but I think we can do better—this place just needs a firm hand, and it will double in size within the year. Unfortunately, with growth comes additional expense. Did I mention I paid top dollar for this place?" Dr. Green suddenly stops and smiles—one of the most artificial smiles Adam has ever seen. "Here's what I'm thinking, Adam. Rather than wasting money on notepads and pens that the other reps give me by the case, I'd like some support—we can call it marketing funds if you'd like—in decorating my office. Some high-end furniture worthy of a doctor with a growing practice—what do you think?"

Adam coughs, trying desperately to come up with an answer: "Well, sir, that's a very unusual request, um, and while we greatly appreciate your support of our medicines, um, I don't think I could get that approved by my regional manager."

Dr. Green's fake smile disappears as quickly as it had arrived. "Here's the deal, Adam. I had a very productive meeting with a delightful young man named Zachary this morning. He works for your competition, I believe."

Adam winces at the mention of Zach's name.

"Zachary didn't seem to think there would be a problem with such an unusual request. In fact, he has a friend who is an interior designer, and he was confident that her services could be included in those 'marketing funds.' So what are we going to do here?"

QUESTIONS

1. The four key points of a code of ethics are outlined in the "Making It Stick—Key Components of an Ethics Policy" section. If we assume that Adam's company has such a code, what guidance could Adam find in those four key points?

2. Do you think Zachary is willing to provide those "marketing funds" to win the business away from Adam, or is Dr. Green just bluffing?

3. What should Adam do now?

>> If ethics are poor at the top, that behavior is copied down through the organization.

Robert Noyce, inventor

>> Making It Stick— Key Components of an Ethics Policy

Ask any CEO to describe the market she is working in, and she will probably describe the same set of characteristics:

- *Demanding customers* who want new and better products and services at lower prices.
- *Impatient stockholders* who want the stock price to rise each and every quarter.
- *Aggressive vendors* who want to sell you more of everything.
- *Demanding federal, state, and local officials* who want to burden you with more rules and regulations while encouraging you to hire more people and pay more taxes.
- *Demanding creditors* who want their loan payments on time.
- *Aggressive competitors* who want to steal your customers from you.

When you are operating a business in such a tough environment, holding on to your promise to run an ethical business and to do "the right thing" for all your stakeholders can be very challenging. It's easy to see why so many executives, after the unethical behavior of their companies has been exposed, point to the ruthless competition of the business world as their excuse for not doing the right thing.

Sustainable Ethics Ethical behavior that persists long after the latest public scandal or the latest management buzzword.

So how do you make it stick? How do you make sure your company holds on to its ethical principles even if everyone else in your marketplace doesn't? **Sustainable ethics** in a culture are those that persist within the operational policies of the organization long after the latest public scandal or the latest management buzzword.

We have seen in the previous nine chapters how a company's commitment to ethical behavior impacts every managerial level and every department of the organization. So making ethical behavior *sustainable* requires the involvement of every member of the organization in committing to a formal structure to support an ongoing

© Stockbyte/PunchStock RF

process of monitoring and enforcement. This can be summarized in the following six stages:

1. Establish a code of ethics.
2. Support the code of ethics with extensive training for every member of the organization.
3. Hire an ethics officer.
4. Celebrate and reward the ethical behavior demonstrated by your employees.
5. Promote your organization's commitment to ethical behavior.
6. Continue to monitor the behavior as you grow.

ESTABLISH A CODE OF ETHICS

For everyone to begin from the same starting point, the organization's commitment to ethical behavior must be documented in a code of ethics. A well-written code of ethics can do several things:

- It can capture what the organization understands ethical behavior to mean—your values statement.
- It can establish a detailed guide to acceptable behavior.
- It can state policies for behavior in specific situations.
- It can document punishments for violations of those policies.

The audience for the code of ethics would be every stakeholder of the organization. Investors, customers, and suppliers would see how serious you are about ethical performance, and employees would understand clearly the standard of behavior expected from them and the consequences for failing to meet that standard.

Review the following online material for examples of codes of ethics from the following organizations:

- Society of Professional Journalists (SPJ), Online Ethics Code 1.
- Association for Computing Machinery (ACM), Online Ethics Code 2.
- The Institute of Internal Auditors (IIA), Online Ethics Code 3.
- American Society of Civil Engineers (ASCE), Online Ethics Code 4.

As you can see from those four examples featured online, there is no perfect model for a code of ethics: Some are very specific in their commitments to their profession (consider the "Canons" of the ASCE code), and others are operational in their focus, giving very clear guidance as to the consequences if employees transgress the code.

If you are involved in creating a code of ethics from scratch, consider the following advice from the Institute of Business Ethics:[1]

1. *Find a champion.* Unless a senior person—hopefully the CEO—is prepared to drive the introduction of a business ethics policy, the chances of it being a useful tool are not high.
2. *Get endorsement from the chairperson and the board.* Corporate values and ethics are matters of governance. The board must be enthusiastic not only about having such a policy but also about receiving regular reports on its operation.
3. *Find out what bothers people.* Merely endorsing a standard code or copying that of another will not suffice. It is important to find out on what topics employees require guidance.
4. *Pick a well-tested model.* Use a framework that addresses issues as they affect different constituents or stakeholders of the company. The usual ones are shareholders, employees, customers, suppliers, and local/national community. Some might even include competitors.
5. *Produce a company code of conduct.* This should be distributed in booklet form or via a company intranet. Existing policies, for example on giving and receiving gifts or the private use of company software, can be incorporated. Guidance on how the code works should also be included.
6. *Try it out first.* The code needs piloting—perhaps with a sample of employees drawn from all levels and different locations. An external party such as the Institute of Business Ethics will comment on drafts.
7. *Issue the code and make it known.* Publish and send the code to all employees, suppliers, and others. State publicly that the company has a code and implementation program that covers the whole company. Put it on your website, and send it to joint venture and other partners.
8. *Make it work.* Practical examples of the code in action should be introduced into all company internal (and external) training programs as well as induction courses. Managers should sign off on the code regularly, and a review mechanism should be established. A code "master" needs to be appointed.

SUPPORT THE CODE OF ETHICS WITH EXTENSIVE TRAINING FOR EVERY MEMBER OF THE ORGANIZATION

Writing the code of ethics is the easy part. Getting your commitment to ethical performance down on paper and specifying the standards of behavior you will accept and the punishments you will enforce is a good starting point. However, the code can only be a guide—it cannot cover every possible event. The real test of any company's ethics policy comes when one of your employees is presented with a potentially unethical situation.

Moreover, even though your code of ethics is written for employees to follow, your stakeholders aren't required to follow it.

For example, what do you do when a supplier offers one of your employees a bribe or kickback for signing an order, or a customer asks for a kickback from you for giving you his business? Is that example going to be in your code? If not, what guidance are you going to offer your employees?

This is where an extensive training program to support the published code of ethics becomes so important. Since the code can't capture every possible example, each department of the organization should take the code and apply it to examples that could arise in its area. In these department or team meetings, employees can work on:

- Recognizing the ethical issue.
- Discussing options for an appropriate response.
- Selecting the best option for the organization.

Employees in all job functions need to be familiar with their company's code of ethics. How might a code of ethics apply to these workers?

PROGRESS ✓ QUESTIONS

1. List six characteristics of a tough market.
2. List four key items in a code of ethics.
3. Provide three examples of unethical behavior by a customer.
4. Provide three examples of unethical behavior by a supplier.

Smaller organizations can strengthen this employee training with additional training for supervisors and managers in ethical conflict resolution. If an individual employee or team of employees is unable to resolve an ethical issue, they can then turn to their supervisor or manager for guidance and support. In

>> A lone voice

For an organization to operate ethically, senior executives must commit to developing a culture that supports ethical principles beyond minimal compliance to federal legislation. Ultimately, however, ethical conduct comes down to the actions of individual employees each and every day. "Doing the right thing" becomes an individual interpretation based on personal ethics and a series of guidelines from a company code of ethics. Can you make that work? What if you work with colleagues who don't share that perspective? If they operate from the perspective that it's a "dog-eat-dog world" with "'victory at all costs,'" you may find yourself as the lone voice in trying to do the right thing. How will you handle that?

Check List

---

larger organizations, that role is made more significant by the creation of the position of ethics officer.

HIRE AN ETHICS OFFICER

The hiring of an **ethics officer** represents a formal commitment to the management and leadership of an organization's ethics program. The role is usually developed as a separate department with the responsibility of enforcing the code of ethics and providing support to any employees who witness unethical behavior. It sends a clear message to your stakeholders and provides an appropriate person for employees and their managers to turn to when they need additional guidance and support. This person can be promoted from within the organization (selecting a familiar face who can be trusted) or hired from outside (selecting an independent face who is new to company history and office politics).

The Ethics and Compliance Officers Association (a professional group of ethics and compliance officers with more than 1,000 members) documented the chief responsibilities of their members in a survey, which may be summarized as follows:

89% Oversight of hotline/guideline/internal reporting.

89% Preparation and delivery of internal presentations.

88% Organizationwide communications.

85% Senior management and/or board briefings/communications.

84% Training design.

83% Assessing/reviewing vulnerabilities.

83% Assessing/reviewing success/failure of initiatives.

79% Overseeing investigations of wrongdoing.

79% Management of program documentation.

77% Direct handling of hotline/guideline/internal reporting.

72% Preparation and delivery of external presentations.

68% Establishing company policy and procedures.

64% International program development.

61% Training delivery.

56% International program implementation.

52% Conducting investigations of wrongdoing.

Ethics Officer A senior executive responsible for monitoring the ethical performance of the organization both internally and externally.

> ### ! Key Point
>
> How much authority should a chief ethics officer (CEO) have in an organization? If the company is committed to doing the right thing, should the CEO be able to challenge or even overrule the other CEO—the chief executive officer? How would you resolve a disagreement between the two positions?

CELEBRATE AND REWARD THE ETHICAL BEHAVIOR DEMONSTRATED BY YOUR EMPLOYEES

With standards of behavior specified in the code of ethics, along with the punishment served for failing to follow those standards, your ethics program can become harsh. This goes against your goal of increasing employee loyalty and customer satisfaction. So the threats of punishment must be balanced with promised rewards for successful behavior:

- Celebrate examples of good ethical behavior in your company newsletter.
- Award prizes for ethical behavior—and let the employee choose the reward.
- Award prizes for new and creative ideas—and let the employee choose the reward.
- Recognize employees who represent the standard of behavior to which you are committing.
- Declare an Ethics Day, and allow every department to share success stories.

PROMOTE YOUR ORGANIZATION'S COMMITMENT TO ETHICAL BEHAVIOR

An ethics policy commits you to doing the right thing for all your stakeholders, so that message must be shared with *all* your stakeholders—both inside and outside the

PROGRESS ✔ QUESTIONS

5. When hiring an ethics officer, is it better to promote someone from within the company or hire someone from outside? Explain your answer.
6. List six key responsibilities of an ethics officer.
7. Give three examples of celebrating ethical behavior.
8. If you publicly celebrate ethical behavior, should you also publish punishment for unethical behavior? Why or why not?

© Digital Vision RF

© Bloomberg/Getty Images

THE PRICE OF PROFIT MAXIMIZATION

On April 5, 2010, a series of explosions at the Upper Big Branch (UBB) coal mine in southern West Virginia resulted in the deaths of 29 miners. It was the worst domestic mining disaster in 40 years. The mine was owned by Massey Energy. In 2008, UBB had been ranked by the Mine Safety and Health Administration (MSHA) as one of the worst mines in the country. In 2009, the company received 249 safety reports detailing hundreds of safety violations.

Those violations landed on the desk of Chief Executive Donald Blankenship, a man renowned for tracking every detail of mining operations in order to minimize costs and maximize revenue. With 2009 revenue of $331 million, and the UBB mine bringing in $600,000 of high-priced metallurgical coal every day, there was a lot of revenue to maximize and, based on MSHA reports, lots of opportunities to cut corners and to directly ignore safety standards in the mine. Blankenship had been cited 835 times for safety violations in the 28 months leading up to the disaster.

The fatal explosions in 2010 were assessed to have been caused by a spark igniting accumulated methane gas. The situation was exacerbated by the presence of

coal dust and the failure to dampen the dust with limestone rock powder that combined to expand the initial gas ignition into a series of flaming fireballs. The MSHA had cited UBB 29 times in 2009 alone for insufficient dusting, but a

CONTINUED >>

more detailed investigation after the explosions revealed a more systematic pattern of safety avoidance (methane gas alarms switched off, coal dust allowed to pile up, and insufficient water pressure to dampen down the dust) and overdue equipment maintenance (the limestone dusting equipment was over 25 years old).

In November 2014, Blankenship and Massey Energy were presented with a 43-page indictment by a federal grand jury alleging that he knew about the safety violations (something he denied) and had directly ordered every violation in order to keep costs down and to maximize revenue. However, by the time of the indictment, Blankenship had moved on from Massey. He had chosen to retire at the end of 2010, and in a securities filing, the terms of that retirement package were outlined in detail:

- $12 million severance package—$2 million in 2010 and $10 million in July 2011.
- Two-year consulting agreement at $5,000 a month that required him to work no more than 32 hours per month.
- $5.7 million pension.
- $27.2 million in deferred compensation.

All of this was in addition to the $17.8 million he was paid in 2009. Massey Energy, in the meantime, was sold to Alpha Natural Resources in a deal worth over $8.5 billion. As part of the deal, Alpha agreed to pay $209 million in penalties for Massey's role in the explosion and to invest $80 million to improve safety infrastructure at the mine.

Blankenship consistently refused to cooperate with investigators, claiming that he knew nothing about the violations, and that the explosions were caused by an uncontrollable flood of methane gas. He faced up to 31 years in prison, prompting his legal defense team to argue that he was being targeted for a broader industrywide problem of poor safety practices. In December 2015, Blankenship was found guilty on one of three counts—conspiring to willfully violate safety standards, a misdemeanor. He was found not guilty of the other two counts of securities fraud and making

false statements. The jury in the case deliberated for nine days after the 24-day trial, and twice reported to the judge that they were deadlocked.

On April 6, 2016, Blankenship was sentenced to the maximum term of one year in prison for the misdemeanor charge, followed by a year of supervised release, and a fine of $250,000, a verdict that his legal team immediately announced that they would appeal. Requests for restitution payments to the victims of the UBB disaster were denied.

Terry Scarbro, a 14-year veteran MSHA mine inspector who inspected 20 mines including the UBB, took a very pragmatic view of the industry: "Is there any way Don Blankenship doesn't know this is going on? No, there's no way," Scarbro said. "He knows it's going on. All management knows it's going on and the employees are guilty and they know it's going on. It's a cat-and-mouse game. You catch me, I'll fix it. If I can get ahead of you and fix it before you catch it, then you didn't see it." He says many other coal-mining firms play the same game.

QUESTIONS

1. Is maximum profit a sufficient rationalization for cutting corners on safety? Why or why not?
2. Does that fact that "other coal mining firms play the same game" make a difference? Why or why not?
3. Do you think the mining industry will change its safety practices as a result of the UBB verdict? Why or why not?
4. Should the issue be addressed at the federal level or corporate level? Explain your answer.

Sources: Frank Lanfitt, "Ex-Miners Say Massey Skirted Inspection Rules," *NPR,* May 27, 2010; Len Boselovic, "Massey Sends Blankenship off in Style," *Pittsburgh Post-Gazette,* December 12, 2010; Gael O'Brien, "Culture Kills: The Legacy of Massey Energy," *The Week In Ethics,* December 7, 2011; Gail Sullivan, "Ex-Massey CEO Don Blankenship Indicted for Coal Mine Disaster that Killed 29," *The Washington Post,* November 14, 2014; Bouree Lam, "A Guilty Verdict in Don Blankenship's Trial," *The Atlantic,* December 3, 2015; Alan Blinder, "Donald Blankenship Prosecutors Urge Jail in Mine Safety Case," *The New York Times,* March 29, 2016; Laura Wagner, "Former Coal Executive Don Blankenship Sentenced to 1 Year in Prison," *NPR,* April 6, 2016; and Alan Blinder, "Donald Blankenship Sentenced to a Year in Prison in Mine Safety Case," *The New York Times,* April 6, 2016.

company. Make clear and firm promises to them, and then deliver on those promises. Offer concrete examples that your organization is committed to winning the trust (and the business) of your customers by building a reputation they can count on. For example:

- Offer a no-questions-asked refund policy like Lands' End.
- Offer a 110-percent price-match guarantee like Home Depot.
- If you overcharge clients by mistake, give them a refund *plus* interest *before* their accounting department figures out the error and asks for the money.

- Get your clients involved in the development of your ethics policies. Ask them to tell you what forms of behavior or guarantees will make them feel reassured that they are dealing with an ethical company.
- Let your employees visit client sites to talk about your code of ethics in person.
- Share your success stories with all your stakeholders, not just your employees.
- Invite your stakeholders to your Ethics Day celebration.

THE PRICE OF PROFIT MAXIMIZATION CONTINUED

Business Ethics Now

NESTLÉ WATER: A CRISIS PROFITEER?

In March 2015, a California newspaper, *The Desert Sun,* published a report revealing that companies were tapping aquifers and springs for bottled water with little state or federal oversight. The release of the report during California's worst drought on record and the imposition of tough water usage restrictions created an inevitable public outcry.

Nestlé Waters North America came under particular scrutiny when it was revealed that the company was transporting water across the San Bernadino National Forest for bottling under a permit that had expired in 1988, 27 years earlier. Activists were quick to respond, and an online petition to stop Nestlé's operations drew 27,000 signatures, with some prompted to picket the entrance to Nestlé's bottling plant in Sacramento.

Although Nestlé only operates 12 out of 108 private water-bottling plants in California, the company's less-than-stellar reputation for ethical conduct appeared to place it at the top of the list for activists seeking a response to the state's serious drought problem. A critical article on Salon.com described Nestlé's business practices as "despicable," claiming that the company was drawing water from some of the hardest-hit areas in California's four-year drought.

However, when the scale of Governor Jerry Brown's water restrictions, designed to save 500 billion gallons per year, were compared against Nestlé's reported pumping figures of 200 to 250 million gallons per year, advocates of the private bottling agreements argued that the situation was being blown out of proportion. Critics argued that there was a larger moral issue. Nestlé generated revenues of $4 billion from its 29 facilities across the United States in 2012. There was room, critics argued, for them to share in the sacrifice and cut back on their California operations during such a hard time.

In October 2015, a group of environmental organizations filed suit against the U.S. Forest Service for allowing Nestlé to operate under the expired permit and demanded the immediate shutdown of the four-mile pipeline that the company used to transport water to its bottling facility. Eddie Kurtz, executive director of one of the groups involved in the lawsuit, the Courage Campaign Institute, made his organization's position very clear: "Nestlé's actions aren't just morally bankrupt, they are illegal."

The plaintiff's argument was that the amount paid by Nestlé to siphon water from the Strawberry Creek was only $524 per year, less than the average Californian's water bill. The fact that water levels at the creek were measured to be at record lows appeared to be of no concern to Nestlé Water North America CEO Tim Brown.

© Glow Images RF

When asked if the company would stop bottling water in California, he replied, "Absolutely not. In fact, if I could increase it, I would."

When a May 2015 *Mother Jones* report identified that Starbucks' Ethos brand water was being bottled in Merced, California, the company took a dramatically different approach, announcing that bottling operations would be moved to Pennsylvania within six months as a show of support for the residents of California.

QUESTIONS

1. Is this issue being blown out of proportion? Why or why not?
2. Does Nestlé bear any responsibility for not notifying the Forest Service about the expired permit? Why or why not?
3. If Governor Jerry Brown had included water bottling plants in his water use reduction plans, do you think Nestlé would have agreed? Explain your answer.
4. Find two other examples of Nestlé's poor reputation on ethical conduct. What could Tim Brown do differently here to help to restore faith and trust in the brand?

Sources: Ian James, "Bottling Water without Scrutiny," *The Desert Sun,* March 8, 2015; Zoe Schlanger, "Nestle's California Water Permit Expired 27 Years Ago," *Newsweek,* April 13, 2015; David Dayen, "Nestlé's Despicable Water-Crisis Profiteering: How It's Making a Killing while California Is Dying of Thirst," *Salon,* April 7, 2015; Katie Lobosco, "Drought Turns Californians against Water Bottling Companies," *CNN Money,* May 26, 2015; Geoffrey Mohan, "Nestle Drawing Millions of Gallons of California Water on Expired Permit, Suit Claims," *Los Angeles Times,* October 13, 2015; Justin Worland, "Lawsuit Alleges Illegal Water Use by Nestle in Drought-Stricken California," *Time,* October 14, 2015; and Julia Lurie, "The Feds Just Got Sued for Letting Nestle Bottle Water in California's Drought Country," *Mother Jones,* October 14, 2015.

Real World Applications

Randall has been offered the position of chief ethics officer for an insurance company that recently settled a large lawsuit for unethical business practices (without admitting any wrongdoing) brought by several state insurance regulators. The creation of the ethics officer position was part of the agreed settlement, and the company has committed to several specific action items by agreed deadlines. However, when Randall asked detailed questions about those action items in his final round of interviews, the answers he received were very vague. The position would represent a significant promotion for Randall, with a nice salary to match, but his wife is concerned that the insurance company has no plans to change, and if the unethical behavior is caught again, the chief ethics officer would be blamed for poor leadership and he would be fired as the sacrificial lamb. Should Randall take the job?

Reactive Ethical Policies Policies that result when organizations are driven by events and/or a fear of future events.

Proactive Ethical Policies Policies that result when the company develops a clear sense of what it stands for as an ethical organization.

Transparency Characteristic of an organization that maintains open and honest communications with all stakeholders.

CONTINUE TO MONITOR THE BEHAVIOR AS YOU GROW

Any organization's commitment to ethical performance must be watched constantly. It is easy for other business issues to take priority and for the code of ethics to become taken for granted. Also, the continued growth of technology will present new situations for ethical dilemmas such as policies on e-mail monitoring and web surfing, so your code may need to be rewritten on a regular basis. A large organization can make that one of the responsibilities of its designated ethics officer. Smaller companies need to include their code of ethics as part of any strategic planning exercise to make sure it is as up to date as possible.

PROGRESS ✓ QUESTIONS

9. List six examples of commitments that companies can make to win the trust of their stakeholders.
10. Provide four of your own examples.
11. Why would a code of ethics need to be updated?
12. Find out when your company's code of ethics was last updated.

>> Becoming a Transparent Organization

Many organizations have been prompted to introduce or modify their codes of ethics by the sight of CEOs pleading the Fifth Amendment in front of congressional committees. Others have been inspired by the large number of zeroes that can now be tacked onto financial penalties for corporate misconduct. Unfortunately, neither motivation is enough. These are examples of **reactive policies**, which result when organizations are driven by events and/or a fear of future events. True ethical policies are **proactive**, which occur when the company develops a clear sense of what it stands for as an ethical organization—not only what ethics means to that company and its stakeholders but also the extent of the actions it will take (and the necessary punishments it will enforce) to get there.

One characteristic that is common to such organizations is a commitment to organizational **transparency**, which means the company is open and honest in all its communications with all its stakeholders. However, the financial markets that govern stock prices (and the profits to be made as corporate executives cash in their stock options) have proved to be remarkably indifferent to "open and honest communications."

As Microsoft's 2006 white paper, "The New World of Work: Transparent Organizations," summarized:[2]

Transparency in business means that stakeholders have visibility deep into the processes and information of an organization. This is becoming an important focus for businesses in several ways. Important qualities of transparency include the following:

- A requirement that is being enforced on markets and companies through regulation.
- An enabler of better relationships with partners and customers (that is soon to be an expectation).
- A great opportunity to rework business processes to increase efficiency.
- A risk to confidential intellectual property.

It is the risk factor of becoming too transparent that still remains as the biggest obstacle to change in this area. Managers may be able to break through their business school teachings and start sharing cost and revenue figures with employees, and even produce honest appraisals of organizational performance in annual reports (rather than polished, vetted PR documents), but giving away too much information, from their perspective, leads to the inevitable conclusion of the loss of market advantage through corporate espionage, for if you give away your secrets, what do you have left? Ultimately, however, organizations can only build trust with their stakeholders if there are "open and honest communications."

PROGRESS ✔ QUESTIONS

13. What is a *reactive* ethical policy?

14. What is a *proactive* ethical policy?

15. Why would a company want to be transparent?

16. Would you say the company you work for is transparent? Explain your answer.

>> Conclusion: Organizational Integrity

The intense media coverage of the many corporate scandals that have been uncovered over the past few years has brought the subject of business ethics to the attention of a large portion of this country's population. That increased attention has proved to be something of a mixed blessing.

On the one hand, the average investor can be forgiven for thinking that the business world is full of crooks whose only purpose is to make as much money as possible. Problems with product quality, poor customer service, made-up financial reports, and out-of-court settlements with no admission of guilt paint a very negative picture.

The response to this negative picture has been new rules (Sarbanes-Oxley and others) and tighter controls that now represent a greater risk for organizations that fail to comply with the expected standard of behavior. Large financial penalties and expensive lawsuits can now place a substantial dollar figure on the cost of unethical behavior.

On the other hand, ethics has also become an issue that positively impacts the business world. Stockholders want to invest in companies with solid reputations and strong ethical programs. Employees prefer to work for companies they can trust and where they feel valued. That sense of value results in increased commitment and reduced turnover, which means greater profits for the company. Customers prefer to buy from companies with proven track records of integrity in their business dealings—even if that choice costs them a little more. So if the threat of negative publicity, ruined reputations, and million-dollar legal settlements won't lead a company into developing an ethics policy, perhaps the promise of increased profits, happy stockholders, happy employees, and happy customers will!

Recognizing the concept of *business ethics* allows us to categorize behavior as unethical, but when you are looking to manage the reputation and policies of an organization, the commitment to doing the right thing becomes more about **organizational integrity** than any sense of a written ethics policy. As such, carefully "wordsmithed"

> **Key Point** !
>
> Many manufacturing companies in the United States have seen tremendous success from the Japanese business practice of *kaizen* (a Japanese word meaning "continuous improvement"). The constant search for ways to improve their internal processes has led these companies to significant cost reductions and sales growth. Could you apply the same practice to ethical business practices? How would an already ethical company become *more* ethical?

> **Organizational Integrity** A characteristic of publicly committing to the highest professional standards and sticking to that commitment.

documents and carefully positioned press releases suggest you have something to hide, and if you have something to hide, how can you be trusted? Understanding that your company does not operate independently from its community, its customers, its employees, its stockholders, and its suppliers is vital to the long-term survival of the organization. Winning the trust and confidence of all your stakeholders would be a great achievement in today's business world, but *keeping* that trust and confidence over the long term would be an even greater one.

FRONTLINE FOCUS
You Scratch My Back—Adam Makes a Decision

Dr. Green continued to stare at Adam. He was obviously looking for an answer now, and Adam knew that if he tried to stall by asking to check with his regional manager, Green would show him the door.

One small part of Adam wanted to laugh out loud at this ridiculous situation. Doctors had asked him for extra free samples before, and the industry had always been willing to underwrite lunches and tickets to sports events or shows as appropriate marketing expenses, but no one had ever asked him outright for money to decorate his office—and this guy was dead serious!

For a moment Adam wondered if he was bluffing about Zach. He knew Zach was a tough competitor, and they fought a tough battle in this region, usually managing to win clients away from each other on a couple of occasions. *Come to think of it,* thought Adam, *Zach probably would go along with this deal. Winning this practice would be a real catch for his territory.*

Then Adam looked at Dr. Green again. Something was bothering him about this guy. He got the feeling that this wasn't a onetime special request. If Adam gave in on this, he knew there would be other requests for "marketing funds" in the future, always with the threat of switching to the competition.

Suddenly Adam, almost as a surprise to himself, knew what he had to do: "I'm sorry Dr. Green. We value our relationships with our doctors very highly—that's how we were able to work so closely with Dr. Stevens for as long as we did. Unfortunately, that type of relationship doesn't include 'marketing funds.' I hope Zach's interior designer friend does a good job for you."

With that, Adam got up and turned to leave.

Six weeks later, the local paper featured a very unflattering picture of Dr. Green and Zach on the front page. Dr. Green had developed a very close relationship with Zach and his company—so close, in fact, that Dr. Green had been willing to massage some of his patient data to help Zach's company in a new drug trial.

QUESTIONS

1. What do you think the reaction of Adam's regional manager was to the initial news of the loss of Dr. Green's business?
2. Do you think Zach's company supported his willingness to provide Dr. Green's "marketing funds"?
3. What do you think will happen to Zach and Dr. Green now?

[For Review]

1. **Develop the key components of an ethics policy.**

   For an organization to develop an ethical culture, and for that culture to be sustainable, an ethics policy requires the involvement of every member of the organization in committing to a formal structure to support an ongoing process of monitoring and enforcement. This can be achieved through six initiatives:

   - Establish a code of ethics *that presents a common understanding of organizational values and provides clear guidance on acceptable behavior.*
   - Support the code of ethics *with extensive training for every member of the organization.*
   - Hire an ethics officer *to formalize the management and leadership of the organization's commitment to an ethical culture.*
   - Celebrate and reward ethical behavior *so that employees come to see ethical behavior as a positive event rather than an avoidance of punishment.*
   - Promote your organization's commitment to ethical behavior *so that all your stakeholders can learn what to expect from you.*
   - Continue to monitor the behavior as you grow *so that ethical conduct remains ingrained in the organizational culture.*

2. **Analyze the ramifications of becoming a *transparent* organization.**

   Organizational transparency represents a commitment to honest and open communication with all stakeholders, and can often be the hardest adjustment in any ethics policy. Trusting your employees enough to share your cost and revenue figures with them goes against most business school teachings. Similarly, presenting an honest picture of organizational performance in a detailed annual report can generate paranoia about proprietary information and the dangers of corporate espionage. However, carefully "wordsmithed" documents and carefully positioned press releases suggest you have something to hide, and if you have something to hide, how can you be trusted?

3. **Understand the difference between *reactive* and *proactive* ethical policies.**

   A reactive ethical policy exists when organizational decisions are driven by events or the fear of future events.

A proactive ethical policy is established when the company develops a clear sense of what it stands for as an ethical organization and what actions will be taken (and what punishments will be enforced, if necessary) to get there.

4. Discuss the challenges of a commitment to organizational integrity.

Organizational integrity is very easy to commit to, but very difficult to enforce. Integrity involves winning the trust and confidence of all your stakeholders and working to keep that trust over the long term. In practice, that means understanding that the company does not operate independently from its community, its customers, its employees, its stockholders, and its suppliers. Any and all decisions should be made with those partners in mind. As such, doing the right thing has a much broader reach than just doing the right thing for the company.

[Key Terms]

Ethics Officer 210

Organizational Integrity 215

Proactive Ethical Policies 214

Reactive Ethical Policies 214

Sustainable Ethics 208

Transparency 214

[Review Questions]

1. You have been asked to join a team as the representative of your department. The team has been tasked with the development of an ethics training program to support the company's new code of ethics. What would your recommendations be?

2. Your company wrote its code of ethics in 1986. You have been assigned to a team that has been tasked with updating the code to make it more representative of current business ethics issues such as the Internet and modern business technology. What are your recommendations?

3. Does the role of an ethics officer bring real value to an organization, or is it just "window dressing" to make the company look good?

4. Do you think you could be an ethics officer? Why or why not?

5. When you go shopping, do you pay attention to how *transparent* the company is in its business practices? Why or why not?

6. Would *organizational integrity* make a difference in your loyalty to a company? Why or why not?

[Review Exercise]

When Hurricane Sandy hit the eastern seaboard of the United States at the end of October 2012, the sheer size and force of the storm had already earned it the name "Superstorm Sandy." Reaching over 1,100 miles in diameter at its peak, the storm claimed 285 lives in seven countries on its journey from the western Caribbean.

On the New Jersey shore, entire towns were wiped out, with houses floating off their foundations into the bay and streets being buried under tons of sand blown in from the beach. It took Brad O'Connell two months to get back to what was left of his house, and another month before it could be repaired enough to be habitable. You can imagine his surprise, then, when he received a letter from his local city council advising him that his property taxes for 2013–2014 would be increasing by 9 percent.

When he called the city finance office to complain that his house was now worth *less,* not more, he was told that the increase was part of a five-year budget plan that included predetermined tax increases.

1. Which ethical theories could be applied here?

2. When Brad took his complaint to the local media, a spokesperson for the city finance office pointed out that the city's property taxes were paying for the emergency services that were currently working overtime to help everyone impacted by the storm. Is that an ethical argument? Why or why not?

3. If you were in Brad's situation, how would you react?

4. How would you resolve the situation?

Internet Exercises

1. Review the website of the Charity Commission (the regulator for charities in England and Wales) at https://www.gov.uk/government/organisations/charity-commission/about.

   a. What are the stated priorities of the commission?

   b. What guidance does the commission offer in managing a conflict of interest?

   c. What guidance does the commission offer for the role of a trustee?

2. Review the website of the United States Department of Justice (DOJ) at https://www.justice.gov/oip/government-transparency.

   a. What was the message of President Obama's FOIA Memorandum?

   b. What are the three principles of the Open Government Directive?

   c. Select and summarize three example initiatives of how transparency is being promoted across the government.

Team Exercises

1. **A different Massey Energy.**
   Divide into two teams. One team must defend the decision made in the lawsuit against Don Blankenship from Massey Energy. The other team must critique the decision and come up with an alternative resolution to the mine explosions.

2. **An ethics charter.**
   Divide into groups of three or four. Each group develops a charter that documents its company's commitment to ethical behavior. What industry is your company in? What does ethical behavior look like in that industry? What will your company's commitment consist of? A code of ethics? Performance guarantees? Corporate governance policies?

>> MOTT'S: SOUR APPLES

In 2009, the Dr Pepper Snapple Group (DPS) reported a net income of $555 million, compared with a loss of $312 million in 2008, with sales down 3 percent at $5.5 billion. The beverage conglomerate owns 50 brands including 7UP, A&W Root Beer, and Hawaiian Punch, but in 2010 it was receiving the most media attention for its Mott's apple juice plant in the Rochester area of upstate New York. The 305 hourly workers at the plant went on strike on Monday, May 24, 2010, in response to a new contract offer by the plant's senior management that reduced production wages by $1.50 per hour, froze pension benefits, ended pension benefits for new hires, reduced employer contributions to the 401(k) plan, and increased employee copays in the health care plan.

© C Squared Studio/Getty Images RF

The rationale for the pay decrease was that the Mott's workers—all members of the Retail, Wholesale, and Department Store Union (RWDSU)—were overpaid in relation to the other blue-collar production workers in the Rochester area, where companies such as Xerox and Kodak have made large layoffs resulting in high unemployment. This negotiation, in line with "local industry norms," had been quite transparent. The parent company had confirmed that its finances were very healthy and that there were no plans to close the plant or move production operations overseas. When the company was spun off as a separate entity from UK conglomerate Cadbury Schweppes in 2007, the stock stood at $25 a share—it was then in the high 30s. DPS's three highest paid executives, including CEO Larry Young, all saw pay increases of more than 100 percent in 2009.

The average hourly production wage in the area, according to a U.S. Bureau of Labor Statistics National Compensation Survey conducted in 2009, was just over $14 an hour. Union officials estimated that 70 percent of Mott's production workers earned less than $19 an hour under the contract that expired in mid-April 2010. Many had reached that level after more than a decade of service.

Chris Barnes, a spokesman for the Plano, Texas-based DPS, insisted that the company approached the contract negotiations in good faith: "We offered to keep wages unchanged after three years of salary increases and, unfortunately, the union rejected this offer. . . . We have to manage our costs the same as everyone else and ensure that they remain sustainable over the long term."

RWDSU President Stuart Appelbaum had a different perspective. He had seen financially strapped companies needing to cut costs and had agreed to concessions in some dire situations, but to have a profitable company with strong prospects seeking to leverage high local unemployment rates to reduce wage costs was a first for him.

The striking workers saw this as more than just a strike over money. They didn't begrudge the company profits or high executive salaries, or even the 67 percent increase in the dividend paid to shareholders in April 2010. What they saw was an attitude of unfettered corporate greed. "When you get down to it, this situation is much bigger than just some unhappy workers at a Mott's apple juice plant in upstate New York," Applebaum said. "This is about a large company doing extraordinarily well demonstrating outrageously greedy behavior. It's beyond outrageous. It's un-American."

The strike ended after 16 weeks in mid-September. In a three-year deal, the union agreed to a wage freeze, but not the cuts in hourly rates that the company had demanded. Pensions for current workers were preserved (the company had wanted to freeze them), in return for a concession from the union that new workers would be offered 401(k) plans instead of pensions.

Mike LeBerth, president of the local branch of the RWDSU, admitted, "Nobody wins in a strike . . . neither side is happy with what we got. Was it worth it? Yes, because we stood strong and the company knows we're a force to be reckoned with."

In March 2013, the RWDSU announced that Mott's workers had ratified a new three-year contract without any need for industrial action (strikes). The new contract increased wage rates by $1.60 per hour, introduced signing bonuses of over $3,000, and secured health care benefits for all 300 employees. Representatives of the Local 220 chapter of the RWDSU commented that the show of strength in the 2010 strikes exhibited a "resolve [that produced] a good contract that recognizes their [members'] contributions to making [Mott's] a successful, profitable facility."

CONTINUED >>

1. When you consider Milton Friedman's position on corporate responsibility in Chapter 4, is it possible to defend DPS's demand for lower hourly wages?

2. Was DPS considering the interests of all stakeholders in this battle? Explain why or why not.

3. How could senior executives have approached this situation differently?

4. Both sides claimed in media interviews that they had won their case. Was there a victory here? Explain why or why not.

Sources: Rich Blake, "Sour Apples: Strike at Mott's Plant Underscores Disconnect in Corporate America, Union Says," *ABC News,* May 26, 2010; Norma Ridley, "The Mott's Strike: Arguing the Workers' Case," www.MPNnow.com, June 9, 2010; John Egan, "Rep. Doggett Weighs in on Mott's Labor Strike in Upstate New York," *Austin Market Examiner,* August 16, 2010; Steven Greenhouse, "In Mott's Strike, More Than Pay at Stake," *The New York Times,* August 17, 2010; Steven Greenhouse, "Ending Strike, Mott's Plant Union Accepts Deal," *The New York Times,* September 13, 2010; and "Mott's Workers Ratify New Contract," www.rwdsu.info, March 24, 2013.

Thinking Critically 10.2

>> THE FAILED TRANSFORMATION OF BP

In 2000, the chief executive of British Petroleum (BP), Lord John Browne, who had transformed the company from a small oil producer into a global giant with the acquisitions of Amoco and Atlantic Richfield, rebranded the company as "Beyond Petroleum" to portray a company that was environmentally conscious and committed to the development of alternative energy sources such as wind and solar power. The new "blooming flower" corporate logo was intended to convey a company that was responsive to growing public concerns about climate change.

However, that commitment to environmental awareness did not seem to extend to the safe operation of BP facilities around the world. In 2005 an explosion at an oil refinery in Texas City, Texas, killed 15 workers and injured hundreds more. The Occupational Safety and Health Administration (OSHA) fined BP a record $21 million for failing to correct safety violations. In 2006, a leaking BP pipeline in Alaska forced the shutdown of one of the nation's biggest oil fields. Prosecutors later fined BP $20 million for failing to correct corroding pipelines.

Browne's replacement, Tony Hayward, a geologist who had previously overseen BP's exploration and oil production, promised to refocus the company on safety, committing to spending $500 million to address the problems at the Texas City refinery and settling a series of criminal charges against BP operations totaling $370 million. Unfortunately, an emissions release at the refinery in early 2010 confirmed OSHA suspicions that the changes promised as part of the 2005 settlement were not being addressed, and BP was fined another $50.6 million that the company paid without an admission of violations.

Source: U.S. Navy Photo by Mass Communication Specialist 2nd Justin E. Stumberg

Critics have argued that BP's aggressive acquisition strategy under Browne created a focus on cost containment as a means to maximize profit margins. That mentality is now ingrained in the corporate culture to the extent that fines are simply addressed as a cost of doing business. April 20, 2010, brought yet another example of this argument and the largest oil spill in history.

The explosion on the newly completed Deepwater Horizon rig in the Gulf of Mexico resulted in 11 deaths and broke open the Macondo well, allowing an estimated 19 million gallons of crude oil to flow into the Gulf of Mexico, threatening a fragile ecosystem and the livelihoods of thousands of businesses along the entire Gulf Coast. The terrifying scale of this event only becomes clear when the size of the *Exxon Valdez* spill in Prince William Sound in Alaska in 1989 is considered. That tanker spill released an estimated 500,000 gallons of oil.

To some extent the practice of drilling in the deep water of the Gulf of Mexico brings extreme operational risks—risks that environmentalists believe should prompt a nationwide move away from a clear dependence on oil. However, what the Gulf spill made clear was just how unprepared oil companies appear to be to handle any miscalculations in these risks. BP's response to the Deepwater Horizon explosion was described by all the agencies involved as "a scramble." A succession of attempts with strange names like "junk shot," "top hat," and "kill shot" delayed the eventual capping of the Macondo well until July 15—a total of 87 days. Estimates of how much oil was allowed to flow remain under dispute, with scientists arguing that access to the video footage of the wellhead (which they would need to calculate flow rates of the oil) had been restricted by BP.

Inevitably, accurate accounts of BP's response to the spill were marred by global media outlets enjoying the biggest story since Hurricane Katrina. BP committed to "putting everything right" and doing "whatever it takes" to restore the Gulf region to the same condition it was in before the spill. However, alongside those promises came legal posturing to spread the blame as much as possible. BP was the majority owner of the Macondo well, with Anadarko and Mitsui as minority partners; the Deepwater Horizon was owned by Transocean (and leased to BP); Cameron International was the manufacturer of the "blowout preventer" that was alleged to have failed, causing the explosion; and Halliburton engineers worked on the rig equipment the day before the explosion. Multiple lawsuits were settled in the next two years between all the parties involved, though none included any admission of accountability as part of the settlement.

The question remains, however, as to how well Tony Hayward delivered on his commitment to a safer BP. At the time of the Deepwater Horizon spill, Exxon, the former poster child for reckless oil companies, had only one OSHA fine in place. BP, by comparison, had 760. Hayward was reassigned during the response to the spill to a nonexecutive role with BP's Russian joint venture TNK-BP. The terms of his departure included immediate access to his pension of $1 million annually and full entitlement to a compensation package estimated to be $18 million.

For BP, the spill continued to dominate the company's operations. A total of $42 billion was set aside for the payment of fines, compensation to victims, and ongoing cleanup operations in the Gulf of Mexico. Of that amount, almost $36 billion has already been paid out or earmarked in settled lawsuits. However, the U.S. government was asking for $21 billion in compensation for its costs in the cleanup, and the Gulf states impacted by the spill (Florida, Alabama, Louisiana, and Mississippi) were seeking another $34 billion for economic losses and property damage. Under the Clean Water Act, the federal government could have fined BP between $1,100 and $4,300 per barrel of oil spilled. Since no accurate figure existed for the total size of the spill, that fine could have run BP between $5 billion and $21 billion.

In July 2015, BP announced an $18.7 billion settlement of all federal, state, and local claims arising from the 2010 spill—the largest single settlement with any civil entity in the nation's history. Of that $18.7 billion, $5.5 billion represented a civil penalty under the Clean Water Act, to be paid over 15 years, $7.1 billion under a Natural Resource Damage Assessment, with the remainder going to settle outstanding economic damage claims.

Critics argued that BP's willingness to settle was driven more by the economic reality of lower oil prices than by any commitment to safer operations or ethical conduct. In an April 2015 interview with National Public Radio (NPR), Geoff Morrell, BP senior vice president, attempted to draw a line under the event by stating that the signs were good for a healthy Gulf: "There is nothing to suggest other than that the Gulf is a resilient body of water that has bounced back strongly . . . the Gulf has not been damaged anywhere near the degree some people feared it would have in the midst of the spill." Marine scientists disagree with such a rosy assessment, arguing that the impact may continue to be felt for generations to come.

QUESTIONS

1. What evidence is there in this case that BP simply addresses fines "as a cost of doing business"?

2. BP Chief Executive Officer Tony Hayward argued that "changing the culture of a 100,000-person company couldn't happen overnight." He had been in charge for three years before the Deepwater Horizon spill. Were critics right to expect more change than they saw?

3. Has BP been successful in its move "Beyond Petroleum"?

4. How can BP begin to restore its reputation going forward?

Sources: Clifford Krauss, "Oil Spill's Blow to BP's Image May Eclipse Costs," *The New York Times,* April 29, 2010; Jad Mouawad, "For BP, a History of Spills and Safety Lapses," *The New York Times,* May 8, 2010; "The Oil Well and the Damage Done," *The Economist,* June 17, 2010; Susan Thompson, Helen Power, and Robin Pagnamenta, "Hayward Exit Leaves BP with £21 Billion Oil Spill Write-Off," *The Times,* July 27, 2010; Sheila McNulty and Sylvia Pfeifer, "BP Listed 390 Problems on Gulf Rig," *Financial Times,* August 23, 2010; Juliet Eilperin and Scott Higham, "How the Minerals Management Service's Partnership with Industry Led to Failure," *The Washington Post,* August 24, 2010; "BP and the Deepwater Horizon Disaster: Cleaning Up the Legal Spill," *The Economist,* November 15, 2012; "The Deepwater Horizon Disaster: Spills and Bills," *The Economist,* February 9, 2013; Campbell Robertson, John Schwartz, and Richard Perez-Pena, "BP to Pay $18.7 Billion for Deepwater Horizon Oil Spill," *The New York Times,* July 2, 2015; and Debbie Elliott, "5 Years after BP Oil Spill, Effects Linger and Recovery Is Slow," *NPR,* April 21, 2015.

Thinking Critically

>> UNPROFESSIONAL CONDUCT

At the age of 14 months old, most children in North America and Europe receive a triple vaccination against three diseases: measles, mumps, and rubella (also known as German measles). Abbreviated as MMR, the vaccination has come under increased scrutiny over the past two decades for concerns over a potential link between MMR and autism (a neural disorder

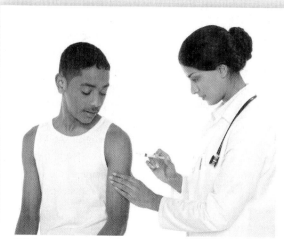

© Science Photo Library/Getty Images RF

affecting behavioral and cognitive skills). Concerned parents have become vocal advocates on both sides of the argument. On one side, parents of autistic children believe that MMR, or specifically the preservative agent thimerosal (a mercury-containing chemical compound), causes significant intestinal problems and behavioral changes shortly after administration of the vaccination. On the other side of the debate, parents are concerned that a choice not to vaccinate exposes children to diseases that have long been controlled in our population.

This debate over a connection between MMR and autism began in earnest in 1998 after the publication in the British medical journal *The Lancet* of a research paper by Dr. Andrew Wakefield of the Royal Free Hospital in London. The paper proposed a new syndrome with two conditions: chronic intestinal disease and the loss of behavioral skills that had already been acquired as part of normal child development. Out of 12 cases in the paper, parents of eight of the children associated the behavioral problems with the administration of the MMR vaccine. While the paper clearly stated that no association between the MMR and the condition had been proved, the implication was there, and that was apparently enough to set off a media storm.

Parents began to question the composition of the vaccination itself (specifically the thimerosal compound), and the justification for administration of all three vaccines in one dose at such a young age. Inevitably, many parents started to choose not to vaccinate their children. In Britain, 91 percent of age-eligible children were vaccinated in 1998. By 2004 that number had fallen to 80 percent which, doctors warned, was far below the 90 percent rate needed to keep the diseases under control.

Despite reassurances from the Medical Research Council in Britain and the U.S. Institute of Medicine that there was no evidence of a link between MMR and autism, emotions continued to escalate. Even study data from Finland (1.8 million children over a 14-year period) and Denmark (537,303 children) showing no evidence of a connection failed to have a calming effect, and Wakefield's reputation as a parent advocate continued to grow, even though his study had included only 12 cases.

However, in 2004, a four-month investigation by Brian Deer, a journalist at England's *Sunday Times* newspaper, revealed information that brought Wakefield's work into serious question:

- While actively warning parents to avoid MMR as the senior author on the *Lancet* paper, Wakefield failed to disclose that a follow-up study was funded by a legal aid group helping parents who believed that their children had been harmed by the MMR vaccines. Wakefield received £55,000 ($90,000) from the group but did not disclose the relationship with his coauthors of the paper or with editors at *The Lancet*.

- In addition, Wakefield's support for three separate vaccinations, rather than the triple MMR (which he believed could be overloading children's immune systems), included an experimental product under development by a company in which he had a financial interest.

This information prompted a partial retraction of the 1998 paper by *The Lancet* on grounds of "a fatal conflict of interest." In addition, persistent media scrutiny of Prime Minister Tony Blair's decision not to reveal whether or not his son Leo had received the MMR vaccination kept the story alive in the British press. In 2006 the death of a 13-year-old boy who had not received the MMR, the first person in Britain in 14 years to die from measles, prompted calls for a full investigation from the General Medical Council (GMC).

After a two-and-a-half year investigation (the longest medical misconduct case in the GMC's 147-year history), at a cost of over £1 million ($1.6 million), the GMC removed Wakefield's license to practice medicine. Evidence for the decision included the conflicts of interest discovered by the *Sunday Times* investigation and other concerns:

- Wakefield was working at the Royal Free Hospital as a gastroenterologist at the time of the studies, which, the GMC found, did not give him the ethical approval or medical permission to conduct tests outside of his approved area, including brain scans, spinal taps (lumbar punctures), and colonoscopies.
- While conducting his follow-up study, Wakefield was found to have acted unprofessionally after taking blood samples from children of fellow medical professionals at his son's birthday party in return for payments of £5.

Despite losing his license to practice medicine, Wakefield continued to remain unrepentant, despite being named one of *Time* magazine's top 10 "Science Frauds" in 2012. He continued to argue that the conflicts of interest did not discredit the research in the original *Lancet* paper. He also pointed out that the GMC ruling was based not on the conclusions he made but for the way in which those conclusions were reached. *The Lancet,* in response to the GMC ruling, fully retracted the paper from the journal, effectively erasing it from public record. In January 2011, the *British Medical Journal* (BMJ) published an article by Brian Deer, titled "Secrets of the MMR Scare: How the Case against the MMR Vaccine Was Fixed," along with an editorial by BMJ Editor-in-Chief Fiona Godlee. The damage to Wakefield's reputation by an assessment from the *BMJ* that his work was "an elaborate fraud" was increased even further by a follow-up *BMJ* article in November 2011 claiming that several of the children in his study didn't have the inflammatory bowel disease that he claimed. Wakefield responded with a lawsuit filed in a Texas circuit court in January 2012, suing the *BMJ* for defamation. The lawsuit and subsequent appeal motion were both denied on the grounds that the articles in question did not concern Texas or any activities that occurred in Texas.

Wakefield remains a popular advocate with parents who are convinced that there is a link between MMR and autism. In a February 2015 *Newsweek* magazine interview in which an earlier measles outbreak that began at Disneyland in December 2014 was referenced, Wakefield adamantly defended his views: "The responsibility lies squarely on the shoulders of those that have been involved in vaccine policymaking, which is totally inadequate and bordering on dangerous . . . the government has only themselves to blame."

When asked to comment on plummeting vaccination rates and the fact that there were more cases of measles in the United States in January 2015 than in all of 2012, Wakefield remained dismissive of any responsibility: "The people who put the blame on me are really just displacing their inadequacy on others."

QUESTIONS

1. What were the perceived conflicts of interest in Wakefield's research activities?
2. If Wakefield had disclosed the source of the funding of his study and his interest in the experimental vaccine, would that have added credibility to his campaign against MMR? Why or why not?
3. Why did Wakefield lose his license to practice medicine?
4. The GMC found that Wakefield brought his profession into disrepute with his conduct. What could he have done differently to share his concerns about MMR?

Sources: Brian Deer, "Revealed: MMR Research Scandal," *The Times,* February 22, 2004; "A Dose of Dissent," *The Economist,* February 26, 2004; "Sow the Wind," *The Economist,* December 4, 2008; David Rose, "Fall of Andrew Wakefield, 'Dishonest' Doctor Who Started MMR Scare," *The Times,* January 29, 2010; Andrew Jack, "Lancet Retracts MMR Link to Autism," *Financial Times,* February 2, 2010; "A Nasty Rash," *The Economist,* May 27, 2010; Brian Deer, "Secrets of the MMR Scare: How the Case against the MMR Vaccine Was Fixed," *British Medical Journal,* January 6, 2011; Alice Park, "Great Science Frauds: Andrew Wakefield," *Time: Health and Family,* January 13, 2012; Ian Sample, "Andrew Wakefield Sues BMJ for Claiming MMR Study Was Fraudulent," *The Guardian,* January 5, 2012; and Stav Ziv, "Andrew Wakefield, Father of the Anti-Vaccine Movement, Responds to the Current Measles Outbreak for the First Time," *Newsweek,* February 10, 2015.

[References]

1. Simon Webley, "Eight Steps for a Company Wishing to Develop Its Own Corporate Ethics Program," www.ibe.org.uk/developing.html.

2. Dan Rasmus, "The New World of Work: Transparent Organizations," White Paper, Microsoft Business Division, February 2006.

A

Accounting Function The function that keeps track of all the company's financial transactions by documenting the money coming in (credits) and money going out (debits) and balancing the accounts at the end of the period (daily, weekly, monthly, quarterly, annually).

Altruistic CSR Philanthropic approach to CSR in which organizations underwrite specific initiatives to give back to the company's local community or to designated national or international programs.

Applied Ethics The study of how ethical theories are put into practice.

Audit Committee An operating committee staffed by members of the board of directors plus independent or outside directors. The committee is responsible for monitoring the financial policies and procedures of the organization—specifically the accounting policies, internal controls, and the hiring of external auditors.

Auditing Function The certification of an organization's financial statements, or "books," as being accurate by an impartial third-party professional. An organization can be large enough to have internal auditors on staff as well as using external professionals—typically certified professional accountants and/or auditing specialists.

B

Board of Directors A group of individuals who oversee governance of an organization. Elected by vote of the shareholders at the annual general meeting (AGM), the true power of the board can vary from institution to institution from a powerful unit that closely monitors the management of the organization to a body that merely rubber-stamps the decisions of the chief executive officer (CEO) and executive team.

Business Ethics The application of ethical standards to business behavior.

C

Code of Ethics A company's written standards of ethical behavior that are designed to guide managers and employees in making the decisions and choices they face every day.

Compensation Committee An operating committee staffed by members of the board of directors plus independent or outside directors. The committee is responsible for setting the compensation for the CEO and other senior executives. Typically, this compensation will consist of a base salary, performance bonus, stock options, and other perks.

"Comply or Else" Guidelines that require companies to abide by a set of operating standards or face stiff financial penalties.

"Comply or Explain" Guidelines that require companies to abide by a set of operating standards or explain why they choose not to.

Conflict of Interest A situation in which one relationship or obligation places you in direct conflict with an existing relationship or obligation.

Consumer Financial Protection Bureau (CFPB) A government agency within the Federal Reserve that oversees financial products and services.

Corporate Governance The system by which business corporations are directed and controlled.

Corporate Governance Committee Committee (staffed by board members and specialists) that monitors the ethical performance of the corporation and oversees compliance with the company's internal code of ethics as well as any federal and state regulations on corporate conduct.

Corporate Social Responsibility (CSR) The actions of an organization that are targeted toward achieving a social benefit over and above maximizing profits for its shareholders and meeting all its legal obligations. Also known as *corporate citizenship* and *corporate conscience*.

Culpability Score (FSGO) The calculation of a degree of blame or guilt that is used as a multiplier of up to four times the base fine. The culpability score can be adjusted according to aggravating or mitigating factors.

Culture A particular set of attitudes, beliefs, and practices that characterize a group of individuals.

Cyberliability A legal concept that employers can be held liable for the actions of their employees in their Internet communications to the same degree as if those employers had written those communications on company letterhead.

D

Death Penalty (FSGO) A fine that is set high enough to match all the organization's assets—and basically put the organization out of business. This is warranted where the organization was operating primarily for a criminal purpose.

Developed Nation A country that enjoys a high standard of living as measured by economic, social, and technological criteria.

Disclosure (FCPA) The FCPA requirement that corporations fully disclose any and all transactions conducted with foreign officials and politicians.

Dodd-Frank Wall Street Reform and Consumer Protection Act Legislation that was promoted as the "fix" for the extreme mismanagement of risk in the financial sector that led to a global financial crisis in 2008–2010.

E

Ethical CSR Purest or most legitmate type of CSR in which organizations pursue a clearly defined sense of social conscience in managing their financial responsibilities to shareholders, their legal responsibilities to their local community and society as a whole, and their ethical responsibilities to do the right thing for all their stakeholders.

Ethical Dilemma A situation in which there is no obvious right or wrong decision, but rather a right or right answer.

Ethical Reasoning Looking at the information available to us in resolving an ethical dilemma, and drawing conclusions based on that information in relation to our own ethical standards.

Ethical Relativism Gray area in which your ethical principles are defined by the traditions of your society, your personal opinions, and the circumstances of the present moment.

Ethics The manner by which we try to live our lives according to a standard of "right" or "wrong" behavior—in both how we think and behave toward others and how we would like them to think and behave toward us.

Ethics Officer A senior executive responsible for monitoring the ethical performance of the organization both internally and externally.

External Whistle-Blowing An employee discovering corporate misconduct and choosing to bring it to the attention of law enforcement agencies and/or the media.

Extranet A private piece of a company's Internet network that is made available to customers and/or vendor partners on the basis of secured access by unique password.

F

Facilitation Payments (FCPA) Payments that are acceptable (legal) provided they expedite or secure the performance of a routine governmental action.

Federal Sentencing Guidelines for Organizations (FSGO) Chapter 8 of the guidelines that hold businesses liable for the criminal acts of their employees and agents.

Financial Stability Oversight Council (FSOC) A government agency established to prevent banks from failing and otherwise threatening the stability of the U.S. economy.

Foreign Corrupt Practices Act (FCPA) Legislation introduced to control bribery and other less obvious forms of payment to foreign officials and politicians by American publicly traded companies.

G

GAAP The generally accepted accounting principles that govern the accounting profession—not a set of laws and established legal precedents but a set of standard operating procedures within the profession.

Global Code of Conduct A general standard of business practice that can be applied equally to all countries over and above their local customs and social norms.

Globalization The expansion of international trade to a point where national markets have been overtaken by regional trade blocs (Latin America, Europe, Africa), leading eventually to a global marketplace.

The Golden Rule Do unto others as you would have them do unto you.

I

Instrumental Approach The perspective that the only obligation of a corporation is to maximize profits for its shareholders in providing goods and services that meet the needs of its customers.

Instrumental Value The quality by which the pursuit of one value is a good way to reach another value. For example, money is valued for what it can buy rather than for itself.

Internal Whistle-Blowing An employee discovering corporate misconduct and bringing it to the attention of his or her supervisor, who then follows established procedures to address the misconduct within the organization.

Intranet A company's internal website, containing information for employee access only.

Intrinsic Value The quality by which a value is a good thing in itself and is pursued for its own sake, whether anything comes from that pursuit or not.

L

Less-Developed Nation A country that lacks the economic, social, and technological infrastructure of a developed nation.

M

Multinational Corporation (MNC) A company that provides and sells products and services across multiple national borders. Also known as *transnational corporations*.

O

OECD Guidelines for Multinational Enterprises Guidelines that promote principles and standards of behavior in the following areas: human rights, information disclosure, anticorruption, taxation, labor relations, environment, competition, and consumer protection; a governmental initiative endorsed by 30 members of the Organization for Economic Cooperation and Development and 9 nonmembers (Argentina, Brazil, Chile, Estonia, Israel, Latvia, Lithuania, Romania, and Slovenia).

Organizational Culture The values, beliefs, and norms that all the employees of that organization share.

Organizational Integrity A characteristic of publicly committing to the highest professional standards and sticking to that commitment.

Oxymoron The combination of two contradictory terms, such as "deafening silence" or "jumbo shrimp."

P

Proactive Ethical Policies Policies that result when the company develops a clear sense of what it stands for as an ethical organization.

Prohibition (FCPA) The FCPA inclusion of wording from the Bank Secrecy Act and the Mail Fraud Act to prevent the movement of funds overseas for the express purpose of conducting a fraudulent scheme.

Public Company Accounting Oversight Board (PCAOB) An independent oversight body for auditing companies.

Q

Qui Tam **Lawsuit** A lawsuit brought on behalf of the federal government by a whistle-blower under the False Claims Act of 1863.

R

Reactive Ethical Policies Policies that result when organizations are driven by events and/or a fear of future events.

Routine Governmental Action (FCPA) Any regular administrative process or procedure, excluding any action taken by a foreign official in the decision to award new or continuing business.

S

Sarbanes-Oxley Act (SOX) A legislative response to the corporate accounting scandals of the early 2000s that covers the financial management of businesses.

Social Contract Approach The perspective that a corporation has an obligation to society over and above the expectations of its shareholders.

Society A structured community of people bound together by similar traditions and customs.

Stakeholder Someone with a share or interest in a business enterprise.

Strategic CSR Philanthropic approach to CSR in which organizations target programs that will generate the most positive publicity or goodwill for the organization but that run the greatest risk of being perceived as self-serving behavior on the part of the organization.

Sustainable Ethics Ethical behavior that persists long after the latest public scandal or the latest management buzzword.

T

Telecommuting The ability to work outside of your office (from your home or anywhere else) and log in to your company network (usually via a secure gateway such as a virtual private network, or VPN).

Thick Consent Consent in which the employee has an alternative to unacceptable monitoring. For example, if jobs are plentiful and the employee would have no difficulty in finding another position, then the employee has a realistic alternative for avoiding an unacceptable policy.

Thin Consent Consent in which the employee has little choice. For example, when an employee receives formal notification that the company will be monitoring all e-mail and web activity—either at the time of hire or during employment—and it is made clear in that notification that his or her continued employment with the company will be dependent on the employee's agreement to abide by that monitoring.

Transparency Characteristic of an organization that maintains open and honest communications with all stakeholders.

U

UN Global Compact A voluntary corporate citizenship initiative endorsing 10 key principles that focus on four key areas of concern: the environment, anticorruption, the welfare of workers around the world, and global human rights.

Universal Ethics Actions that are taken out of *duty* and *obligation* to a purely moral ideal, rather than based on the needs of the situation, since the universal principles are seen to apply to everyone, everywhere, all the time.

Utilitarianism Ethical choices that offer the greatest good for the greatest number of people.

V

Value Chain The key functional inputs that an organization provides in the transformation of raw materials into a delivered product or service.

Value System A set of personal principles formalized into a code of behavior.

Vicarious Liability A legal concept that means a party may be held responsible for injury or damage even when he or she was not actively involved in an incident.

Virtue Ethics A concept of living your life according to a commitment to the achievement of a clear ideal—*what sort of person would I like to become, and how do I go about becoming that person?*

W

Whistle-Blower An employee who discovers corporate misconduct and chooses to bring it to the attention of others.

Whistle-Blower Hotline A telephone line by which employees can leave messages to alert a company of suspected misconduct without revealing their identity.